BRINGING

DOWN

THE TEMPLE

HOUSE

. . .

HBI SERIES ON JEWISH WOMEN
Lisa Fishbayn Joffe, General Editor
Ronit Irshai, Associate Editor

The HBI Series on Jewish Women, created by the Hadassah-Brandeis Institute, publishes a wide range of books by and about Jewish women in diverse contexts and time periods. Of interest to scholars and the educated public, the HBI Series on Jewish Women fills major gaps in Jewish Studies and in Women and Gender Studies as well as their intersection. The HBI Series on Jewish Women is supported by a generous gift from Dr. Laura S. Schor.
For the complete list of books that are available in this series, please see https://brandeisuniversitypress.com/series-list/

Marjorie Lehman, *Bringing Down the Temple House: Engendering Tractate Yoma*

Tamar Ross, *Expanding the Palace of Torah: Orthodoxy and Feminism*, Second Edition

Hadassah Lieberman, *Hadassah: An American Story*

ChaeRan Y. Freeze, *A Jewish Woman of Distinction: The Life and Diaries of Zinaida Poliakova*

Chava Turniansky, *Glikl: Memoirs 1691–1719*

Joy Ladin, *The Soul of the Stranger: Reading God and Torah from a Transgender Perspective*

Joanna Beata Michlic, editor, *Jewish Families in Europe, 1939–Present: History, Representation, and Memory*

Sarah M. Ross, *A Season of Singing: Creating Feminist Jewish Music in the United States*

Margalit Shilo, *Girls of Liberty: The Struggle for Suffrage in Mandatory Palestine*

Sylvia Barack Fishman, editor, *Love, Marriage, and Jewish Families: Paradoxes of a Social Revolution*

Cynthia Kaplan Shamash, *The Strangers We Became: Lessons in Exile from One of Iraq's Last Jews*

Marcia Falk, *The Days Between: Blessings, Poems, and Directions of the Heart for the Jewish High Holiday Season*

Inbar Raveh, *Feminist Rereadings of Rabbinic Literature*

Laura Silver, *The Book of Knish: In Search of the Jewish Soul Food*

Sharon R. Siegel, *A Jewish Ceremony for Newborn Girls: The Torah's Covenant Affirmed*

Laura S. Schor, *The Best School in Jerusalem: Annie Landau's School for Girls, 1900–1960*

BRINGING DOWN THE TEMPLE HOUSE

...

Engendering Tractate Yoma

...

MARJORIE LEHMAN

BRANDEIS UNIVERSITY PRESS

Waltham, Massachusetts

Brandeis University Press
© 2022 by Marjorie Lehman
All rights reserved
Manufactured in the United States of America
Designed by Richard Hendel
Typeset in Arnhem by Passumpsic Publishing

For permission to reproduce any of the material
in this book, contact Brandeis University Press, 415 South Street,
Waltham MA 02453, or visit brandeisuniversitypress.com

Library of Congress Cataloging-in-publishing Data
NAMES: Lehman, Marjorie Suzan, author.
TITLE: Bringing down the Temple house:
engendering Tractate Yoma/Marjorie Lehman.
DESCRIPTION: Waltham, Massachusetts: Brandeis University Press, [2022]
SERIES: HBI series on Jewish women │
Includes bibliographical references and index.
SUMMARY: "A feminist project that privileges the Babylonian Talmudic
tractate as culturally significant. While the use of feminist analysis
as a methodological lens is not new to the study of Talmudic literature
or to the study of individual tractates, this book demonstrates that such
an intervention reveals new perspectives on the rabbis' relationship
with the temple and its priesthood" — Provided by publisher.
IDENTIFIERS: LCCN 2021047531 │ ISBN 9781684580897 (paperback) │
ISBN 9781684580880 (cloth) │ ISBN 9781684580903 (ebook)
SUBJECTS: LCSH: Talmud. Yoma—Criticism, interpretation, etc. │
Talmud. Yoma—Feminist criticism. │ Women in rabbinical literature. │
Rabbinical literature—History and criticism.
CLASSIFICATION: LCC BM506.Y83 L45 2022 │
DDC 296.1/252—dc23/eng/20211018
LC record available at https://lccn.loc.gov/2021047531

5 4 3 2 1

For Ari, Jonah, and Gabriel

CONTENTS

· · ·

Introduction 1

CHAPTER 1
Unsettling the Temple Bayit 19

CHAPTER 2
Violence in the Temple: Priest-Fathers and Their Sons 36

CHAPTER 3
Mothers and Sons: Broken Houses 55

CHAPTER 4
From Inside Out: Kimḥit's House 71

CHAPTER 5
Intergenerational Transmission and the Problem of Mothers 87

CHAPTER 6
Sexuality Inside and Outside the Temple House 103

CHAPTER 7
Sustaining the Rabbinic Household 125

CHAPTER 8
Vulnerable Bodies in Vulnerable Houses 144

CHAPTER 9
The Case of Purity and Impurity 164

Afterword 181

Acknowledgments 189

Notes 195

Bibliography 313

Index 339

BRINGING
DOWN
THE TEMPLE
HOUSE
...

INTRODUCTION

. . .

This study of tractate Yoma is a feminist project that privileges the Babylonian Talmud (Bavli) as a culturally significant unit of material. It began as a feminist commentary project on the tractates of the Bavli spearheaded by Tal Ilan.[1] Tasked with commenting on every place in the tractate that mentions women, I began to detect points of cohesion that challenged my prior conceptions regarding the redaction of Babylonian tractates. The very first mishnah of Bavli Yoma containing the rabbinic metaphorical association between "house" and "wife" set the stage for the development of an argument that runs through the entire tractate, suggesting that this Babylonian tractate was the result of a conscious editorial endeavor. The semantic equation made between "wife" and "house," in that a man's wife is referred to as "his house (*beito*)," is a common rabbinic word linkage. It is used for heralding a well-formed house rooted in the gendered idea that a man's wife is "his house" because she sustains it. Without his wife, the very foundation of the house is destabilized. As this tractate unfolded, the examination of the metaphorical linkage between wives and houses shaped my approach to feminist analysis. I noticed that the rabbis' exploration of their relationship to the Temple house was predicated not only on this association of "wife as house" but also on all that the household conjures — marriage, progeny, kinship, domesticity, and sexuality (including sexual purity laws).[2] Each time women or men were associated with an issue or concept that was typically connected with the household, I looked for the ideas within the text that had triggered the connection. Against the backdrop of Yom Kippur, the house and all that the house as a gendered space invokes revealed that the shift from the Temple house to the rabbinic household was complex.[3] Interwoven into the textual layers of Bavli Yoma was a perspective on the rabbis' struggle with their relationship to the Temple house, as well as a marked concern regarding the stability of the everyday houses they inhabited.[4]

The examination of the metaphorical linkage between wives and houses shaped my approach to feminist analysis. As rhetorical markers of a literary sort, these were textual moments that disclosed more about the ideas of the Bavli's male authors than about the people who were at the center of these texts.[5] Women and priests, in particular, emerged as loci for the rabbis in their attempt to express a need for power as well as a fear of losing (or not having) the very control that they desired.[6] Employing this type of feminist analysis, I was able to detect, document, and trace a narrative arc in Bavli Yoma, distinct from the larger thematic structure of the tractate governed by Mishnah Yoma.[7] Enmeshed within the rabbis' description of the performative aspects of the Temple service of Yom Kippur, I located another discourse in which the semantic universe of the house and the relationships that are associated with it[8] operated to disconnect the Temple house from the rabbinic one.[9] In other words, I found little to support the idea that the Temple *bayit* (house) was re-created or remembered in the everyday rabbinic bayit.[10] The fact that there was a semantic connection between the Temple house, referred to as the *beit hamikdash*, and all of the other institutions, places, and things in rabbinic literature that are also labeled "bayit," did not reflect a desire to infuse an all-encompassing sense of sacredness and geographical rootedness into all the activities in which the rabbis were engaged, the rituals they observed, or the places they inhabited.[11] Instead, a feminist methodology revealed a discourse of empowerment structured around the disempowerment of the priests and the destabilization of the Temple. Indeed, a focus on the Bavli's "others," in this case women and priests, brought ideological issues to the surface, pointing to the role of the stammaim (anonymous redactors) in molding rabbinic perspectives that ran through the entire tractate.[12]

However, quite strikingly, the through line apparent in the first seven chapters of the tractate took on a different character in the final chapter of Bavli Yoma. The holiday of Yom Kippur and its definition as a day of self-denial, treated extensively in this concluding chapter, became an analytical frame through which the rabbis admitted their own vulnerability and their lack of power in the face of life in the everyday household. Prompted by the work of Daniel Boyarin and Charlotte Fonrobert, I found myself thinking about the rabbis' shift in focus in chapter eight as a moment of rupture in the androcentric discourse of the rabbis.[13] In addition to a desire to marginalize the priests and shift power toward themselves, the rabbis expressed anxiety over the implications of their very own claims. They were pushing back against their own patriarchal structures. Male insecurity bound up in the indispensable role women had in the making and subsistence of the rabbinic

Bringing Down the Temple House

household consequently surfaced. This insecurity was intertwined with the fear that their leadership might be entirely unsuccessful. As well, they were concerned about fathering future progeny.[14] Hence, a seven-chapter-long literary presentation about one regal house with a secure patriline reached its climax in the final chapter. Destabilizing the Temple and its priesthood served as a literary ploy of sorts to confront real-life instability and human frailty centered, as it often is, on the household.

MARGINALIZING WOMEN, MARGINALIZING MEN

Through this analysis, it became apparent to me that the rabbis' marginalization of women drove a wedge between men and men, specifically priests and rabbis. Difference and inequality are constitutive of both masculinity and femininity, and in the case of Bavli Yoma, one feeds on the other.[15] Constructing masculinity, like constructing femininity, is a strategy the rabbis use to develop a distinct image of themselves over and against an "other" they wish to render less authoritative and, at times, powerless. Toward this end, the rabbis capitalize on the idea of the priests as a separate class of men,[16] often through references made to priests' relationships with their wives, mothers, fathers, brothers, and other priests. Additionally, in constructing the priests as "other" men, the rabbis create a one-sided, stilted relationship with them.[17] Stigmatized, the priests are pushed aside as the rabbis impose their own memory of the way things were onto them. The priests are described as foolish,[18] inept,[19] unseemly,[20] corrupt,[21] even violent.[22] The rabbis dress and undress them and decide what they should eat. They claim to have knowledge of the priests' bodily secretions (such as semen, urine, and excrement),[23] show preference for physically big-handed priests over small-handed ones,[24] determine whom they can marry and when they must divorce, and decide with whom they have sex and when.[25] Temple procedures offer no latitude for error in the rabbis' vision of them, and blemished priests are disqualified from serving.[26] All decision making, especially in Temple-related ritual matters, falls to the rabbis despite its being beyond their purview. It is the rabbis who decide that the high priest needs to be sequestered for seven days prior to performing the Yom Kippur *avodah* (Temple service). It is they who create a biblical framework to make it look as though the decision for a seven-day separation was biblically mandated.[27] It is the rabbis who look to biblical

Introduction

3

verses and to each other for authority rather than looking to the priests for solutions, validation, or change. Robbing the priests of any effective voice or avenue to object and meaningfully participate in the process leaves a tractate chock-full of textual manifestations of the rabbis' desire to disempower the priests, to emasculate them. In Bavli Yoma, by the time the rabbis discuss the non-Temple Yom Kippur in the eighth and final chapter, priests are known to be exploited, infantilized, and neglected.

Bavli Yoma also underscores the rabbis' struggles with the patrilineal framework of the priesthood.[28] The priests are a caste of men with a legitimate biblical ancestry connected to Aaron. However, in tractate Yoma, they cannot conduct Temple rites without the supervisory skills of the rabbis. Knowledge of Temple rites is firmly in the hands of the rabbis beginning in the earliest rabbinic (tannaitic) sources and reflected in future layers of Babylonian Talmudic material as well. In this way, the rabbis create disorder in the male-male/father-son bloodline, making room for an additional model of relatedness: that of the master-disciple relationship.[29] While the rabbis produce a new type of hierarchy and level of insularity, they appropriate the idea of familial kinship, committed as they are to both legitimizing and reproducing themselves; their disciples will be those linked one to the other by a common cultural and religious commitment to Torah study, whether or not they are blood related.[30] Rabbi-rabbi colleagues become kin of a different sort—linked one to the other by what they know, a move that expands the definition of kinship beyond a bloodline through the father.[31]

Kinship, like gender, is a classification system, a grammar, of the most basic elements of relatedness that can be mobilized to signify not only specific kinds of connection and inclusion but also disconnection and exclusion, often driven by gender.[32] For the rabbis, cultural reproduction overshadows the biological relatedness between the priests. Cultural reproduction weakens the significance of the priestly bloodline and opens the door for crossing the select classificatory boundaries defined by biological relatedness.[33] In a post-tannaitic vignette marking the end of the Yom Kippur service, instigated by linking Mishnah Yoma 7:4 to a tannaitic *baraita* (a source from the same period as the Mishnah), Bavli Yoma brings this tension to a head, advantaging the proto-rabbis, Shema'yah, and Avtalyon, over the high priest:

4 *Bringing Down the Temple House*

[It was taught in the mishnah: They escort the high priest to his house after the Temple Yom Kippur service in the Holy of Holies is complete.] And he would make a feast for his fellows.[34]

The Sages taught [in a baraita]: There was an incident involving one high priest who exited the Holy Temple.

And everyone followed him. When they saw Shema'yah and Avtalyon [heads of the Sanhedrin and predecessors of Hillel and Shammai], they left him [the high priest] and walked after Shema'yah and Avtalyon.

Ultimately, Shema'yah and Avtalyon came to take leave of the high priest. [When this occurred, the high priest] said to them [mockingly]: "Let [Shema'yah and Avtalyon], the descendants of [the non-Jewish] nations, come in peace." They said [back] to him [the high priest]: "Better let the descendants of the nations, who perform the acts of Aaron, come in peace; and let not a descendant of Aaron, who does not perform the acts of Aaron, come in peace." (BT Yoma 71b)

When making leadership choices in this passage, the people gravitate toward the rabbis' direct ancestors rather than to the high priest responsible for their atonement on Yom Kippur. The interchange revolves around the viability of Shema'yah and Avtalyon as alternative leaders to the priests, given their ancestry as non-Jews and now as, presumably, Torah-learned converts to (rabbinic) Judaism.[35] The rabbis depict the high priest as one who mocks the "faulty" lineage of Shema'yah and Avtalyon, shaming them as outsiders. But Shema'yah and Avtalyon, despite their status as proto-rabbis, comfortably cross over into rabbinic ranks, drawing everyone, including the priests, away from the celebration of the high priest. This signals that these two men have devoted followers. The high priest represents a pure priestly bloodline, while Shama'yah and Avtalyon represent those who can perform the functions of the Aaronite priesthood even if they are not direct descendants of Aaron. The story implies that one need not be a priest to perform the acts of the high priesthood, that is, to connect with God through the performance of ritual. Cultural constructions of kinship are enmeshed within an expanded context of reproduction linked to personages and roles, but legitimacy and prestige are earned, not born.

Introduction

This analysis of Bavli Yoma thus not only contributes to the significance of using gender as an analytic category when studying references to women, but also to the ways that religious men privilege and legitimize themselves by differentiating other men from themselves, biologically and socially, albeit to their detriment.[36] Focusing on how women are marginalized without recognizing that the rabbis sideline other men masks the scope of the rabbis' attempts to assert power and cultivate a sense of esteem. Attaining and building priority and privilege as religious leaders is not bound or limited to marginalizing women but includes the marginalization of men legitimately tasked with running the Temple. Presenting the priests as a caste of men who cannot conduct Temple rites without the managerial skills of the rabbis means that something is wrong with priestly leadership and its ties to a patriline lineage where generations are connected through the father's line.

For the rabbis, privileging their male selves is directly connected to making claims about "knowing" more than the priests in conducting Temple rituals, such as that of Yom Kippur.[37] In remembering the Temple, albeit in their own way, the rabbis are arguing for their own legitimacy in an environment where competing claims to leadership continued to surface. In a world inhabited by many groups, each vying for power, including Judaeans, Christians, Romans, and Persians, the Babylonian rabbis represented in Bavli Yoma take every opportunity to prioritize their knowledge over that of others, such as the priests. Their goal is to carve out a niche, hoping that their version of tradition will be embraced by all.[38]

And while this goal may explain the rabbis' desire to reimagine Temple narratives—like the one that extends over seven chapters in tractate Yoma—it does not entirely capture the reasons for the rabbis' rhetoric of utter condescension toward the priests. More than the claim that the priests do not know enough to conduct the Temple rite of Yom Kippur is the rabbis' injurious description of the priests' very personhood. The historical possibility that Temple priests were corrupt does not explain away the degree of disparagement in evidence in rabbinic sources included in tractate Yoma, or even the priests' virtual absence from the final chapter where the non-Temple Yom Kippur rite is discussed.[39] Possibly, in couching the priests as they do, weak in knowledge of the Temple rites, versus themselves, as familiar with Temple practice, the rabbis are offering themselves as needed replacements for an ineffectual priesthood or as perpetuators of a past high standard for which the

6   *Bringing Down the Temple House*

priests once stood.[40] The rabbis cannot claim the Temple as their legislative domain unless they can argue that it is being controlled by others unworthy of such a role.

But a feminist analysis pushes this argument one step further, highlighting the complex power dynamics at play when one group, in this case, a gendered male group, wishes to move another group, also gendered male, "out of their house," so to speak. Once the rabbis undercut the priests, who are the keepers of the Temple house, critiquing everything the priests do to make the Temple "household" run, the overall effect accentuates the lack of viability and usefulness of the Temple house. The priests then become deeply entangled with the image the rabbis' construct of the Temple. Consequently, in criticizing the men who are biblically tasked to supervise its rituals (the priests), the rabbis legitimize not only a shift in leadership but also point to the need for a different type of house.

Repeatedly, in all of the historical layers found in the Bavli, the rabbis not only denigrate the priests with respect to their Temple-related responsibilities, othering them, but they unravel the relationships most often associated with everyday houses, including family relationships —those between priests and their wives, mothers, and their priest-sons, fathers and their priest-sons, and priests and their brothers. From wives who have no agency to affect their priest husbands unless they die or menstruate,[41] to mothers who make transparent clothing for their priest-sons,[42] to priest-fathers who take responsibility for their sons' crimes,[43] and to brothers who can only replace brothers as high priests on the disqualification or the death of the other,[44] relationships, especially blood relationships, are presented as strained. In evidence are multiple cases where the rabbis chip away at the patrilineal framework that defines the priesthood and connects the priests to the Temple by negatively affecting their marriages and fulfillment of their sexual needs, cutting them off from being with and bearing the children who can take their place, separating them from their mothers and fathers and from their own bodies, as well as from their ability to conduct Temple ritual by maintaining ritual purity. Stripping the priests of everything the rabbis value, they are able to justify carving out a space for their own meritocracy to make the argument that leaders are not born; they are made within the framework of functioning houses— unless, of course, circumstances circumvent the plan. Ultimately, the arc of the tractate reveals the rabbis' concerns that they may have no

Introduction

more power or success than the priests, not even in producing biological kin.

STUDYING THE WHOLE AS THE SUM OF
ITS PARTS: THE TALMUD AS LITERATURE

This analysis of Bavli Yoma presents one reading of it that emerges from the study of the tractate as a single complete literary unit.[45] Indeed, the tractate has been a defined unit of knowledge transmission for generations. To this day, the Talmud is bought and sold, gifted, collected, and studied not only set by set but volume by volume. One's claim to "knowing" Talmud continues to be measured tractate by tractate as many readers and students of Talmud continue to engage in seven-year daily folio (*daf-yomi*) cycles following the traditional structural formulation of the Talmudic corpus. That said, academic Talmud scholarship has tended to focus on the parts that make up a given tractate, comparing them to parallel external sources, rather than linking them to recurring ideas that run through the tractate as a whole. In this book, however, the application of a feminist methodology of interpretation, an approach that calls attention specifically to certain texts connected to gender and not others, drives this reading of one tractate. Examining Bavli Yoma for such sources and thinking about them through the lens of one tractate alone exposed a thematic arc woven through it: that of the household. Such a literary approach, using the tractate to set up the boundary of analysis, revealed a perspective that I might have overlooked in comparing rabbinic sources across tractates.

Because the academic study of the Talmud developed within the context of Wissenschaft des Judentums, a nineteenth-century German intellectual movement focused on the intersection of texts, culture, and history, the centrality of the tractate as a culturally significant unit of material lost ground.[46] Linking methods taught in the secular university with traditional Talmud study produced a new way to examine, if not interpret, the Talmud and paved the way for the view that the Talmuds, both the Bavli and the Yerushalmi (Jerusalem Talmud), were composite documents.[47] The objective of study became one of describing the formation of the Talmud's literary passages one by one, laying the foundation for a larger understanding of the role of the anonymous redactors, either in the Land of Israel in the fourth century as contributors to the Jerusalem Talmud (Yerushalmi) or in sixth- and seventh-

8   *Bringing Down the Temple House*

century Mesopotamia as contributors to the making of the Bavli. Early contributors to this academic approach, such as David Weiss Halivni and Shamma Friedman, focused their attention more on the Bavli, given its stylized form, its wider use as part of the curriculum in the Jewish academies of the past, and its pronounced impact on the development of Jewish law (*halakhah*). Each offered theories about its redaction. In studying the Bavli, both scholars argued that earlier sources authored in the Land of Israel and in Babylonia were woven into the later anonymous discursive framework.[48] Relying on their separate theories meant that one developed philological tools to recognize textual seams, distinguishing earlier layers of sugyot (self-contained units of Talmudic discussion) from later ones, using historical dating to gain access to the development of ideas. Both scholars left a significant mark on the field, training scholars to identify and examine tannaitic sources (authored by early rabbis contemporaneous with the Mishnah) and amoraic sources (authored by rabbis who lived between 220 CE and 500 CE approximately) preserved in the Talmud's anonymous layer. By extracting such sources from the larger whole and identifying chronological differences, they pointed future scholars in the direction of finding a reliable testament to the period prior to the composition of the Bavli.[49] The essence of Talmud scholarship tended toward finding the "genuine," or "early," Talmud, prior to the construction of the Babylonian sugya (Talmudic passage).[50]

The debate that ensued between Halivni and Friedman regarding the formation of the Bavli continues to play out among scholars of Talmud. For Friedman, the Bavli's authors were "creative transmitters" who reshaped earlier traditions, improving on them. For Halivni, the stammaim, as he referred to the anonymous authors, received traditions from the tannaim and amoraim in "apodictic" form, that is, without reasoning and justification.[51] The anonymous layer reflected the reconstruction of discussions that undergirded these apodictic statements.[52] More to the point, the scholarly conversation about Talmud redaction was rooted in how much literary license the Talmud's editors embraced. As Mira Wasserman clearly observes, positions continue to run the gamut from scholars who see the editors of Talmudic tractates as "weavers, creating passages of whole cloth," and those who think of the redactors as "quilters, stitching discrete units of material into larger compositions." For decades, scholars have debated whether the Talmud's editors took on a more authorial role or drew together many

Introduction

disparate texts to generate anthologies of miscellanies, and there is evidence to support both possibilities.[53] Many have extrapolated from their textual analyses of the Bavli both universal features and innate discrete characteristics in the anonymous layer. However, as Moulie Vidas has most recently cautioned, we need to pay more acute attention to the "author's voice" in the Bavli. The scope of the activity of the anonymous authors of the Talmud is more varied and innovative than many have argued. The stammaim played a far more inventive role in constructing what we have always considered the Bavli's distinct historical layers. These layers therefore belong to them.[54]

I join Vidas and Wasserman here in my study of Bavli Yoma, thinking of the stammaim not simply as composing the anonymous layer but also as engaged in juxtaposing sources, arranging them, reformulating traditions, and adapting and integrating narratives into the larger context of the tractate.[55] It is these Babylonian authors who make decisions about which sources to include and exclude.[56] Understanding that the Bavli's redactors exhibited an authorial role encourages a reading of earlier tannaitic and amoraic sources that looks beyond the stammaitic layer into which this material is embedded. Once thematic threads begin to emerge, the lens of the tractate as a whole plays a significant role in explaining the additions and emendations—for example, to tannaitic material. As such, when I refer to Bavli Yoma in this book, I am pointing to the redactors who assume a role closer to that of authors who shape earlier material to create thematic arcs.

Even as great advances have been made in the variety of literary analyses that scholars have adopted, Talmud source criticism, as represented by Halivni and Friedman, continues to have a strong impact. Continually associated with meticulous reading, vigilant manuscript analyses, and comparisons between rabbinic texts that belong to the same historical time period, such studies still guide scholars in producing invaluable work tracing the development of rabbinic ideas and uncovering significant rabbinic trends across time periods and locales. At the same time, scholars engaged in this type of research continue to raise criticisms of literary efforts reminiscent of Jacob Neusner's view of the Bavli as a systematic and homogeneous text that makes it worthy of being studied as a whole. Neusner argued that the Bavli should be viewed as a reflection of the ideas communicated by its latest editors.[57] Vidas's contribution lies in his ability not to discount source criticism entirely or to attribute the Bavli's authorship to one flattened

10   *Bringing Down the Temple House*

view of the whole, like Neusner. Rather, he prepares us to think more carefully about the self-consciousness of the Bavli's redactors, that is, to reconsider the reasons for why and how earlier sources are included in a given literary context, revised or unrevised, and what that means for our understanding of a larger unit of material—in this case, Bavli Yoma.[58] In making these substantive contributions to the study of the Bavli, Vidas joined others, including Julia Watts Belser, Daniel Boyarin, Jeffrey Rubenstein, and Barry Wimpfheimer, in considering the literary contexts into which Talmudic sources were embedded, focusing on the creative interventions of the Bavli's editors.[59] But unlike Wasserman, none of these scholars made the case for the tractate to be considered as a whole unit.[60]

This study of Bavli Yoma premises a reading practice in which redactors function more as authors than as mere editors of earlier material. And while I do not ignore the historical layers in evidence, the discovery of a larger thread running through the material rooted in the gendered aspects of the concept of the house has convinced me of the value of reading a tractate at the macro level. The boundaries of my analysis were the same as those chosen by the editors of Bavli Yoma as distinct from Mishnah Yoma, Tosefta Yoma, and Yerushalmi Yoma. Indeed, my observations emerge from a reading strategy similar to that of Wasserman, who discovered a unique narrative arc running through Bavli Avodah Zarah.[61] In the case of Bavli Yoma, there is a level of thematic congruity imposed on the material that points to redactors who took on a more authorial role than an editorial one, quite distinct from Yerushalmi Yoma.[62] I also concur with scholars like Wimpfheimer who detect in the stammaitic endeavor an attempt to rework earlier sources so as to transmit specific agendas.[63]

Methodologically I join a host of scholars who have also defined the boundary of their literary analyses by a single tractate, including Charlotte Fonrobert (Nidah), Alyssa Gray (Avodah Zarah), Christine Hayes (Avodah Zarah), and Julia Watts Belser (Gittin and Ta'anit). Each, however, approaches the tractate, even the same tractate, differently. Whereas Hayes and Gray are interested in what a comparison between the Yerushalmi and the Bavli contributes to our understanding of the way the Bavli took shape, Wasserman is more focused on exposing the artful coherence of the Bavli's redactors/authors. While Fonrobert observes a rabbinic science of bloodstains in her work on tractate Nidah, highlighting both rabbinic authority and the places where the rabbis

Introduction

push back on their own androcentric rhetoric, Belser notices that tractates Ta'anit and Gittin offer significant reflections on rabbinic theology and ethics, couched within a concern for natural disasters and political destruction.[64] Along with them, however, I am participating in a similar literary move that, while hearkening back to the more traditional approach to Talmud study, reveals significant insights into the nature of the Bavli and the perspectives of the rabbis. Admittedly, the more atomistic approach of the medievals who authored commentaries on entire tractates is not the template any of those mentioned here have followed to date. Instead, the contemporary scholarly objective is to produce thesis-driven analyses using a variety of modern critical methodologies that emerge out of studying the tractate as a whole unit. I have no doubt that for those who use other theoretical frameworks and literary approaches to unpack the complexity of Bavli Yoma, different connective threads will emerge from what I put forth in this book. Such analyses will surely put additional interdependent elements into relief, and I encourage this work, as it too needs to be done.

BAVLI YOMA AND LEVITICUS

Reading the tractate from end to end exposes divergent treatments of Yom Kippur in the first seven chapters of Bavli Yoma as compared to the final, eighth, chapter. In fact, two very distinct visions of Yom Kippur emerge that reflect two biblical rites associated with Yom Kippur and that are described in Leviticus 16. The first seven chapters serve as a lengthy commentary on the rite of expiation described in Leviticus 16:1–28, 32–34, where the rabbis add their own set of details and procedures to the biblical account. They narrate the structure of the Temple rite textually, including the high priests' preparations prior to Yom Kippur: extensive purification rites, changes of priestly garments, sacrificial offerings, the sprinkling of blood, preparation of the scapegoat, and their entry into the Holy of Holies to confess the sins of the people. A glorified representation of the Temple surfaces in Yoma, with miracles occurring within its confines, cherubim embracing God behind the Temple curtain (standing for God's love for Israel), and angels preparing the way for a future Temple.[65] The final chapter, however, is an examination of Leviticus 16:29–31 and 23:27–29, specifically the concept of self-denial (*inui*). A separate discussion of repentance appears toward the chapter's end. Although biblical scholars have argued that

12 *Bringing Down the Temple House*

Leviticus reflects two different rites—one of self-denial and purgation that took place to reverse calamity brought about by sinfulness, and the other a day of merriment that took place on the 10th of Tishrei—eventually the two were connected to one another and celebrated as Yom Kippur.[66] Tractate Yoma reflects that the priestly rite of atonement in chapters one to seven and the rite of personal self-denial in chapter eight all took place on the 10th of Tishrei. As such, the tractate offers the illusion of a Temple rite that developed into a post-Temple observance involving bodily self-denial and prayer.

These two visions of Yom Kippur, however, do not intersect, overlap, or build one from the other in Bavli Yoma. The rabbis do not integrate the two Yom Kippur visions into any part of the eighth chapter of the tractate.[67] More pointed, there is a striking shift: the most hierarchical Temple rite, wholly dependent on one high priest who ensures atonement for all, becomes the most equitable of rabbinic rites in chapter eight, where both men and women are required to abide by the prohibitions related to self-denial on Yom Kippur. In the final chapter of Bavli Yoma, with the exception of the priestly blessing bestowed on Yom Kippur, the priests are hardly mentioned.[68] The grandiosity of the Temple Yom Kippur rite and any memory or mention of the Temple structure seem irrelevant.[69] Instead, at the center of the chapter, a lengthy midrashic passage integrates Ezekiel's vision of the sinful behavior that occurred in the Temple with the actions of the angel Gabriel, who cast fire coals on the Temple to destroy it (BT Yoma 77a).[70] When Gabriel is removed, as the midrash narrates, he is replaced by the Persian angel Dubiel, and Dubiel is then replaced by the angel of the Greeks, recalling the prophecy in the book of Daniel that the Israelites will lose sovereignty.[71] A cry for help and protection (עוּי עוּי) goes unheeded. The Temple in Jerusalem is cast aside.[72]

Furthermore, in chapter eight there is no rabbinic leadership role discussed that parallels the function of the high priest who atoned for the people. There is no attempt to create a sense that in observing a non-Temple-centered Yom Kippur, one is reenacting the Yom Kippur Temple service. Noteworthy is the absence of a discussion of the liturgy that was developing during the tannaitic period and recalled the Yom Kippur avodah as presented in the Mishnah.[73] Material objects associated with the sacrificial rite on Yom Kippur, not to mention the fanciful priestly garb, do not appear as symbols needed to reclaim a memory of the Temple. In the final chapter of the Bavli, the observance of Yom

Introduction 13

Kippur is no longer connected to the Temple bayit. As distinct from the development of Passover in Bavli Pesaḥim, where sacrificial rites were incorporated into a home-based meal, the rite of the Temple Yom Kippur and the rabbinic Yom Kippur feel entirely disconnected.[74]

Moreover, reading backward from the end to the beginning of the tractate, none of the prohibitions that define inui play a role in the priests' observance of the holiday in the Temple in the first seven chapters of the tractate. The high priests' frequent immersions seem odd in light of prohibitions against washing on Yom Kippur. Priests who confess their sins using a liturgical formula stating, "Please, God I have sinned willfully, rebelliously and inadvertently before [Y]ou, me and my household," are never depicted as fasting or engaging in any forms of inui.[75] There is no attempt to align this central Temple confession formula with the words of confession that appear in a brief discussion in chapter eight.[76] In addition, the priests' ability to confess the sins of the people and confer atonement onto the Jewish community is not connected to any behavior associated with the main ritual prohibitions that define self-denial.[77] When considering Bavli Yoma as one whole unit, this disconnect suggests that some rabbis wished to put distance between themselves and the Temple. That the rabbinic household surfaces throughout chapter eight without referencing the Temple house spotlights a narrative arc working its way through the material that builds on Yom Kippur but also points beyond the rite itself.

SCOPE AND STRUCTURE

In choosing to think about Bavli Yoma as one literary unit, I have premised literary analysis over descriptive history. I agree with Daniel Stökl Ben Ezra, who has studied Yom Kippur comprehensively, that tractate Yoma does not provide a reliable account of actual Temple worship as conducted by the priests. Many of the details are anachronisms created by the rabbis to generate their own image of the priesthood and do not reflect the biblical narrative.[78] Ishay Rosen-Zvi provides further support for this argument, claiming that the majority of sources about the Temple were "adapted, recreated and reformed in the tannaitic house of study."[79] Naftali Cohn argues that the rabbis used ritual narratives to retell the past as they wanted to see it, reconstructing it in accordance with their current needs. In fact, as Dalia Marx points out, rabbinic literature describes priestly service in the Temple as limited to two weeks a year, despite the fact that sources throughout Bavli Yoma offer up an anachronistic image of priests who serve continuously unless disqualified.[80] Generating such memories and thereby shaping a Temple narrative to their specifications was the rabbis' means through which they argued for their legitimacy as leaders and made claims to an imagined sense of power in the present despite no biblical mandate.[81]

In much the same way that Wasserman views the texts of the Talmud, which she analyzes as a textual creation, I too resist relying on Bavli Yoma for the purposes of drawing historical or ethnographic conclusions about the priests or the history of the development of Yom Kippur.[82] Admittedly, the perspective I present regarding the priesthood and the Temple reflects a literary reading of Bavli Yoma alone. I do not make any claims that what I have uncovered reflects the attitudes conveyed throughout rabbinic literature. There is an enormous amount of scholarship on the relationship between the Temple and rabbinic Judaism, and I do not summarize it or attempt to challenge it by extrapolating from my reading of Bavli Yoma here.[83] Rather, my intention is to reveal a perspective that runs specifically through Bavli Yoma regarding the rabbis' view of the priesthood and the Temple via a feminist methodological intervention into the tractate. We can easily overlook thematic arcs in approaching the tractate piecemeal, cross-referencing sources between tractates to compare and contrast them, studying rabbinic literature diachronically in search of material on the development of the holiday of Yom Kippur, as significant as that is.[84] However, the exercise in reading the tractate synchronically, that is, through the eyes of redactors asserting an authorial role, has enabled me to see the rabbis from another perspective. I now hear their voices differently. I read Talmudic material thinking about the larger literary framework of the tractate. In the wake of the rabbinic Yom Kippur—a rite that is all about the absence of food, drink, and sexual relations—the extravagant Temple bayit is pushed aside. By the final chapter in the tractate, the idea of the Temple's return, or the features of Yom Kippur that emerge as reminders of a Temple past, become insignificant in light of considerations of what is minimally necessary for the subsistence of everyday households.

Admittedly, my view of the rabbinic household is narrow. It is confined by the limits of the tractate, which focuses more on the survival of parents and children within the household than on others who inhabited rabbinic dwellings.[85] The extensive details about the complexion

Introduction   15

of the household, including how many wives lived in a rabbinic house, whether there were adult children or servants (Jewish and non-Jewish), or whether students lived with their teachers, are not apparent in any of the historical layers in Bavli Yoma. What stands out, however, is the fact that the sanctity of the Temple and its associated Yom Kippur rituals are not read into everyday household practices.[86] For example, the discourse regarding the significance of the purity of the high priest on Yom Kippur does not become central to the holiness of the household or the people who inhabit this mundane space on Yom Kippur in the final chapter of the tractate.[87] A potential lack of food and concerns about caring for children and pregnant women figure more prominently.

According to Maurice Halbwach's theory of collective memory, "Even at the moment that [a religion] is evolving, society returns to its past [and] enframes the new elements that it pushes to the forefront in a totality of remembrances, traditions, and familiar ideas." Religion, for Halbwach, is a form of cultural memory work with a "heightened importance attached to religion's complex and potentially paradoxical relationship to the past." We see many instances in rabbinic literature of the rabbis' attempt to reconnect to the Temple as they engage in a post-Temple project marked by institutional and ideological shifts.[88] And yet, in Bavli Yoma, we observe the rabbis discarding past Temple practices altogether.[89] When the rabbis of Greco-Roman Palestine or Babylonia face an incomplete world following the destruction of the Temple, much is deficient and insecure—from their claims to leadership to their ability to ensure the safety of their households.[90] The rabbis make it eminently clear that remembering the Temple will not secure their daily household life, nor will Torah study necessarily produce future sages.[91] In the end, the only thing that secures their future is the birth of children, and on that "reproductive" note, the tractate ends.[92]

Beginning with an analysis of the rabbinic use of the term *bayit* to refer to the high priest's wife—she is "his house"—chapter one of this book highlights not only instances where the high priest cannot perform the Yom Kippur avodah but also accentuates the need for him to remain ritually pure while serving in the Temple. His sexless character comes to the fore, controlled by the rabbinic ruling to sequester himself for seven days before the start of Yom Kippur, only to be completely reversed in the final sugya of the tractate where the *ba'al keri* (a man who has a seminal emission) on Yom Kippur is promised future progeny. In chapter one of this book, the rabbis import tropes that conjure the rabbis' sense of house, including marriage, the *mezuzah*, and house impurity (*nega'im*), to reflect on the Temple house. In so doing, they reveal that their conceptualizations of bayit do not map smoothly onto the holy bayit of the Temple. This juxtaposition presents the rabbis as elevating themselves at the expense of their so-called forebearers, the Temple priests, rendering the priesthood as flawed and the Temple house as a troubled space.

Shifting from the physical structures of the Temple and the rabbinic bayit to the relationships that define each of these spaces, chapters two through five focus on the fathers and sons and mothers and sons of Bavli Yoma. Through these relationships, the rabbis critique the institution of the priesthood as they undermine and disrupt the exclusively male bloodline that transmits priestly privilege. Each relationship foregrounds aspects of the complicated shift from a Temple-centered Judaism to one defined by everyday houses. Each relationship represents a move in tractate Yoma from the social-religious institution of the Temple and its narration of the Yom Kippur Temple rite to the symbolic construction of persons and relations significant to, and challenging for, the continuity of the rabbinic project.

In chapter six, I explore the ways that sexuality, prevalent in many of the tractates of the Babylonian Talmud, weaves its way through Bavli Yoma.[93] Here I discuss how sexuality is specifically integrated into the larger redactional agenda, thinking about how the pieces fit together into an overarching perspective regarding sexuality unique to the tractate's thematic arc. Situated within a Syrian Christian culture where sexual abstinence was widespread and a Zoroastrian culture critical of such extreme attitudes toward sexuality, the Babylonian rabbis navigate the contours of a larger world orbit struggling with their relationship to asceticism.[94] The seepage of ideas from the Roman context where celibacy was firmly rooted in a developing Christianity also had an impact.[95] The Temple on Yom Kippur becomes a viable entry point. It provides an avenue for the rabbis to construct the priests as their masculine "others" by differentiating them as sexless while describing themselves as quite the opposite. Despite the fact that Yom Kippur observance is rooted in bodily self-denial, including abstention from sexual relations, and that Babylonian rabbis live in a cultural orbit where ascetic behavior is a locus of attention among religious groups, in Bavli

Introduction 17

Yoma, the rabbis present themselves as having, needing, and wanting sex. This discourse around sexuality not only underscores the rabbis' desire to differentiate their own virility from that of the priests but differentiates the sexuality of women from priests as well. In so doing, the rabbis locate moments where women use their sexuality for positive self-fulfilling aims, inasmuch as they are sexually enticing; the priests, however, are completely emasculated. This thread leads us to the final chapter of the tractate where the priests are pushed aside, sexual relations become allowable on Yom Kippur in certain instances (chapter seven), and sexual purity law, once intimately tied to the Temple, is rendered an entirely separate category of law with no impact on the observance of Yom Kippur (chapter nine).

Chapters seven, eight, and nine focus on the lengthy eighth and final chapter of the tractate. In the final chapter of Bavli Yoma, the rabbis construct the rabbinic household not as one that replaces the Temple or as a space where Temple ritual is reimagined. Instead, they imagine what, at a minimum, is necessary for the subsistence of the daily household. Toward this end, they not only point to their own vulnerability as rabbis, medical experts, and fathers but also to their dependence on women, at the very least, to care for their children and to bear healthy progeny.[96]

CHAPTER 1

UNSETTLING THE

TEMPLE BAYIT

. . .

The holiday of Yom Kippur is the dominant thematic arc that runs through Bavli Yoma. Readers of this tractate are readily drawn to the drama taking place in the *beit hamikdash* (the Jerusalem Temple) connected to the observance of Yom Kippur and to the priestly caste responsible for it.[1] Despite the fact that the Temple was destroyed in 70 CE, the rabbis of all generations who appear in this tractate couch themselves as eyewitnesses to Temple practices that seem fully operational.[2] But this is not the only through line that binds this tractate into a literary whole. A feminist analysis leads readers to locate what can be overlooked when approaching a tractate such as this one, built as it is around the narration of the Temple Yom Kippur as outlined initially in Mishnah Yoma. Turning to the idea that the Temple is also a bayit draws feminist readers to think about all that is associated with households. Such connections offer another perspective on the Temple that will draw from references to women and to the houses where they can be found.[3] In this chapter, ideas linked to functioning houses are projected onto the Temple bayit revealing this alternative view. Looking to the ways that the final redactors piece together tannaitic and amoriac material into larger passages exposes a memory of the Temple's intactness alongside an image of disorder over which the rabbis wish they can control but admittedly cannot entirely regulate.

Functionality turns houses into enduring home spaces.[4] But a space that cannot be effectively and harmoniously lived in cannot function as intended. More specifically, while anthropologists argue that houses stand for social groups, the rabbis work toward separating the Temple house from its social group, its keepers, the priests.[5] From the relationship of marriage to the most significant rabbinic spatial marker, the mezuzah, Bavli Yoma's redactors import tropes from their own legal system that draw attention to cracks in the Temple's ritual operation as well as to fault lines in the actions of the priests overseeing it. House impurity (nega'im) becomes yet another method for unsettling the Temple house, revealing that the rabbis' conceptualizations of bayit do not necessarily map smoothly onto the holy bayit of the Temple. But the reverse is also true: the Temple does not map onto the rabbinic household either. This sets the stage for the final chapter of Bavli Yoma where the Temple and the rabbis' priestly forebearers become insignificant by omission. Instead, in chapter eight of this tractate, the everyday household rises to the surface against the backdrop of the rite of bodily self-denial (*inui nefesh*) on Yom Kippur.[6]

Inasmuch as the rabbis highlight deficiencies in the operation of the Temple bayit and its priesthood, such shortcomings come to the surface in Bavli Yoma in conjunction with women's bodies and the legal categories that naturally or unnaturally revolve around or include them. Paying attention to where women appear, not as a lens into women's experience in Jewish antiquity or in rabbinic society but as a literary force used by the rabbis to "think with," exposes a perspective on the priests and the Temple. Placed in a dialectical relationship, the house metaphor and women's bodies intersect,[7] becoming a way for the rabbis to dissect their built environment by contemplating where women exist within it.[8] By proceeding from whether wives are needed to effectuate atonement on Yom Kippur to examining spaces that need *mezuzot*, women's bodies and the spaces women inhabit become a literary way for the rabbis to think through their relationship with the priests and the centrality of the Temple. From the very first mishnah in tractate Yoma, women prove to be indispensable for thinking about the very fabric of the house—both in their absence from the Temple house and, quite remarkably, in their association with it as well.[9]

This chapter focuses on the use of the Hebrew term *bayit* in material found in connection with the Babylonian sugyot that are connected to M. Yoma 1:1. Beginning with an analysis of the rabbinic use of this term to refer to the high priest's wife—she is "his house"—she becomes the literary linchpin, the fulcrum highlighting the possibility that the high priest might be unable to perform the Yom Kippur ritual service. In addition, the rabbis' use of the mezuzah in juxtaposition with house walls that can become contaminated serves to differentiate the Temple from other lived Jewish spaces, including the house spaces that women use daily.

20   *Bringing Down the Temple House*

THE RABBINIC BAYIT

As a spatial term, *bayit* is used throughout rabbinic literature to connect people, cultural and religious institutions, and other spaces with one another.[10] That being said, "Bayit is never just a space," argues Cynthia Baker in *Rebuilding the House of Israel: Architectures of Gender in Jewish Antiquity*; rather, it "signifies a whole complex of intersecting routines and relations." Everything from altars to chambers to people associated with the Temple takes on the name *bayit* in rabbinic literature.[11] As a multipurpose term, *bayit* also refers to the many institutions that ideally define rabbinic life, such as *beit hakeneset* (the synagogue), *beit hamidrash* (the house of study), *beit hasefer* (the school), *beit din* (court), and, of course, the actual bayit, or private dwelling place.[12] Furthermore, in its construct form, the word *beit* also designates nation or ethnos (as in *beit yisra'el*) as well as the rabbinic "houses" of masters and their disciples (for example, Beit Hillel and Beit Shammai). People's livelihoods, their ritual, economic, and social lives, not to mention their commitment to study, form an interconnected living web, linked by their relationship to bayit. Arguably, the persistent use of the word *bayit* as a descriptive term conjures an identity for the rabbis that is defined by a pervading desire for all that the Temple connotes as the bayit par excellence. In using this spatial term so pervasively, the rabbis convey a desire to infuse an all-encompassing sense of sacredness and geographical rootedness into all the places they inhabit as well as into the activities in which they engage. Reflecting a sense of yearning for the Temple, for Zion, and for Jerusalem, the word *bayit* triggers feelings of connection and belonging. And yet when Bavli Yoma sets up discussions about the Temple bayit, it disrupts this synchrony.[13] The husband-wife relationship, the household spatial marker, the mezuzah, and the threat of contracting house impurity, import images of the household onto the Temple that function textually to desacralize it rather than glorify it.[14] So what does it mean to categorize so much in rabbinic literature using the term *bayit*? What is Bavli Yoma saying about the idea of the bayit given how common the term is in the rabbis' world and how often they think with it and about it?

HIS WIFE IS HIS HOUSE

In the spatial discourse of rabbinic literature, beginning as early as the tannaitic period (pre-220 CE), houses are gendered: a man's wife

Unsettling the Temple Bayit

is referred to as "his house."[15] As Cynthia Baker notes, "In a number of rabbinic constructions, a house is not *where* a woman/wife is, but rather a house is, in part, *who* and *what* she is,"[16] resulting in a blending of the constructs wife and house. The first mishnah of tractate Yoma, which begins with the preparation for Yom Kippur of the high priest seven days prior to Yom Kippur, mentions "his bayit," referring to a substitute or "backup wife."[17] The mishnah is as follows:

> Seven days before Yom Kippur they set apart the high priest from his house [and send him] to the Parhedrin[18] chamber. And they also appoint another priest as his substitute in case some cause of invalidation should overtake him.

> Rabbi Yehudah says: "They also appoint another woman as a substitute for his wife, in case [his wife] dies," as it says, "And he shall make atonement for himself and for his house" (Leviticus 16:6). "His house," this refers to his wife.

> They said to him, "If so, there is no end to the matter." (M. Yoma 1:1)

According to M. Yoma 1:1, the high priest was sequestered for seven days, removed from his home (although we are not sure where he resides), and placed in a separate chamber in the Temple precincts to ensure that he remained in a state of purity.[19] He was required to adopt a temporary ascetic lifestyle in preparation for his performance of the Yom Kippur avodah rite (the Temple service). In addition to having another high priest prepared to replace him in the event that he became disqualified, Rabbi Yehudah notes that an additional wife must be readied for the high priest in case his present wife dies. M. Yoma 1:1 then quotes Leviticus 16:6 as a proof text: "And he shall make atonement for himself and for "his house [beito]," making the exegetical leap from beito, which in the biblical text refers to Aaron's larger household, to the high priest's wife in the mishnah. The high priest, it is said here, must create a household; that is, he must be married when he performs the Yom Kippur avodah (service) without exception, and atone for all.[20]

When the Bavli steps in to comment on this mishnah, it focuses on justifying both the seven-day sequestration of the high priest and ensuring that he has only one wife when he performs the Yom Kippur rite.[21] A tannaitic source, T. Yoma 1:1, that is quoted on Bavli Yoma 6a attributes to Rabbi Yehudah ben Beteirah the reason for the mish-

22   *Bringing Down the Temple House*

nah's requirement of separation: "Lest his wife come to be in doubt as to whether she is menstruating and he [the high priest] has sexual relations with her, he will be impure for seven days."[22] A seminal emission that occurs on Yom Kippur eve would render the high priest impure until after sunset the following day. This too disqualifies the high priest from conducting the rite of Yom Kippur.[23] The contingency plan devised by the rabbis seems straightforward: according to M. Yoma 1:1, a substitute high priest is prepared to take over if needed. The Yom Kippur rite can then take place.

So important is the marriage of the high priest, however, that according to the minority opinion of Rabbi Yehudah in M. Yoma 1:1, the proper execution of the avodah is dependent on whether the high priest has a substitute "just-in-case" wife. While Yerushalmi Yoma 1:1, 38d is comfortable with this legal strategy, allowing for the high priest to marry on Yom Kippur if his first wife dies, the Bavli problematizes the case, creating a legal demand that makes R. Yehudah's position untenable. For the Bavli, the high priest must have only one wife, that is, only one household (one bayit) at a time. The Bavli is clear: a high priest's wife is his bayit, and without her to complete his house, he cannot atone—he cannot perform the Yom Kippur avodah.[24] There can be no moment during Yom Kippur when the high priest is wifeless. A gap in time disqualifies the avodah, as do two wives and therefore two households. The presence of a substitute wife, just in case, would run the risk that the high priest would perform the Yom Kippur avodah while having two wives. Despite an allowance for men to have more than one wife, the rabbis propose a different rule for the high priest.

The anonymous redactors of the Bavli devote enormous literary energy to resolving the conundrum of making sure that the high priest is always married to one wife while ensuring another wife is available who can seamlessly (without time gaps) protect his married status to one wife at a time.[25] The complexity of this case—rather than simply replacing the high priest with another priest who is married, which is the position of Yerushalmi Yoma—sets the Bavli into a tailspin, a crisis. The stammaim creatively propose one possibility after another. In doing so, they show more concern for ensuring the high priest's marriage to one wife than for explicating the rules governing priest substitutions so that the high priest can be replaced by another who shares his priestly bloodline.[26]

Unsettling the Temple Bayit

In the lengthy Babylonian stammaitic sugya on BT Yoma 13a–14a that has little earlier tannaitic or amoraic material, the Bavli spends an enormous amount of time trying to figure out how the priest can ensure that no interruptions will prevent his Yom Kippur ritual performance because of his marriage to two wives. Imposing legal categories with respect to marriage, divorce, levirate marriage, and *aninut* (the period before the burial of a relative when a mourner is exempt from certain commandments), not to mention exploring possibilities that involve the space of the synagogue, the rabbis offer many imaginative legal propositions in an effort to find a resolution. Consider three examples: The high priest betroths a second wife and offers his first wife a conditional divorce that will take effect retroactively, saying to her, "This is your *get* [divorce document] on the condition that you die." In other words, if his first wife dies, she will be retroactively divorced from him extending back to the beginning of Yom Kippur and allowing the second wife to be his "one household," closing the all-important gap of time. The problem is that his first wife might remain alive, and then he would effectively have two wives. Offering another possible solution, Bavli Yoma suggests that he marry a second wife and give her a conditional *get*, saying, "This is your *get* in the event that you do not die." In this way, if both wives remain alive on Yom Kippur, the second wife is automatically divorced from him as she satisfies the terms of the *get*, and the first wife enables him to perform the avodah. But this alternative solution is also problematic. If his first wife dies, he is stuck in an untenable position because he will not have any wives—one will have died; the other will effectively be divorced from him. The Bavli tries again. The priest says to his second wife, "This is your *get* on the condition that one of you dies." Once again, if neither of them dies, the high priest has two wives. The Bavli perseveres, offering several other solutions to the problem, but none of them work.

As the sugya progresses, the rabbis explore the high priest's legal status as an *onein* (BT Yoma 13b–14a) should his wife die.[27] In such a case he would not be able to atone for himself and his household even if he had another wife waiting, because an onein cannot eat sacrificial meat. Since Yom Kippur is a fast day (this being the only instance in Bavli Yoma where the priest's Yom Kippur fast is specifically mentioned),[28] an argument is made for overriding his status as an onein, giving him the right to continue offering sacrifices despite the loss of his first wife

24   *Bringing Down the Temple House*

or the backup wife. However, this suggestion too is challenged in an attempt to halt a conversation that inches toward removing any obstacles impeding the high priest's continuous married status so that the avodah rite can occur. It cannot be done.

At the end of the sugya (BT Yoma 14a), the personhood of the high priest is finally considered, that is, the idea that he might be saddened by the death of his wife. In one final comment of just a few words, Rabbi Yehudah's case as interpreted by the Bavli is undone: נהי דאנינות לא חיילא עליה, אטרודי מי לא מיטריד—"Granted that [the legal status of] aninut does not take effect on him [and does not affect his ability to offer sacrifices], but isn't he troubled [by the death of his wife]!?" Rabbi Yehudah's position cannot be resolved. The anonymous redactor uses a rhetorical tone to end this argument as if to say: "Did you, Rabbi Yehudah, really suggest that a priest take a backup wife? If his wife dies, would he be emotionally able to conduct the avodah at all?" It is the high priest's emotional state after the loss of his wife that disqualifies him from fulfilling his responsibilities in performing the avodah. In this way, his emotional state stands in the way of his larger participatory role, and the sugya cannot find a resolution to support Rabbi Yehudah's opinion that a backup wife is necessary.

That said, for much of this sugya, the discourse is informed by a disruption to the high priest's house/bayit due to his wife's death. Here the Bavli expresses that the high priest's ability to perform the avodah in the Temple bayit, or not, is dependent on his relationship with his wife — specifically with regard to whether he is distraught or not over her death. She is the linchpin even in death. She enables or prevents the proper performance of her husband's high priest responsibilities. If she dies, his connection to the Temple house on Yom Kippur can be interrupted. It is perhaps better that the high priest is replaced with another priest, in keeping with the majority opinion in M. Yoma 1:1 and parallel to the position presented in Yerushalmi Yoma (JT Yoma 1:1, 38d). It would seem simpler to rely on a male-male transfer of power from one high priest to another. However, for the Bavli, this strategy receives brief attention in comparison to the discussion about the high priest's need for one wife.[29] In the case of the Bavli, the stammaim push the discussion toward the male-female relationship of marriage, calling significant attention to the death of the high priest's wife and the threat that ensues to the Temple service relative to the high priest's emotional stability on the most significant day of the year.

Unsettling the Temple Bayit

The overarching message that weaves its way through the Babylonian layers of anonymous material is that high priests cannot control for the unexpected variables of real life. Despite their position in the Temple, they cannot prevent or control for the death of their wives. They are unable to ensure that the Yom Kippur avodah rite will function properly every year, year after year, a point that does not emerge in the Mishnah or in the Yerushalmi's analysis of the same mishnah. In the end, not only does a wife's potential status as a menstruant threaten her husband's qualification for performing the avodah, but her death can also threaten his emotional state, posing obstacles to his ritual performance. More to the point, the high priest's "wife," who signifies his "house," is not congruent with his ritual "house," in that a high priest can never be assured that one house (his marriage to one wife) will remain intact for the sake of the other. Thinking with women, specifically about the high priest's marriage to one wife, underscores that something about the Temple observance of Yom Kippur is awry. But what does that mean? As Jonathan Smith has argued, ritual represents a "controlled environment" where the variables of ordinary life are pushed aside so that one engages in a perfect performance knowing full well that it is ideal.[30] In this case, the priests cannot perform the Yom Kippur Temple rite in the face of the unresolvable precariousness of daily life. Without an assurance that high priests can remain married to one wife, the Bavli unsettles the Yom Kippur avodah as well as the ideal integrity of the Temple house necessary for its performance.

THE MEZUZAH: MARKING SPACE

In a shift from the relationship of marriage to the space of the Temple itself, the Bavli engages in a comparison between the Temple and all of the commonplace houses—storehouses, barns, tanneries, and bathhouses—that can be considered Jewish space.[31] The Temple's chambers or the rooms within it that make Temple practice functional are juxtaposed with the mundane ancillary houses outside its walls that make the daily life of the rabbinic household run. Using the mezuzah, a prominent spatial marker essential for fulfilling the biblical commandment to "inscribe" the words of Torah on the doorposts of one's house (Deuteronomy 6:9, 11:21), the Bavli's anonymous redactors proceed to differentiate Temple house spaces from other house spaces.[32]

26   *Bringing Down the Temple House*

Not all "houses" require a mezuzah despite being labeled as bayit/ beit. While Gaston Bachelard argues that houses and the rooms within them (or supplementary to them) are extensions of persons, meaning that they are "felicitous" spaces with "protective and comforting associations,"[33] the rabbinic exploration of the term *bayit* in Bavli Yoma illustrates that rabbinic notions of houses are quite messy (literally and figuratively). Making determinations about whether a space requires a mezuzah at all depends on what occurs within its walls. Rather than thinking about the mezuzah as a material signpost used to distinguish between holy and profane spaces, what emerges is a desire to use this object to differentiate dignified from undignified spaces based on the activities that occur within them. The use of the term *bayit* as a descriptive label does not link every space deemed a bayit to another, nor does it preside over or govern the laws of mezuzah.

Mishnah Yoma 1:1 opens with a commandment to separate the high priest from his house, sending him to the Temple's Parhedrin chamber for a weeklong separation from his wife and household before Yom Kippur, to ensure his purity for the service. No mention of a mezuzah for the chamber appears in Mishnah Yoma, although the Tosefta (T. Yoma 1:1–2), on which the Babylonian sugya is constructed, begins with a description of the sequestration of the high priest and is followed immediately by the exemption of chambers of the Temple from the requirement of mezuzah.[34]

Based on BT Yoma 8b–9a and Yoma 19a, the Bavli asserts two things about the Parhedrin chamber. First, its name, Parhedrin, carries a negative connotation (8b). Second, as the Bavli attributes to the amora Rav Pappa, it is one of the central chambers where the high priest dwells before performing the Yom Kippur avodah.[35] Bavli Yoma quotes a baraita on 8b noting that the Parhedrin chamber was associated with unsavory high priests who bought themselves positions via bribery. Such behavior necessitated the removal of these priests every twelve months just like the non-Jewish "Parhedrin," where officials needed to be replaced every twelve months (BT Yoma 8b). This baraita then sets off further discussion about the disreputable behaviors of high priests, who, especially during the Second Temple period, were replaced before the end of a year (BT Yoma 9a).[36] Later in the first chapter of the tractate, a lengthy passage attributed to the Babylonian rabbi Rav Pappa focuses on what the high priest did inside the chamber, intimating that he slept in the Parhedrin chamber during the seven-day period prior to

Unsettling the Temple Bayit   27

Yom Kippur.[37] Each day the priest would rise, leave the chamber, relieve himself, and then immerse before going to the Avtinas chamber to fill his hands with incense. Then he would perform the daily Temple service, be sprinkled with water, immerse, and return to the chamber to sleep (BT Yoma 19a). Each stage of the procedure during his sequestration appears to be subject to oversight by others, creating an image of the high priest as lacking the knowledge and the memory to prepare for the avodah properly on his own. The image of the high priest that emerges here in the Bavli's collection of tannaitic and amoraic material is of the high priest as a member of an inferior class in comparison to the rabbis, not only needing assistance with all aspects of Temple procedure but also as one who needed to be confined to dwelling in a specific space for the seven-day sequestration period in order to protect him, and therefore the holiness of Yom Kippur.[38]

The discussion about the mezuzah begins inside the walls of the Temple with the Parhedrin chamber, setting the stage for distinguishing the Temple from the chambers found within it and the spaces outside it. Only the Parhedrin chamber is singled out and requires a mezuzah:

> The Rabbis taught [in a baraita]: None of the chambers in the Temple had a *mezuzah* except for the Chamber of Parhedrin, because this was the place of residence of the high priest.

> Rabbi Yehudah said: Were there not several chambers in the Temple that were place[s] of residence and yet they did not have a mezuzah? Rather, [the mezuzah] in the Chamber of Parhedrin [was required by] rabbinic decree. (CBT Yoma 10a)

So despite the fact that the high priest was housed in the Parhedrin chamber temporarily, a mezuzah *was* required by both the rabbis and Rabbi Yehudah, according to the baraita cited above. The disagreement between them is merely over whether the mezuzah is required by biblical or rabbinic decree. According to the way the stammaim understand Rabbi Yehudah, biblically one cannot place a mezuzah on a structure where one is legally forced to reside. For Rabbi Yehudah, a mezuzah is generally required only on the doorposts of permanent spaces where one's residence is voluntary and not required by law (BT Yoma 10b). In this regard, the Parhedrin chamber needs no mezuzah, at least according to Rabbi Yehudah.[39] But because the high priest's se-

28   *Bringing Down the Temple House*

questration residence, due to a required weeklong separation from his wife to maintain his purity status, appears to be forced on him, Rabbi Yehudah makes an exception and requires a mezuzah on the chamber. The reason for this, according to the stammaim, is a concern for outward appearances.[40] How would it look if there was no mezuzah? Would people think that the high priest was being kept in the Parhedrin chamber against his will?

The Bavli imagines that those who turn their gaze toward the Parhedrin chamber might presume that the high priest was imprisoned there if they do not see a mezuzah.[41] Such individuals, who are presumed to know rabbinic law, might link together the notion that in the absence of a mezuzah, the high priest's seven-day residence would appear forced on him. Seeing the mezuzah, however, would indicate that the high priest is in the chamber, willingly sequestering himself for a week before the Yom Kippur rite. The rhetoric here seems to point to a group of Babylonian rabbis who want to assert their control over the Temple but are worried about that control as well. After all, the mezuzah, as the stammaim argue, hangs on the doorpost of the Parhedrin chamber because of a rabbinic ruling, not because of a decision made by the priests themselves. The mezuzah functions as no more than a necessary prop, commandeered by the stammaim through their interpretation of Rabbi Yehudah, to convince themselves and others in the Temple courtyards that they have protected the high priest from impurity and thus ensured that the rite of Yom Kippur can in fact take place. More to the point, Rabbi Yehudah's position is, for the stammaim, an opportunity to make an argument for a priesthood that consents to rabbinic decrees.[42]

Oddly, of all the chambers in the Temple referred to as *batim* (houses)—chambers for incense preparation, immersion, and preparing sacrifices—only the Parhedrin chamber needs a mezuzah. Interestingly, the Parhedrin chamber is also the one space where no specific Temple practices occur. This is a dwelling place for the priest to sleep and eat. It is his house for a week. In the absence of his wife, this space spotlights what matters for the larger redactional agenda at play in this tractate. Interweaving tannaitic and amoraic material into a larger stammaitic discussion about the mezuzah also brings the absence of the high priest's sexual activity to the fore, that is, the requirement incumbent on the high priest to remain ritually pure in order to perform the Temple Yom Kippur service. This sexless state, albeit temporary in

Unsettling the Temple Bayit

29

this case, is one that the rabbis wish to associate with the Temple and the priesthood—but not with themselves—as will become evident as the tractate unfolds.

On BT Yoma 11a, the rabbis widen this discussion of the mezuzah to compare the Temple with houses outside its walls, leaving the Temple's internal chambers aside. It is here that places where women are found surface alongside other mundane spaces—for example, *beit ha-teven* (a storehouse for hay), *beit habakar* (a storehouse for cattle), *beit ha'eitzim* (a storehouse for wood), and *beit ha'otzarot* (a general storehouse). After focusing on the Parhedrin chamber, an all-male space within the Temple precincts, the Bavli moves on to discuss the requirement of the mezuzah as contingent on wherever women dwell.[43] In the hands of the Bavli's editors, "dwelling" means that these "houses" are places women use to bathe themselves, a factor that designates them as "undignified spaces"—whether they are public bathhouses or private ones. A shift then occurs in the Bavli as it moves from requiring mezuzot in spaces where people reside, to spaces where the nature of what occurs within them is or is not decorous or respectful.[44] Whereas the demarcation of a house or space as bayit alone may not link all similar-named spaces to one another, a bathroom (*beit hakise*), a tannery (*beit haburski*), a bathhouse (*beit hamerhatz*), and a house of immersion (*beit hatevilah*) are connected or linked by virtue of the foul smells, blood, dirty water, and bodily excrement that make them unfit for a mezuzah (משום דנפיש זוהמיה), as BT Yoma 11ab states. Nonsacred houses, in contrast, made specifically for "dignified" uses, must have mezuzot (בית עשוי לכבוד).

Imposing this discussion about spaces outside the Temple back onto the Parhedrin chamber located inside the Temple labels this chamber with its mezuzah as a dignified space. But no Temple-related practices happen there. The high priest merely sleeps and eats. Sexual relations do not happen there. The Temple's bayit within a bayit with a mezuzah on its lintel becomes a nested space where "dignified" behavior occurs in preparation for the ritual of atonement on Yom Kippur, as the rabbis orchestrate it. But the rabbis stop short of extrapolating from the Parhedrin chamber to the larger Temple bayit and the remainder of its chambers and gates in the requirement of mezuzah.[45] In contrast to the Parhedrin chamber, the holy space of the Temple and its chambers do not need mezuzot, despite their understood demarcation as spaces intended for the "dignified" worship of God:

30   *Bringing Down the Temple House*

I might have thought to include in the obligation of mezuzah even the Temple Mount and its chambers and courtyards. Therefore, the verse states: "House"; just as a house is a [structure] that is non-sacred, so too any place that is non-sacred is obligated in the mitzvah of mezuzah, excluding those [structures] that are sacred. (BT Yoma 11b)

On one level, exempting the Temple from the commandment of mezuzah highlights the exceptionalism of the Temple space, sacralizing it by differentiating it from all other spaces that define the rabbis' built environment. However, recognizing the redactor's decision to link a discussion about ancillary houses outside the Temple's walls to a discussion about whether the Temple Mount, including the Temple and its chambers, requires a mezuzah, suggests something through its redactional design. The textual and comparative juxtaposition of tannaitic and amoraic material about which houses are to have mezuzot prompts consideration of which houses align with which houses. More specifically, an outhouse, a tannery, a bathhouse, a place of immersion, and places that women use, quite ironically, parallel the Temple space in the sense that they all happen to be spaces that do not require mezuzot.[46] This comparison then suggests that these spaces have something in common. While the rabbis do not label the Temple outright as an unseemly place, the way the stammaim construct their sources highlights by way of comparison that the Temple also has qualities that deem it an undignified space. Its potent smells, muck, dirty water, blood, and excrement discharge the need for a mezuzah (BT Yoma 11a). From the Temple's foul-smelling animals that were sacrificed in great numbers, the blood that flowed from the bodies of these animals, the excrement, and the dirty water coursing through the Temple's grounds, there was much material disgust.[47] By mapping foul mundane spaces onto the Temple via the absence of a mezuzah, the rabbis desacralize the Temple house and intimate that something new should replace it.[48]

Biblically, houses that require mezuzot promise reward. According to Deuteronomy 11:21, inscribing God's words onto "your house" (ביתך) with a mezuzah grants long life. To make this point, BT Yoma 11b introduces additional spaces distinct from the Temple, pointing to those that in fact require a mezuzah. Each one—a synagogue, a house where women gather, and a house jointly owned—connects people

Unsettling the Temple Bayit   31

with others who might not necessarily be members of the same family or bloodline. That these "houses," even in cases where women gather, must have mezuzot reveals a belief in God's biblical promise of longevity. Houses with mezuzot are spaces that grant those within them a future. The absence of a mezuzah suggests not only that these are spaces where people do not reside, but like the Temple house, they are precarious and fragile structures.

PROFANE HOUSES

Material about mezuzot proceeds right into a discussion of house leprosy, a type of mildew that taints the walls of private houses. By doing so, the sugya highlights a profound threat to everyday households and their material contents (BT Yoma 11b). Cleverly, the Bavli inserts two parallel baraitot into its larger discussion in order to move from spaces requiring mezuzot to house spaces afflicted with house leprosy (nega'im). The integration of these two baraitot into the larger framework, however, taps into a concern as to why synagogues must have a mezuzah whereas the Temple does not. Resolving this issue depends on a comparison between them. Strikingly, the comparison is linked to whether these two spaces are subject to house impurity. The two baraitot that form the skeleton of the remainder of the sugya are as follows:

> It was taught in a baraita: A synagogue, a house [where] women [gather] and a house owned by partners are required for mezuzah. . . .
>
> As it is taught in another baraita: A synagogue, a house owned by partners and a house [where] women [gather] become impure with [house] leprosy. (BT Yoma 11b)[49]

According to Leviticus 14:35-37, responsibility for the purification of houses outside the Temple walls that contract impurity is placed entirely in the hands of a priest.[50] Reversing the trajectory that brings the priest into the Parhedrin chamber to protect him from "his house," that is, from "his wife," before Yom Kippur, house impurity introduces the priests' responsibilities in ridding private houses where non-priests can reside from impurity. Priests are accountable for the inspection of such houses and for ensuring that the contamination is removed properly. In moving beyond the discussion of whether the entryway of different types of houses need mezuzot and into the physical space of a house tainted by leprosy, the sugya calls attention to a threat to the subsistence of the daily household. The mildew that seeps into the walls of a house, rendering it impure, can be utterly destructive. It can spread to the very contents of the house. In the face of such a damaging force, householders are required to remove the objects within their houses prior to the priest's inspection, protecting them, they hope, from the spread of impurity. In the end, if the mildew cannot be eliminated entirely, the house must be destroyed (Leviticus 14:45). Indeed, in comparison to rabbis who make decisions about Temple spaces and mezuzot, priests appear to have more power outside the Temple than they do within its walls. They can leave their Temple house, go outside Jerusalem, and declare a house impure or pure.

That said, not all house spaces are contaminable. While spaces that require a mezuzah, such as a synagogue, a house owned by two people, or a place where women gather, are prone to house leprosy, the Temple itself cannot be defiled with this type of impurity. Tied to the idea of landownership and derived from midrashic readings of Leviticus 14:34–35, house leprosy applies only to houses that people physically own and within which they permanently reside.[51] In contrast, the Temple belongs to no one other than God, and therefore it possesses a level of sanctity absent from mundane houses. In addition, the walls of houses in Jerusalem, as opposed to Jewish homes in other locales, fit into the same category as the Temple. Their inability to contract house leprosy signifies that Jerusalem bears a similar degree of holiness. Ultimately the Bavli returns to the issue of whether synagogues can contract house leprosy, reversing the position found in the tannaitic material cited earlier. By introducing the category of sacred space (מקום מקודש), the anonymous redactors include the synagogue and the house of study, equating them with the Temple by virtue of the fact that they too cannot contract house leprosy.

Unexpectedly, this conclusion seems to overturn the idea presented earlier in the sugya that the Temple in the absence of a requirement for a mezuzah aligns closely with other houses that are not required for mezuzot. The stammaim had aligned various houses that did not require mezuzot alongside one another to call attention to the idea that Temple ritual turned the Temple into an undignified space filled with dirt and muck and blood. However, by introducing one more category of law, house leprosy, these rabbis quite ironically turn something as

Unsettling the Temple Bayit

physical and impure as house mold into an avenue for locating the core of Temple sacredness. They find it not in the material and physical nature of the Temple's ritual performances or in its walls but in the metaphysical idea of holiness that can be infused into spaces outside the Temple, such as into the synagogue and the house of study. That said, for whatever sacredness the synagogue and the house of study might share with the Temple as determined by their inability to contract house leprosy, in requiring a mezuzah, these spaces align far more closely with the everyday bayit than with the Temple itself.[52]

CONCLUSION

The body and the house are webs of signification that profoundly inform one another in Bavli Yoma to express a perspective regarding the Temple and its priesthood.[53] A husband creates a house both metaphorically and physically when he marries a wife. She is "his house."[54] So significant is this equation that a high priest must be married to one wife in order to ensure that the atonement for "his household" is acceptable. The effort made by the stammaim to challenge the priest's ability to maintain his marriage to one wife upends the husband-wife-house linkage and, with it, the structure of the Temple. Nothing will guarantee that the high priest's wife will remain alive for the duration of Yom Kippur, a fact that accentuates the instability of the role of the high priest while serving in the Temple, as well as the potential ineffectiveness of the Temple rite of atonement itself.[55] In other words, the husband-wife relationship that most signifies the construction of a solid "house" does not map onto the Temple house. Not only does the priest inhabit the Parhedrin chamber without his wife, but he is confronted with the possibility of disqualification if he does not remain married to her throughout Yom Kippur.

From the relationship of the high priest and his wife to other more common spaces that are also referred to as bayit, Bavli Yoma's anonymous redactors weave together an assemblage of different "houses" connected via the requirement of the mezuzah. Most of these houses are storehouses or places where livelihoods are made, such as the tannery. But houses designated specifically for women, used for bathing and ritual immersion, also become the means through which the Bavli's redactors conjure an image of an indecorous all-male Temple space by comparison. Effectively, their continuous associative logic and rea-

34 *Bringing Down the Temple House*

soning move from the consequences of deceased wives to the repercussions of smelly spaces to moldy walls, calling into question whether they wish for the return of the Temple and the authority of the priesthood at all.

And yet, quite conspicuously, the stammaim infuse the synagogue and the house of study with the Temple's holiness, not through comparisons made through the mezuzah but through a discussion of the category of house impurity associated with the destruction of houses and their material contents. The undertaking of this feat is far from smooth. An element of equivocation surfaces: Why choose a household mold to make a point about the infusion of Temple sacredness into the synagogue and the house of study? Having begun with the Parhedrin chamber and the requirement to place a mezuzah on its entryway, Bavli Yoma introduces house impurity, signifying the extent to which it also strains to acknowledge the Temple's holiness. In addition, this redactional decision to introduce a category of law that has no bearing on M. Yoma 1:1 and nothing to do with the Temple indicates that the redactors are fashioning earlier material into discourse that points in a particular direction shaped by them. House impurity brings the everyday household into view, foreshadowing Bavli Yoma's final chapter. By chapter eight of the tractate, the Temple as well as the synagogue and the house of study fall from view. The focus shifts to the everyday house, not through an examination of house impurity but through the Yom Kippur practice of self-denial that brings human and household fragility to the fore.

Unsettling the Temple Bayit

CHAPTER 2

VIOLENCE IN
THE TEMPLE

Priest-Fathers and

Their Sons

• • •

The rabbinic critique of the priests reaches its apex as holy ritual turns to bloodshed.[1] In chapter two of Bavli Yoma, the necessary Temple housekeeping task of removing ash left by the sacrifices (*terumat hadeshen*) devolves into an act of carnage that pits priest against priest within the Temple walls. Mishnah Yoma 2:1–2 and an accompanying baraita on BT Yoma 23a present parallel versions of this story, narrating the actions of zealous priests rushing to gain an advantage over their fellow priests by running up the ramp to the Temple altar.[2] Highlighting uncharitable behavior, the versions of the story that are worked into the Bavli illuminate how the Temple cannot effectively "house" these types of priest-priest relationships. Priests housed within the Temple precincts undermine their priestly community and the rites that connect them. A portrait of dysfunctionality surfaces, creating a need for the rabbis to intervene. Paying attention to the differences introduced into Bavli Yoma's version of the tannaitic story, as well as additional stammaitic comments added to analyze the tannaitic narrative, the narrative thread of instability that is layered onto the Temple house and its priests emerges.[3]

Widening the scope of feminist studies to reveal instances of how and where the rabbis marginalize other males—in this case, the priests—illuminates early on in Bavli Yoma the ways in which the rabbis wish to define and augment their own masculinity in contrast to the men who make up the all-male house of the Temple. Fellow priests, arguably part of a familial clan, not to mention priest-fathers and their sons, spark the rabbis' thinking about a rabbinic masculinity tied to the creation of themselves as new father-like figures in the hope of augmenting their own image.[4] Rabbis will emerge here as nothing like the priests. Priest-fathers will point to relationships with sons that need to be replaced, built instead on something other than Temple rites.

Moreover, this tannaitic story of priests vying to be the first to clean the ritual ashes and the way that the redactors of Bavli Yoma embed it into a larger sugya linked to Mishnah Yoma 2:1–2 enables this Temple vignette to function as a literary climax to a far longer story about past challenges to biological kinship and successful leadership. Collating some of the most pivotal events in the lives of the Israelite kings, Saul and David, Bavli Yoma brings to the fore the ways that leadership can promise stability and yet still falter. Before introducing misbehaving priests, the anonymous redactors navigate through biblical material about the establishment of institutional houses and the negotiation of power by male elites who are chosen by God and who, even with the strength of a bloodline to support them, stumble into committing unforgiveable sins.

MISHNAH YOMA 2:1–2 AND THE
RITE OF TERUMAT HADESHEN

In biblical law, the first daily procedure connected to the offering of sacrifices on the altar, performed each morning before the sun rose, was the removal of ash from sacrifices burned the day before, this in accordance with the commandment in Leviticus 6:3: "The priest shall dress in linen raiment, with linen breeches on his body; and he shall take up the ashes (*heirim et hadeshen*) to which the fire has reduced the burnt offering (*'olah*) on the altar and place them beside the altar." A priest would ascend to the altar, gather a shovelful of ash, descend, and place the ash next to the altar. The image of this ancient, biblically mandated act of symbolic ritual housekeeping, for which the priests needed to dress appropriately, linked male priests to the daily upkeep of cultic life. Bavli Yoma, in commenting on the M. Yoma 2:1–2 where this rite is mentioned, takes this rite apart to look at it from many angles, from the space next to the altar where the priests prepared to ascend to collect the ash to the procedure itself. The progression of the Bavli's discourse homes in on who would collect the ash, the garments that needed to be worn, whether non-priests could perform the rite, whether priests who had been disqualified could perform the rite, whether the removal of ash was considered an official Temple service

Violence in the Temple

(avodah), and finally, how much ash needed to be gathered (BT Yoma 22a–24b). M. Yoma 2:1–2 begins with a narrative description of this procedure of ash removal. It reveals an image constructed initially by the tannaim of the way the priests "kept" their holy "house":

> At first, any [priest] who wanted to separate [the ash] from the altar separated it. And when the [priests who sought this privilege] became many, they would run up the ramp [of the altar, and] whoever preceded his fellow into the [top] four cubits [of the ramp] won [the privilege]. (Mishnah Yoma 2:1)

The Mishnah describes the rite of ash removal as a form of ritual housekeeping. In an archetypical way, just as a man's wife is "his house (beito)," male priests "were" the Temple.[5] They were responsible for its daily maintenance; they were its keepers.[6] While there is a degree of slipperiness with regard to the distinction between male and female labors in rabbinic sources, as both men and women laundered and mended clothing, for example,[7] this never stopped the rabbis from trying to distinguish men's from women's tasks.[8] Like the quotidian tasks of the rabbinic wife, which connected her to her husband and made her "his house," the priests' housekeeping tasks, such as removing ash from the altar, powerfully associated the priests with their Temple house. As Dalia Marx argues, the Temple was the domestic realm of God, where an all-male priesthood took on the domestic tasks often associated with women, such as washing, sweeping, gathering, and cooking.[9] But rather than turning the priests into the "best" of men for performing the chores necessary for serving God in the holy space of the Temple, the domestic responsibility of removing the leftover ash from the sacrifices performed on the altar displays the priests as men competing for a privilege that was not available to all of them unless they reached the ramp of the altar first.[10]

More to the point, the rite of ash removal turns the priests who wish to execute it into forceful men vying for the right to perform a biblical commandment. The mishnah relates that when the number of priests serving in the Temple came to outnumber the rites available for each to perform, they introduced a competition.[11] The priest who could beat his fellow priests on their way up the ramp to the altar would merit the right to perform the ash removal. These men ritualize their competitive behavior, turning the performance of a Temple rite into an earthly game in which the most athletic priest is rewarded with the ability to perform a domestic Temple house rite.[12] This literary move couches the priests' masculinity in physical terms in that they become "hot-blooded" and aggressive.[13] M. Yoma 2:2 accentuates the potential dangers of this model of masculinity by highlighting what can occur when priests use their male bodies to outshine one another in the name of performing a Temple rite:

> A story is told of two priests who were running up the ramp simultaneously, and one of them pushed his colleague, who fell, and his leg was broken. When the *beit din* [court] realized that [the priests] were getting into danger, they decreed that they would [be selected to] separate [the ash from] the altar only by lot. Four lots were cast there [in the Temple], and this was the first lot. (Mishnah Yoma 2:2)

Here the priests embody a type of masculinity, rooted in bodily strength, that has unfavorable consequences. Realizing the hazards of a priestly race up the ramp to determine who removes the ash, the beit din steps in to change the procedure. The composition of this court could very well have been a group of rabbis, which makes sense in the context here. Admittedly, some might argue that this beit din was composed instead of priests making decisions regarding their own rite, given sources such as M. Ketubot 1:5, which describes a court of priests supervising family ritual matters related to women's claims of virginity. However, it is also the case that judges, going back to the biblical period, were not necessarily priests.[14] M. Sanhedrin 1:1, which describes the makeup of various courts, indicates that even in cases where priests were required on the court, they were always outnumbered by non-priests. M. Yoma 1:5 suggests that the rabbis referred to themselves as "agents of the court" along with the high priest and declared themselves its full-fledged members. It is surely possible that the rabbis imagined themselves as controlling the courts, granting themselves the decision-making power to oversee matters connected to Temple rites and the priesthood.[15] In fact, tractate Yoma makes it clear that the priests needed rabbinic supervision. M. Yoma 1:3 intimates that the high priest was illiterate and needed the *zekeinim*, the rabbinic sages, to read the Torah portion containing the Yom Kippur service to him during the seven days of sequestration;[16] similarly, a tannaitic source on BT Yoma 4a describes the high priest as requiring "two *talmidei ḥakhamim* of the disciples of Moses, to the exclusion of the

Violence in the Temple   39

Sadducees, to [transmit the laws of the Yom Kippur service]." Arguably, it is the rabbis who introduce the noncompetitive approach of drawing lots. They envision themselves as having authority over priests who could not manage to complete a daily Temple ritual task without pushing aside a fellow priest, as BT Yoma 22a clarifies (see below).

The drawing of lots generates a sense of parity among the priests, preventing the more physically able from gaining an advantage over weaker individuals. As such, the rabbis (represented by the beit din here) imagine themselves as instituting a less dangerous and more equitable way to perform Temple ritual, in comparison to the priests, who, when left to their own devices, opt for a more aggressive, competitive approach in a display of invented machismo. The Temple procedure is thus made to seem open to the impulse of the individual, each man out for himself; by contrast, the rabbis of the Mishnah imagine themselves here as capable of asserting their own decision-making abilities as a legal community, functioning as a rabbinic court of men who initiate a more equitable Temple system. The point that rabbinic cerebral, communal masculinity, rooted in legal decision making, is preferable to the priests' individual exhibitions of cutthroat behavior is made on and through the priests' bodies.

BT YOMA 22A–23A: THE SINS
OF THE PRIESTS IN CONTEXT

The development of the sugya that comments on M. Yoma 2:1–2, beginning with BT Yoma 22a and leading up to the second version of the story of two priests who chase one another up a ramp (found in a baraita on BT Yoma 23a), has two large interlocking threads that need to be considered. The first is an attempt by the Bavli to credit the rabbis with the decision to enforce the casting of lots and, in so doing, make the priests look more inferior to them than they do in the Mishnah. The second is a memory of the sins of the two competitive Israelite kings, Saul and David, turning an original tannaitic story into a cautionary tale about viable leadership. Starting out with a stammaitic question as to why the rabbis did not institute the practice of lots before any priests were harmed, the stammaim clear the rabbis of wrongdoing making the following point:

> Why didn't the rabbis institute the casting of lots at the beginning [before there was trouble]?

40   *Bringing Down the Temple House*

At first [they—the rabbis] thought that because the service [of separating the ash] occurred at night, it would not be considered [important to the priests] and they would not come [all at once]. [Therefore, the rabbis did not institute a lottery].

But when they [the rabbis] saw that they [the priests] did come and they came to danger, they instituted lots . . .

[Later in the sugya it states]: After they instituted the casting of lots, the priests did not come [because] they said [to themselves]: Who can say that [the lot] will fall on us (me)?

Therefore, the rabbis revised [the procedure saying] whoever wins [the right] of separating the ash, [also] wins [the right of] arranging [the wood for the] fire and placing two blocks of wood [on it].

This was so that they [the priests] would come and cast lots [in order to participate]. (BT Yoma 22a)

Faced with a baraita that connects winning the right to ash removal with another Temple rite on BT Yoma 22a, specifically that of arranging the wood for the pyre and placing two wood planks on it (Leviticus 6:2), the Bavli makes clear that it is the rabbis who keep adjusting Temple procedures to ensure that the priests draw lots. It is the rabbis who are not only most concerned with protecting the priests from harm, but it is they who claim the right to make enactments that govern priestly behavior. Here the stammaim are clear to point out that additional privileges tied to preparing the altar pyre for sacrifice needed to be added to motivate the priests to take on their priestly responsibilities.

When the Bavli moves on to discuss the actual procedure of casting lots, a process that involved each priest putting out their fingers in order to be counted, the sugya bristles at the idea of counting Israelites/Jews. Along the way, the Bavli weaves in references to King Saul's wartime experiences of counting, quoting 1 Samuel 11:8, where after a successful battle against the Ammonites, Samuel, the prophet, inaugurates Saul as king. This is coupled with a reference to 1 Samuel 15:4, where the very idea of keeping tallies of troops brings the Bavli to mention Saul and his refusal to carry out God's instructions in the battle with Amalek (BT Yoma 22b).[17] Saul's choice to save the choicest animals and not kill the king of Amalek, Agag, countering God's command that he should destroy the entire city (1 Samuel 15:3), leads to

Violence in the Temple   41

Saul's ultimate downfall and to the removal of kingship from his familial line. In 1 Samuel 15:11, as Bavli Yoma points out, God says, "I regret that I made Saul king."

Saul's invocation of the *eglah arufah*, a rite performed to atone for a murder when the murderer is unknown, is a way to atone for his own sins and, more specifically, to explain his decision to save the Amalekites' animals. It is the Bavli's way of foreshadowing the transgressions of the priests whose race up the Temple ramp will be introduced in a baraita on BT Yoma 23a. To mention the eglah arufah is for Saul, according to the Bavli,[18] a way for him to atone for his errors. In response, he receives a warning from God: not to be overly righteous. No doubt, the response is rhetorical because the eglah arufah cannot atone for murder in Saul's case.[19] Bloodshed in the war with Amalek is premeditated and the murderers surely known. Invoking the eglah arufah signifies that there is nothing Saul can do to reverse his failure to follow God's instructions, prefiguring Rabbi Tzadok's use of the same image later in the sugya (BT Yoma 23a).

Immediately before transitioning to discuss David's sins, Bavli Yoma 22b spotlights a pronounced moment of competition between King Saul and David that results in the death of the community of priests living in the city of Nov (1 Samuel 22:18). Fleeing from Saul, David travels though this city and relies on them for food and supplies. Infused by jealousy and unrestrained rivalry with David, Saul punishes the priests of Nov for aligning themselves with his adversary. He commands one of his courtiers, Doeg, to kill them all (BT Yoma 22b). As such, the power of Saul rises to the surface: kings have more power than priests. At the same time, the admiration of the priests for David, who is not yet their king, and the competitive surge that rises in Saul in response, pinpoints what can unsettle the institution of kingship. This presages the adversarial relationships that are central to the tannaitic portrayals of the priests and will be quoted by the Bavli on BT Yoma 23a.

When BT Yoma 22b moves on to recognize David as the king who replaces Saul, it does so by measuring the sins of both, one against the other. As the Bavli recalls, David's sins are greater in number than Saul's. From David's sexual relationship with Batsheva, his killing of her husband, Uriah, and his wrongful decision to take a census of the people that resulted in the death of thousands by plague, David epitomizes the dangers of power (2 Samuel 24:1). In the story that the anonymous redactors weave, they offer both an explanation of why the

Bringing Down the Temple House

kingship of the House of Saul does not continue and conclude their discussion regarding David by mentioning the division of his kingdom into two during the reign of his grandson Reḥav'am (1 Kings 11–12).[20] The idea that God disrupts bloodlines in response to sinful behavior and that leadership roles such as kingships are not always successful become narrative fodder used by the anonymous redactors to set the stage for the upcoming baraita about the tension between rabbis and priests. Both Saul and David shook the foundations of their houses in ways that were not reversible. Recalling them draws attention to the possibility that the priesthood, like Israelite kingship, needs to be replaced.

Finally, before transitioning to share two baraitot that expose egregious behavior on the part of the priests, Rabbi Yoḥanan states, in the name of the priest-turned-rabbi Shim'on ben Yehotzadak,[21] "Any Torah scholar who does not take revenge or harbor [enmity] like a snake is not a Torah scholar" (BT Yoma 22b–23a).[22] It is here that the sugya shifts to consider the reactions of rabbis to being personally mistreated in an attempt to imagine what is different about rabbinic leadership. The anonymous redactors struggle with Shim'on ben Yehotzadak's description, challenging it with the commandment in Leviticus 19:18, "You shall not take vengeance or bear a grudge." However, in the brief piece of back-and-forth that ensues, the stammaim reinterpret Rabbi Shim'on ben Yehotzadak as stating that Torah scholars "keep [resentments] in their hearts," presumably without acting on any sense of ill will they harbor. In the end, after citing Rava's position about the importance of forgiving everyone, the discussion ends with the caveat that the one who has been harmed forgives only those who reach out to appease him (BT Yoma 23a).[23]

Unlike King Saul who acted on his feeling of resentment against David, and unlike both kings who act vengefully against others who threaten them, the rabbis present themselves as capable of similar feelings but also as able to control them. Using Shim'on ben Yehotzadak as the foil, this priest-turned-rabbi becomes, in the hands of the stammaim, a symbol of what rabbis hope they can accomplish as compared to priests. Priests so imaged cannot keep their feelings close to their hearts; instead, they act physically to harm another, letting their egos over performing the rite of ash removal govern their decision-making processes.[24] Even though some priests had become rabbis, there remained a sense of insecurity and concern among the rabbis that their

Violence in the Temple   43

male leadership role might be provisional, even questionable, in view of a biblically mandated priestly caste governed by heredity and a Temple that could be rebuilt. However, if the rabbis can make the case that priests, as keepers of the homosocial male Temple home, are corrupt, as opposed to the rabbis whose behavior is controlled by a different moral standard, they can secure a vision of an entirely distinct world from one where ritual devolved upon a priest, and a priest alone in the space of the Temple.[25]

And so at this juncture, two baraitot are introduced that pit the character of the priests against that of the rabbis (BT Yoma 23a). The stammaim use this first baraita to link back to the procedure of lots proposed by the rabbis of the Mishnah:

> But was it not taught in a baraita—they [the priests] may not put out a middle finger or a thumb because of the cheaters. And if they put out a middle finger, we count it for him; if a thumb, we do not count it for him. And not only [do we not count his thumb] but he receives lashes from the appointee of the *peki'a*. (BT Yoma 23a)

Priests, during the casting of lots, point their fingers to determine, through a system of counting, who will be picked to remove the ash. According to this baraita, in doing so, they can cheat the system by putting out a finger as well as a thumb, hoping to increase their chances to win the right to perform the ash removal. For such behavior, they are lashed. The amora Abaye then steps in to define the word, *peki'a*, used in the baraita in association with the person responsible for this punishment. Abaye, however, drives home the point that priests are lashed not by the maker of wicks (referred to as a peki'a) but with actual whips (also referred to as peki'a).[26] Unfortunately, if not ironically, the image generated is that the rabbis' introduction of lots has accomplished little in terms of sparing priests from harm. They continue to cheat the system, and for that they are punished.

But dishonest priests are not as grievous as priests who stab their fellow priests, murdering them. A more violent tannaitic version of the same story as that which appeared in M. Yoma 2:1–2 functions as the climax of this sugya and one around which its most salient messages turn. When one priest tries to outperform another, this time he will inflict injury upon his fellow with a knife.[27] Bavli Yoma, recognizing that the baraita has a different description of the events of the mishnah,

Bringing Down the Temple House

clarifies that these are not to be viewed as two different records of the same story. Rather, they are two separate events entirely—one instance of ash removal followed the other. Seen this way, the priests surface as men who fail to respond to the early signs of danger that occurred in the competition that ensued around the rite of ash removal. The rabbis then construct themselves to be men who recognize the gravity of the situation, imagining priests who have sunk so low that they need outsiders, such as the rabbis, to fix what is wrong. In response, the rabbis introduce the system of lots, a system that also fails to prevent priests from cheating, as noted in the baraita quote above. Alongside the material about Saul and David, the baraitan material offers further evidence of the notion that leaders stumble and the institutions they represent suffer irreversible consequences.

The Bavli's account of the story of two priests competing for the right to remove ash from the altar on BT Yoma 23a is an amalgam of pieces drawn from T. Yoma 1:12,[28] T. Shevu'ot 1:4,[29] Sifrei Bamidbar, Mas'ei 161, and Yerushalmi Yoma 2:1, 39d, making the Bavli's version distinct. Presumably, it is the latest of them all:

> The rabbis taught in a *baraita*: A story is told of two priests who were running up the ramp simultaneously. [When] one of them came within four cubits [of the altar] before his fellow [priest], [the other] took a knife and drove it into his [fellow's] heart. (BT Yoma 23a)

Following the stabbing, Rabbi Tzadok spoke out to a gathering of people from the steps leading up to the hall of the Temple:

> Rabbi Tzadok stood on the steps of the hall and said: "Hear, our brothers of the House of Israel.[30] Behold He [God] said [in Deuteronomy 21:1–2]: "If . . . someone slain is found lying in the open, the identity of the slayer not being known, your elders and your judges will go forth" [to perform the rite of the eglah arufah]. [As for] us, upon whom is it incumbent to bring the eglah arufah? Upon [the people of the] city or upon [the priests in the] Temple courtyards?!"[31]

All of the people burst out weeping.[32]

Rabbi Tzadok, whose name aptly means "justice," is, like Shim'on ben Yehotzadak, a priest-turned-rabbi. He is positioned here to reverse

Violence in the Temple

45

all that has transpired by doing what rabbis do: use Torah to instruct those who have committed wrongful acts.[33] He chooses the laws related to the eglah arufah rite that, according to Deuteronomy 21:1–9, enables a group of elders to atone for the sin of an unknown murderer by breaking the neck of a heifer. The heifer bears the sin and removes the community from responsibility, functioning as a scapegoat. Forestalling damaging accusations against innocent individuals is the purpose of the eglah arufah rite by eradicating the contamination of an unexpiated murder and displacing blame. The heifer, functioning as a scapegoat, bears the sin and removes responsibility from the community. This choice of biblical law to instruct the community at this moment—whether that community is a group of priests or a larger gathering of Jews (which is not clear in the narrative)—suggests that Rabbi Tzadok wishes to address the priests using familiar images. The notion that sin can be transferred onto an animal to absolve an entire community conjures the "scapegoat" ritual performed on Yom Kippur (Leviticus 16:10). Furthermore, Rabbi Tzadok can point out that while one priest has stabbed another, the entire community is responsible for tolerating competitive and zealous behavior, accentuating the notion of collective guilt.[34]

The association of the eglah arufah with the public stabbing of one priest by his fellow priest seems odd and wrongly placed. Similar to the way that Saul misuses the eglah arufah following his sinful behavior in the battle with Amalek, Rabbi Tzadok captures the people's attention with this same law that also happens not to be applicable to the situation at hand. The baraita highlights this very point. The eglah arufah cannot be performed by the people in Jerusalem or in the Temple.[35] Why would Rabbi Tzadok choose to teach this ruling? In fact, as the Bavli's stammaitic redactors point out, the perpetrator is a known individual; the stabbing is done in full view of those racing to the altar.

Rabbi Tzadok's goal is to accentuate that there is no mechanism, no scapegoat, and therefore no physical means of turning back the evil that has emerged. That is, there is no way to atone in the Temple. Furthermore, the responsibility falls on everyone—"my brothers of the house of Israel"—not just the priests. Together they had supported the continuity of a broken ritual system that instigated aggressive behavior. Rabbi Tzadok's rhetorical question makes sense: "Upon whom is it incumbent to bring the eglah arufah?" The answer is self-evident: just as there was no way for Saul to activate a process of atonement through

46   *Bringing Down the Temple House*

the eglah arufah, the same is true here in the case of the priests and the Temple.

Perplexed by Rabbi Tzadok's use of the case of the eglah arufah to make his point, the anonymous redactors in Bavli Yoma question the baraita's use of the analogy and conclude that he meant only to induce the wailing of the people, which is the response he evokes on the part of the people. His intentional misuse of biblical law brings tears of sorrow and remorse in a way that, as the Bavli sees it, signifies that much is awry, not only for the people whose atonement occurs through a priest in the Temple but also in the relationship between priests. While the act of weeping recalls a rabbinic type of repentance in the manner of a wail used to call on God, weeping also surfaces in M. Yoma 1:5 and BT Yoma 19b as a sign of utter frustration.[36] *Ziknei beit din*, presumably the rabbinic elders of the court,[37] impose an oath on the high priest, whereby he must promise not to change any of the instructions given to him by these rabbinic elders regarding the preparation of the *ketoret* (the incense).[38] In response, according to the Bavli's understanding of M. Yoma 1:5, the high priest and the rabbinic elders weep simultaneously, the high priest because of the suspicion lodged on him that he might not prepare the incense correctly and the rabbinic elders out of fear that they mistakenly accused him. Apparently weeping indicates that the relationship between the priests and the rabbis is strained. The rabbis, who feel responsible for making sure that the incense is prepared perfectly, cannot trust the high priest or themselves, and the high priest weeps because he too is not viewed as reliable to prepare the incense for which he is tasked. Returning to BT Yoma 23b, Rabbi Tzadok intentionally instigates intense weeping when he mentions the eglah arufah, referring to a rite that can never be performed in Jerusalem. His objective is to convey that the relationships between himself and the priesthood, between priest and priest, as well as between the community and the priests, have all broken down. Wailing is a cry of frustration by a people unable to set things straight.

PRIEST-FATHERS AND THEIR SONS

The actions of the father of the priest who has been stabbed is symbolic of the failure to transmit appropriate values from father to son. Intended to discredit the priestly patriline, the Bavli's rendition of this tannaitic narrative calls attention to what is wrong with the Temple

Violence in the Temple   47

through a parent-child relationship. As a rabbi among priests in the Temple, rather than as a rabbi among rabbis, Rabbi Tzadok is directly challenged by the victim's father, who approaches the priests to offer another solution, one of his own. A spark of male competition is re-introduced as the victim's priest-father tries to set things right where Rabbi Tzadok seems to have failed:

> The father of the boy came and found that he was still writhing [in death throes]. He [the father] said: "Behold, he is your atone-ment. My son is still writhing, and [therefore] the knife has not become impure [from corpse-contact]." This teaches you that they [the priests] regarded the purity of utensils more seriously than bloodshed. And so, Scripture states: "Menasseh also shed very much innocent blood, until it filled Jerusalem from end to end." (2 Kings 21:16)

Accentuating what divides them, the priest-father steps in to over-turn a rabbi immediately following this rabbi's attempt to reprimand the priests. Where Rabbi Tzadok relies on his Torah knowledge to as-sert his authority, in the name of evoking change within the commu-nity of priests and ultimately linking them to the larger community of Jews, the victim's father relies on his connection to the physicality of the sacrificial cult. In contrast to the emotional reaction of the people, this priest-father does not shed a tear for his son. He is willing to claim his son's death as the people's atonement, ignoring the personal as-pect of the tragedy and thinking only of the need for the ongoing func-tionality of the Temple. He willingly offers his son as a human sacrifice to atone for the sins of his community, superseding Rabbi Tzadok and producing, on some level, the sacrifice that is otherwise conspicuously absent from the story.[39] For this father, the male body of his son with a knife in his heart, and not a sacrificial animal, will remove the per-petrator's guilt as well as the priests' shame. In consonance with the religious structure of the Temple, where offerings clear individuals and the community of sin, this father offers up his own son. Unlike in the biblical story of Abraham and Isaac, God will not intercede to spare this son from death. The image of a protective, father-like, all-controlling God never emerges. This father's emotionless but bold ac-tions do not have the strength to muster a divine response. Sacrifice, especially human sacrifice, is not a way to interact with God. Therefore, when the anonymous redactors step in to comment on this tannaitic

48   *Bringing Down the Temple House*

story, they side with Rabbi Tzadok. Reminding the people of the eglah arufah to evoke cries of remorse, the stammaim use Rabbi Tzadok to accentuate that the priests can offer no remedy for wrongful behavior even when they try to offer up their own sons. The relationship between a father and his son, which easily calls to mind the priestly bloodline, cannot set things right.

On one level, the rabbis poke fun at this priest-father–son relationship, highlighting the utter absurdity of a father who thinks he can absolve a murderer simply by declaring that his son's death removes the sins of an entire community, not to mention an individual. Mocking the idea prevalent among the early church fathers that Jesus died for the sins of the people and that God is the eternal father of Jesus, the rabbis present this father's actions as lacking the ability to exact punishment on a priest who brought violence into the Temple precincts and, ultimately, as valuing the Temple and its rituals over and above the survival of his son.[40] The father's act of claiming his son as the priests' atonement conjures an image that is percolating in Pauline literature of the first century CE, although I make no claims for a direct influence on the rabbis, given the challenges of dating these documents.[41] It is the case, however, that according to Galatians 3:13 and 4:4–5, Paul considers Jesus a scapegoat who, by being sent to his death, redeemed people from their sins. In Romans 8:32, God does not spare his own son but "gives him up" for humankind. And Colossians 1:13–17 states that God transferred to the people the kingdom of God's beloved son, who offers redemption and the forgiveness of sins. 1 Peter 2:24 indicates that Jesus bore the sins of the people on the cross so that they might "die to sin and live in righteousness," for "by Jesus's wounds they were healed."[42] Indeed, in wishing to undermine the priesthood and dissuade Jews, who in rejecting the Temple could align themselves with early Christians, the tannaitic source included in the Bavli may represent a desire for distance from the ideological tenets fueling early Christianity.[43]

In all of the versions of this tannaitic story of the priest-father and his murdered son, the version found in Bavli Yoma is the only one where the father claims his son as the people's atonement. By comparison, versions of this narrative that appear in collections associated with the Land of Israel, such as Tosefta Yoma, Yerushalmi Yoma, and Midrash Sifrei Bamidbar, present a less severe image of the priest-father. Rather than claiming that his son has died for the people, in the

Violence in the Temple

Yerushalmi, the father says, "I am your atonement," taking the blame for the incident.[44] He turns himself into a scapegoat but with far less resonance to a Jesus-like figure because in the end, he is no martyr; he lives.[45] He also recalls the community members described in M. Sanhedrin 2:1 who come to pay their respects to a priest in mourning and say, "We are your atonement," that is, we take upon ourselves the sins for which you are being punished by the death of your family member. A non-priest can absolve the guilt of a priest, indicating that one human being can take on the guilt of another.[46] Yet the Yerushalmi's version of the story is still disheartening in that the father expresses no sense of loss as he watches his son writhe in pain with a knife stuck in his heart. That said, in what seems to be an intentional emendation to the baraita by the Bavli's editors, a more disturbing perspective rises to the surface when a priest-father is willing to claim his son as a human sacrifice.

This trajectory of critique heaped on the Temple and the priests is intensified as the narrative ends. The victim's father continues to assert himself over Rabbi Tzadok in suggesting that the knife be removed from his son's body while in the throes of death. If the son dies with the knife stuck into his body, that knife will need to be purified before it can be used again. The concern for the purity of the knife, given the ease with which an impure knife can be rendered pure by immersing it in water, belittles the father and his request to have the knife immediately removed.[47] Temple implements appear to be more important than the individual lives of those responsible for ensuring the ongoing operation of the Temple. Remarkably, not only are some priests utterly corrupt in their willingness to murder solely for the right to perform a Temple rite like removing the altar's ash, but other priests, specifically this priest-father, are willing to cast corruption aside so that Temple procedure can continue as though nothing has happened. Ultimately, however, there will be a dead body in the Temple, desecrating its sanctity and upstaging anything the father has tried to accomplish.

And then the baraita in Bavli Yoma, drawing from T. Yoma 1:12, in marked contrast to the Yerushalmi's version of the same story, makes one more literary move to castigate the Temple and the priesthood still further. The baraita ends by referring to Menasseh, who was king of Judah during the period of the first Temple; 2 Kings 21 describes him as one of the most evil kings, not only desecrating the Temple with idols but killing many innocent people and shedding blood until Je-

50   *Bringing Down the Temple House*

rusalem was filled end to end (2 Kings 21:16).[48] The inclusion of King Menasseh, for whom bloody violence and idolatry go hand in hand, intimates that the priests are tantamount to idolaters, tainting the very precincts of the Temple by looking to the Temple implements as more important than human life itself.[49]

That said, it is Bavli Yoma's anonymous redactors who, in explicating the baraita, drive home the point that this father was a priest among others, with nothing to distinguish him from other priests. His behavior was in keeping with the overarching attitudes already associated with the Temple. After requoting the portion of the baraita where the father exclaims that they must remove the knife from his son's body before he dies, the stammaim add the following:

> The father of the boy came and found that he was still writhing [in death throes]. He [the father] said: "Behold, he is your atonement. My son is still alive,[50] etc., . . ." to teach that they [the priests] regarded the purity of utensils more seriously than bloodshed.

> They asked: Was it that they [the priests] treated murder lightly but [treated] the purity of the utensils [just] as the [utensils] had been [treated] originally? Or perhaps they treated murder as they had originally, but [regarding the] purity of utensils they were [even] stricter.

> Come and hear: Since the teaching [in the baraita] brought [the following verse]: "Menasseh also shed very much innocent blood," learn from it that it was murder that they treated lightly, but [the] purity of utensils remained [as it was] originally. (BT Yoma 23b)

Here, the Bavli wants to expand on the point made in the baraita that "they [the priests] regarded [the] purity of the vessels more seriously than murder," adding a more severe twist and intensifying the critique against the priests. The point of the stammaitic question and its answer is to point out that there was nothing unusual about the way the father reacted to the knife. He was not trying to enforce stricter-than-normal rules governing the ritual status of Temple implements. The laws governing the purity of Temple implements remained as they always had, and the father acted accordingly. However, the act of murder in the temple became a less serious offense over time. Even the priest-father failed to shed a tear over his son. The stammaim bring in

Violence in the Temple

2 Kings 21:16 again to accentuate the point that the Temple was a place where murder occurred. Recalling an utterly violent Menasseh, an association is made between the priests and a king who spilled innocent blood needlessly. The message: murder is endemic to the Temple.

Neither the baraita quoted on BT Yoma 23b nor the stammaitic passage on the same Talmudic page, calls attention to the fact that Menasseh is not a priest but a king. On the surface, he is not a fitting literary foil for the priest-father. The verse seems to be a strange proof text. However, the baraita's inclusion of this very verse, when other versions of the tannaitic narrative about one priest stabbing his fellow exclude it, brings the unsettling nature of kingship directly into the Temple itself.[51] Unlike Saul and David, Menasseh's destructive behavior fills the city of Jerusalem with blood from "end to end." Kings commit murder. Failed leadership is fully possible.[52] When kingship is passed on to Menasseh's son, Amon, 2 Kings 21:20 relates that Amon follows in the path of his father doing what is "displeasing to the Lord." In contrast to Rabbi Tzadok, who stands on the steps of the sanctuary to share words of the Torah that bring the people to recognize the gravity of what has happened and conjuring a rabbinic male figure with many potential disciples, priest-father–son relationships are flawed. This father-son relationship is surely a story of misplaced values. Fathers are not necessarily proper role models for their sons — not King Menasseh for Amon and surely not this priest-father for his son — offering examples of familial relationships included in Bavli Yoma that function literarily to upset the viability of the Temple house as well as the idea of "bloodline" as the sine qua non of priest replacement or inheritance.[53]

CONCLUSION: THE CONSTRUCTION
OF RABBINIC MASCULINITY

Feminist analysis of this Talmud passage draws attention to rabbis who, wishing to see themselves as authoritative figures, create hierarchies among men that parallel their "othering" of women, as will be discussed in the next three chapters. Priest-fathers and their sons are "othered" to disempower them by pointing to knowledge and values that do not transfer from parent to child, diminishing a father's impact. Priests, as the rabbis construct them here, care more for the purity of a physical implement — an object that is here both weapon and

52   *Bringing Down the Temple House*

holy instrument—than they care about a morally upright priesthood. Male kings and priests are authoritative, aggressive, competitive, and even violent. Indeed, not every priest has access to sancta in the same way, and so they resort to trying to beat out their fellow priests. The ideal rabbinic male leader, however, is the man who teaches moral behavior through Torah and controls his desire to avenge those who have sinned against him. Rabbi Tzadok, who can evoke a reaction of wailing on the part of the priests but also on the part of people to whom he is not blood related, emerges as more successful in his leadership role than the priest-father. Critique of the priesthood percolates between the lines of these tannaitic sources. The father enables the rabbis to imagine a house built not only on morally objectionable values such as murder but also on the misplaced use of biblical commandments related to ash removal and the purity of Temple implements, all of which contributes to Temple house instability. In one more addition to the narrative arc building throughout this tractate, the keepers of the Temple house emerge as men unworthy of passing down the priesthood to their sons. The rabbis chip away at the patrilineal framework of the priesthood, cutting priests off from the children who could take their place in the future, that is, from men who are known to be unable to command leadership roles in the Temple without resorting to violence and emotional manipulation.[54]

Naftali Cohn, building on the work of feminists and postcolonial theorists, argues that the rabbis, like others at the margins of power, use "discourse as a strategy of asserting their own agency," employing it as a way to negotiate power relations.[55] In particular, their prolific "Temple discourse," including constructed narratives of Temple rites and extensive legal material no longer viable after the destruction of the Temple, outlines "a claim for legitimacy and authority" over non-rabbis.[56] Reading the larger redacted passage of BT Yoma 22a–23b as a whole illuminates the rabbis' strategies of marginalization that are rooted in the construction of divergent, if not self-serving, conceptions of masculinity. The priests (and kings as well) are intentionally constructed as "different" types of men, exhibiting characteristics and behaviors distinct from the rabbis' own ideals.[57] The stammaim who piece together this larger passage by building on a tannaitic story project an image of whom they imagine themselves to be. Theirs is a masculinity defined by equal access for all males to Torah study and by a master-disciple relationship that parallels the father-son bond.

Violence in the Temple 53

Ultimately, if political and religious leadership is connected to bloodlines, the rabbis have less power through which they can engineer and pass down their own system of knowledge; they have less potential for success in the creation of a new leadership model, even if they too generate an exclusionary caste all their own.[58] The rabbis therefore turn to theorizing something that they can reasonably overturn. In Bavli Yoma it becomes about describing familial relationships that cannot support the Temple and need replacing.[59]

CHAPTER 3

MOTHERS AND SONS

Broken Houses

· · ·

Shifting from the father-son relationship to the relationship of mothers and their sons, the next three chapters focus on the ways that the mother-son relationship is used in Bavli Yoma to critique the Temple and the priesthood, on the one hand, and, on the other, to highlight the rabbis' apprehensions as they theorize about the successful transmission of knowledge from rabbi to disciple. Intimately connected to the makeup of the household, mothers and their progeny, beyond their shared biology, become a literary means for the final redactors of Bavli Yoma to accentuate ruptures created by mothers in the workings of the Temple house and its priesthood.

Found originally in tannaitic material, these mother-son blood ties, when incorporated into Bavli Yoma, play into the larger redactional framework of the tractate and are shaped by it. A common thread emerges: the desire to undermine and disrupt the exclusively male bloodline that transmits priestly privilege from fathers to sons and the power that emanates from it. Mother-son relationships connected to the Temple function here to problematize priestly father-son kinship by casting light on problematic behaviors instigated by these mothers through various gifts to their priest-sons. In drawing attention to these relationships, the rabbis construct a complicated society built around a hierarchical all-male nexus of authority in a manner that implicates themselves as well. As such, mothers and sons represent a move of focus in tractate Yoma from the social/religious institution of the Temple and its narration of the Yom Kippur Temple rite to the symbolic construction of persons and relations significant to the continuity of the rabbinic project but also challenging for the perpetuity of the Temple house.

This chapter focuses on two mothers: the mother of Doeg, the son of Yosef, and Helene, both liminal women in rabbinic literature, who are mentioned in conjunction with their patronage of the Temple house.[1]

The sheer expense of running the Temple fostered opportunities for patronage as well as increased social status. Female patrons, including mothers, with a desire to strengthen their relationship with the Temple gave money and material gifts. Temple-centered rites, such as *mishkal* and the rite of the *sotah*, in juxtaposition with rabbinic practices, such as the recitation of Shema in its proper time and the teaching of Torah, work to differentiate priests from rabbis on the coattails of mothers and their relationships with their sons.

WHY MOTHERS?

Mothers, like priests, are aligned with both nature and culture. Just as mothers are never fully consigned to nature, that is, they take on other "assigned" cultural and domestic roles (e.g., weaving), a priest's relatedness to other priests via a bloodline is inseparable from the Temple culture he represents, performing essential other duties.[2] In terms of cultural in-separateness and the importance of marriage, wives are considered their husband's bayit, or house. There is no "house" without her. But in the case of Yoma, the mothers mentioned, interestingly, appear to have no husbands and their sons no fathers. These mothers thus conjure up images of fractured households caused by unknown circumstances. This brokenness of their "house" serves a rhetorical purpose, calling attention to fault lines in the Temple's central authority, the Temple house, its priesthood, and the rites associated with them.[3] The mothers and sons discussed in Yoma both problematize Temple patronage by highlighting its superficiality and question the importance of blood kinship, which is associated with traditional generational continuity. As extra-rabbinic source material indicates, Helene, in particular, stands out as a mother with no shared bloodline to a priest or rabbi. The rabbis use the figure of Helene, believed to be a convert to Judaism, to illuminate that a connection to the Temple house through blood is not a requirement for communal or institutional belonging. Through her, they diminish the importance of blood kinship in the acquisition of Torah knowledge from one's rabbi teacher.

In fact, the power of the mother-son relationship in and of itself becomes a way—a target, if you will—for the rabbis to express their own anxiety about the formation of rabbi-disciple kinship ties.[4] Without

56   *Bringing Down the Temple House*

identified fathers, "single mothers," like Helene, who have sons, expose the rabbis' concern that their own male-male transfer of knowledge to replace the traditional sense of authority vested in a male-male priestly bloodline might be in danger of misapplication, with unknown future consequence. The master-disciple relationship might not be as strong as blood ties between mothers and their sons. Themselves desirous of the presumed power inherent in mother-child relationships, the Bavli's redactors recast earlier source material to destabilize mothers and highlight the inability of these mothers to pass down correct religious values to their sons. In a world where the rabbis are also a subjugated minority group living in the complicated cultural orbit of Sassanian Babylonia, where Judaism is one religious tradition among others,[5] to take control of the house, whether Temple or domestic, is to imagine a sense of empowerment as disempowered subjects.[6] Mothers of sons who appear without husbands are a malleable literary trope for the rabbis, one that the rabbis exploit for their own ends. The rabbis use them to think about what is at stake in promoting a master-disciple structure that challenges their own definition of bayit, that is, a house with a husband/father figure who can claim his wife as "his house (beito)."

Reminiscent of the more recent vision of the Jewish mother in American Jewish culture discussed by Joyce Antler, mothers described in Bavli Yoma are not entirely dissimilar. Like modern American mothers who became a "vessel" into which the cultural contradictions of a society, grappling with deep-seated anxieties about their relationship to the culture at large and to each other were poured, the rabbis use mothers to come to grips with their own discomfort with the Temple past and concerns about a rabbinic future. Mothers therefore became a foil for rabbinic self-doubt and insecurity.[7] Characterized as either well-to-do or connected to priest families, or, as in the case of Helene, with knowledge of Jewish law, mothers shed light on concerns not only about the priests' ability to pass down Torah knowledge but the rabbis' overall ability in doing their job as well. Here in Bavli Yoma, these relationships are shaped to reflect a thread running through the tractate. The Bavli's redactors use these relationships that represent the household to shake not only the foundations of the Temple house but also the idea of a replacement house in the wake of the Temple's absence.

Mothers and Sons

COLLAPSING HOUSES

M. Yoma 3:11 shames priests for failing to transmit their knowledge of specific Temple-related skills. While the Bavli interweaves additional tannaitic material to reverse the mishnah's negative depictions of these priests (the house of Gamru that prepared the showbread; the house of Avtinas that prepared the incense; and the Levite Hugras, who knew what to sing), it is Ben Kamtzar, fourth in the list, who is censured further for failing to share his unique method of writing. Arguably, writing was a skill that remained useful even after the Temple was destroyed, calling more attention to why the redactors of Bavli Yoma chose to build on tannaitic material that discredited him more than the others. More significant, however, is the fact that the Bavli introduces a well-known ancient story about a mother's patronage of the Jerusalem Temple in conjunction with Ben Kamtzar, right at the center of the Talmudic passage that comments on M. Yoma 3:11.[8] It functions as the pivotal point in the sugya to accentuate fault lines in the institution of the priesthood before moving on to differentiate between righteous and dishonorable individuals more generally, leaving the discussion about these priests aside.[9] Before this occurs, the Bavli presents the story of a mother's repeated donations of her son's weight in gold within the context of a warning: naming a child after a priest such as Bar Kamtzar threatens who this child is and what happens to him:

> The Rabbis taught in a baraita: Ben Kamtzar did not want to teach [his] way of writing.
>
> They said about him that he would take four quills between his fingers and if there was a word of four letters he would write [all of the letters] at one time.
>
> They said to him: Why did you not teach [your way of writing to others]? All of the other [priestly families mentioned in M. Yoma] found an explanation for their actions.
>
> Ben Kamtzar [however] did not find an explanation for his actions.
>
> Concerning the first [families of priests mentioned in M. Yoma 3:11], it is said: "The memory of the righteous shall be for a blessing" (Proverbs 10:7) and about Ben Kamtzar and his fellows it is stated: "But the name of the wicked shall rot. (Proverbs 10:7)"
>
> What is the meaning of "the name of the wicked shall rot"?

58   *Bringing Down the Temple House*

Rabbi Elazer said: Putrefaction will spread on their names; [meaning] we do not use their names [to name their children after them].

[The Babylonian amora] Ravina challenged the idea [that one should not name for an evil person] from a tannaitic source:

A story about Doeg, the son of Yosef, whose father left him as a young son to his mother. Each day his mother would measure him in tefaḥim (handbreaths) and give his weight in gold to the Temple. And when the enemy prevailed, she slaughtered him and ate him. And about her lamented Jeremiah, "Should women eat their own fruit, their newborn babes (*olelei tipuḥim*)?" (Lamentations 2:20). The Holy Spirit responded, "Should priest and prophet be slain in the sanctuary of the Lord?" (Lamentations 2:20).[10]

See what happened to him [Doeg]. (BT Yoma 38b)

The priest with the name of Ben Kamtsar is here called out for his pronounced wickedness. His name, the Bavli intimates, should be forgotten because he failed to pass down the memory of an important Temple skill: writing with four quills at once. The amora, Ravina, then introduces the baraita about Doeg to prove that some children can be named after wicked individuals. Doeg conjures up the biblical figure with the same name, who in 1 Samuel 22:18–19 kills the priests of Nov, along with "men, women, children, infants, oxen, asses and sheep." The priests of Nov had sided with David, inciting the ire of King Saul. In other places in rabbinic literature, he is Doeg the Edomite, a quasi-Jew undeserving of the World to Come.[11] But as the stammaim point out, Doeg, the son of Yosef, meets a horrific end as described in the baraita: his own mother cannibalizes him. Why should anyone be named after such a person? In like fashion, no one should be named for Ben Kamtzar either: Ben Kamtzar's character is deeply flawed and represents a failed transfer of priestly skill to the next generation.

Noticeably, Yerushalmi Yoma 3:9, 41ab, in commenting on the same mishnah, makes no mention of Doeg. The predictions about Ben Kamtzar and the other priests mentioned in M. Yoma 3:11 indicate, on a far more positive note, that these priests will be called back to the Temple in the future by their own names. In this regard, Yerushalmi Yoma points with optimism toward a future priesthood that not only recalls priests of the past but invites them to return. Bavli Yoma's

Mothers and Sons

59

redactors, however, suggest that the memory of some individuals, including some priests, should be wiped out, intimating that select patrilineal lines simply should not continue.

THE MOTHER OF DOEG, THE SON OF YOSEF

The tannaitic story brought in by the Babylonian amora Ravina presents the most horrific image of kinship. Doeg, in this version of the story, appears to have been abandoned by his father and left in the care of his mother, who ultimately eats him.[12] While crystallizing the famine and death that ensued when the Temple was destroyed, this mother-son relationship, as depicted, does far more in this sugya than to make a point about whether to name children after disreputable ancestors like Ben Kamtzar. There are several points of interest. The decision on the part of the stammaitic redactors to place the Doeg story here seems to be an uncomfortable fit. Doeg is acted on by his mother, whereas Ben Kamtzar makes his own decisions. Doeg's mother shares her wealth with the Temple; Ben Kamtzar shares nothing. In addition, placing the story of Doeg here situates it at the center of the sugya and functions as a way to construct a damaging image of both the Temple and its priests by highlighting the interactions of a mother with Temple rites.[13] As a result, the story stands out in the larger frame of the sugya.

In this vignette, a wealthy mother donates her son's weight in gold to the Temple in place of her son. The story recalls a practice referred to as mishkal in rabbinic sources, which is thought to be rooted in a set of rules elucidated in Leviticus 27:1–8 regarding donating the fiscal value of a human being to God.[14] A person could vow to donate a value equivalent to the weight of an individual to the Temple as a sign of devotion, as monetary support for the Temple, or as a means of exchange to prevent that individual from serving in the Temple.[15] As Jacob Milgrom points out, unlike Hannah's decision to give up her son, Samuel, to Eli, the high priest (1 Samuel 1), mishkal may have been a way to circumvent dedicating a son to Temple service.[16]

As the story goes, Yosef, the father of Doeg, disappears.[17] When Doeg's mother vows independent of her husband to donate generously to the Temple, she foolishly believes that her material wealth will connect her to the Temple and buy her household security as well as communal standing in the absence of a father figure.[18] But weighing her son for a financial Temple gift is a calculated gesture and impersonal, mak-

Bringing Down the Temple House

ing Doeg analogous to a material object purchased from the Temple for his mother's own use. Donations of gold do not ensure the longevity of the Temple or protection of her household. Rather, this mother figure embodies the curses predicted in Leviticus 26:28–29: "I [God], for My part, will discipline you seven-fold for your sins; You shall eat the flesh of your sons and the flesh of your daughters." These predictions are then fulfilled as Lamentations 2:20 describes: "Alas, women eat their own fruit." Indeed, this mother destroys the very household that she is mandated to preserve, despite being a single mother in the wake of the Temple destruction. Nothing from the Temple house reaches out to protect this mother-son relationship. And nothing that binds this mother to her son through her strategic donations of gold protects the Temple. Ironically, she assists in God's plan of physical destruction, horrifically cannibalizing her own son as if to say that without a Temple or in the wake of such fierce destruction, one must physically suffer a similar sacrifice: eat one's own kin.[19]

This disturbing mother-son story works together with those of other mothers in Bavli Yoma who, in their relationship with sons, shed negative light on the Temple. Stories such as this one about Doeg and his mother play into the hands of a redactor, who then interweaves the material into the larger tractate to bring attention to how Temple-related kinship and lineage have gone awry. Just as this mother cannot ensure the survival of her own house despite her wealth, so too the Temple cannot perpetuate itself if what it stands for cannot be passed down outside a father-son bloodline (as exemplified in Ben Kamtzar's refusal to share his unique expertise and the Bavli's insistence that his name cannot be passed on). Doeg's mother also calls attention to the need for Temple benefactors, even female benefactors who can support the materiality of Temple upkeep. While these women can buy themselves high-class status through their material contributions rather than through their spiritual connection to the Temple, benefaction does not ensure the Temple's continued existence. Doeg's mother, who "sacrifices" her son so that she can survive the destruction of the Temple, highlights just how much is at stake when the Temple is destroyed. But this mother also alludes to the need for a new Temple house that will be built and sustained with different material resources (not gold coins). It will also require different types of expertise (not Ben Kamtzar's type of writing). Instead, there will be a type of knowledge transfer from one male to another rather than from mother to son. Finally, the trope of

Mothers and Sons

mothers unable to provide food for their starving children amplifies rabbinic anxiety and foreshadows a related discussion about the Yom Kippur rite of fasting and its dangers, discussed in the final chapter of Bavli Yoma.

HELENE AND THE TEMPLE HOUSE

Helene is another female patron of the Temple who emerges in Bavli Yoma with her son, Munbaz, to challenge what the Temple and its priesthood represent in very different ways from the mother of Doeg (M. Yoma 3:10; BT Yoma 37ab).[20] Although referred to in other places in rabbinic literature as a queen, in Bavli Yoma, Helene is only referred to as the mother of King Munbaz, calling more attention to her role as the mother of royalty than to her status as a queen, ruling over a province.[21] She and her son donate material ornaments to the Temple, underscoring its opulence.[22] According to M. Yoma 3:10, Munbaz donates the "handles of the utensils used on Yom Kippur," crafting them of gold. His mother donates a gold *nivreshet* (a lamp of sorts) that she makes for the entrance to the *heikhal* (sanctuary) in the Temple.[23] The absence of the term *nivreshet* in rabbinic literature prompts Yerushalmi Yoma, JT Yoma 3:8, 41a to rely on the word *nivrashta*, mentioned in Daniel 5:5, in an attempt to clarify the nature of this gift. Relying on Daniel, the Yerushalmi intimates that Helene's gift is a lampstand, similar to the one found in the palace of the Babylonian king Belshazzar. In spite of the fact that the Mishnah and Bavli Yoma make no attempt to elucidate what Helene's nivreshet looks like, thinking about it through the lens of Daniel suggests something exceptional about the gift, possibly something not typical of Israelite culture. It was not a regular lamp used in the Temple, such as a menorah, and appears to have no connection to the performance of any Temple-related rite.

Helene also donates a "golden tablet" containing a passage from Numbers 5, the biblical pericope about a woman suspected of adultery (sotah). Presumably the tablet was to hang within the Temple and would assist the high priest in his role of publicly accusing a suspected wife as an adulteress.[24] In contrast to the mother of Doeg and to Helene's own son, Munbaz, Helene's material gifts of gold, according to the Bavli, transmit Torah and signal a behavior the Temple and its priests do not represent.

Notably, in M. Yoma 3:10 and Bavli Yoma 37ab, Helene's Temple

62   *Bringing Down the Temple House*

gifts are different from her son's, albeit no less splendid in appearance, driving a wedge between them relevant to their Temple-related behavior. Indeed, Helene's son is associated with contributing glorious handles made of gold for the utensils used on Yom Kippur. But as the Bavli challenges, "[Instead] let him make them [the entirety of the vessels he donates] of gold" (BT Yoma 37a). The Bavli, by referring to the amora Abaye's interpretation of the mishnah, suggests that gold is too weak a metal for the blades of axes and adzes, as these were tools used for the Temple tasks of cutting, carving, and chopping.[25] Therefore, only the handles could be made of gold. From the Bavli's perspective, Munbaz's patronage was for the purposes of ornamenting Yom Kippur implements through which he could glorify the majesty of the Temple and the rite of Yom Kippur.[26] While this does not discount that other sources such as T. Peah 4:18 describe Munbaz as a generous benefactor who gives his treasures away to help the poor, here in Bavli Yoma, his gifts are viewed as more superficial.[27] To be sure, Bavli Yoma does not suggest that Munbaz was remembered with praise for his donations (a reference to which can be found in T. Yoma 2:3).[28] Rather, the Bavli follows M. Yoma 3:10 more closely in not connecting Munbaz's gift with praise.[29] In fact, here in Bavli Yoma, Munbaz merely adorns these Temple utensils with gold, contributing little to their usefulness in Temple-related tasks.

In contrast, Helene's nivreshet gives off light at the precise time when the community needs to say Shema at sunrise.[30] A tradition that appears in Yerushalmi 3:8, 41a states that "when the sun would rise, sparks would come out of the nivreshet, and they would know that the sun was rising."[31] In the Bavli's expanded version of this baraita on BT Yoma 37b, the sparks that radiate outward from the nivreshet inform everyone that the time has arrived for reciting Shema.[32]

The Bavli makes its point by juxtaposing two baraitot, followed by an amoraic statement also attributed to the Babylonian amora, Abaye. The short sugya invokes a disconnect between the recitation of Shema outside the walls of the Temple and what occurs each morning within its precincts:

> [Mishnah]: Helene, his mother, fashioned a gold nivreshet.
>
> [Baraita]: When the sun rose, sparks of light would emanate from the nivreshet, and everyone knew that the time to recite Shema had arrived.

Mothers and Sons

[A baraita is brought as a challenge]: One who recites Shema in the morning with the men of the priestly watch or with the men of the non-priestly watch does not fulfill his obligation [to recite Shema], because the men of the priestly watch recite Shema too early and the men of the non-priestly watch[33] delay reciting Shema. [This means that the nivreshet did not signal those within the Temple to recite Shema, so what was its purpose?]

Abaye said: [The nivreshet was] for the rest of the people in Jerusalem. (BT Yoma 37b)

More to the point, two baraitot in Bavli Yoma 37b, one serving to challenge the other, with a response by Abaye, disclose that men of the priestly watch recite Shema at the earliest possible moment so as not to forget to say it amid their sacrificial duties. And men of the non-priestly watch, that is, non-priests who accompany the priests and represent the community at large when daily sacrifices were offered, said Shema later because they were involved in watching over the morning sacrificial rites. But as Abaye adds, the remainder of Jews in Jerusalem, who were not involved directly with preparing Temple offerings, said Shema at the correct time because of the sparks that emanated from Helene's Temple lamp. Her lamp was therefore intended for the general public (of Jews), positioned as it was on the front of the heikhal facing outward. It revealed that Helene fully understood the significance of rabbinic time necessary for the proper recitation of Shema, albeit in a way that threatens the significance of the space of the Temple used to offer the morning sacrifice.[34] A light that sparkles to signify a divinely ordained time suggests that Helene takes rabbinic law seriously, while the priests and those associated with them do not, as they recite Shema either too late or too early.

This textual addition of Shema to the baraita appears only in the Bavli and is absent from T. Yoma 2:3, where the lamp is described merely as emitting sparks each morning as the sun rises.[35] Shema is also not mentioned in the version of the baraita that appears in Yerushalmi Yoma 3:8, 41a. A later textual interpolation into the Bavli, along with Abaye's comment, focuses attention on Helene's contribution to enabling others, specifically those outside the Temple, in reciting Torah through Shema and to perform this rite.[36] Indeed, Shema is composed of biblical verses that include the commandment to teach them to one's children.[37] In comparison to Munbaz's gifts of gold that were entirely ornamental and intended to glorify the Temple, Helene's lamp captures what matters to the rabbis: the recitation of Shema at its proper time. Helene's gift integrates the memory of the seven-branched menorah that adorned the Temple with the everyday household oil lamp in a way that points beyond the Temple and the priests.[38] The light that emerges from the rising sun as it hits the nivreshet is far more than a Temple adornment or an implement designed for use by a priest. It represents a rabbinic interest in a prayer rite centered on the daily recitation of Torah verses.

In taking responsibility herself for ensuring that individuals say Shema, Helene's act belittles the priests by comparison. When a woman, who is not required by Jewish law to recite Shema,[39] seeks the means for safeguarding the commandment for others to recite it, she is shifting attention from Temple rites to supporting rabbinic practice. But more flagrant than belittling and perhaps outshining the priesthood is the fact that Helene might not be Jewish from birth. Arguably, she is a convert, someone who is believed to be from Adiabene, the northern Mesopotamian province in the Parthian empire, and not a Jerusalemite living proximal to the Temple. One of the strongest ways to attack the priestly patriline is to introduce someone who is praiseworthy and has no blood relationship to the priests or even to the rabbis. Rather, as Josephus suggests, Helene brought Judaism to Adiabene, including to her son Munbaz, leading both to convert.[40] However, she reflects the notion that cultural transference is not dependent on a connection through a bloodline. She can lead Munbaz to Temple Judaism, but his patronage goes only so far. It is Helene alone, in the absence of a father-husband figure,[41] who is associated with ensuring that Shema is recited at the right time and *not* Munbaz. It is she, in the rabbis' imagination, who passes this rabbinic value on to others with whom she has no blood relationship. Munbaz, for his part, is only a full supporter of the magisterial appearance of the Temple.

Intriguingly, in Bavli Sukkah and distinct from Yoma, Helene is depicted as a mother who observes rabbinic law, ensuring that her sons —whether minors or not—have a sukkah in which to sit.[42] Her own sukkah is located in Lod, far from the precincts of the Temple in Jerusalem, characterizing her as a woman without ties to the Temple. Yet she has the title "queen," unlike in Yoma, where she is referred to only as "mother." Her seven sons, unlike Kimhit's seven high-priest-sons, who will be discussed in chapter four, fulfill their sukkah obligation,

Mothers and Sons 65

and Helene does the same. That Tosefta Sukkah 1:1 refers to Helene's sons as sages (*talmidei ḥakhamim*), reinforces the point that outside the Temple context and outside of the rites connected to the Temple that are designed only for priests, rabbinic literature acknowledges that mothers who are presumably converts to Judaism can pass down authentic rabbinic values to their sons.[43] The fact that this is not the case in Bavli Yoma calls attention to an argument running through the tractate. Even with the apparent measure of success Helene had in bringing Judaism to some of her sons in Bavli Sukkah, knowledge transmission between blood relatives is not always successful, as Bavli Yoma's presentation of Helene highlights. The household represented by a mother and her son is not always a fitting educational or spiritual model. This point parallels the critique of priest-fathers who cannot pass down appropriate values to their priest-sons, as discussed in chapter two (BT Yoma 23a).

However, Helene lodges her strongest critique of the priesthood through her gift of a golden tablet with biblical verses engraved on it that describe the rite of the suspected adulteress (sotah) (M. Sotah 3:11). Although the priests pass judgment on women accused of adultery, they need to be reminded of the ritual despite the availability of the Torah to them. Through her gift of the tablet, Helene acts as a teacher to the priests and the community, filling in potential gaps in their knowledge of how to conduct the rite. Notably, she does so using a ritual that demeans women. According to Numbers 5:19–24, the priest utters words publicly to warn the suspected wife of the effects of her alleged adulterous actions if she were to be found guilty. It was the priest who would then curse her, transcribe the curses written in Numbers 5:21–22, rub off the curses in "the water of bitterness," and then require the sotah woman to swallow the mixture of water "with the dissolved curses." If her belly became distended and her thigh sagged, she was considered guilty. If these effects did not occur, she would then be able to bear children (Numbers 5:27–28). Helene exposes the priests as men who cannot remember the instructions for performing the sotah ordeal, the rite, as cited in the Torah. With her gift of the tablet, Helene ensures that the priest would not have to open the Torah and find the place in order to copy it and then read the sotah passage; he could simply turn to the golden tablet, refamiliarize himself with the passage, copy it, and then expound it to the accused woman.[44] This gift of a tablet therefore constructs the priests as men who need

66   *Bringing Down the Temple House*

assistance in performing rites that require them to recall Torah commandments.

Helene is literate, and she knows biblical law. The Bavli on BT Yoma 37b accentuates this point when it suggests that Helene's decision to excise the sotah passage and place it on a tablet signifies that other actions related to knowledge transmission are valid—for example, that preparing scrolls with a biblical passage for the sake of teaching children is allowable.[45] This point intimates that Helene knows more Torah than the priests do, transmitting knowledge to them in a manner that would make it more easily accessible to them, not unlike creating a memory tool. Similar to a teacher preparing instructions for a disciple and, arguably, like a mother teaching a child, Helene passes on Torah to the priests.[46] However, as a single mother who takes it upon herself to prepare such a tablet "for a priest," the act is patronizing. In creating and passing on the golden tablet, she mocks the priests for needing the tablet at all, humiliating the very men whose role it is to bring shame on women suspected of adultery.

And yet Helene's "gift" of the golden tablet goes one step further in casting aspersions on the priests in her choice of the sotah passage rather than, for example, other biblical passages that provide instruction related to Temple rites.[47] After all, why choose to fashion a tablet with the verses about the sotah? How can the Temple house be a functional house if its priests need assistance in conducting the sotah rite aimed at protecting households from adulterous women who threaten to break households apart? And what type of leaders are the priests if they cannot execute the rites commanded of them without the help of a woman who is neither a priest nor a rabbi, a woman who is not married and might not even have been born a Jew? As an outsider who does not represent a bayit herself, given that she is not said to be married in Talmudic sources, Helene is able to unravel the public image of the priest and function as a Temple insider possessing more knowledge than the priests. Her tablet gift spotlights the Temple as an ineffective ritual space where the core relationship of what makes a house a house —the husband-wife relationship—can be torn apart within its walls on the basis of unprovable suspicions.[48]

With this dark veil cast upon the Temple, what can be done to protect future households? There will be a move from sacrifice and materiality to textuality (writing on a tablet), as Helene represents with a plaque that contains the sotah passage inscribed on it. While Munbaz

Mothers and Sons

represents the significance of Temple sacrifice with his gifts of gold, Helene bridges Temple materiality and heuristic rabbinic textuality. The Bavli's expansion of the tannaitic material about Helene's choice of the sotah passage devolves into a discussion about whether Helene might have set a legal precedent for allowing the transcription of sections of Torah verses onto a scroll for the purpose of teaching children. The Bavli concludes its discussion by arguing for the possibility that Helene had recorded only incomplete verses, mnemonics of a sort. But the larger thrust of this sugya is its emphasis on the idea that learning cannot be unmediated. Scrolls that contain passages excised from the Torah or incomplete verses that serve as mnemonics still require the intervention of knowledgeable individuals who can pass Torah down to the next generation. In this regard, Helene emerges as a mother invested in the idea of teaching Torah, although she does not appear to have taught Torah to her son King Munbaz.[49] This is reflected in the fact that the two do not share the same vision of how to support the Temple and its priesthood.

At the same time, Helene recalls a tannaitic teaching found in M. Sotah 3:4 in the name of Ben Azzai. Intent on the idea that fathers should teach their daughters Torah, Ben Azzai argues that knowledge will protect women from the suspicion of adultery and from becoming a sotah. While Helene seems to have had no father who could have taught her Torah, and no husband either, Bavli Yoma co-opts her not only as a teacher of priests but also of women.[50] Somewhere along the way, as the rabbis imagine it, Helene learns Torah, albeit not from someone to whom she is related. By turning Helene into a women who is Torah knowledgeable, the rabbis draw her into their own patriarchal world, not only as a symbol for women who must resist all threats to their marriages (the tablet passage serves as a warning to them) but also as a way for the rabbis to upstage the priests' role in the very same Temple-centered rite through a woman.[51] The golden plaque that she designs simultaneously reminds women of the public humiliation that will befall them on the part of the priests in the Temple as a consequence of allowing adultery to break up their "households." The plaque also guides the priests to perform the rite properly, perhaps an image that presents a double-edged sword to its usefulness.[52] When a husbandless woman such as Helene intervenes in the priesthood and gains the upper hand, she destabilizes the priests' role in safeguarding the sotah tradition, inasmuch as she points women to the significance of enforc-

68   *Bringing Down the Temple House*

ing it themselves (that is, if they too are literate and can read the golden tablet).[53]

The narrative thread that builds on the image of the household is strengthened still further by reading Helene in conjunction with Bavli Yoma 66b. It is here that the tanna Rabbi Eliezer emerges in an interchange with a "wise woman" that reflects what lurks behind the figure of Helene: the rabbis' anxiety about being unable to sustain a house built on Torah, where its members are not blood related. He happens to be the same tanna who argued with Ben Azzai in M. Sotah 3:4. Rabbi Eliezer asserts that Torah study leads women to lascivious behavior, challenging the possibility of a learned Helene entirely.[54] Embedded in a larger passage focused on the goat sent to Azazel, that is, from the Temple and off a cliff on Yom Kippur bearing the sins of Israel, Rabbi Eliezer is baffled by a set of questions about instances when this rite is not executed properly. All he can do is quote a verse from Judges 5:31, "So may all of Your enemies perish, O Lord," in an attempt to evade an admission that he is puzzled.[55] While the sages can respond to the issues at hand, Rabbi Eliezer is presented as a rabbi at a loss for clarity. Ironically, he is also confronted with a question from a "wise woman" about the golden calf.[56] He can only respond by typecasting her as women often are in rabbinic literature—as "wise" with the spindle alone.[57] His insecurities are borne out through this interchange.[58]

When linked one to the other in Bavli Yoma, these two women underscore the difference between the rabbis' view of the priests and their view of themselves. Helene proves that women can learn Torah and not be led astray. When presented within the context of her patronage of the priests in the Temple, her Torah knowledge upstages them. By comparison, a woman who asks to learn Torah from a rabbi and presents him with a question he cannot answer results in identifying her as having no more knowledge than that of the household labor, spinning. Percolating beneath the surface here is the rabbis' anxiety about the nature of Torah transmission. If mothers who are literate and know the laws of Shema and the sotah but nevertheless cannot influence their sons' choices, will rabbis be able to ensure that they can have an impact on their students? Simultaneously, a mother-son relationship, like that of Helene and Munbaz, parallels a failed master-disciple transfer of knowledge, suggesting that Bavli Yoma's final authors feared that in replacing the priests, they (the rabbis) might be ineffectual as well. Rabbi Eliezer, in his interchange with a "wise

Mothers and Sons

woman," draws this point out still further. Making allowances for anyone to learn Torah, such as Helene, suggests that women too can become knowledgeable in more than spinning.

CONCLUSION

Doeg's mother as well as Helene challenge the nature and the integrity of the priesthood and the Temple. Both highlight the failures of the Temple's exclusivity and its authoritative voice. While the priests need wealthy patrons to support the Temple, such patronage does not ensure the Temple's longevity or contribute to reducing afflictions that befall it. In fact, the calamity associated with the Temple's destruction does more than just generate famine and personal suffering. Doeg's mother eats her own son, challenging the idea that parents always can and do protect their children. Relying on bloodlines for generativity can also be seen as not always reliable or inevitable, a pronounced concern to which the final chapter in Bavli Yoma will return. Moreover, women here find a unique model in the most liminal of figures. Helene, a woman who happens to be husbandless as well as a foreigner from Adiabene, is Torah knowledgeable and capable of teaching priests and women about practices that are significant to the rabbis. The daily recitation of Shema denotes, in those who perform it, an absolute commitment to God and Torah. The sotah rite, as disturbing for women as it is, accentuates the rabbis' apprehension around the sustainment of marital bonds and the Temple's somewhat sinuous role in the maintenance of such marriages. Helene, who is not a wife, a priest, or a Jew from birth, challenges the exclusivity of the Temple house in her ability to have an impact from outside the closed Temple caste of priests. She upstages the superficial gift of gold vessel handles that her son Munbaz made for use by the priests in the performance of Temple rites, pointing to another set of values more significant to the rabbinic future: transference of Torah knowledge. Emblematic of Helene and Doeg's mother is the way their behaviors cast light on the fault lines of the Temple and its overseers. In addition, they call into question the authority of a male-male priestly patriline, on the one hand, and, on the other hand, the necessity for blood ties in transmitting Torah from master or rabbi to disciple.

CHAPTER 4

FROM INSIDE OUT

Kimḥit's House

• • •

The Bavli's integration of the story of the mother Kimḥit and her priest-sons into Yoma, building from early source material present in Yerushalmi Yoma, accentuates still further the sense that the rabbis are struggling with the male-male/father-son bloodline of the priesthood (BT Yoma 47a; JT Yoma 1:1, 38d). Kimḥit's contribution to her sons and to the Temple is intimately connected to her modest behavior within the confines of her house rather than to making material donations to the Temple. The story of Kimḥit, like those of Helene and the mother of Doeg, bear out that men cannot become effective priests or knowledgeable rabbis when reared by their mothers at home, especially without fathers. While the story, as told in the Yerushalmi, offers a glimmer of Kimḥit's righteousness, in ways not communicated in the Bavli, both versions underscore that both the Temple bayit and the private bayit are charged spaces for the rabbis—neither can easily replace the other in terms of passing down Torah knowledge or preparing sons for a Temple life.

In addition, Kimḥit brings to the fore the trope and behavior of a mother and her seven sons, intimating that she has an agenda for their advancement. Whereas the overwhelming power that mothers wield in their willingness to martyr themselves (along with their children) surfaces in other Talmudic tractates and rabbinic collections, Bavli Yoma does not connect mothers and their sons to martyrdom. In fact, Kimḥit and her seven sons invert the image of self-sacrifice as suffering. Martyrdom stories intensify the power of the mother-son relationship as mothers empower themselves and their sons to martyr themselves in the name of God, turning the people who victimize them into their victims. However, the trajectory in Bavli Yoma is to weaken the relationship bond between mothers and their sons and, with it, the priests and the Temple. Reworked tannaitic material in the hands of the Babylonian redactors turn Kimḥit into a mother of ineffective priest-sons once again, offering evidence of Bavli Yoma's interest in discrediting the priesthood.

All of the references to Kimḥit in rabbinic literature, from the earliest versions in the Tosefta[1] and Yerushalmi,[2] to the later collections, the Bavli,[3] Vayikra Rabbah,[4] Avot derabi Natan,[5] Tanḥuma,[6] Pesikta derav Kahana,[7] and Bamidbar Rabbah,[8] are versions of a story about a mother able to witness her sons serve as high priests in succession.[9] Only one high priest served at a time, reflecting the fact that daily Temple service and surely the Yom Kippur avodah was a "one man show."[10] When one son was disqualified, the next in line rose to fill his brother's position in the Temple. The largest lacuna in these texts about Kimḥit is the lack of any mention of her "absent" priest husband, leaving her children fatherless. Yishmael in the Bavli and Shim'on in the Tosefta and Yerushalmi material are referred to as sons of their mother, Kimḥit.[11] Even among the sons of rabbis, recalling one's lineage through one's mother is extremely rare, with few parallels elsewhere.[12] No doubt the absence of a patronymic, or family name, suggests something questionable about the father, possibly related to his lineage.[13] That Kimḥit is mentioned heightens her significance, especially in the larger context of the Temple, where only the father's house is meant to prevail.[14]

In keeping with biblical patterns, sons who fail to ascend to the position of heir within their father's house are, thus, "mother-born" rather than "father-born" sons, such as Yishmael (Genesis 21:1–22). They continue to be defined by their mothers throughout their lives. In other instances, mothers disappear from the biblical narrative and, presumably, significance when they assist their sons in becoming successful heirs to their father's line. Their sons, like in the case of Isaac and Jacob, attain an heir status and become "father-begotten-son[s]," who take their father's place within the patriarchal, or male-controlled, lineage of Israel (Genesis 25:19, 28:1).[15] In the case of Kimḥit, each of her sons tries individually, in succession, to take their father's place as high priest. They fail to succeed. Their disqualification turns them into "mother-begotten" children, remembered in their mother's name rather than their father's. This turn-of-events found in tannaitic source material plays into the hands, most especially, of the Bavli's redactors. Kate Cooper has argued, "Wherever a woman is mentioned, a man's character is being judged—and along with it—what he stands for." In the case of Kimḥit, it is the character of the men connected both to her household and the Temple that calls into question the lineage integrity of the priesthood built upon patrilineal blood kinship.[16]

While the latest version of the story of Kimḥit appears in Bavli Yoma (BT Yoma 47a), it is informed by an earlier tradition found in Tosefta Yoma 3:20, as well as in Yerushalmi Yoma (JT Yoma 1:1; 38d).[17] The more positive characterization of Kimḥit in the Yerushalmi influences all later versions of the story, including Rashi's reading of it in the Bavli.[18] In fact, this more oft-quoted version serves as the central motivational source, equating women who cover their hair as a sign of modesty with the reward of birthing righteous sons.[19] The Bavli's distinct treatment of Kimḥit is crystallized through its comparison to the Yerushalmi.[20] Such points of difference reveal that the final redactors of the Bavli had a different agenda in mind when they recharacterized Kimḥit as an ineffectual mother. Such a perspective dovetails with observations made above regarding the mother of Doeg and Helene, although it is Kimḥit who is mentioned in conjunction with the physical space of her house. This reception history suggests that the Babylonian version in Yoma was more critical of the priesthood than earlier sources, especially relative to those authored in the Land of Israel.[21]

Versions of the Kimḥit story are also among the very few sources in rabbinic literature that focus specifically on how and why high priests are replaced. There is no clear-cut rule of succession, which is especially surprising for tractate Yoma, dependent as the Yom Kippur rite is on the presence of an active high priest. For example, a reference to Ben Ilas/Ilam, while mentioned in the Yerushalmi immediately before the story of Kimḥit and her sons, tells us nothing about his relationship to the high priest whom he replaces. Was he a brother, a cousin, or a member of another priest family? The story of Kimḥit, despite no mention of a husband-father, offers some insight, in that her sons replace each other after one is disqualified. And yet, why are the details not disclosed in a legal framework?[22] Furthermore, the tannaitic (Toseftan) source, T. Yoma 1:22, that is reshaped and incorporated into BT Yoma 35b, seems to suggest that a high priest's brothers can remove their brother-priest from his position due to undignified behavior, that is, unless the Hebrew word for brothers (אחיו) refers to fellow priests.[23] Whereas it might seem that responsibility to replace a high priest falls to family members who share the same kinship lines, it is not clear that high priests or backup priests succeed one another in accordance with rules of heredity or are based on a familial role of

From Inside Out: Kimḥit's House

73

supervision. After all, who appointed Ben Ilas/Ilam? Given that the rabbis narrate Temple performance in tractate Yoma as if it is happening in present time, this lacuna provokes the question as to why they would overlook the details related to rights of succession on which the proper execution of Temple rites so depends.[24] Surely without an active high priest the Temple avodah performed on Yom Kippur, vital for repentance and atonement, cannot happen.[25] But this is exactly the point: if there is no instruction regarding how one high priest takes over for another, and there is also material that discredits priests (or their wives) for buying Temple positions for their priest-husbands, acting as facilitators (BT Yoma 18a), what emerges is a desire to weaken the idea of a well-working system of priestly succession that protects the institution from corruption or outside influence.[26]

KIMḤIT'S STORY IN THE YERUSHALMI: THE MOTHER EXEMPLAR

In Yerushalmi Yoma, the story of Kimḥit is situated within a larger discussion about the disqualification of one high priest and the appointment of Ben Ilas/Ilam, a priest from Tzippori (JT Yoma 1:1; 38d).[27] A seminal emission disqualifies the exiting high priest from serving in the Temple on Yom Kippur, requiring Ben Ilas/Ilam to become the replacement priest.[28] The context creates a fitting literary framework for the story of Kimḥit's sons who, subsequently, are also replaced, according to the Yerushalmi. The first of the sons was disqualified because of saliva from a non-Jew that landed on his robes before the beginning of Yom Kippur, as follows:[29]

> There is a story about Shim'on, the son of Kimḥit who went out to speak to the king on the eve of Yom Kippur[30] and a drop of saliva sprayed from [the king's] mouth onto [Shim'on's] garments and he became impure.[31] And his brother Yehudah entered and served as the high priest in his [Shim'on's] stead. And their mother [Kimḥit] saw two of her sons [serve as] high priests on the same day.
>
> Kimḥit had seven sons and all of them served in the position of high priest.
>
> The sages sent [a question to her] and they said to her: "What good deeds have you done?"

74   *Bringing Down the Temple House*

She answered them: "May [evil] befall me if, in my days, the beams of my house saw the hair of my head or the seams of my undergarment."[32]

They said [about Kimḥit]: "All flour is flour, but the flour of Kimḥit is fine flour." And they applied to her the verse, "Every honorable king's daughter is within, and her clothing embroidered with golden mountings." (Psalms 45:14-15;[33] JT Yoma 1:1, 38d)

As noted in chapter one, the high priest could be disqualified if he became impure. Sexual relations with a woman in *nidah* and a seminal emission are mentioned in Yoma as the causes that most often affect a high priest's ritual status. His death would also require a replacement high priest.[34] However, in the case of Kimḥit's son, Shim'on, the impurity is generated by the saliva of a non-Jew[35] that lands on his priestly robes while he is outside the area of the Temple.[36] Non-Jews, because of their automatic classification as *zavim*—meaning they are impure, and all of the fluxes that emerge from them are also impure, including saliva—have the ability to render objects and people impure as well.[37] According to some sources, including the Yerushalmi's version of the Kimḥit story, this occurs right before the beginning of Yom Kippur, leaving no time for the high priest to immerse himself in a ritual bath and clear himself of this impurity in preparation for performing his ritual duties. There are no details explaining why a high priest would leave the confines of the Temple precinct walls to do anything that would threaten his ability to perform the Yom Kippur rite. As high priest, he is also supposed to be sequestered for seven days before Yom Kippur to ensure that he remained pure. If he left the Parhedrin chamber, he potentially forfeited his right to conduct the holiest service of the yearly calendar. Furthermore, in constructing the high priest as a Jewish leader with connections to non-Jews in power, "a king" in this case, the story offers no dialogue.[38] The saliva that passes onto the high priest is no more than spittle, but when the king's saliva lands on Shim'on's garment, it renders him impure, and his brother Yehudah must then replace him.[39] Kimḥit is recorded as fortunate to see not one but two sons who serve as high priests in one day. An additional baraita presents Kimḥit not as a mother of two high priests, but as the mother of seven sons, all of whom serve as high priests.

Despite the mocking tone of the rabbis' description of a negligent high priest, Kimḥit emerges as a righteous mother rewarded for her

From Inside Out: Kimḥit's House

75

modest behavior, presumably with sons who all serve as high priests. When the rabbis send her the following question, "What good deeds have you done [to deserve this]?" Kimḥit argues for her own vigilant modest behavior. She says in response, "May [evil] befall me if, in my days, the beams of my house saw the hair of my head or the seams of my undergarment," at which point the story turns to laud Kimḥit as a mother exemplar.[40] Through a positive play on Kimḥit's name, recalling the Hebrew word for flour, *kemaḥ*, as well as the Temple grain offering, *solet minḥah* (Leviticus 6:13) where only the choicest flour is used, she emerges as possessing the life-sustaining quality of ensuring that her household has the finest bread.[41]

The oft-quoted verse from Psalms 45:15, "Every honorable king's daughter is within," also finds its way into the description of Kimḥit, marking her as an admirable role model. She stabilizes her house by virtue of remaining within it.[42] The positive tenor of the passage about Kimḥit is enhanced by mention made of a woman's garments in Psalms 45:14, "the royal princess, her dress embroidered with golden mountings (ממשבצות זהב לבושה)," which recalls the golden mountings on the priestly vestments in Exodus 28:13, using the same words. This woman in Psalms is also promised the reward of sons who become "princes throughout the land" (Psalms 45: 16–17). A reference to Psalms 45 is intended to reverberate through Kimḥit's story in the Yerushalmi, couching her as a mother whose dress rewards her with "princely" sons. Female modesty, as well as her at-homeness, is intimately tied to her sons' good fortune and to her own. Therefore, what seems to begin as a story about negligent high priests turns into a reflection on how the familial house—and the mother who stays within it—has a positive impact outside herself, that is, on her ability to birth sons for prominent roles. With an absent father, the issue of biology and a hereditary priesthood is overtaken by the deeds performed by Kimḥit. She stands out here as a positive model for the rabbis, feeding the stereotype of a modest mother who remains at home and births and feeds her children, ensuring great reward for them.[43]

THE BAVLI'S KIMḤIT (BT YOMA 47A): UNDOING KINSHIP TIES

The Bavli's sugya that focuses on Kimḥit appears within a discussion about the advantage of priests having large hands. Big hands were useful for the high priest, all of whom were required to scoop up incense (*ketoret*). The larger the priest's hands, the greater the amount of incense he would be able to carry to the Holy of Holies. And more incense meant that a more pleasing odor would emerge. While incense was burned every morning and evening in the Temple (Exodus 30:7–8), on Yom Kippur incense was taken into the Holy of Holies (Leviticus 16:12–13).[44] Coals would be swept up into a separate coal pan that the high priest carried in one hand. He then placed the spoon with incense in his other hand—a task that required great physical strength. The high priest would then place the incense on top of the coals.[45] A priest's able-bodiedness made it easier for him to perform this and various other Temple rites. With this framework in mind, Kimḥit is valorized in the Bavli by her son Yishmael, a priest, who is oddly referred to here in the Bavli as a rabbi. While many manuscripts lack this rabbi title, this version suggests that Yishmael, who was disqualified as a priest, was able to successfully make the shift from priest to rabbi.[46] In marked contrast, the Yerushalmi does not refer to any of Kimḥit's sons as rabbis; indeed, they are all priests.

The sugya begins as follows:

> They said about Rabbi Yishmael, the son of Kimḥit, that he would scoop up four *kav* [of incense], which would fill his hands [because they were large], and [he would say]:
> "All the women have done valiantly, but the valor of my mother rose to the roof (כל הנשים זרדן, וזרד אימא עלה לגג)."[47]

> Some say he was referring to his mother's selection of flour (*arsan*), in accordance with Rabbah bar Yonatan. As Rabbah bar Yonatan said that Rabbi Yeḥiel said: "Flour is beneficial for the sick."

> And some say [that Yishmael was referring to *zered*, a euphemism for the] semen [that formed him], in accordance with Rabbi Abbahu, as Rabbi Abbahu raised a contradiction between two verses. It is written [in one verse]: "For You have girded me (ותזרני)[48] with strength for battle" (2 Samuel 22:40). And it is written in another verse: "Who girds me (ותאזרני)[49] with strength" (Psalms 18:33). David said before the Holy One, Blessed is He: Master of the Universe: You selected me (זריתני) and you fashioned me (וזרזתני) within her. All of the world was created from the

From Inside Out: Kimḥit's House

77

choicest and I [David] from the choicest of the choicest. (translation reflects Bavli Yoma 47a, Enelow 271)[50]

Kimhit is lauded for contributing to the physical strength of her son Yishmael by birthing a son of muscularity. He has the large hands necessary to perform good priestly work. In addition, the sugya uses a house metaphor to symbolically accentuate Kimhit's value. Indeed, as Yishmael points out, his mother's valor rose beyond her house, "to the roof."[51] An opinion attributed to the amoraim Rabbah bar Yonatan and Rabbi Yehiel conveys that Yishmael's strength was the direct result of the arsan Kimhit ate while she was pregnant. This is a foodstuff made from grains that were split and cooked into a type of porridge. Its strength-giving potential enabled Yishmael to develop the body needed to become an exceptional high priest ready to perform Temple rites dependent on his physical strength.[52] Like the tannaitic source in the Yerushalmi, Yishmael is referred to in the name of his mother (as a mother-begotten son), and she is associated with food—food that nurtures her son in a unique way. But in contrast to the Yerushalmi, in the Bavli Kimhit is praised for nothing more than feeding herself while pregnant and for ensuring the birth of a son who had the physical capabilities to perform Temple rites.

Immediately prior to weaving a version of the baraita quoted in the Yerushalmi into its redactional framework, the Bavli cites another possibility for Yishmael's praise, attributing this position to the Babylonian amora Abbahu. His position covers up for the lacunae created by an absent father by turning Kimhit into a fitting "receptacle" for the choicest male seed. As Charlotte Fonrobert has pointed out, a woman's very body is "his [her husband's] house" in the way she completes it.[53] Drawing on 2 Samuel 22:40 and Psalms 18:33 and a play on the words זרע and זרז and זרה,[54] the sugya makes the point that the natural, or biological, aspect of birthing children, heredity, is associated with the father. A son, therefore, is only as prodigious as the semen placed into his mother.[55] Food would nurture Yishmael physically for the demands of the priesthood, but according to Rabbi Abbahu, it is his father who contributes far more in terms of his future. It is the father who determines Yishmael's status as a priest. Details about Yishmael's father appear to be missing; nevertheless, the Bavli has not cast Yishmael's father aside entirely or the significance of his role over and above that of Kimhit.

78   *Bringing Down the Temple House*

Bringing in the baraita about Kimḥit and her sons at this juncture focuses attention on the fact that Kimḥit cannot quite become her husband's "house" in his absence. She can be a receptive vessel for her husband's seed, but she cannot perpetuate the ongoing nature of a functioning male-male bloodline.[56] The emended baraita that appears in the Bavli purposefully problematizes the categories of nature and nurture embedded in the larger Babylonian sugya.[57] In this version of the baraita, there is no reminder that Kimḥit is like what her name connotes, as the Yerushalmi's version presented. Rather than accentuating the fact that she nourishes her sons with food, her priest-sons beginning with Yishmael, shirk their responsibility regarding the purity laws that govern whether they can serve in the Temple. Nothing that Kimḥit does within her household informs her sons or the Temple house, as the Bavli's version of the baraita reflects:

> They said about Rabbi Yishmael, the son of Kimḥit:[58] Once, he conversed with an Arab in the market and a drop of saliva sprayed from [the Arab's] mouth onto [Rabbi Yishmael's] clothing [which rendered him impure for offering sacrifices in the Temple]. And his brother, Yesheivav, entered and served as [the high priest] in his stead, and their mother saw two [of her sons serve as] high priests on the same day![59]

> They further stated about Rabbi Yishmael, the son of Kimḥit: He once went out [of the Temple] and conversed with a certain lord in the market, and a drop of saliva sprayed from the [lord's] mouth onto [Rabbi Yishmael's] garments, and his brother Yosef entered and served as [the high priest] in his stead. And their mother saw two [of her sons serve as] high priests on the same day![60]

> The Rabbis taught in a baraita: Kimḥit had seven sons, and all of them served in the position of the high priest. The sages said to her: "What did you do to merit this?" She replied: "In all my days, the beams of my house did not see the braids of my hair."

> They said to her: "Many [women] did [not show their hair] and they were not raised up (ולא הועילו)" (BT Yoma 47a).

Once again, the high priests emerge as irresponsible men regarding their purity status. Although the tannaitic story is no longer set against

From Inside Out: Kimḥit's House

the backdrop of Yom Kippur where the need for the high priest is so central, the story captures a moment when the high priest, Yishmael, leaves the holy space of the Temple for the unholy space of the market.[61] If priests are given provisions while serving as priests through required donations such as *terumah* and *ma'aser*, what could the high priest possibly need in the market? Regardless of his reason, once saliva falls on him spewing forth from the mouth of either an "Arab" or a "Lord," both of whom, as non-Jews, fall into the category of zavim, his negligence regarding maintaining bodily purity renders his decision to visit the market completely irresponsible. Possibly he is simply unaware of the rules connected to his role. Yishmael is then disqualified for his incompetence. His brother steps in to replace him, and Kimḥit is able to see two of her sons serve as high priests in one day, albeit in succession, not at the same time. The insertion of additional tannaitic source material increases the number of priest-sons hyperbolically to seven, and then Kimḥit is described as a mother able to witness each of her seven sons in the post of high priest.

Kimḥit, even as their mother, however, can do nothing to prevent her sons' lack of attention to the details of their responsibilities as high priests. She simply observes each son step up to his post alongside rabbis who are skeptical about how an unmarried mother can raise son after son ready to assume the leadership role of a high priest. In the Yerushalmi, the rabbis preserve an expected male-female boundary by "sending" Kimḥit this question rather than talking directly to her: "What good deeds have you done [to deserve seeing all seven of your sons serve as high priests]?" However, in the Bavli, the rabbis ask Kimḥit face-to-face: "What have you done to merit this?" In this latter question, the rabbis cross the line into her "female" space, prompting a humbling response from Kimḥit, "In all my days, the beams of my house did not see the braids of my hair." But Kimḥit's modesty is so extreme that in comparison to the Yerushalmi, where Kimḥit mentions that the beams of her house did not see the *hair* on her head, the Bavli's version of the baraita specifically mentions Kimḥit's *braids*. In antiquity, hair braids placed on top of a woman's head were considered modest behavior for women when they ventured outside their homes. Flowing or untidy hair was considered sexually enticing.[62] Therefore, the specific mention of braids intensifies Kimḥit's display of modesty, as even within her house she is careful to braid her hair and then to cover the braids so that the "beams" do not see them. This act of modesty is countered by the rabbis' lack of it. The question that they pose face-to-face sets Kimḥit up for their final jeering response.

IS KIMḤIT'S BEHAVIOR TRUE MODESTY?

The nexus between Kimḥit's head covering and the beams of her house parallels the experience of her son Yishmael when exiting the Temple grounds for the market. While Kimḥit might think that taking on an extreme form of modesty earns her reward for caring about both the gaze of those inside her house on her as well the "stare" from its very structure, the beams, she has misunderstood the legitimate rules of modest behavior. Like her priest-son who misjudged the significance of maintaining bodily purity outside the Temple, Kimḥit has also misconstrued the rules of modesty and their purpose. Yishmael wears priestly robes outside the Temple and becomes impure. Kimḥit wears her modest clothing inside the house structure in a manner that also discredits her judgment as she attempts to argue for her influence on her sons within the Temple house. While head coverings for women were required in public spaces, they were not required in the privacy of their home. When a married woman uncovered her hair in public, she made herself sexually enticing to men who were not her husband.[63] At home, Kimḥit's "modest" behavior is inversely overzealous because she is not required to cover her hair in the domestic household. It also makes no sense in the absence of a husband-father figure. Who is she modest for? Possibly her sons. But her sons appear to learn nothing from this act of presumed piety for themselves; ergo, they, like her, falter.

When Kimḥit responds to the rabbis who set her up with their question, "What did you do to merit this?" she highlights the significance of the very structure of her own house that defines who and what she is, using the beams of her house as part of her modesty narrative. Picking up on what Kimḥit fails to transfer to her sons, a similar type of zealousness about their purity status that would prevent them from becoming disqualified high priests, the rabbis respond to her in a mocking tone, "Many [mothers] did [not show their hair] and they were not raised up."[64] It is as if to say that her actions had not earned her merit, meaning the act itself of extreme modesty was not the catalyst for meriting her sons' successes. In other words, many other women covered their hair and were not rewarded. Kimḥit's unnecessary display of modesty within her household called attention to the failings of the high priests

From Inside Out: Kimḥit's House

when serving in their Temple house. Her misguidedness for believing that the physical structure of her house needed protection from seeing her hair parallels the folly of the priests who think that they can protect the Temple from impurity when they venture outside it into the market, only to return, bringing their impurity into the Temple requiring their disqualification.

The Bavli builds on the notion that rights to the high priesthood come only from a paternal bloodline. Therefore, none of Kimhit's sons have earned the right to serve based on their merit or hers, despite her strategically enacted modest behavior. In truth, only their ancestry made it possible for them to conduct Temple rituals as high priests. Just as their priestly responsibilities are brought into question, Kimhit's role and special status as a mother providing advantages to her sons is questioned as well. She has not "made" them priests, because their priestly status comes from their father alone. In other words, Kimhit "gives" nothing "natural" in terms of priestly heredity and "creates" or nurtures nothing socially or culturally advantageous when it comes to her priest-sons.[65] In this regard, the Bavli presents a very different image of Kimhit from the more positive representation in the Yerushalmi. A social order rooted in hereditary kinship that the son-priests and their mother, Kimhit, represent is undermined in the Bavli, while affirmed in the Yerushalmi.[66]

Moreover, in comparison to the Yerushalmi, the Bavli's redactors include a different version of the baraita about Kimhit and her sons, integrating it into a layer of anonymous material, absent from the Yerushalmi. The Bavli's version of this tannaitic source picks up on the instability of priestly succession evident in the Yerushalmi and the problems with priest-priest succession, but it also moves the Yerushalmi's positive image of Kimhit as a nurturing mother into the anonymous layer referencing amoraic material. Admittedly, this additional piece in the Bavli masks the emotional lacuna left by the absence of a priest-father figure and the fact that her priest-sons are remembered by associating them only with the name of their mother. Conversely, mothers become mere vessels for the seed of fathers. The significance of this redactional move, from the mother-son relationship to the role of fathers in producing progeny, foreshadows the anxiousness of the Bavli's redactors reflected in the final chapter of Bavli Yoma regarding their ability to produce progeny. Reading this passage about Kimhit in the larger context of the tractate enables the rabbis to communicate

82   *Bringing Down the Temple House*

what must be present to construct viable households. At a minimum, there must be women who can bear children and nurture them by preparing quality food. But even more so, the future is tied to men who can implant the choicest seed.

FOR BAVLI YOMA IT IS A MATTER OF LIFE AND NOT DEATH

Kimḥit, like Helene (see chapter three), is a mother of seven sons.[67] This familiar seven-son trope calls attention to the narrative thread in Bavli Yoma linked to mothers and their sons. Few other images are as provocative as the mothers who martyr themselves along with their sons in the name of God.[68] While the overarching power of these mothers appears in other Talmudic tractates and rabbinic collections, the image of the mother martyr is absent from Bavli Yoma. Instead, Kimḥit and her seven sons turn this image on its head. Kimḥit's motherly role proves inconsequential as her sons continue to be disqualified, one after the other.[69] Presumably they have failed to maintain the required purity status needed to conduct Temple rites while serving in the Temple.

No doubt, redactors of rabbinic texts drew from various written and oral traditions in circulation in constructing their stories about martyrs.[70] BT Gittin 57b, for example, builds on the mother-son martyrdom image, constructing an image of a heroic mother.[71] Seven sons, one after another, resist pleas to worship idols and, in keeping with rabbinic law, choose death rather than succumb to idolatry.[72] They are willing to die rather than cast Jewish practice aside. As BT Gittin 57b points out, in comparison to Abraham, who placed one son on the altar to sacrifice him and both lived, the mother of this story is conceptualized as a courageous instigator as well as a fearless witness to her sons' martyrdom. Bavli Gittin's mother has raised exemplary sons, so much so that God extols her, citing Psalms 113:9: "He sets the childless woman among her household as a happy mother of children." Death is a praiseworthy act of resistance to a foreign, unjust regime that threatens the lives of Jews if they fail to commit transgressions against God —they must betray God or die. As a rebellion against this type of unreasonable religious authority, the choice of martyrdom shifts the power dynamic from the oppressor to the oppressed.[73] Therefore, the mother in Bavli Gittin emerges as a heroine remembered for reversing her victimhood and that of her sons through their public martyrdom.[74]

From Inside Out: Kimḥit's House

And yet martyrdom also raises suspicion and derision.[75] Martyrs create anxiety and fear in others because their actions contradict systems of rationality, not to mention that martyrs have the power to encourage others to act like them, perhaps taking the same actions.[76] For this reason, Bavli Gittin wavers, underscoring that choosing death over sinning is akin to becoming like "sheep" going to their slaughter (Psalms 44:23).[77] Martyrdom does not prevail as a clear choice worthy of emulation in rabbinic literature. The rabbis convey that this type of theology, dependent as it is on suffering and death, is laden with difficulties.[78] Therefore, it is not surprising to find mothers with seven sons such as Helene (see chapter three) presented in Bavli Sukkah as ensuring her sons observe the commandment of sukkah.[79]

Turning back to Kimḥit, while she is utterly distinct from the mother-martyr image in BT Gittin, she is not like Helene of tractate Sukkah either. More parallel to the Helene of BT Yoma, who has little impact on her son Mundbaz despite her commitment to calling attention to the Torah verses of Shema and sotah, Kimḥit also has no impact on her sons' priestly behaviors; she asserts no authority over them. Even when her valor is described as raising her "to the roof," she is couched as the mother who can serve as no more than a natural vessel for priestly seed. While Helene appears to be more powerful than Kimḥit in her own commitment to Torah knowledge, Kimḥit is powerless in the Bavli's presentation of her, reduced to a mother who does nothing beyond nourishing her fetus with the food that gives him physical strength (as important as that is). In the absence of the mother-martyr image, her ineffectiveness as a mother of seven sons intensifies by comparison. While the mother who martyrs herself and sways her sons to do so as well is the most pronounced example of sons who do what their mother tells them, in Bavli Yoma the rabbis prefer to imagine a far weaker mother-son bond. In fact, the very way in which the rabbis mock Kimḥit's desire to link her modesty with her sons' ability to become high priests is also suggestive of a certain discomfort on the rabbis' part. Fully aware of the need for a strong emotional bond in their own rearing of disciples, the rabbis are caught here in the Bavli looking to mothers like Kimḥit and Helene with envy, wishing to diminish the power of the bonds they can form with their sons. As well, their role in bearing and caring for children is also taken over by the idea that mothers, as seen through Kimḥit, are the receptacles for fathers' seed.

CONCLUSION

Bavli Yoma reshapes earlier sources that refer to Kimḥit, reiterating her story. She is linked to her own household and to the Temple house in order to think about the succession of priestly authority and who bears responsibility for it. But in the redactional layers of Bavli Yoma, there is also a desire to challenge this notion, even as the rabbis propose it. The insecurity of the Temple house brought to the fore through Kimḥit destabilizes the Temple house as well as mundane houses where mothers can be found with their sons and not their husbands. Not only do the rabbis drive a wedge between Kimḥit and her sons; they also suggest that the power of mothers might not be so strong either. Kimḥit is not like the martyr mothers who can sway their sons to die in the name of God or like Helene who raises her seven sons to sit in the sukkah (BT Sukkah 2b). Kimḥit, along with BT Yoma's characterization of Helene, stand out by comparison in ways that call attention to a larger redactional agenda where the rabbis question the power of the priestly bloodline and express concern about their own role in cultivating the next generation. What happens if Torah knowledge is not conveyed? What if it is not transmitted within the "house"? Do rabbis need the mothers of households in rabbinic culture to ensure that a transfer of knowledge occurs? If not, what falters? If yes, what power structures are challenged? Will the rabbis go the way of the priesthood? Will their houses suffer a similar fate to the Temple?

Like bodies, houses are often taken for granted; they are so commonplace and familiar and so much a part of the way things are that at times their significance is overlooked. Kimḥit calls extreme attention to the beams of her house, not only in their function as a witness to her modesty but also in their inability to transfer values to her sons. She gives her house great significance—indeed, anthropomorphic attribution—without success. Kimḥit's body calls attention to her sons' bodies. Her sons, in turn, call attention to the Temple house through behavior that disregards its sanctity. In this regard, anecdotes about Kimḥit in the Bavli support the notion that "houses" are symbolic and conceptual. These "houses" are able to stand for "individuals" who "stare" and for social groups that represent institutional structures, such as a Temple.[80] The private house, housing the modest mother, and the Temple house, housing only ritually pure priests, are juxtaposed here, neither structure, neither institution able, if not unwilling,

From Inside Out: Kimḥit's House 85

to reinforce the other. What is left is the space in between, that is, a space, a place where rabbis may interject questions and "receive" (albeit constructed) answers—the space where knowledge gets built and a new sense of kinship challenges traditional kinship forms.

Chapter five joins mothers and their priest-sons together in a different way. Turning from the influence of shared biology on priest-sons, it focuses instead on the garments that the high priests wear. A marker of status, gender, and class, these garments define priests, so much so that if they do not wear them properly, they are threatened biblically with death (Exodus 28:35). While the female body was the subject of rabbinic anxiety, as well as the motivating factor behind rabbinic laws such as women's head coverings, the mother discussed in the next chapter casts aspersions on her son when she provides immodest clothing for him to use in Temple service. This mother-son relationship once again spotlights a problematic priesthood, but also a concern for mothers who jeopardize their sons' abilities to perform central rites.

CHAPTER 5

INTERGENERATIONAL TRANSMISSION AND THE PROBLEM OF MOTHERS

· · ·

Issues of transmission, familial and Temple house related, frame Bavli Yoma. Woven into the larger narrative initiated by the Mishnah, the Bavli charts the transference of sin onto animals for the purpose of atonement by male priests.[1] The mothers of Bavli Yoma parallel this concept of transference in their desire to pass on something of value to their priest-sons or to the Temple itself. These mothers are uniquely constructed to highlight their gifts of material and nonmaterial transference to their sons and illuminate behavior that ultimately results in their sons' disqualification from priestly duties, if not their Temple role. The story of Kimhit, mother of seven high priests (see chapter four), celebrates a belief that her extreme modesty will pass along special merit to her priest-sons. In contrast, the mother of Doeg, the son of Yosef, and Helene donate material objects to their priest-sons and the Temple, trusting that such gifts not only will connect them to the Temple but enhance its ongoing operation.

The skill of the loom and weaving in this chapter also rises to great prominence in the endeavors of mothers who wish to promote their sons and ingratiate themselves to those who represent the societal elite. As mothers, they weave expensive priestly garments for their sons to wear, fashioning the necessary clothing their sons need to serve in the Temple.[2] However, the actions of these mothers, found initially in tannaitic material and woven into the Bavli, not only reflect on the nature of the priesthood but also reveal concerns about the transference of values from the outside Roman, Jewish, and Babylonian cultures.[3] Filtering through this material is a complicated balancing act, whereby the Bavli's redactors denigrate the priests but also express insecurities

87

about their own ability to transmit knowledge authoritatively from one rabbi to another.

Tying the mother-son trope to evidence in Bavli Yoma, specifically to the labor of weaving, the anonymous redactors tap into their own anxieties about their ability to transmit Torah from one generation to the next, related to their awareness of the strength of the relationship between a mother and her son. As the rabbis consider the powerful cultural, spiritual, and consequential associations of mothers with the continuity of their project,[4] their fears about the nature of, if not adherence to, rabbinic discipleship come to the fore.[5] For the rabbinic elite seeking to control the transference of knowledge from male to male, weakening the power of the mother-son relationship feeds into their desire to spotlight, if not further secure, their own role. The ways that the female-gendered image of the spindle and the labor of weaving differentiate women from men in rabbinic literature play into the rabbis' hands in Yoma as well.[6] Here too, referring once again to Joyce Antler, the mother is a "vessel" for the rabbis, into which their deep-seated anxieties are poured.[7] Can the rabbis reproduce themselves in perpetuity? Who and what stand in their way?

THE BACKGROUND: BIBLICAL
AND TALMUDIC ANTECEDENTS

The mother-son relationship in evidence in Bavli Yoma 35b and its connection to the domestic labor of weaving clothing are informed by various biblical antecedents. The special tunic that Jacob makes for Joseph (Genesis 37:3) connects him to this son over and above his other sons. The elaborate tunic (*ketonet pasim*), while not intended for ritual performance, symbolizes Joseph's salvific power and marks him as the son who will lead the Israelites to Egypt, saving them from famine. Resonating with this story is the biblical image of the prophet Samuel's mother, Hannah, who, on the annual pilgrimage to Shiloh, brings her son a robe that she has made for him, presumably to wear while engaging in his priestly duties (1 Samuel 2:18–19).

Both stories suggest that clothing has the power not only to forge significant connections between parents and their children but also to confer political and religious authority. Jacob's favoritism for Joseph, expressed through the gift of a beautiful robe, for example, parallels the way a mother's gift of clothing, as told in Yoma, is given only to the

Bringing Down the Temple House

one son who is the high priest, to the exclusion of his siblings. Noteworthy is that there will only ever be one high priest at a time. Where there are priest brothers, according to the tannaitic material below, they remain ready to take over when and if the high priest is disqualified. A mother who crafts a priestly garment for her son, so that he can fittingly worship in the Temple with "her" garment, builds on the images extolled in the biblical material. Hannah's show of favoritism for Samuel, however, as compared to Jacob's, signifies a desire to elevate her own status within the priestly family as she calls attention to the status of her son and to herself.[8]

Talmudic discussions about priests' vestments are also built on Exodus 28 and 39, which, bearing witness to the intimate link between particular garments and the proper execution of cultic practice, provide elaborate details regarding the clothing that must be prepared for Aaron to serve God properly.[9] Nowhere in Israelite/Jewish tradition is the link between clothing and ritual practice as strong as in the context of the performance of the sacrificial cult.[10] Biblical accounts describe priestly wardrobes as quite extensive, requiring a breast piece, an ephod, a robe, a fringed tunic, a headdress, a sash, and undergarments for the purposes of dignity and adornment.[11] The apocryphal book of Ben Sira describes the radiance of the high priest as he ascends to the Holy of Holies on Yom Kippur "as a vessel of beaten gold set with all manner of precious stones," clothed "with perfection" in his robe (Ben Sira 5:9, 11).[12]

Expanding on biblical material, the rabbis of tractate Yoma draw on biblical sources to describe lavish priestly vestments woven of gold, blue, purple, and crimson yarns, as well as garments of fine twisted linen. The intricate details, as well as the careful instructions for preparing priestly vestments in Exodus 28, enable the rabbis to imagine majestic clothing unlike anything they choose to emulate for themselves. Like the *parokhet* (the veil covering the ark), such woven materials functioned as holy vessels, separating the holy from the unholy (or, as in the case of the parokhet, the holy from the less holy).[13] The priests' elaborate robes, breastplates, and hats set them apart, distinguishing not only priests from non-priests and women, but high priests from regular priests, and priests serving in the Temple from those not serving. Mishnah Yoma 3:4, 6–7 and a baraita on BT Yoma 32ab describe priests' clothing of gold and fine white linen with as many as four outer garments and four inner ones.[14] BT Yoma 32b points to five Yom Kippur ceremonies, distinguished one from the other by the priests' change of garments.[15] Sources such as JT Yoma 7:3, 44b and BT Yoma 32b and 35b reveal that priestly garments had a power of atonement similar to sacrifices.[16] So consequential is priestly dress to Temple ritual that in linking priestly vestments to atonement, Bavli Yoma states, "If not for the priestly clothing there would not remain one remnant or survivor from the people of Israel."[17]

But more than the fact that priestly garments connect priests to sancta, the very act of spinning and weaving has, for the rabbis, the power to create as well as threaten the core relationships that define rabbinic society.[18] According to M. Ketubot 5:9, "The works of a woman's hands" protect her if her husband does not provide adequately for her. She has the right to sell them if he denies her a silver coin weekly for her daily needs.[19] The amount of monies that she must in turn provide for her husband is measured according to the weight of the yarn of either the warp or the woof of a loom, signifying that through wool work, a wife shows fidelity to her husband.[20] Even if she is wealthy, she still must spin. According to Rabbi Eliezer, a wife must engage in spinning wool, no matter how many servants she has. The laboriousness involved in creating just one garment was thought to keep women from a type of idleness that threatened their personhood. Without daily wool working, Rabbi Eliezer feared, a wife could become dull-minded and therefore capable of jeopardizing her marriage.[21] Miriam Peskowitz has noted that spinning was "an antidote" to the rabbis' concerns about their wives' desiring other men sexually. Through her labor, she communicated her loyalty to her husband. The idea that she might earn needed money from her handiwork is less significant than the fact that weaving keeps her from idleness and idleness from sexual behavior outside her marriage.[22]

Furthermore, women would spin with other women in public. The sitting position used in spinning incited worry that women would be exposing their bodies in a dishonorable manner. The observation of such an action granted husbands grounds for divorce without needing to give their wives the monies promised in their *ketubot* (marriage contracts), thereby depriving them of financial support.[23] But more significant is Mishnah Sotah's revelation that women who gather at night to spin their wool, protected by the darkness, become a community of women who pass information to one another, gossiping as they spin.[24] The content of such transfers of knowledge endangered women outside the circle as gossip could be spoken and spread without their immediate knowledge. In M. Sotah 6:1, Rabbi Eliezer states that men can accuse their wives of adultery based on hearsay,[25] but Rabbi Joshua adds that a husband cannot divorce his wife until that information emerges from a circle of women spinning at night. Such information is admissible, and a husband can act on what he hears, divorcing his wife. Hence, women weave to stay out of trouble as well as to protect themselves from idleness. But engaging in the domestic chore of spinning is therefore as protective to women as it is damaging. As such, this rabbinic view of spinning is more reflective of what the rabbis think about women than it is an expression of the essential nature and domestic objective of the task of spinning itself.

When Bavli Yoma brings up the image of women spinning, it intersects with the trope of the "wise woman." In this text, a wise woman poses a question to Rabbi Eliezer about the biblical incident of the golden calf, and he dismisses her with the claim that "woman only have wisdom [regarding] the spindle" (BT Yoma 66b).[26] While women can transmit to others the techniques of spinning and weaving, along with the products they create, Rabbi Eliezer, in the larger context of BT Yoma 66b, struggles to assert his knowledge and pass it on to other rabbis. He answers neither the question of the wise woman nor any other queries posed to him. Against the backdrop of the high priest's transference of the people's sins onto a goat sent off a cliff to its death, with all of the added concern regarding whether the rite can be executed without any hitches, the question of how knowledge is passed from rabbi to student surfaces when questions posed are not answered.[27] Prior to the wise woman's question about the golden calf, other questions are presented to Rabbi Eliezer that are related specifically to the rite of the goat: "What if the goat takes ill?" "What if the one designated to take the goat out [of the Temple and lead it off the cliff] becomes sick?" "What if in pushing the goat [off the cliff] it does not die?" Is the process of atonement ineffective? The sages have answers. Rabbi Eliezer does not.

These questions devolve into a list of additional queries to Rabbi Eliezer that range from the existential—whether a certain man would receive the reward of the World to Come for his behavior—to more practical inquiries such as saving ewes and shepherds from lions in the wake of a threat to one's life, laws concerning *mamzerim* (children born from adulteress relationships), and plastering one's house. Rabbi Eliezer deflects all of them until the anonymous voice in the Bavli points out that Rabbi Eliezer "never said anything that he did not hear from the mouth of his [rabbi] teacher," that is, Rabbi Eliezer would only pass on knowledge that was given to him by his mentor. Therefore, according to this sugya, the transmission of knowledge moves in a direct line from master to disciple. Under this method of transmission, knowledge itself remains static. It does not change. Answers have already been set by Rabbi Eliezer's teachers; there is nothing that this rabbi can add. And yet the questions keep coming. The final question is that of the "wise woman," which Rabbi Eliezer also evades. Offering no direct answer, he typecasts her and all other women as spinners with wisdom only for the tool used in weaving: the spindle. On some level, the message is that women are better off than male rabbis or their disciples. They can create and produce and freely transmit knowledge, skills, and product. Rabbi Eliezer, however, can do no more than pass on the knowledge he was given, preventing him from responding to any new questions that arise. The tension reverberating throughout this sugya highlights an insecurity that the rabbis feel, especially in the wake of a discussion of Temple ritual. If they wish to move the priests aside, if Temple rites were to fail to persist, do the rabbis have what it takes to replace the priesthood? Could it be that there are others who are more capable of transmitting knowledge? Perhaps the women who spin?[28]

In BT Yoma 35b, the connection between a women's knowledge of spinning and the transference of the products of this wisdom from mother to son links her household to the Temple house. In fact, for the Bavli, mothers who craft tunics for their sons are brought into the discussion to highlight the significance of transferring privately owned objects, such as priestly garments, to the Temple for private and public Temple ritual use.[29] "You might think," the anonymous redactors point out, that in donning a garment, a priest might fail to transfer it to the Temple for priestly use there. He might continue to wear it and keep it as his own garment. Such a worry seems unfounded, as the Bavli points out, bringing the case of a priest, Yishmael ben Pabi, who wore tunics crafted by his mother to serve in the Temple.[30] Surely, the Bavli assumes, he had transferred ownership of it to the Temple. This image, however, of a priest wearing the tunic made by his mother while serving in the Temple speaks to the role of the household in cultural transmission. How does that transfer occur? Who gives what to whom? And what is its nature? According to the rabbis, is the transfer successful? That mothers are the ones giving priestly vestments to their sons, and that these sons transfer their ownership of them to the Temple house, brings to mind what it is that priest-fathers transfer to their sons beyond biological relatedness.

PROBLEMATIZING THE MOTHER:
BAVLI YOMA 35B AND ITS BUILDING BLOCKS

Scholars have long mined Talmudic material for indications of the presence of women within the Temple precincts. They have argued that women had a far greater presence in Temple ritual than in the institutions associated with the rabbis, such as the beit midrash from which women were excluded.[31] Women offered sacrifices, participated in pilgrimage festivals,[32] and brought offerings after they gave birth or if they miscarried,[33] placing them in the Temple precincts on a regular basis.[34] On the surface, the portrayal of mothers engaged in the preparation of their sons' priestly clothing connects them to the sancta.[35] And yet the mothers referred to in Bavli 35b do more than dress their sons. They instigate a process whereby vestments are turned over to the Temple so that their sons can wear them and effectuate, in this case, Temple rites.[36] However, when this transfer of a garment to her son occurs, the mother's role ends; she remains on the outskirts of Temple life, relegated to a purely domestic role.[37] She is dependent on her son to manage the gift's ritual transfer to the Temple house. While it is not clear in this case how or when a priestly garment transitions from private ownership to Temple ownership,[38] as BT Yoma does not elaborate on this matter, the integration of this ownership transfer with the story about Yishmael ben Pabi's mother is a mark of the Bavli's intervention.[39] Bavli 35b builds on the earlier Toseftan and Yerushalmi parallels (T. Yoma 1:21–23 and JT Yoma 3:6, 40d), incorporating details from each.[40] It makes conscious choices that play into the larger narrative arc of Bavli Yoma.[41] The Yerushalmi is as follows:

> There was a story about Rabbi Yishmael ben Piabi in which he wore a tunic worth one hundred maneh and went up and offered sacrifices on the altar.
>
> There was a story about Rabbi Eleazar ben Ḥarsom, in which he wore a tunic worth twenty thousand (maneh) and went up and offered sacrifices on the altar. But his brothers, the priests, removed him because he appeared naked in it. What did [Rabbi

Intergenerational Transmission

Eleazar] do? He soaked [the tunic] in water, and he circled the altar seven times. (JT Yoma 3:6, 40d)

Both Yishmael ben Piabi and Eleazar ben Ḥarsom are high priests who offer sacrifices on the Temple altar wearing expensive priestly garments.[42] Eleazar ben Ḥarsom, however, is removed from the role of high priest by his brothers because he appears naked during the rite, presumably an affront to his position. Eleazar ben Ḥarsom proactively reacts, however, saving his position. He soaks his tunic in water, causing it to become thicker, which happens to linen when wet.[43] In an attempt to defend himself further, he circles the altar seven times, conjuring up the circumambulations with willow branches performed on the holiday of Sukkot, reclaiming his position by performing a Temple rite. That he marches in circles also means he can be seen from all angles in priestly clothing that, while unacceptable to his brothers, can be transformed into functional holy clothing. The Yerushalmi's Eleazar ben Ḥarsom turns out to be a practical high priest capable of preserving his position. This stands in marked distinction to the characterization of the same priest in T. Yoma 1:21–22, who willingly dons the transparent tunic his mother crafts for him and is deposed by his priestly brothers with no dispute. The presence of a mother in the Tosefta weakens her son's decision making, while her absence from the Yerushalmi appears to make room for the high priest to rectify his errors.

The sugya in BT Yoma 35b ties together details from the Tosefta and the Yerushalmi, bringing mothers from the Tosefta to the forefront and interweaving their gifts with the idea of transferring individually owned garments to the "public," that is to the Temple, for use:[44]

> Rav Huna bar Yehudah taught [in a baraita] and some say it was Rav Shmuel bar Yehudah: After the public [Temple] service was completed, a priest whose mother made a tunic for him, would wear it and perform an "individual service" (*avodat yaḥid*) in it. And [the priest could wear this tunic for communal services] only if he transfers [ownership of it] to the public [for Temple use].

> This is obvious; [once he transfers it to the public, it is Temple property like any other vessel that an individual donates to the Temple. What is novel in this statement]?

> What might you have thought? We might be concerned that perhaps [the priest] would not transfer [the tunic] in an accept-

94   *Bringing Down the Temple House*

able way. [The baraita therefore] teaches us [that one need not be concerned about this.]

They said of Rabbi Ishmael ben Pabi that his mother made him a tunic worth one hundred maneh, and he donned it and performed the individual service in it. And he transferred it to the public.[45]

And they said [in a baraita] of Rabbi Eleazar ben Harsom[46] that his mother made for him a tunic worth twenty thousand maneh, but his brothers, the priests, did not allow him to wear it because he appeared naked [in it].

Could one really see [his body through the tunic]? But wasn't it already stated that the threads [of a priestly garment] were sixfold [in thickness]?[47]

Abaye said: As [clear as] wine [shining through] a glass cup.[48] (BT Yoma 35b)

The mishnah (M. Yoma 3:7) to which BT Yoma 35b is connected sets the stage for what follows regarding mothers and sons. It refers to the leeway granted to priests concerning their Temple apparel.[49] According to the mishnah, priestly garments were given to them by "the community," and as priests, they could add additional funds if they wished to wear finer clothing when worshipping in the Temple. The excessive amounts of money spent by the mothers of Yishmael ben Piabi/Pabi (100 maneh) and Eleazar ben Harsom (20,000 maneh) on the materials necessary to weave these elaborate Temple garments raise concerns: maybe these priests will not want to part with the utterly fine vestments, turning them over to the Temple. Indeed, the garments have great value. That said, the Bavli is confident—of course the priests did turn the garments over to the Temple—for, indeed, the Bavli has tannaitic evidence that high priests wore garments made by their mothers. Yishmael ben Pabi made the necessary transfer to the Temple and performed his duties in them.

That said, these very same holy garments, so essential to Temple ritual, made Eleazar ben Harsom appear naked at the altar, turning his mother's finely crafted gift to the Temple via her son into a sham, despite its cost of 20,000 maneh. In addition, this tannaitic mother-son vignette does nothing to prove that high priests transferred garments

Intergenerational Transmission

to the public, as in the first story about Rabbi Yishmael ben Pabi.[50] So why include it? Eleazar ben Ḥarsom's brothers must step in to inform him that he cannot wear such a garment, and the Bavli moves on to offer confirmation that in fact the material was transparent. Unlike the Yerushalmi, where the brothers remove (הורידו) the same Eleazar ben Ḥarsom from his post, prompting him as high priest to turn the garment into something "convincingly" wearable, here in the Bavli's version of the baraita, the brothers do not allow him to wear the tunic at all.[51] In the Bavli, Eleazar ben Ḥarsom does nothing. As such, he stands out as a son who dons what his mother made for him. In addition, the Bavli's version accentuates his ignorance of Temple clothing requirements and calls attention to his mother's misplaced motives.[52]

Furthermore, the transparent garment invokes the Greco-Roman artistic style of wet drapery, dating back to the fifth century BCE when the intention was to create a "diaphanously clinging" cloth, exposing the body beneath it "as if through a thin, wet veil," while simultaneously "pretending" to hide the male body.[53] This deceptive gesture connects mother and son here in a sexual and provocative way. Rather than women exposing their own bodies when they spin wool in public,[54] here a mother exposes her son's body through the clothing she weaves—an act that has incestuous overtones. It calls to mind not only the significance of the naked male body in Greco-Roman culture, where it was extolled, but also the Babylonian Zoroastrian understanding of incestual relationships as pious acts.[55] For a mother to display her son's body in the public space of the Temple—to show him off, so to speak—was to represent the successful transmission of another set of values to him that were surely not priestly and not rabbinic.[56] The Temple was a public ritual space where nakedness was prohibited.[57] Exodus 28:42–43 specifically states that priests must "cover their nakedness" or incur the punishment of death. Rabbinic literature is replete with references warning against nakedness in the Temple and in synagogues while studying Torah. There are clothing requirements even when engaged in sexual relations.[58] Eleazar ben Ḥarsom's mother emerges as a mother willing to violate biblical law and pass this transgression on to her son in the guise of a traditionally acceptable behavior of gifting a woven garment. Her son follows suit; he intends to wear the garment. Only his brothers stand in his way. With resonance to the Joseph story, showing off the majestic robe made for him by his father and instigating the ire of his brothers, here too a mother and her gift

Bringing Down the Temple House

of elaborate clothing highlight the inequities that the priesthood can generate when one brother is singled out over the others.

The final comment added to BT Yoma 35b by the Babylonian amora, Abaye, drives home the gravity of this mother's use of the spindle. Abaye offers a more perceptible visualization of the holy garment in response to the anonymous redactor's shock: "Could one really see [Eleazar ben Ḥarsom's body]?" Weren't the priests' vestments woven to be six times as thick as any normal article of clothing? Abaye argues that thickness is not the issue. One could see through the cloth because presumably the thread used was as clear as glass, so no matter how thick the material, it did not hide the naked body over which it was worn. The image of wine, which is metaphorized here to the naked body, also happens to be dangerously alluring in the sense that wine can entice one to drink. Hence, through Abaye, Bavli Yoma pushes the image of the fabric mentioned in the tannaitic material to the point where these extraordinarily expensive materials do more than cling to the body of a priest. The cloth is utterly transparent, and the male body is visible as an object to desire.

Here the Bavli reflects on both the strength and threatening nature of a mother's ability to connect with her son and a son's desire to create an attachment to his mother. For the rabbis, this is a close and dangerous pairing.[59] This mother is more than a prototypical enabler who spins needed clothing for her family or even a woman who wants to involve herself in Temple worship in the limited ways open to her. The relationship she forges with her son, with all of its sexual overtones, is both enviable in the way it conjures an intense and intimate connection but also threatening in that strong bonds mean dangerous lines can be crossed.[60]

As the rabbis make efforts to implant a rabbinic hierarchy rooted in a male-male transfer of knowledge and create a different identity from that of the priests, they struggle with the extent to which men are what their mothers make them or even make for them. In keeping with the notion that "the human body is never seen as a body without being treated as an image of society," the rabbis here construct the naked body of the high priest in a rhetorical move, symbolizing their own desire to diminish the powerful role of the mother in order to make room for a different set of gendered power relations: male-male.[61] Can they take control away from mothers?[62] Can they, the rabbis, promote a social status centered on themselves—as men who pass down a

Intergenerational Transmission

particular legacy and take full responsibility for the religious development of other males who may or may not be their sons?[63] Can the symbolism of bloodlines and birth be transferred to the rabbis from the priests and the mothers who enable their priest husbands to continue the priestly line?[64]

The Bavli's inclusion of a mother connected to a Temple life that no longer exists, crafting an article of clothing that has no use in rabbinic society, also functions as a critique of the priesthood. While Eleazar ben Ḥarsom's mother can weave a garment that her priest-son does not object to wearing, her expertise with the loom cannot prepare her son for proper priestly service as a nontransparent, properly woven garment would. He accepts and projects the cultural value of nakedness proffered by her without objection. A mother who eroticizes her son and, even more so, a son who allows it, vividly constructs an image of a flawed relationship, disclosing the problems that for the rabbis inhere in a system reliant on a (Temple house) material garment for an effective ritual performance. The rabbis set up a "house" of their own making, this time with a mother and son who function to reveal its flimsy foundations. A dysfunctional mother-son relationship thwarts the possibility of a functioning Temple rite and generates the possibility that maybe something better can, and should, replace it.

Moreover, Eleazar ben Ḥarsom's mother cannot prepare him for Torah study, from which she is, for the most part, generally excluded.[65] Even the financial freedom that the rabbis construct for her—indeed, she has her own funds that enable her to donate gifts to the Temple, essential for worship—does not allow her to purchase or acquire any kind of Torah knowledge that she could then pass on. As well, Eleazar ben Ḥarsom's brothers,[66] who refuse to allow him to wear the transparent garment crafted for him and not for them, have a stake in his disqualification.[67] One of them can step into the role as high priest, testifying to the fact that the high priesthood is not a permanent position for any one person. A high priest can, like Joseph, be pushed away and other blood relatives step in to take his place. For the rabbis, though, the significance of distinguishing the cultural universe of the priesthood from their own rabbinic sphere of influence is paramount.[68] They defend and promote a social status built on an inner knowledge of Torah, open to all men and not on crafting an outer wardrobe. In the movement from one house to another, in this case, from the Temple to the house of study (the beit midrash), relationships will be formed be-

98   *Bringing Down the Temple House*

tween rabbis and their students through study and not through sacred clothing worn exteriorly.

Proper Temple worship is also made to turn on the way a mother, like the mother of Doeg and Helene, with extensive means, donates to the Temple with no positive result for Temple worship. Each gift underscores the precariousness of the Temple, especially in the case of Eleazar ben Ḥarsom, where a Temple rite depends on an expensive garment for its success. No doubt such mothers call attention to the fact that a tie to the Temple boosts their social standing as both a sign of their wealth and a way to align themselves with the distinct social status of the priesthood. However, whether a matter of Kimhit's extreme modesty, or the nakedness imposed on the high priest by his mother, neither one can ensure that what the Temple house stands for can be passed down through their actions, surely not by material support.

In the next and final passage of this sugya, Eleazar ben Ḥarsom rejects his family's wealth and his role as high priest in favor of Torah study, walking from town to town to study and carrying only a flask of flour. Here, neither wealth nor poverty is a deterrent to becoming a rabbi, as the remainder of BT Yoma 35b shows through a lengthy baraita that links Hillel's destitution to that of Eleazar ben Ḥarsom's fortune. With no parallel in Tosefta or Yerushalmi Yoma, the redactional decision to include this final baraita fleshes out the narrative thread running through Bavli Yoma—that familial relationships connected to the Temple are troubled and insecure, whereas relationships formed outside the Temple through Torah are more resolute and constant, even if they require the rejection of one's biological father. Indeed, the Bavli's sources construct Eleazar ben Ḥarsom as the prototypical Torah scholar, the son who rejects his father's priestly status and his wealth to study passionately among father-like figures who are rabbis. By contrast, in the Yerushalmi, no mention is made of the pursuit of Torah knowledge on the part of Eleazar ben Ḥarsom.[69]

BUILDING A NEW HOUSE: ELEAZAR
BEN ḤARSOM REJECTS HIS FATHER

While the passivity of Eleazar ben Ḥarsom is apparent in his decision to don the transparent tunic crafted for him by his mother, in the continuation of the sugya on BT Yoma 35b, he rejects the personal management of his father's estate in the name of Torah. Here, an additional

Intergenerational Transmission

baraita included in Bavli Yoma recalls that his father "left him one thousand cities on dry land and, corresponding to them, one thousand ships at sea."[70] Each day Eleazar ben Ḥarsom would travel from "town to town and from province to province to study Torah." He became so engaged in his studies that by the time he returned home, his own servants did not recognize him. Mistakenly forcing him to work, these servants learn that he is their master who has chosen to study day and night instead of administering to the property he inherited from his father. The effects of this baraita, appearing in the sugya immediately after Abaye's comment highlighting Eleazar ben Ḥarsom's nakedness, spotlight the high priest's double abandonment. Eleazar ben Ḥarsom rejects both the management of his inheritance by wearing a see-through tunic and the familial connection through his father to the priesthood.

Alongside Eleazar ben Ḥarsom's return home in this baraita is the story of the poverty-stricken and noteworthy rabbinic figure Hillel, who peers through an aperture in the roof of the house of study to hear the learned words of Shema'yah and Avtalyon. That Shema'yah and Avtalyon are themselves converts to Judaism highlights the idea that one needs only determination to study Torah and not a connection through a father. While Eleazar ben Ḥarsom walks away from the Temple, Hillel grasps at the very structure of the house of study, resolute to learn Torah. This baraita then moves on to the seduction of Potiphar's wife. Unlike Eleazar ben Ḥarsom, who could not refuse his mother, Joseph resists the advances of Potiphar's wife and the influences of the Egyptian court. According to the biblical narrative (Genesis 39), Joseph recognizes that to give in to Potiphar's wife means to shake the foundations of the house that Pharaoh had entrusted him to oversee. But the baraita homes in on the detail of Potiphar's wife's clothing, which in the biblical narrative she used to accuse Joseph, resulting in his imprisonment. In the baraita, however, Potiphar's wife attempts to entice Joseph day and night with her clothing. Joseph resists, recognizing that his future punishment for succumbing to Potiphar's wife's advances would connect him to her in the World to Come. The message of the passage is to choose Torah study over wealth and in spite of poverty. It is to resist the temptations of "wicked" women, like Potiphar's wife, who lure men with provocative clothing or, like Eleazar ben Ḥarsom's mother, who tempt their sons to wear see-through garments in the holiest of places.

100 *Bringing Down the Temple House*

The concluding baraita also accentuates the potential power and increased danger inherent in the mother-son relationship as compared to all other relationships that appear in the final baraita—including the master-servant relationship (Eleazar ben Ḥarsom and his servants), the teacher-disciple relationship (Shema'yah and Avtalyon with Hillel), and the male-female seductress relationship (Joseph and Potiphar's wife). Neither Eleazar ben Ḥarsom's father nor his servants play any influential role in his choices. Hillel refuses to break off his relationship with his teachers for lack of funds, and Joseph resists the temptations of Potiphar's wife. The relationship that is most fraught is the mother-son relationship, contextualized as it is within the life of the Temple and connected as it is to the labor of spinning, which women are able to and need to pass on. Weaving a son's garments when linked to the Temple, however, does not engender or foster a functional familial relationship between Eleazar ben Ḥarsom and his mother. He wears what his mother makes for him until his brothers step in. Eleazar ben Ḥarsom can resist his father and all of his father's wealth, but he cannot resist the overtones and values that his mother transmits to him through a garment intended to show off his naked body publicly. It seems quite strategic that the Bavli omits any reference to Eleazar ben Ḥarsom's father in its discussion of the tunic and chooses to append a baraita that disregards any reference to his mother when ultimately portraying Eleazar as a student of Torah following his exit as a high priest.

In recognizing the power of transmission that mothers have when it comes to their sons, the rabbis in Bavli Yoma limit this transmission to a mother's work with the spindle and the loom. But the wisdom of spinning pales in comparison to the wisdom passed on through Torah study. Interweaving a mother's knowledge of spinning with Temple practice and connecting that to what other values she can successfully transfer to her son not only reflect and contribute to the rabbis' envy and fear of the strength of the mother-son relationship but also cast a negative light on the requirements associated with priestly service.[71] Indeed, the material object, the tunic that Eleazar ben Ḥarsom takes from his mother without self-reflection, indicates that he not only has a different relationship with his mother than his father but also a different connection to the Temple than to Torah study. The same individual who as a high priest is submissive in the space of the Temple asserts himself in the name of Torah study outside the Temple, earning the

Intergenerational Transmission

title "rabbi." He, like Hillel and Joseph, resists the forces that stand in the way of the pursuit of Torah wisdom.

CONCLUSION

In Roman-period and Babylonian Jewish culture, there was an integral link between the labor of spinning and gender.[72] By way of the image of mothers weaving garments for their sons, the mothers of these priest-sons are constructed by the rabbis as women who participate in their sons' religious lives and hinder them as well, as in the case of Eleazar ben Ḥarsom. Interestingly, when the rabbis consider the male-male blood relationships that are the basis of a functioning priesthood, they also underscore concerns about the significance of maternal kin-ship.[73] For a rabbinic elite looking for social control in the transference of knowledge from male to male and fully aware that mothers play a large role in raising their sons—mothers who make tunics for their priest-sons who willingly wear them—enable the rabbis to construct a circumstance where a mother-son transfer of values goes completely awry. A mother who prepares see-through priestly garments for her son conjures an image drawn from the late antique world of men display-ing their naked bodies publicly. Although she performs domestic du-ties typically associated with nurturing children, she exposes rather than protects her son's body by passing down values that are not rab-binic—this against the construction of an all-male rabbinic program where Torah is central. The rabbis' anxieties about the strength of their own authority and the nature of rabbinic discipleship come to the fore.[74] The mother-son relationship is a bond that while enviable to the rabbis is also threatening to the relationship of master and dis-ciple on which their own success depends. This supports a recurrent thread in Bavli Yoma, that is, an interest in using relationships identi-fied with the household—like that of mother and son—among others, to think about whether such relationships sustain the Temple bayit or challenge its foundations.

Bringing Down the Temple House

CHAPTER 6

SEXUALITY INSIDE AND OUTSIDE THE TEMPLE HOUSE

...

The overarching narrative that runs through the first seven chapters of Bavli Yoma is focused on events surrounding the service of Yom Kippur, beginning with the separation of the high priest in the Parhedrin chamber seven days prior to the start of the holiday. Building on Mishnah Yoma, the Bavli offers many details that dramatize this grand event, so much so that rabbinic passages from Yoma form the basis of Yom Kippur liturgy still recited today.[1] But not unlike many other Talmudic tractates, Bavli Yoma has material interspersed within its treatment of the Temple Yom Kippur performance that might appear marginal but in truth forms a central arc within the larger redactional whole.[2] Keeping in mind the idea of the household and the relationships between its members as anchoring context, Bavli Yoma brings to the fore instances where both licit and illicit sexual relations link to or upend the very definition of a functional household. Sexuality is used by the stammaim both to eroticize the Temple house inhabited by sexless priests and to construct an image of the rabbis as sexed by comparison. Along the way, the image of Yom Kippur outside the Temple as compared to its observance within the Temple walls pits sexually allowable and promiscuous behaviors against the ascetic behavior of the priests. As a result, a different image of Yom Kippur emerges. This image differs both from the Temple Yom Kippur and the practice of self-denial that comes to define Yom Kippur, as discussed in chapter eight of the tractate. Sexuality surfaces over and over again in Bavli Yoma not only as a reminder that there might have been more than one way in which Yom Kippur was observed but also to shed light on whether the Temple is a ritually effective space.[3]

Additionally, the rhetoric around sexuality that winds its way through Bavli Yoma not only underscores the rabbis' desire to differentiate their own masculinity from that of the priests but points beyond it as well. It reflects a rabbinic perspective constructed not only within the cultural orbit of Sassanian Babylonia, where the rabbis' status as a minority was acutely felt,[4] but also where priests continued to live alongside them as a reminder of the Temple past and its priestly leadership.[5] Moreover, situated within a Syrian Christian culture where sexual abstinence was widespread and a Zoroastrian culture critical of such extreme attitudes toward sexuality, the Babylonian rabbis navigate the contours of a larger world orbit struggling with their relationship to asceticism.[6] The seepage of ideas from the Roman context where celibacy was firmly rooted in a developing Christianity also had an impact.[7] Turning to the Temple, which for the rabbis is a site defined by asceticism and sexual renunciation, is a viable entry point. It provides an avenue for the rabbis to construct the priests as their masculine "others" by differentiating them as sexless while describing themselves as quite the opposite. Potentially fueled by a reaction to the Mishnah (M. Yoma 8:1) and the development of a Yom Kippur rite of self-denial with all the trappings of ascetic behavior, Bavli Yoma speaks through the Temple and its priests to carve out its own concerns about sexual abstinence even for brief periods of time.[8] As such, the goal of this chapter is to think about Bavli Yoma and its objectives when sexuality is factored into the larger framework of the tractate.[9] What role does sexuality play in enabling the rabbis to think about the viable rabbinic household? Indeed, sexuality brings to the fore what it takes at a minimum to sustain households (including the Temple) and what can lead to their ultimate destruction.

SEXUALITY IN THE BAVLI

Scholars, including Daniel Boyarin, Michael Satlow, and Ishay Rosen-Zvi, have all argued that Babylonian sources, as compared to parallel sources compiled in the Land of Israel, reflect a deep interest in sexuality. Bavli Yoma supports this observation.[10] Speaking through texts that mention women and priests, the rabbis legitimate having, needing, and wanting sex in ways that parallel other Babylonian tractates. That said, the question is: How do the rabbis use the idea of sexual desire in Bavli Yoma? When does it surface? How do the pieces that treat sexuality fit together in ways that are unique to Yoma?

These questions are particularly critical when recognizing that male sexual desire and female sexual enticement work their way through a tractate bent on narrating a rite, Yom Kippur, that requires priests to abstain from sexual relations while serving in the Temple. Moreover, the observance of the non-Temple Yom Kippur, as described in Mishnah Yoma and discussed in the final chapter of the tractate, prohibits sex (M. Yoma 8:1).[11] In fact, this tension between sexuality and ascetic behavior bookends the tractate, beginning with the directive to sequester the high priest for seven days prior to the holiday in M. Yoma 1:1 and ending hoping that men experience seminal emissions on Yom Kippur in the tractate's final passage.[12] In between, the Bavli constructs various male paradigms using sexuality as a way to highlight both the asexual nature of the high priest while serving in the Temple and the highly sexual nature of the rabbinic male. What emerges is a permissive attitude toward rabbinic sexuality in comparison to the priests serving in the Temple, especially for a tractate devoted to a holiday linked to a prohibition regarding sexual relations.[13]

To draw from Mieke Bal's study of the biblical book of Judges is to detect a social revolution of sorts that plays out in literary moves aimed to create distance from the Temple. The Babylonian rabbis appear to be working not to link themselves organically to the priesthood but rather to understand what makes them distinctly rabbinic Jews.[14] Rather than connecting the ritually pure priest and his ascetic behavior with parallel requirements for non-priests on Yom Kippur, the rabbis work to differentiate priest from non-priest and the Temple house from the rabbinic household. Priests are men who must keep their sexual lives separate from their ritual responsibilities in the Temple. The Babylonian rabbis, however, are encouraged to act on their sexual urges. This chapter examines Bavli Yoma as a whole and the way its redactors use sexuality to couch the Temple and its priests as different from themselves. Beginning with the ways in which the priests are desexualized within an eroticized Temple structure, and then moving on to discuss the idea that for the rabbis sexual relations are valued as part of functioning households, highlights this distinction.

AN ASCETIC RELIGIOUS ORBIT

In the culture of late antiquity, asceticism emerges as a key religious issue. Jews, along with pagan philosophers and early Christians, struggle to understand the relationship between sexuality and one's ability

Sexuality Inside and Outside the Temple House

to develop a close relationship with God. The Stoics and Cynics argue for the importance of distancing oneself from the "distracting and weakening influences of the passions," believing that the control of physical and sensual impulses can bring about a type of spiritual perfection.[15] Some Jews and Christians believed that celibacy had the power to make "the human body a more appropriate vessel to receive divine inspiration."[16] There appeared, in their eyes, to be a direct relationship between "the negative denial of world, body, senses, pleasure, and emotion" and the "positive pursuit of moral and spiritual perfection."[17] And yet not all Jews, pagans, or Christians, or even all rabbis, shared one understanding of asceticism and its religious benefits.[18] By the second century, when Christian communities lay scattered throughout the Roman world, they attached various meanings to the idea of Christian chastity, some allowing for marriage and some arguing for complete sexual renunciation.[19] While sexual abstinence was an ideal among Syriac Christians in the Babylonian neighboring culture, Zoroastrians were more critical of such behavior.[20] Even within rabbinic literature, different attitudes toward asceticism emerged, understandable given that its sources are from different time periods and locales.[21] No doubt this makes it difficult to draw conclusions as to the rabbis' precise interlocutors, and no attempt will be made to do so here.[22] That said, it is also true that Bavli Yoma reflects the degree to which the rabbis were struggling with questions, not unique to them, about the relationship between ascetic behaviors and religious piety.[23] Indeed, this tractate brings to the fore the personal, social, and religious exigencies that made this tension so palpable and also unresolvable.[24]

SEXLESS PRIESTS IN A SEXED TEMPLE

As tractate Yoma begins, M. Yoma 1:1 requires a seven-day period of separation between the high priest and his wife before Yom Kippur, when the stakes are the highest with regard to his bodily purity.[25] Effectively, someone had the responsibility to separate the high priest to protect him from any voluntary or involuntary seminal fluxes, nonseminal discharges, or contact with menstrual blood.[26] Although not the only cause of impurity, the ritual purity of the high priest (or any priest for that matter), necessary to perform their duties within the Temple, was tied to his sexual restraint. While his impurity was ameliorable in that he could immerse in a *mikveh* (ritual bath), the rabbis accentuate

106   *Bringing Down the Temple House*

in the early sugyot of the tractate that measures needed to be taken to ensure that the high priest remained pure, going so far as to prevent him from eating certain foods that might prompt seminal emissions "on the eve of Yom Kippur toward nightfall." The idea was to keep the priest awake all night before the day of the Yom Kippur Temple service. A seminal emission on the eve of Yom Kippur would disqualify the high priest from his Temple responsibilities until after he immersed himself and waited until the following evening to be considered ritually pure (after Yom Kippur ended).[27] Furthermore, the high priest had to immerse five times over the course of the day of Yom Kippur, accentuating the steps that were taken to ensure that his bodily purity was intact.[28] In presenting the rules regarding the purity of the high priest on Yom Kippur, as well as the rules for regular priests, the rabbis couch the priests in general as a closed male group with a different set of responsibilities and therefore a stricter purity code than non-priests.[29] Only the priests can perform the public rituals of the Temple. Only they can enter certain precincts of the Temple, like the Inner Court or the Holy of Holies.[30] In this way, the rabbis couch the priests as sexless during the time when they serve in the Temple, distancing the priest from his body and his sexuality for this period of time.[31]

However, the Bavli in a sugya, beginning on BT Yoma 54a, imposes erotic images onto the holy space of the Temple, despite arguing for sexual restraint on the part of the priests.[32] In a Temple space where purity is primary such that chambers are specifically designed to protect priests from fluxes that can emerge from their own and their wives' bodies, poles that protrude from the Ark's curtain (*parokhet*) resemble breasts,[33] and *keruvim* (cherubim) in a sexual embrace are found behind the curtain where the Ark was kept.[34] The passage about the keruvim reads as follows:

> Rav Katina said: When Israel would make pilgrimage, they [the priests] would roll aside the curtain for them [the pilgrims] and show them the keruvim, which were entwined (מעורים)[35] with one another [in a sexual way], and would say to them, "See how beloved you [Israel] are before God, like the love of a man and a woman." (BT Yoma 54a)[36]

This sugya is rooted in 1 Kings 8:6–8, where the priests bring the Ark to the Holy of Holies in the context of Solomon's dedication of the Temple. To look at Kings is to notice no overt sexual overtones.[37] In

Sexuality Inside and Outside the Temple House   107

fact, most often biblical images of keruvim are winged figures. Both Philo and Josephus draw no such image of these figures clasping each other. Other instances in the Bavli such as BT Sukkah 5b, where keruvim are referenced specifically with respect to the Ark in the tabernacle, also bear no such sexual imagery. These erotic images are interpolated into the image presented in Kings to form a passage in Bavli Yoma that is sexually charged.[38] More specifically, the Babylonian amora Rav Ketina indicates that the priests would roll up the curtain (parokhet) for the people of Israel who made pilgrimages to the Temple, revealing the keruvim in a sexual embrace and then say, "See how beloved you are before God; like the love of a male and female." This image of male-female sexual intimacy that the priests reveal in the Temple is intended to metaphorize the relationship between God and the people.[39] Those who enter the Temple precincts should understand that God's love is ever so intimate, modeled after the closeness of a man and woman engaged in a sexual embrace.

And yet as BT Yoma 54ab expresses, the image of these keruvim does not comfortably sacralize the Temple house. The erotic pose does not parallel the experience of the priests while serving in the Temple. As the conduits between the people and God, the priests were beset with strict purity laws that did not allow them to have any sexual contact while serving in the Temple—so why use the male-female sexual embrace of the keruvim to signify the nature of God's relationship with the people and, in turn, the people's relationship with God? The image seems an odd fit for a priesthood required to remain sexless at the precise time that they are serving in the Temple. The rabbis, as they peer into the domain of the priests (albeit literarily), reveal priests who are eyewitnesses to the eroticism of the keruvim, albeit while denied earthly sex themselves.[40]

The interchange that brings several Babylonian amoraim into conversation on BT Yoma 54ab also raises concerns about why images of God were revealed to Israel in the Temple at all.[41] Citing Numbers 4:20, a thread of discomfort emerges regarding whether one should see any image that represents God, let alone a sexual one. Capturing both the positive nature of a sexual embrace and the problematic aspects of conceptualizing God's love by seeing the nakedness of the keruvim, the Babylonian amora Rav Naḥman introduces the non-Temple household of a bride and groom hoping to cast a sense of reasonableness onto this erotic scene.[42] Differentiating between the modesty of a bride

108   *Bringing Down the Temple House*

in her father's house, who is betrothed (*kidushin*) but not yet married (*nesu'in*), and a woman in her father-in-law's house, who is married and therefore no longer modest in the company of her husband, Rav Naḥman points out that the keruvim are similar:

> [The matter is] analogous to a bride. All the time that she is in her father's house she is modest before her husband. Once she arrives at her father-in-law's house, she is no longer modest before her husband. (BT Yoma 54a)

When a woman is fully married and leaves her house to join her husband in her father-in-law's house, sex is fine; this is equal to the Temple where sex is fine if it occurs. In other words, in the "married" chamber of the Temple God and the people can experience intimate relations. Just as in the non-Temple household, where there is no problem with a wife who welcomes the sexual embrace of her husband outside her father's house, there is also no difficulty with the sexual imagery presented by the keruvim. Rav Naḥman's comparison to the non-Temple husband-wife relationship suggests that a functional house is where women's sexual availability to her husband is entirely legitimate. It is where, in the absence of her own father, she can act on her sexuality, presumably exposing her nakedness to her husband without concern for her own modesty.[43] Mapped onto the image of the keruvim, Rav Naḥman argues that within the Temple house, that is, in the Holy of Holies as compared to the everyday household, God's intimate relationship with the people can be respectfully presented through male and female figures appearing as though they are clinging to one another sexually.[44] Sex happens in the Temple to reflect the very nature of God's intimacy with human beings, but all the priests can do is lift the curtain to expose it. While the keruvim inhabit the space behind the curtain and are, for Rav Naḥman, symbolically in their father-in-law's house, the priests "remain" in their father's house, that is, in God's house. As such, keruvim can exhibit sexuality, but the priests, in their relationship with God in the Temple house, can do no more than remain modest. Their relationship with God fails to take on the same degree of intensity as those who visit as pilgrims, presumably those who are non-priests.

The Babylonian amora Rav Ḥana bar Katina is not convinced and pushes back, recalling the tannaitic source known to Rav Naḥman (BT Yoma 54a) about a priest who is consumed by fire upon thinking that he discovered the place where the Ark was hidden in the Temple. The

Sexuality Inside and Outside the Temple House

lesson: certain sacred objects like the Ark, covered by a curtain with keruvim behind it, must remain hidden. But Rav Naḥman continues to defend his position, reintroducing the husband and wife again. He warns Rav Ḥana bar Katina that the period after the destruction of the First Temple was like a woman divorced from her husband. Before there was a new Temple, not only did she return to her original modest and sexless state, but she had no connection to her father or her husband. It was during this period after the destruction of the First Temple and before the Second Temple was built that the priest of the tannaitic source quoted in BT Yoma 54a wrongly sought the Ark. At that time, in the absence of any Temple, all images or objects associated with God had to remain concealed. The relationship of the people and God was strained. But once the Temple is rebuilt, as Rav Naḥman intimates, the keruvim and all of their sexual overtones can be on view for all of Israel. He locates God's presence within the Temple, comfortable with the provocative visual image of the keruvim and the way that they represent the intimacy of God's relationship with the people.

The Bavli, however, is far from done. The discomfort brought to the surface by the inclusion of a reference to the keruvim continues to surface in an attribution, this time to an amora from the Land of Israel:

> Reish Lakish said: When gentiles entered the Sanctuary, they saw [images of] keruvim entwined with one another [sexually].[45] [They] took them out to the market, and said: These Jews, whose blessing is a blessing and whose curse is a curse, should they be occupied with such matters? They immediately debased them, as it is stated: "All who admired her despise her, for they have seen her nakedness (*ervata*)." (Lamentations 1:8) (BT Yoma 54b)

According to Reish Lakish, when non-Jews entered the Second Temple, they saw images of the keruvim carved onto its walls.[46] Stripping them from the Temple, they brought the keruvim to the market and put them on public display. They were utterly perplexed by how such sexually provocative images could be present in the Temple at all. In quoting Lamentations 1:8, which references the destruction of the Temple and Jerusalem, the Bavli uses this verse to accentuate that the embrace of the keruvim is a symbol of disgrace. Non-Jews have seen Israel's *ervah*, her nakedness. In this way, the Temple house becomes a house of ill repute. Reish Lakish, an amora living in the Land of Israel, effectively admits that non-Jews had a credible reason for destroying

Bringing Down the Temple House

the Temple, a reason that is tied to the display of sexually provocative images on the part of the priests. Once sexuality is taken out from behind the curtain, that is, out of the Holy of Holies, and placed on display before the public, it becomes a mockery worthy of punishment.

This passage is central to Bavli Yoma's redactional concerns. The rabbis create a Temple house in this passage where sex and abstinence are both presented as being in tension with the other. Is one closer to God when imagining God as an intimate sexual partner? Is one's relationship with God best understood by visualizing two figures entwined with one another in a sexually intimate and provocative way behind a curtain in the Holy of Holies? Maybe the "immodest" married woman having sexual relations in her father-in-law's house is the better model for channeling the intimacy between human beings and God. Or, is the Temple priest closer to God because of his ability to remain sexless while serving the people? Possibly, celibate behavior generates the most intimate relationship with God. Maybe the paradigm of the ascetic priest should be acted on? Tapping into the cultural and religious conversations percolating in Babylonia at the time with respect to the role of sexual renunciation in defining one's relationship with God, the Bavli's stammaim present their own struggles using the Temple as the locus. In the end, the gaze of the non-Jewish outsider is by far the most critical of the Temple's erotic imagery, functioning as a reminder that while sex can be holy, it can also be unholy, that is, depending on the one who views it (or engages in it).[47]

Indeed, examining the instances in Bavli Yoma where the rabbis deal with issues related to sexuality occurring within the Temple reveals that they were concerned about the connection between sexual renunciation and rabbinic Judaism. Not only was there a memory of a priesthood that would, albeit for short periods of time, remain abstinent while connecting with God in the Temple; there was also a calendar marked by fast days, such as Yom Kippur, that generated concern for what it meant to take on ascetic behaviors. At the same time, the rabbis were struggling with when sexuality crosses the line from an acceptable act, even a holy act, to a sinful one. Is imagining a relationship with God through the intense embrace of keruvim in the Temple problematic when, as Rav Naḥman wants to show, sexual relations are entirely permissible between a husband and wife? Does sexual desire legitimize sexual relations? Does marriage? Does procreation?[48] To speak about what is percolating within the narrative about the Yom

Sexuality Inside and Outside the Temple House   111

Kippur service in the Temple is to recognize a discourse that is explored through the very question of what type of sexuality can and should construct the household and also what has the power to tear it down.

DIFFERENTIATING "OTHERS" FROM "OTHERS": BAVLI YOMA'S DISCOURSE ON WOMEN VERSUS PRIESTS

Bavli Yoma is full of textual moments when sexuality seems surprisingly legitimate and times when it is called into question. The rabbis keep returning to the Temple and its priests to examine both the necessity for and the dangers of sexuality. To look more closely at the sources that are brought together in Bavli Yoma is to recognize that while the Temple is eroticized through the sexual embrace of the keruvim, the tractate also uses sexuality to marginalize women and priests, albeit in distinct ways. Women are depicted as sexually enticing and responsible for the destruction of the First Temple. In addition, powerful biblical women who use their sexuality for political gain also appear in Bavli Yoma. In contrast, priests are couched as unaffected by the sexually arousing aromas that waft from the daily incense offered on the Temple altar. They are also described as anatomically defective. And they are deceptive about the most important aspect of the priesthood, their lineage, emerging as weak figures unable to maintain their family line.

More specifically, BT Yoma 9b reiterates a perspective that appears in many places in rabbinic literature, blaming women for instigating illicit sexual behavior (*giluy arayot*) from men. In this case, the aroma that wafts from a woman's feet is sexually arousing, rather than, for example, in the case of Kimhit, who raises the issue of hair as sexually provocative (BT Yoma 47a):[49]

> On what basis was the First Temple destroyed? Because of three things that existed there: idol worship, illicit sexual behavior (*giluy arayot*), and spilling of blood.
>
> Illicit sexual behavior: [As it says in Isaiah 3:16], "Moreover the Lord said: because the daughters of Zion are so vain and walk with their heads thrown back/outstretched necks, with roving eyes and with mincing gait, making a tinkling with their feet." . . . "Making a tinkling with their feet" — Rabbi Yitzhak said: They would take myrrh and balsam, place them in their shoes and when they reached the young men of Israel, they would stamp

Bringing Down the Temple House

[their feet] and spray them, driving into them the evil inclination, like the venom of an angry [snake].[50] (BT Yoma 9b)

Here, women use their bodies to entice young men to commit forbidden sex; they arouse the evil inclinations of these men, luring them with the smells of myrrh and balsam coming from their feet as a result of stamping their feet intentionally.[51] Men, in and of themselves, are upright until led astray, weakened by the sexual advances of the smells that emerge from the feet of women.[52] These women awaken impulses that promote chaos and bring about the destruction of the Temple house.

Paralleling the image of fragrant smells rising from women's feet in Bavli Yoma, the Temple itself emits aromas that arouse the senses. Aromatic smells rise from the incense that accompanied the sacrifices and was thought to reach as far as the city of Jericho. So strong were these fragrances that they stimulated the senses of both animals and men.[53] Capable of perfuming the bodies of women, including brides in Jerusalem, such scents made additional personal adornment unnecessary (BT Yoma 39b).[54] Once again in Bavli Yoma, the Temple is eroticized, emitting smells that provoke arousal. Read together with BT Yoma 9b, the stammaitic thread keeps testing the boundaries for both priests and men. The tractate uses fragrance to call attention to a spectrum of sexual behavior. Women who fill their shoes with sensual spices are so dangerously enticing to men that their behavior causes the destruction of the First Temple. On the other hand, the Temple's daily effusion of aromas from incense that has the power to turn brides as far away as Jericho into sexually desirable women for the men they marry appears to have no effect on the priests who perform the incense rites. Such smells happen to be emitted at the precise moments when the bodily purity of the priests within the Temple is crucial for effective Temple performance. Moving back and forth between discussions of illicit and licit sexual behavior, Bavli Yoma places the Temple at the center of its discourse as it explores both the dangers of sexuality and the necessity for it as well.[55]

The rabbis further weaponize female sexuality, pointing to the ways that women use it for additional and particular ends. In fact, the three biblical women who receive attention in Bavli Yoma are Potiphar's wife, Batsheva, and Esther, each of whom uses her sexual prowess to achieve desired goals. They do this by reinforcing the notion that

Sexuality Inside and Outside the Temple House　　　113

female sexuality can be forceful enough to threaten monarchies and powerful enough to reverse political fortunes. Joseph successfully resists Potiphar's wife's sexual advances. Ultimately the interchange sets off a series of events that contributes to the Israelites' survival. David, however, is drawn to Batsheva, who is married. He loses three of his children as punishment for having sex with her.[56] Equally so, sexuality can have the kind of salvific power that brings about miracles, as, for example, through Esther, who functions to validate the Babylonian rabbis' diasporic post-Temple world. Adding to that, Esther's sexual relationship with Ahashverosh in BT Yoma capitalizes on but also exploits the highly provocative nature of female sexuality (BT Yoma 29a). On the one hand, Esther is the enabler. She saves the diasporic community in Babylonia. However, reference made to Esther in Bavli Yoma is also rooted in the similarity made between Esther's womb and that of an *ayalah* (a ram). Esther's "narrow womb," according to the Bavli, is the physical feature that results in multiple acts of pleasurable sex for Ahashverosh, but it is also what saves the Jews from Haman's evil decree by winning over the king. As Mieke Bal argues, through sex women can gain access to and influence men.[57] In this way, through the constructed dangers and uses of the female body, the rabbis point to the possibility that women can bring about destruction as well as redemption using the power rooted in their sexuality.

Priests, however, while also marginalized, are, with constancy, opposed to women, in that their bodily imperfections emerge to highlight their sexual limitations rather than their sexual prowess to accomplish needed objectives.[58] In addition to the protocol to change from one set of beautiful vestments into another during Yom Kippur (M. Yoma 3:4, BT Yoma 30b and 31b, JT Yoma 1:4, 39a), the high priest is required to perform several full-body immersions. Each immersion separated each of the five services conducted on Yom Kippur one from the other. A linen sheet became a necessary implement to hide the high priest's naked body (Leviticus 16:4; M. Yoma 3:3, 3:4, 3:6; BT Yoma 31b; BT Yoma 35a; and BT Yoma 30b–31b). The ritual bath water was warmed for him in case he was too old or fussy and might feel chilled (M. Yoma 3:4–6; BT Yoma 31b–32b; JT Yoma 3:6, 40c).[59] Ten sanctifications (hand and foot washings called *kiddushin*) accompanied these five full-body immersions and required that the high priest wash his hands and feet each time a priest removed his vestments and then again prior to donning the new ones for the next service (M. Yoma 3:3–4, 3:6; BT Yoma

Bringing Down the Temple House

31b–32b).[60] A detailed discussion explores exactly when the high priest was to perform these sanctifications so as to ensure that he washed his hands and feet properly.[61] However, when the Bavli examines this Temple rite, intended for reasons of maintaining Temple purity, the rabbis choose to highlight a problematic feature of the priest's naked body. Different from the way that the rabbis couch women, these men have physical defects that prevent them from having any sex at all.

According to M. Yoma 3:2, "everyone (*kol*)," that is, every priest who serves in the Temple, must perform this rite of hand and foot washing after he urinates, whether it is Yom Kippur or not. In bringing this to the fore, the Mishnah interrupts the overall narrative describing the Yom Kippur service to discuss a daily purification rite incumbent on every priest before serving in the Temple—one that also must be observed on Yom Kippur. M. Yoma 3:2 states:

> They took the high priest down to the house of immersion.
> This was the general rule in the Temple: Anyone who moves his bowels requires immersion and anyone who urinates requires sanctification of the hands and feet.[62]

Remarkably, BT Yoma 29b–30a extrapolates further, turning hand and foot washing into a precautionary move aimed to protect priests from being judged improperly (also see M. Yoma 7:3; BT Yoma 70b):

> The general rule in the Temple was: It is understandable [why the] feet [must be washed]. [It is] because droplets [of urine fall onto one's feet]. However, what is the reason [one needs to wash his] hands? Rabbi Abba said: [This] indicates [that there is] a commandment to rub off [droplets of urine that fell on one's feet with one's hands]. [Rabbi Abba's explanation] supports Rabbi Ami, for Rabbi Ami said: It is forbidden to go out with droplets [of urine] on his feet, because he will appear like a person with a crushed penis (Deut. 23:2)[63] and [thus] cast aspersions on his children— that they are *mamzerim*[64] (children born from an adulterous relationship between a man and a married women or children born from an incestuous relationship).[65]

A mere gaze at the feet of a priest can inform an onlooker about the health of the most intimate part of a priest's anatomy, his penis.[66] When the Bavli labels, or calls out, a priest who neglects to perform the rite of hand and foot washing and therefore fails to remove droplets

Sexuality Inside and Outside the Temple House

of urine from his feet, a *kerut shofkhah*, it invokes Deuteronomy 23:2 in a powerful literary move. Deuteronomy 23:2 commands that a man without a penis or with a crushed penis cannot be "admitted into the congregation of the Lord." Rashi, in trying to figure out why droplets of urine would land on a priest's feet, not to mention the connection between this and mamzerut, notes that it is a sign of an anatomical defect responsible for impotence when a man's penis can only point straight downward. Droplets of urine on a priest's feet would therefore serve as a sign of his inability to have children, deeming him an outsider to an institution built on the rules of kinship. Any children he claims as his own would be suspected as mamzerim. In other words, there would be doubts about the paternity of his children and concerns that they were born to a different father who had engaged in an adulterous relationship with this priest's wife. However, if he had rubbed off the droplets and performed the rite of hand and foot washing, no one would be suspicious.

Perhaps the remedy is compassionate in that priests can undergo a rite of sanctification that protects them from the judgment of others. However, introducing physical defects undercuts the holiness of the rite of sanctification and its function as an act of purification associated with the performance of the Yom Kippur rite. On BT Yoma 29b–30a, "urine droplets" and "feet" become the means of contextualizing the priests as men who cover up their imperfections, allowing sons without priestly blood to become priests. Furthermore, this text casts aspersions on the priests, constructing them as men who cannot have sex—and this within a tractate where the identity of the male rabbi is positively connected to his wanting, needing, and having sex, as will become clearer below.[67]

Images of the priests washing their hands and feet to purify themselves from defecating and urinating in M. Yoma become, for the Bavli, an opportunity to call attention to the priests' sexual impotence and to their manipulative behavior in hiding challenges to the purity of the patriline by claiming mamzerim (born to possible non-priest-fathers) as sons. Highlighting the physical features of the priests' bodies reinforces rabbinic desires to assert authority and control in ways that sideline the priests, making them look weak, fastidious,[68] and committed to a Yom Kippur rite that is overrun with different types of ritual immersions. It is also another discursive moment for the Bavli to question the priestly bloodline in suggesting that their lineage might be tainted.

Moreover, the mere suggestion that priests might falsify their sons' lineage enables the rabbis to construct imagined deficiencies in priestly leadership. No doubt there is a level of rabbinic insecurity peering through the veil of this critique of the priestly patriline.[69] Priests were indeed a threat, more real than imagined, even in Babylonia after the destruction of the Temple.[70] Recasting a purification rite into one whose purpose it is to remove droplets of urine from a priest's feet in order to construct not only the possibility of sexual weakness on the part of priests, but also a way for the priests to hide that weakness, makes claims for rabbinic power over priestly control reasonable. When the rabbis conjure up the impotent priest who seeks to hide his failings with the rite of foot washing, they reveal a desire for authority in the wake of a scripturally sanctioned group of leaders who can serve as priests only because they are related to one another. Inherited leadership was an issue of concern to the Babylonian rabbinic elite for whom religious and cultural reproduction were rooted in a master-disciple relationship and not a bloodline; the accepted sources of authority for priests and rabbis were fundamentally at odds.[71] As such, they denigrate the priests in the wake of vivid and seemingly nostalgic descriptions of Temple ritual, convincing themselves not only that religious authority rightfully belongs to them but also that maintaining rabbinic households is dependent on sexual relationships that produce legitimate progeny.[72] That said, and in contrast to their rejection of patriliny, the rabbis envy the priestly bloodline. They recognize that passing on Torah knowledge is in fact deeply dependent on producing offspring. Fatherhood is entirely dependent on sex and women, and because both can be fraught with problems for access, the making of and birthing of children was a profoundly fragile endeavor.[73] The social revolution that rears its head in Bavli Yoma is about the rabbis unsettling the priestly patriarchy, disempowering the priests, and empowering themselves. But to do so means to construct a new house as sexed fathers with an ability to have children. For this reason, the rabbis present themselves as virile men, in comparison to the priests.

VIRILE RABBIS

While scholars, including Daniel Boyarin and Ishay Rosen-Zvi, have noted the more positive attitude toward sexuality in Babylonian rabbinic sources, the fact that sexuality surfaces in Bavli Yoma within the

Sexuality Inside and Outside the Temple House   117

context of Yom Kippur communicates its pronounced significance in the minds of Yoma's redactors.[74] While priests serving in the Temple must maintain a status of ritual purity, and the observance of Yom Kippur is associated with sexual abstinence, Bavli Yoma includes one of the most provocative sources about rabbis who in their travels are looking for sexual partners "for a day." The assumption that the stammaim make by bringing in a baraita with the opinion of Rabbi Eliezer ben Yaakov is that these amoraic rabbis are looking to marry "temporary" wives so that they can engage in legally permissive sex:

> When Rav came to Darshish, he would announce, "Who will be mine for a day?" Whenever Rav Naḥman would come to Shakhnetziv, he would announce: "Who will be mine for a day?"
>
> But has it not been taught [in a baraita]: Rabbi Eliezer ben Ya'akov says: No man should marry a woman in this country and then go and marry a woman in another country lest [their children] marry one another with the result that a brother would marry his sister [or a father his daughter][75] and [thereby] filling the whole world with illegitimacy. And about this it is written: "And the land will become filled with depravity" (Lev. 19:29).
>
> I will tell you that the affairs of the rabbis are well known [and people know of their second wives and the identities of their children].
>
> But didn't Rava say, if one has proposed marriage to a woman and she has consented then she must await seven clean days [before the wedding to make sure that she is not a nidah]?[76]
>
> [This problem was resolved] because the rabbis sent a messenger in advance to them [these women].
>
> Or if you like, say: They would [only] live in seclusion with [their new wives and would not have marital relations with them] because you cannot compare one who has bread in his basket to one who does not have bread in his basket.[77] (BT Yoma 18b)

In this passage as a whole unit, Bavli Yoma acknowledges and sanctions the idea that men need to be satisfied sexually, even while traveling, so much so that every potential threat to engaging in this practice of marrying for a day is removed.[78] For example, men do not have to worry about incestual marriages between their sons from one mar-

118 *Bringing Down the Temple House*

riage and their daughters from another because the "affairs of rabbis are well known." More than the fact that sexual relations "for a day" are completely permissible with a "temporary" wife, the potential children born of the union are always identifiable and their lineages clear in cases where the men are rabbis. In contrast to the priest who might lie about his progeny, claiming them as part of his patriline (BT Yoma 29b–30a), rabbinic lineages remain intact. The reason? The rabbis are well known to all. Concerns that temporary wives might be niddot (menstruants) also falls by the wayside because rabbis always prepare for their brief marriages in advance, sending messages regarding their intentions to these women. It might even happen that they do not actually have sexual relations, but that too is not an issue because by marrying a woman ever so briefly, these men have "bread in their baskets."[79] In the rabbinic mind-set, where a wife is metaphorized to "his [a husband's] house" by marrying just for a day, even if only for the purpose of companionship, men create temporary houses where their sexual desire can be sated merely by being together — she is the "bread" in his "basket."[80] Temporary marriage legitimizes this encounter. In contrast to the high priest, who could have only one wife on Yom Kippur, the redactors of Bavli Yoma convey that other men may have many wives for the purpose of controlling their sexual urges.[81]

Moreover, just as the rabbis can build "houses" with provisional wives wherever they go, there were instances when men had sex on Yom Kippur with Nehardean virgins (Nehardea, a center of Babylonian Judaism). BT Yoma 19b–20a points to the need to keep the high priest awake all night to prevent him from having a nocturnal emission before performing the Yom Kippur service in the Temple.[82] Here in Bavli Yoma, the tanna Abba Shaul describes a loud noise coming from "prominent" people (יקירי ירושלים) around Jerusalem aimed at disturbing the priests so that they would not sleep. The implication: the priestly rite could not be easily sustained without the assistance of outsiders who supervised priestly behavior and were probably not priests. Making noise, however, devolved into sexual revelry. Reconstructing the events, the Babylonian rabbis (Abaye and Rav Naḥman bar Yitzhak) argue, quite surprisingly, that in Nehardea, people continued to stay awake on the night of Yom Kippur and had sexual relations with virgins in this Babylonian town. The Bavli intimates that their actions deserved punishment, possibly even using this to explain why the Messiah had not yet come. But Elijah the prophet interjects:

Sexuality Inside and Outside the Temple House   119

"Satan does not prosecute on Yom Kippur," a statement that intimates that these acts of sexual intercourse are excusable. What occurred in Jerusalem among "prominent" non-priests on Yom Kippur is permissible in a Babylonian context.

In the Babylonian rabbinic imagination, keeping priests up all night so that they would not have seminal emissions transformed over time into an occasion for sex on Yom Kippur among those who had no relationship to the Temple and were surely not in Jerusalem at the time. Possibly the image is linked to M. Ta'anit 4:8, which describes virgin women engaged in a day of merriment attempting to attract men on Yom Kippur. Tal Ilan, in commenting on M. Ta'anit, points out that the Mishnah's description of Yom Kippur is more reminiscent of pagan wine and fertility orgies than of an ascetic holiday defined by a list of prohibitions. In fact, the Syrian Church father John Chrysostom, albeit in the context of polemicizing against the Jews, described Yom Kippur as a fast day that had turned into a day devoted to "sensuality and licentiousness," where Jews danced with naked feet in the marketplace.[83] Was this reference to the Nehardeans a way to legitimize a practice that Chrysostom utterly denounced and rendered perverse?[84] The image of women dancing publicly in vineyards and mentioned in M. Ta'anit also parallels to some extent the Bavli's vision of the eve of Yom Kippur in Nehardea. It is therefore possible that the stammaim intentionally weave different ways of observing Yom Kippur that were either cast aside or neglected once the idea of self-denial on Yom Kippur became paramount. While sexual relations with virgin women by Nehardean men might recall elements of merrymaking on this holiday, as M. Ta'anit also suggests, this image parallels the tension in evidence on BT Yoma 54a. Keruvim entwined sexually in the Temple alongside ascetic priests captures the tension between sexuality and sexual renunciation and its ties to a divine-human relationship percolating in the Babylonian cultural orbit. Here too the stammaim capitalize on a similar tension, thinking about the extent to which self-denial and its association with the observance of Yom Kippur grant the idea of sexual abstinence for any period of time in the Jewish calendar credibility (see chapter seven).

That said, for BT Yoma 19b–20a, a reference to the Nehardeans constructs a significant distinction between priests and regular Jewish men, disfavoring the priesthood. Men connected with the Temple cannot even fall asleep for fear that a seminal emission will endanger their ability to connect with God on behalf of the people. Men in Nehardea, with the same sexual urges, can act on them on Yom Kippur without fear that they will endanger their relationship with God. Satan will not punish them, and their behavior will not prevent the future arrival of the Messiah. Satisfying the oversexed male is more important here than reappropriating the ascetic experience of the priest on Yom Kippur. In this regard, the non-Temple Yom Kippur excuses men for acting on their sexual urges, in comparison to the priests, who needed to maintain sexual control.

But what centers so much of the material found in Balvi Yoma with respect to sexuality is an imaginative Babylonian aggadic narrative about the consequence, even benefit, of sexual immorality. This complicated story links many of the other passages about sexuality found in Yoma together, disclosing what is at the core of the rabbis' fears of sexual renunciation. Here on BT Yoma 69b, sexual immorality is personified to challenge the merit of maintaining a celibate world, bringing these two impulses into dialogue with one another. Within a larger stammaitic passage, this aggadic story raises the idea that the "Inclination" (*yetzer*) for sexual immorality should be quieted. Despite murky details as to who is speaking, a request is made: "Let us pray for the Inclination that promotes [sexual] transgression [to be subdued]." The prayer is answered, and the opportunity is granted to destroy the penchant for immoral sexual behavior. Then the Inclination speaks out in warning, "See if you kill me the world will end [as no one will have offspring]," because the same passion required for sexual transgressions such as adultery and incest is also required for licit sex.[85] In response, they imprisoned the Inclination for three days to see what the world would be like without it. They looked for a sign from hens and roosters who lay fertilized eggs shortly after insemination. Not finding even one fertilized egg, they realized that "killing" the Inclination would have disastrous results. Indeed, the world would be deserted of life. And yet, recognizably, it is not possible to restrain the Inclination in instances of transgressive sex and enable it only for licit procreative sexual relations. The aggadic story rules this out. Opting to blind the Inclination instead, the story ultimately allows for a man to have sexual relations but never to become "aroused by it [to the point where he would have sex] with his relatives."[86] There would be sex for the purpose of procreation alone, to the exclusion of incestual relationships, even if such an incestual relationship was "intended" for the purpose of birthing offspring.

Sexuality Inside and Outside the Temple House

While incest could always ensure future progeny, it also meant that families, such as priestly families, might inbreed. As part of a narrative arc connecting viable households to licit sexuality, the ultimate concern, as will become more evident in the eighth and final chapter of the tractate, is future offspring. The Babylonian rabbis stake their claim here in a cultural orbit where Syriac Christians, for example, were embracing ascetic behaviors. But these rabbis want nothing to stand in the way of procreative sex.[87] And while the disciplined nature of Torah study, both mental and physical, can be viewed as a rabbinic form of ascetic practice that required men to leave home and replace priestly service in the Temple, Bavli Yoma does not advocate for the acquisition of Torah knowledge as more significant than progeny. Yom Kippur in the Bavli becomes an ideal platform, a perfect jumping-off point, given the mishnaic dictum prohibiting sexual relations in M. Yoma 8:1, for assessing the nature and limits of rabbinic ascetic behaviors and their link, not to Torah study but to rabbinic sexuality as connected to procreative sex.[88]

More to the point, the position that Bavli Yoma takes in the debate over whether one is to study Torah before marriage or marry first is resolved in the name of the Babylonian amora Rabbi Ḥanina: studying Torah requires marrying a woman first (BT Yoma 72b).[89] BT Yoma 77a praises wives for their commitments to their husbands, lauding the fact that "they chase away sleep in this world (שממנדדות שינה בעולם הזה),"[90] that is, they lose sleep waiting up each night for their husbands to return from their studies in an act that grants them merit in the World to Come. In other words, husbands who are Torah scholars leave the Beit Midrash each day according to Bavli Yoma. The wives who wait for them to return home are dutiful, and for that they are praised.[91] As compared to the wives of high priests, who do no more than exist in a married relationship so that their husbands can atone for their "households," the wives of Torah scholars are described as women who value their husband's pursuit of Torah study. High priests are sequestered from their wives, so their wives are mere objects in a role they play two weeks of the year; a rabbi's wife, however, is integrally linked to his commitment to Torah study, a commitment that is ongoing with no time limits attached to it.

That said, part of a wife's commitment to her husband is to fulfill his sexual needs, even if it means waiting up all night for him to return. The tension in the Bavli that Boyarin and others have so aptly docu-

122 *Bringing Down the Temple House*

mented, associated with a monastic life devoted to Torah, where husbands leave their wives for long periods of time to study, interestingly does not surface in Bavli Yoma.[92] In addition, while Yom Kippur reappears several times in other tractates as the time in the Jewish calendar when men would return home to their wives after periods studying in the Beit Midrash, no reference is made to such a tradition of returning home on Yom Kippur in Bavli Yoma. Instead, men return home every night, creating greater opportunity for more frequent sexual relations. As a counterpoint to husbands' lengthy monastic-like periods of time in the Beit Midrash that appear in other tractates, here in Bavli Yoma, rabbis not only marry wives for a day when traveling and have sexual relations on Yom Kippur with Nehardean virgins, they are also characterized as men who study close to home.[93] In an environment where sexual renunciation was highly valued, Bavli Yoma's redactors construct moments of opportunity where rabbis can act on their sexual urges, but more important, they construct rabbis as men with ample opportunity to engage in sex that will lead to future progeny.

CONCLUSION

Yom Kippur and its association with observing a day of sexual abstinence sets the stage for drawing out larger tensions over the connection between sexual relations and sexual renunciation with one's relationship with God. Within an environment where the rabbis were pulled in both directions regarding sexuality, Bavli Yoma uses the ascetic nature of the Temple and its priests as a lens through which to think through this struggle. The placement of keruvim in the Temple in a provocative embrace highlights a central question reverberating throughout the tractate: Is the intensity of sexual intimacy the model for understanding God's relationship with human beings? Or is the behavior of the priest who needed to remain ascetic preferable for connecting with God?

Although there is evidence throughout the tractate of a group of men grappling with how to respond to their earthly biological urges and their commitment to God and Torah, the issue that generates the greatest degree of anxiety is the lack of assurance of future offspring. Offspring legitimize sex and ensure a lasting household.[94] Forms of sexuality that do not ensure progeny and that in Bavli Yoma happen to be connected to the Temple and its priests, including keruvim in

Sexuality Inside and Outside the Temple House

a sexual embrace, aromas wafting from the Temple that cause sexual arousal, disqualifications from priestly service due to seminal emissions, and priests' deformed sexual organs, shake the foundation of the Temple house and its priesthood. In this way, using sexuality to distinguish priests from rabbis, as well as priests from women, does more than marginalize them. It also highlights what is at the core of the rabbis' struggles in Bavli Yoma, which is where ascetic behavior ultimately points, having no kin at all.

As Mieke Bal detects in the book of Judges, a social revolution is underfoot here. The discourse around sexuality woven into the tractate ultimately moves the priests to the periphery of the rabbinic household, that is, to a place where they have little to no relevance unless they become rabbis. The rabbinic conceptualization of the non-Temple rite of Yom Kippur in the final chapter of Bavli Yoma, where worries about birthing progeny emerge again against the backdrop of a rite contingent on bodily self-denial of sex and food, does not bring the priests back into the discussion. Instead, what rises to the surface are the challenges that ascetic behaviors raise for the rabbis not so much as rabbinic leaders but as human beings. These struggles prompt them to think about themselves as persons living lives as members of households threatened by everyday critical problems, such as a lack of food and water, sickness, and, of course, their greatest fear: having no progeny.

CHAPTER 7

SUSTAINING
THE RABBINIC
HOUSEHOLD

· · ·

The final chapter of Yoma begins with M. Yoma 8:1, the locus classicus for rules governing Yom Kippur that remain in force today, saying: "On Yom Kippur it is forbidden to eat, drink, wash, anoint, wear sandals and have sexual relations." This is one of the earliest records where the prohibitions associated with Yom Kippur are defined in rabbinic literature, specifying what is meant by the commandment in Leviticus to practice self-denial (inui nefesh) on the tenth day of the seventh month (Leviticus 16:29, 31; 23:29, 32; Numbers 29:7). While ascetic behavior can be a means toward transcending and overcoming difficult life experiences, the Bavli's treatment of Yom Kippur in its final chapter questions whether any individual can assert control over the exigencies and trials of daily life. Returning to the relationships that are at the core of household life, this last chapter uses the prohibitions associated with the non-Temple observance of Yom Kippur to examine what threatens and also sustains the earthbound body in the everyday household. After many chapters in Bavli Yoma that critique the Temple and its priesthood, the rabbis shift their lens and use the Mishnah's list of Yom Kippur prohibitions to think through what maintains (and does not maintain) the familial household, pushing the discussion about the Temple to the wayside.

In discussing Mishnah Yoma in its entirety, Gunther Stemberger describes its last chapter as "nothing but an appendix that shows how, in a time without the Temple, one can still obtain atonement." The final mishnah (M. Yoma 8:9), which presents the image of a mikveh to effect ritual purification, supports Stemberger. The mikveh is used metaphorically to describe the ability of Yom Kippur to change individuals through the process of repentance. The quote "I [God] will sprinkle clean water upon you and you shall be clean" (Ezekiel 36:25) is followed

125

by a verse that uses the word *mikveh* to refer to God as the "Hope of Israel" (Jeremiah 17:13), to strengthen the point that God will give individuals "new heart[s]" and "new spirit[s]" (Ezekiel 36:26). However, a closer look at this chapter in the Mishnah in comparison to the Bavli reveals that repentance and atonement, the central themes of Yom Kippur, as practiced both within and outside the Temple, are not the central focus of the Bavli's final chapter. Rather, a different view unfolds building on the narrative arc of the "house" that captures the rabbis as fragile men, not focused on the priesthood and the Temple house but more concerned about the subsistence of their own households.[1]

THE TRACTATE'S TORN SEAMS

A disjuncture is in evidence between the first seven chapters and the final, eighth chapter of Bavli Yoma. In this last chapter there is no narrative describing the execution of a Yom Kippur rite as in the first seven chapters of the tractate, and no specific symbol or Temple memory fuels the discussions.[2] Here, the rabbis seem uninterested in the priests, especially the high priest, giving him no visible role in the observance of the rabbinic Yom Kippur.[3] Salt to the wound, no rabbinic leadership role is described paralleling the function of the high priest who, in prior chapters, atoned for the people. There is no attempt to create a sense that in observing the rabbinic Yom Kippur, one is reenacting the Temple service.[4] There is also no evidence of liturgical passages, such as a requirement to recite parts of the mishnah's narration of the Yom Kippur avodah, as was already developing during the tannaitic and amoraic eras, according to scholars such as Michael Swartz.[5] Additionally, the commandment of inui nefesh and the verses that mention this commandment do not surface in the tractate until here. More specifically, the Yom Kippur Temple rite that was addressed in detail in earlier chapters of the tractate is not connected to the everyday bayit. In other words, the rabbinic household does not emerge as a replacement ritual space for the Temple house, at least not in Bavli Yoma, and the independent householder, by observing ascetic behavior, is not couched as a replacement high priest. Yom Kippur might be about individual atonement for the one who takes on a list of temporary ascetic practices, but the issues percolating in chapter eight bring to the fore the rabbis' concerns regarding what is needed, at a minimum, to sustain their own households. The rabbis' assertion of power over every detail

126   *Bringing Down the Temple House*

of the extravagant public Temple Yom Kippur rite is transmuted into a vigorous reflection on maintaining the everyday house and the people within it.[6] More specifically, fasting and the prohibition of sexual relations, ascetic behaviors that also permeated the cultural orbit of Sassanian Babylonia, were recognized by the rabbis as practices that could threaten the construction of viable everyday households.[7]

MISHNAH YOMA 8:1: INUI NEFESH

The observance of Yom Kippur, as discussed in the final chapter of Yoma, when centered on bodily self-denial is incumbent on all individuals, regardless of gender, class, or ancestry, thereby completely reversing the traditionally observed hierarchical image generated by the high priest in the Temple house. Women are not the inevitable victims of a rabbinic attempt to marginalize them. They are no more at risk than anyone else, unless they are pregnant, a new mother, or a recent bride (as discussed in chapter eight).[8] In fact, women in this chapter have agency over their bodies, and they prove to be no more or less resilient in protecting the family against life's crises than men are.[9] While anachronistic houses, rather than temporary huts (sukkot), rise from the desert, it is manna that brings the narrative threads connected to the household that run through the tractate—of family relationships, sexuality, and embodiment—to the fore.[10] Manna, a foodstuff prepared by God that requires no domestic preparation, also crystallizes the Israelites' experience in the most vulnerable and temporary of spaces, the desert, calling attention to a life that at a minimum requires sufficient nourishment and, uniquely, draws no distinction between men and women.[11] It is not the memory of the temple or the maintenance of a rabbi-disciple transmission of Torah that establishes continuity in this chapter but something far more tangible: food and sexual relations. While never fully dismissing more typical rabbinic gender paradigms, whereby women's bodies have the power to entice men sexually, the focus in this final chapter turns to the power of individuals to mediate their own bodily experiences and ensure the survival and integrity of the household, whether they are male or female, rabbi or not.[12]

To create the religious and cultural rabbinic individual, households need to be built of people who take responsibility to sustain themselves and their children.[13] God sets up this paradigm of answerability when providing the Israelites with manna in the desert. By sending

Sustaining the Rabbinic Household

manna, God is taking care of "God's household" and enabling its very survival. Therefore, in Bavli Yoma, manna sets the stage for examining the Bavli's understanding of self-denial. It enables the rabbis to grapple with the idea of rabbinic asceticism, specifically their anxieties over behaviors that threaten the very substance of what makes a house a viable household.

THE CASE OF MANNA

Bavli Yoma is not concerned with how fasting is connected to attaining atonement. Paradoxically, the final chapter is more focused on discussing examples of eating, most specifically God's delivery of manna to the Israelites in the desert. Integrating tannaitic material into a lengthy passage, the Bavli presents a detailed examination of how manna fell, what messages it conveyed to the people based on where it landed, what it looked like, and how indeed, it had a taste.[14] But more than to grant God with utter power, manna captures a unique liminal moment in history when the absence and presence of food occur simultaneously. At the precise time when the people are living outside a regular home and cannot be typical householders with domestic responsibilities for preparing foodstuffs, the Israelites receive a portion of food daily. Manna does not look like anything that resembles food in their experience and cannot be cooked or stored away except for Shabbat. More to the point, this discussion brings the rabbis' emotional stresses to the fore, not of suffering from starvation but suffering the fear that what they have today might not be available tomorrow. Therefore, manna becomes a symbol of turning fear into trust and anxiety into faith.

In struggling to define self-denial, the rabbis examine forms of the Hebrew word *inui* (עינוי), relating back to the biblical commandment to practice self-denial on Yom Kippur where this word appears.[15] BT Yoma 74b refers to Deuteronomy 8:3 because of its inclusion of a form of the word *inui*, citing a tradition associated with the tannaitic academy of Rabbi Yishmael. Deuteronomy 8:3 mentions the affliction of hunger alongside manna in the same verse: "[God] subjected you to the affliction of hunger (ויענך וירעבך) and gave you manna to eat, which neither you nor your fathers had ever known, in order to teach you that man does not live on bread alone, but that man may live on anything the Lord decrees." Manna is the food that reverses the hardship of hunger. Because of the presence of a form of the word *inui* (עינוי) in Deuteron-

128   *Bringing Down the Temple House*

omy 8:3, the Bavli, like the Yerushalmi, juxtaposes this verse with Leviticus 16:29 — "On the tenth day of the seventh month, you shall practice self-denial (תענו את נפשתיכם)" — using a typical rabbinic hermeneutical tool, the *gezeirah shavah*.[16] Linking the two verses that mention inui, the tanna Rabbi Yishmael (or possibly the tannaitic school of Rabbi Yishmael) offers proof for understanding the commandment of inui as hunger. Just as ויענך in Deuteronomy 8:3 referred to the fact that the Israelites experienced hunger in the desert, inui in Leviticus 16:29 must also refer to hunger. Therefore, the word *inui* must mean that one is biblically commanded to experience hunger on Yom Kippur.[17]

While the Yerushalmi quickly abandons the discussion of manna, the Bavli explores inui, using the concept of manna in a far more expansive way. On BT Yoma 74b, the Bavli goes on to juxtapose Deuteronomy 8:3 with the following verse from the same chapter in Deuteronomy: "[God] . . . fed you in the wilderness with manna, which your fathers had never known, in order to test you by hardships (ענותך)" (Deuteronomy 8:16). According to Deuteronomy 8:16, manna in and of itself generated hardship in the desert, setting up an exegetical quandary for the rabbis to build on; manna could reverse hunger but also generated an experience of hardship (Deuteronomy 8:3). As Deuteronomy 8:16 indicates, living without actual food and relying on manna alone as a stand-in for food is also a privation. The question then arises as to how these contradictory verses work to explain the meaning of *inui nefesh*. BT Yoma 74b states:

> "[God] . . . fed you in the wilderness [with manna, which your fathers had never known], in order that by hardships (למען ענותך) you would be tested." (Deuteronomy 8:16)
> Rabbi Ami and Rabbi Asi [disagreed on the definition of *hardship* and its connection to *manna*]:
> One said: There is no comparison between one who has bread in his basket and one who does not have bread in his basket.
> And one said: There is no similarity between one who sees [the food] and eats it and one who does not see [the food] and eats it.
>
> [To build upon this] Rav Yosef said: From here there is an allusion to blind people who eat but are not fully satisfied.
>
> [To support this] Abaye said: Therefore, one who has a meal should eat it only during the daytime.[18]

Sustaining the Rabbinic Household   129

Rabbi Zeira said: What is the verse? "Feasting of the eyes is better than the pursuit of desire" (Ecclesiastes 6:9).

And Reish Lakish said: The sight of a woman is better than the actual act [of sexual relations], as it is stated: "Feasting of the eyes is better than the pursuit of desire" (Ecclesiastes 6:9).

In this passage, the opinions of several Babylonian amoraim are interwoven to call attention to the fact that manna, while capable of sustaining the Israelites in the desert, does not seize on the senses or whet the appetites of the Israelites.[19] The mere sight of manna and its failure to resemble actual food evokes feelings of deficiency and want, according to these amoraim. For the rabbis, the human instinct to judge with one's eyes, rather than to reserve judgment until after one engages in the actual experience of eating, is a very real aspect of human nature. Likened to feelings of sexual desire caused merely by seeing a woman, the rabbis drive home the point that suffering is caused not by the absence of sustenance (sexual or otherwise) but by the absence of images that have the power to induce appetites (images can be a partial fulfillment).[20] Were they eating "food" if it did not resemble food? Because manna delivered in the desert robbed the Israelites of this sensorial experience, it generated feelings of additional hardship among the Israelites, despite being a source of nourishment.[21]

Anthropologists and scholars of linguistics have shown that embodiment and the lived experience of individuals in their bodies play roles in communicating how people understand, articulate, and process their own experience.[22] Metaphor, in particular, facilitates greater understanding and communication, evidenced here by the rabbis, who become proficient in equating the image of food (the source of the metaphorical comparison) with sexual relations (the target of the comparison) so as to make greater sense of what it means to desire something.[23]

Likening food to women's bodies accentuates the male gaze, not to mention the image of consumption. Men have the power to see, the entitlement to look; women are seen, their images consumed, like food. The cultural power of associations between food and sexuality common throughout rabbinic literature reinvokes male power and agency in the objectification of women.[24] These amoraic rabbis use women's bodies to conjure up the experience of wanting something, desiring something, in order to problematize the experience of fasting. In so doing, they turn fasting into more than the desistance from eating food. Just as

130   *Bringing Down the Temple House*

in some males the mere sight of a woman may evoke a desire stronger than the act of having sexual relations, seeing food can evoke a sense of longing to eat that is more pleasurable than eating itself.

In a Foucauldian sense, the body is a creation of culture manufactured through discourse.[25] Therefore, while the rabbis imagine inui nefesh, albeit paradoxically, as a commandment that women are required to observe, in defining the essence of the prohibitions encapsulated by this category of self-denial, the amoraim fall back on more typical rabbinic images of women's bodies as sexually enticing. The physically disabled body, blinded to any sense of pleasure, surfaces prominently as well. Without complete power, both within and outside their households, the amoraim mentioned on BT Yoma 74b attempt to capture in words an imagined sense of power.[26] Quite disturbingly, by relying on cultural constructions of the female body and those with disabled bodies, they turn those who ironically share the same hardships of want with them into metaphorical constructs. This they do both to assert a sense of control and displace their own feelings of vulnerability.[27]

Manna, when understood as a hardship, turns the definition of inui or, more specifically, the denial of food on Yom Kippur, into an experience that ensures baseline sustenance without any of the mechanisms that evoke desire or enjoyment. The mishnah's seemingly full-fledged demand to refrain from eating[28] therefore becomes an allowance for the minimal amount of food needed to maintain oneself. As such, the redactors of the Bavli seem to distance inui nefesh from the idea of complete abnegation, redefining what it means to experience the suffering body. To practice inui nefesh on Yom Kippur is merely to deny the body its daily pleasures, but not to the point of absolute privation.[29]

Noticeably, thinking with manna in the Bavli invites greater reflection on eating than on fasting. The debate between Rav Ami and Rav Assi (BT Yoma 74b) presents a host of arguments related to interpretations of biblical verses that mention food. Proverbs 23:31, for example, discloses that persons should not set their eyes on wine as it inflames the appetite; Isaiah 65:25 presents the serpent of the Genesis narrative as doomed to eat dust; Numbers 11:5 points to the Israelites' complaints in the wilderness recalling the food that was once available to them in Egypt.[30] Each mention of food or wine here in Bavli Yoma is coupled with sexual innuendos linked to women in a manner that objectifies them. Such references reinforce the point that the rabbis are

Sustaining the Rabbinic Household   131

searching for a way to control what is not in their control. While wishing to believe in their own power and authority over women, they also recognize their powerlessness. Similarly, such powerlessness is deeply evident in their inability to steward the consistent availability of food in ways that are fleshed out further as the sugya continues to unfold (BT Yoma 75a).[31]

In the wake of the spread of Christianity eastward and the rabbis' familiarity with monastic practices, as Michal Bar-Asher Siegal argues, as well as the Jewish cultural interactions with Sassanian culture, as Simcha Gross observes, it is not surprising that the rabbis were participating in a larger conversation about ascetic behavior.[32] While, arguably, the rabbis of the Bavli have an interest in defining rabbinic asceticism to distinguish themselves from other religious groups, their discourse here within the context of discussing Yom Kippur presents them as deeply concerned with their own survival as able-bodied, fertile men who are responsible for their own functional households. Like the Bavli's discussion of manna, the following exegetical examination of Numbers 11:5, which oddly connects the memory of eating fish in Egypt with incestuous relations, brings to light the complex tension that surfaces as the rabbis think about the possibility of limited food supplies. Capitalizing on the Israelites' complaints in the desert after leaving Egypt that are fueled by the memory of home and the insecurities of homelessness, Bavli Yoma proceeds with the following analysis of Numbers 11:5–6 accentuating still further the tensions that ensue when thinking about food and sex:

> "We remember the fish (דגה) that we ate [for] free in Egypt . . . [Now our gullets are shriveled. There is nothing at all. Nothing but manna to look to]" (Numbers 11:5–6).
>
> Rav and Shmuel [argue]: One said: [the word (דגה) refers to actual] fish [that the Israelites no longer had in the desert].
> And one said: [the word (דגה) refers to] illicit relations [that they could have in Egypt but not after they left].[33]
>
> [Explanation]: The one who said [that (דגה) refers to actual fish derives it from] that which is written [in Numbers 11:5], "We used to eat."
> And the one who said [that (דגה)] refers to illicit relations [derives it from] that which is written [in the same verse], "[for] free."

132   *Bringing Down the Temple House*

[Challenge]: And according to the one who said "illicit relations," isn't it written, "we [actually] ate (אשר נאכל)?" [Therefore, how can the verse be referring to illicit relations?]

[Refutation]: The language [used in the verse is] a more appropriate expression [for sexual relations], as it is written: [Such is the way of an adulteress]—she eats (אכלה), wipes her mouth and says, "I have done no wrong" (Proverbs 30:20).

[Challenge]: And according to the one who said that [the word (דגה) refers to actual] fish, what does "free" [mean]?

[Refutation]: [The Israelites in Egypt did not have to purchase fish], since they would bring them from [the rivers which were] ownerless property. As it has been said previously [in BT Sotah 11b]—when the Israelites [in Egypt] would draw water, the Holy One Blessed is He would prepare small fish for them in the water to be drawn [from the rivers] in their jugs.

[Challenge]: It is well according to the one who said that [the word (דגה) refers to actual] fish, but [about] illicit relations [in Egypt, they had no reason to complain because] the Israelites did not promiscuously engage in them. [And therefore] this is what is written [to praise the Israelites]: A garden locked, is my sister, my bride; [a fountain locked, a sealed-up spring] (Song of Songs 4:12). But, according to the one who said [the Israelites conducted] illicit relations [in Egypt], what [does the phrase] "garden locked" [mean]? [It suggests chaste behavior].

[Refutation]: [It means that in Egypt they were] not promiscuous [with] relatives who were [already] forbidden [to them by the Noahide laws, but did have relations with relatives that were forbidden later to them when they received the Torah].[34]

[Challenge]: It is well according to the one who said [that the word (דגה) refers to] illicit relations. [And therefore] this is what is written [in support]: Moses heard the people weeping for their families (Numbers 11:10). [This means they wept] with regard to their families, because, now [after the Exodus], it became prohibited for them to cohabit with them. But according to the one who says that [the word (דגה) refers to] fish, what does "weeping for their families" mean?

Sustaining the Rabbinic Household   133

[Refutation]: [The Bavli concludes that]: Both this and that happened. [They wept over both the unavailability of fish and the increased prohibitions regarding sexual conduct]. (BT Yoma 75a)

This predominantly stammaitic Babylonian sugya builds on the earlier amoraic passage about manna focusing not on what God provided to the Israelites in the desert but on what they had while in Egypt and have no longer. In fact, Numbers 11 exposes the discontent of the Israelites with respect to manna in verse 10 as they realize and suffer what they left behind. This fuels the exegetical construction of the sugya so as to differentiate between the pre-Exodus and post-Exodus experiences. The stammaitic dialectic places food/fish and sexual relations in virtual competition with one another in an attempt to understand the nature of the Israelites' longing for their prior homes, a longing that threatened the success of their journey through the desert. In so doing, the Bavli continues to accentuate two of the most concerning aspects of self-denial: food and sex.

Relying on the word *dagah* in Numbers 11:5 prompts an exegetical discussion by the stammaim focused on the meaning of this word. While the word can simply be a reference to fish within this context, the verse also refers to the cucumbers, melons, leeks, onions, and garlic that were readily available to the Israelites in Egypt, expanding the implication of the loss of many foods. As well, it was said, "The dagah that we used to eat (נאכל)" can also refer euphemistically to sexual relations. Proverbs 30:20 then serves as the proof text to associate "eating (אכלה)" with cohabitation of an illicit nature. This is all to couch an Israelite woman in Egypt as similar to an adulteress who "eats," "wipes her mouth," as if she has eaten without any sense of manners, and then thinks she does no wrong, that is, she has sex, wipes her sexual organs, and forgives herself.[35] In contrast, the aggadic passage also conveys by relying on Song of Songs 4:12 that an Israelite woman in Egypt was like a "locked garden," that is, she was chaste. Song of Songs 4:12 then challenges the very idea that the Israelites had ever acted illicitly by shedding a different light on the meaning of the word *dagah*. Hence, as the aggadic passage in Bavli Yoma shows, dagah can refer to actual fish or illicit sexual behavior, depending on the verse to which it is compared: Proverbs 30:20 or Song of Songs 4:13.

When Bavli Yoma 75a turns to Numbers 11:10, stating that "Moses heard the people weeping for their families," it takes the verse out of

Bringing Down the Temple House

context to make another significant point. In Numbers, the weeping is directly related to the manna that fell, and Moses is distressed over why this is so. In the aggadic passage, however, the people weep in the desert because of their inability to have sexual relations with members of their families, projecting a different reading onto Numbers 11:10.[36] While it is unclear for which family members the Israelites longed, Rashi presumes that in Egypt, the Israelites were subject to the Noahide laws. These laws were more permissive than the later Toraitic law in terms of incest.[37] Therefore, the Israelites were crying out to have sexual relations with family members who became prohibited to them after they had left Egypt and received the Torah.

This sugya concludes by reading the events of Numbers 11 both ways: "Both this and that happened." The people not only cried out for the sexual relationships that they could no longer have, but also for the food that was not available to them in the desert. Yearning for fish serves to explain the reasons that the people view manna as a hardship. It did not resemble the food that was easily available to them in their past lives or the sexual relationships that were once permissable. However, the conclusion to this exegetical difficulty over the meaning of the word *dagah* begs the question as to why the Babylonian stammaim raise and offer hermeneutical support for the possibility that the Israelites engaged in incestuous sexual relationships in Egypt, which by their time were considered prohibited.

The permissibility of incestual relationships as the rabbis build their Egyptian past means that sisters and brothers and other close relatives could protect their bloodline in a culture where, according to Exodus 1:12, the more the Israelites were oppressed, the more they increased.[38] Perhaps in the Babylonian world, where Zoroastrians, for example, valued incest,[39] the rabbis were giving some thought to incestuous relationships. Possibly they were thinking about how to increase in number in a world where they were in the minority. However, to recall the passage where the yetzer (the sexual inclination) is personified on BT Yoma 69b is to remember that with regard to sexuality, there is a line that cannot be crossed. While there must be an allowance for sexual relations if the world is to continue, incestuous relationships were not part of the equation. In tandem with this perspective, the trope of incest recedes from prominence after the Israelites leave Egypt, as the aggadic passage on BT Yoma 74a indicates. But before doing so, it uses the idea of sexuality to signify a successful shift from one culture

Sustaining the Rabbinic Household

135

to another. Just as the Israelites before leaving Egypt were entirely distinct from the Israelite people who wandered through the desert in the way they had sexual relations, the insular caste of the priests connected via a priestly bloodline, who must remain ascetic while serving in the Temple, are also distinct from the rabbinic Jews in Babylonia. As manna becomes food in the desert and the definition of allowable sexual partners changes, the rabbis suggest that a shift from one cultural way of being to another is, indeed, possible.

Tying this back to the larger context of inui nefesh, it is significant that the rabbis rely on the Israelites' experience in the desert to pinpoint, perhaps to transpose for their purposes, what it means to practice self-denial on Yom Kippur. In this context, it appears from BT Yoma 75a that the rabbis' understanding of bodily self-denial is not one of complete lack. Rather, reading inui nefesh through the lens of the Israelites' view of hardship is to see it as the denial of satiety. It is about taking control of one's body, rejecting want and replacing it with absolute need.[40] Just as manna constructs that complicated moment when one can be minimally sustained but not entirely satisfied, denying rights to incest captures a point of liminality as an in-between stage as well. It strikes that balance between having and not having. It is not about complete sexual self-abnegation or about having sex with a family member just to ensure the continuity of one's bloodline.[41] In this way, the final redacted discussion that is connected to manna not only evokes the sense of absence connected to the ritual fulfillment of inui nefesh but also carries a deep concern for how to ensure continuity, dependent as it is not only on food but on producing offspring in the face of limitations like incest.[42]

IMAGINATIVE BODIES IN IMAGINATIVE HOUSES IN THE DESERT

Tractate Yoma begins with sugyot that focus on the Temple bayit, followed by chapters that regale readers with events taking place within the Temple as if it is still standing. These events evoke a sense of pageantry and in "their time" required enormous material prosperity to execute. Animals that have no blemishes, luxurious garments, the availability of water for multiple immersions and for cleansing the altar, incense, coal, as well as an infrastructure for individuals to travel to Jerusalem, whether to serve in the Temple or witness its events, all

Bringing Down the Temple House

image the Temple as a place of excess, requiring many resources for its successful upkeep.[43] In marked contrast, by recalling the manna in the desert, the last chapter of Bavli Yoma underscores the precarious and fleeting nature of the Israelites' sojourn in the desert, signaling images of deprivation and want. The disjuncture is palpable.

Nonetheless, something productive occurs in the desert as the redactors of the final chapter of Bavli Yoma imagine the experience. In the absence of resources that a desert experience conjures, houses (batim), rather than temporary huts (sukkot), become places where God makes legal judgments. Manna becomes the conduit through which God sends messages to the people. In a place of homelessness and profound insecurity, desert households are nourished, even fortified, by the signs that God sends via the very location of where manna falls. Manna fell at the entrance of the houses of the righteous. For average people, manna fell outside the camp. The wicked, however, had to roam even farther to collect their portions, connecting sinfulness with greater burden, if not penance.[44] The site of fallen manna identified the rightful masters of the slaves who belonged to them if under dispute and resolved accusations of adultery, whether it be regarding husband or wife.

Whereas manna evoked feelings of uncertainty among the Israelites according to the biblical narrative, in Bavli Yoma, Rabbi Yose conversely argues that manna had the power to clarify "what was in the holes and what was in the cracks" of someone's soul. Using this structural house-like imagery, he argues that manna could distinguish between truth and falsehood. For example, according to a baraita on BT Yoma 75a, one master accuses another of stealing his slave, prompting his fellow Israelite to argue back, "You sold him to me!" Moses relies on manna for determining the rightful household of the slave. "Morning will come," Moses informs them, "and manna will appear in the house of the rightful master." That the Israelites had recently been slaves themselves and now had the ability to construct households and own slaves in the desert is a highly anachronistic literary move. Surely it reflects more about the rabbis' present time than an Israelite past. But the point is clear: while household stability requires God, a household's daily functionality depends as well on workable master-slave, neighbor-neighbor, and judge-defendant relationships that interact effectively with one another.

Similarly, a judgment in the case of a husband and wife who come

Sustaining the Rabbinic Household

before Moses together to accuse one another of adultery is also determined by the appearance of manna. A measure of manna would appear in the house of the husband if his wife committed adultery but would appear in her father's house if he was the adulterer. Both spouses are potential culprits, and in a surprising twist, wives can accuse husbands of adultery just as husbands can accuse their wives, challenging the sole power typically granted men to cast suspicions on their wives' fidelity, as in the case of the sotah.[45] When Moses uses the Hebrew word הידוע, meaning, "it is certain," to refer to the level of certitude manna can convey by virtue of where it lands, manna becomes a resource capable of ensuring not only household "truth," and therefore functionality, but also familial stability in the face of potential adultery. Moses can, with the help of the delivery of God's manna, litigate cases that threaten the very stability of households, potentially supporting those who are marginalized in other chapters of Yoma, specifically women.[46] Indeed, manna, quite unlike the sacrifices offered by the priests in the Temple, is powerful enough to signify with certainty who is right and who is wrong, who has sinned and who has not. And yet manna in and of itself is collected, consumed, and gone as quickly as it comes. There is never a surplus.[47] There is only ever just enough.

SEXUAL RELATIONS AND INUI NEFESH

For the Bavli, the prohibition against sexual relations on Yom Kippur —despite being only one day—signifies what threatens the continuity of the rabbinic household. In the first chapter of Bavli Yoma, the rabbis use the insecurity and precarious nature of the high priest's marriage to "one wife" (see chapter one) to highlight the dysfunctionality and instability of the Temple house. Here, too, relative to Yom Kippur, there is concern that the absence of sexual relations challenges the very idea of the productive household. Paralleling their discussion of manna, the redactors of chapter eight of Bavli Yoma use the Mishnaic dictum in M. Yoma 8:1 to think in terms of what it means to allow just enough sex to secure the rabbinic household.

Interestingly, the rabbis draw no connection between the Temple requirements of the high priest and the Mishnah's prohibition. Refraining from sexual relations on Yom Kippur, which was required of everyone—men and women—is not connected to the practice of sequestering the high priest or to the prohibitions related to protect-

138   *Bringing Down the Temple House*

ing his sexual purity on Yom Kippur. As the rabbis struggle to define what the biblical concept of inui nefesh means in Leviticus 16:29, 31; 23:29, 32 and Numbers 29:7, they also convey that what disqualified the high priest, that is, various types of sexual impurity, did not disrupt the attainment of atonement in the rabbinic practice observed outside the Temple (see chapter nine). Nor was sexuality on Yom Kippur completely forbidden either.

In discussing the prohibition of sexual relations in Mishnah 8:1, the stammaitic redactors of the Bavli grapple with the many instances in which the biblical word *inui* (ענוי) appears in the Bible. BT Yoma 74b points to Deuteronomy 26:7—"And God saw our affliction in Egypt (וירא את־ענינו)." The stammaim interpret this as a reference to the suffering of the Israelites in Egypt who were not allowed to have conjugal relations. Alternatively, the Hebrew root "ענה," as the Bavli suggests, can also mean nonconsensual sex, as in the case of Shekhem's rape of Dinah (Genesis 34:2),[48] or illicit sex, as in the case of Laban's entreaty that Jacob not mistreat his daughters (Genesis 31:50). The fact that even in nonsexual biblical contexts, this verb form has negative connotations, such as to treat someone harshly or exploitatively or abusively, prompts the rabbis to think about whether the experience of inui requires something closer to suffering or mere self-denial.[49]

Picking up on the ambiguity of the word ע.נ.ה, Bavli Yoma 77b attempts to use Genesis 34:2, regarding Shekhem and Dinah, to flesh out the implication of Laban's words to Jacob, not to mistreat his daughters. If Shekhem raped Dinah, then the same word used in the case of Laban must mean that Laban was worried Jacob would treat his daughters in a similar sexually inappropriate way. In reading this back into M. Yoma 8:1, several questions arise: Are the rabbis suggesting that the tannaim were forbidding nonconsensual or forbidden sexual relations on Yom Kippur, but not licit sex?[50] What were the stammaitic redactors trying to communicate about inui? If, according to the Bavli, when Shekhem "afflicted Dinah (ויענה)," he had "different relations (שעינה מביאות אחרות)" with her, how does this understanding explain what M. Yoma 8:1 means by its prohibition of sexual relations?[51] The Bavli's point is that Shekhem did not have sexual intercourse with Dinah in a natural way, specifically in a manner that brings forth children. Rather, he had "different relations" with her: either rape, anal intercourse, or nonprocreative relations.[52] Reading this back into Mishnah 8:1, the prohibition is against having nonprocreative sex or anal sex or,

Sustaining the Rabbinic Household   139

possibly, rape on Yom Kippur, which means that "natural sex," defined as sex for producing progeny, is allowable.[53]

Returning to BT Yoma 74b, it now makes sense that the Bavli's anonymous redactors reject using Deuteronomy 26:7 "and God saw our affliction," to understand inui nefesh. Pharaoh, who feared the Israelites were becoming too numerous, instructed midwives to destroy all male babies (Exodus 1:9–17). Therefore, when the rabbis interpret Deuteronomy 26:7, observing that the Israelites were calling out to God regarding their plight, that plight was the requirement to abstain from sexual relations so as to subvert Pharaoh's decree. Reading this interpretation into M. Yoma 8:1 would then mean that the term *inui nefesh* reflects a prohibition to not have sex at all on Yom Kippur.

The Babylonian stammaim reject this interpretation and argue, "We do not derive an affliction commanded by God from an affliction caused by a human being [Pharaoh]," meaning that God's commandment of inui nefesh on Yom Kippur cannot be derived from Pharaoh's decree and the Israelites' response to it, which was to abstain from sexual intercourse. Another understanding of inui is therefore needed.[54] Thus, the Bavli grasps a small interpretive window regarding Shekhem and Dinah to permit procreative sexual relations on Yom Kippur and therefore to support the notion that at a minimum, sex to produce progeny is allowable because it sustains the rabbinic household. With the destruction of the Temple looming in the background, the observance of Yom Kippur, despite its ascetic character, then comes to symbolize the potential longevity of the household as realized in the necessity for procreative sexual relations, even on Yom Kippur. This stands in contrast to the Temple as the rabbis imagine it, where priests were required to abstain from sexual relations.

THE ABSENCE OF THE SUFFERING BODY

Significantly, in the rabbis' discussions of inui nefesh, there is also no link between fasting, sexuality, and the concept in antiquity of the suffering body.[55] Fasting, in particular, has long held a central religious role that surfaces not only in the Bible but in rabbinic sources.[56] Undeniably, there are many stories about rabbis who intentionally fast out of concern that they transgressed, believing that fasting is a form of suffering capable of bringing about repentance and atonement.[57] Julia Watts Belser in her discussion about drought fasts in tractate Ta'anit

140   *Bringing Down the Temple House*

argues that the fasting body is self-empowering, engaged in becoming a speaking body aimed to reestablish right relations with God.[58] However, the idea that bodily affliction can be a means of atonement replacing sacrifices, and that the sinner is absolved as a result of suffering through fasting or sexual abstinence, is not mentioned in the final chapter of Bavli Yoma.[59] There is nothing explicit here that directly connects suffering to repentance and atonement—not fasting, or any of the other prohibitions associated with Yom Kippur.[60] Curiously, sugyot that do examine the idea of repentance and appear later in the final chapter of Bavli Yoma fail to link back to inui nefesh.[61]

The scholarship of Moshe Beer and Elisheva Baumgarten supports this tension in rabbinic sources, arguing that fasting was not solidly linked to repentance until the early medieval period.[62] Beer argues that while some individuals practiced extreme fasting, the rabbis often ridicule or dismiss such behavior.[63] BT Ta'anit 11a–11b reflects that Babylonian amoraim were not all in agreement about the benefits of fasting. In fact, Rabbi Yirmiyah bar Abba argues that Torah scholars should not engage in individual fasts because they will become too weak to study Torah.[64]

From the very beginning of chapter eight of Yoma, the rabbis push back on the strictures of inui, locating leniencies wherever possible. In fact, the eighth chapter opens with a desire to ease the punishment for transgressing the Mishnah's prohibitions by distinguishing, or selecting out some prohibitions from others, making some punishable by *karet* (the punishment of spiritual removal from the community of Israel) and others not (BT Yoma 73b; 74a).[65] In the end, only eating and drinking (not the remaining prohibitions listed in M. Yoma 8:1) render one liable for karet but only if one eats a "full measure" of food. A half-measure, while still forbidden, does not invite the same level of punishment (BT Yoma 73b). Eventually the rabbis make allowances for the greatest volume of food possible while still considering what it means to fast. As trivial an amount as this might be, the discussion reveals the rabbis' concern for what it takes for the body, at a minimum, to remain nourished enough not to become ill.[66] Fasting never becomes a requirement demanding the absolute absence of food and drink in Bavli Yoma.[67]

One is also warned against forcibly afflicting their bodies, such as by moving from the shade into the sun to generate suffering from the heat (BT Yoma 74b). Additionally, under certain circumstances, washing

Sustaining the Rabbinic Household   141

and wearing shoes become allowable.[68] A discussion about using rags to bring comfort to someone wearing a prosthetic foot results in a rhetorical comment attributed to Rava: "Is any pleasure that is not footwear prohibited on Yom Kippur?!" The implication based on the larger sugya is that some pleasures, including wearing certain types of shoes, are indeed permitted as a way to protect the body (BT Yoma 78b). Overall, inui nefesh is not presented as an experience of utter suffering that requires bodily self-transformation but one of generating and maintaining a disposition of minimal comfort.

Admittedly, BT Yoma 86a mentions that suffering cleanses the body of sin (יסורין ממרקים), inviting God's forgiveness, but nowhere in the Bavli's discussion of inui is it clear that the prohibitions associated with Yom Kippur are intended to generate the type of suffering that brings about forgiveness. Personal or communal suffering is seen as either a punishment for iniquity or a sign of God's parental love, and is not something one brings on one's own body.[69] Here in BT Yoma 86a, however, Psalms 89:33 is invoked to "prove" that suffering is brought upon the people by God when they forsake God's teaching and do not observe the commandments. God "will punish their transgression with the rod, their iniquity with plagues." God's children are not, however, required to impose bodily suffering upon themselves. Rather, as the baraita included on BT Yoma 74b indicates, the commandment of inui is one that falls into the legal category of "sit and not do" (שב ואל תעשה), which means that individuals should not go out of their way to impose undue suffering upon themselves.

CONCLUSION

Chapter eight, the chapter of the non-Temple Yom Kippur, speaks back to all of the preceding chapters, which constructed a Yom Kippur observance steeped in opulence, embellished rites, and beautiful vestments. In contrast to the Temple rite of Yom Kippur, which is utterly dependent on an abundance of material goods—everything from animals without blemishes, elaborate clothing made of gold, a host of implements, and a great supply of water—the observance of the non-Temple Yom Kippur is about what is minimally necessary to maintain people and their households without suffering. In this way, the non-Temple Yom Kippur that is presented here is not, to use Jonathan Klawans's words, "templisized" or "sacrificialized."[70] In fact, the

142   *Bringing Down the Temple House*

image is just the opposite. Yom Kippur is presented in Bavli Yoma as entirely distinct from its Temple precursor. When the concern is the Temple house in comparison to the houses the rabbis domestically inhabit, all of the pageantry associated with the Temple is replaced by a ritual that acknowledges what is fundamentally needed to maintain the everyday household: food and sexual relations.[71] Moreover, the dysfunctionality of families with socially elite or financial connections to the Temple that appeared in the tractate's earlier chapters to critique priestly kinship, is here replaced, interestingly, not by Torah study, not by male-male/teacher-disciple transmission, but by discussions about what is absolutely necessary to ensure a future everyday household in perpetuity.

Against the backdrop of a Yom Kippur rite that is required of both men and women and within a discourse on sustaining daily households, the rabbis continue to engender authority and agency by relying on gendered and ableist stereotypes.[72] Disturbingly, women "still" entice men, who "still" yield to sexual desire. And men remain active in their illicit natures; they act on passive, unwilling women, such as in the case of Shekhem's rape of Dinah. To reveal what is for the Bavli at the center of Yom Kippur observance, that is, an ability to distance oneself from the sheer desire for food and sex, the rabbis rely on the male attraction to women's bodies and the bodily sense of sight. This they do to distinguish inui nefesh from an experience of complete self-abnegation, unfortunately building legal discussions around unsettling notions of the female body and the male gaze. This they do to communicate a sense of power and control. But such images of rabbinic judgment in Bavli Yoma are entangled within Babylonian stammaitic passages where the rabbis also expose their fears and frailties in ways that disempower themselves, as will become clear in the next chapter. The passages that refocus the discussion of Yom Kippur from the Temple house to the rabbinic household point to what it is the rabbis most desired and also feared: that they would not produce biological kin. Ironically, the rabbis' greatest critique of the priesthood—its rootedness in a patriline dependent on biological kinship—becomes what the rabbis yearn for most. The remainder of this book focuses on the rabbis' concerns about their own frailties and their hope that progeny might reverse such fears.

Sustaining the Rabbinic Household

CHAPTER 8

VULNERABLE
BODIES IN
VULNERABLE
HOUSES

· · ·

The semantic and cultural equation found in the first mishnah of tractate Yoma, where a man's wife is referred to as "his house [beito]," underscores the rabbinic idea that without a "wife," the very foundation of a husband's household is destabilized.[1] As this tractate unfolded, the rabbis used the image of the household and all that is associated with it—marriage, progeny, kinship, domesticity, and sexuality (including sexual purity laws)—to unsettle the Temple house and its priesthood. There are many examples where redactors reworked earlier sources or aligned tannaitic and amoraic material in ways that rendered the Temple as a nonworking, dysfunctional household, unable to sustain relationships typically associated with functioning households.

Such a narrative arc represents a potential destructuring of Temple culture, lending itself to the possibility that in the final chapter of the tractate, a replacement household will emerge.[2] The Babylonian rabbis, who by the time of the redaction of the Bavli were living Jewish lives without a Temple, might have opted to weave a thread of continuity, offering up hope that out of destruction, they could symbolically rebuild the Temple in their houses. Jonathan Klawans, for example, argues that the rabbis' nostalgia for the Temple manifested itself in their "templization" of various rites, including the purity laws.[3] Synagogues were "templisized," and the rites connected to food and prayer were "sacrificialized." However, the Temple house—its sacrifices, its upkeep, and its pageantry—does not find a symbolic place in the treatment of the household in the final chapter of Bavli Yoma. No attempt is made to resurrect Temple rites or priestly ritual procedures in the observance of the non-Temple Yom Kippur; there is no "templization"

144

of the rabbinic household. In addition, the rabbis do not bring up the priests in order to zealously undermine them, arguing to become their replacements. In fact, the most hierarchical Temple rite of the calendar year, Yom Kippur, that centered on the well-orchestrated performance of the high priest, in its non-Temple iteration is required of all —both men and women.

Despite the rabbis' desire to assert authority over the priests, marginalizing them along with women and their past success in doing so, the rabbis drop the reins in chapter eight. They disempower themselves in an admission that they have little control over the stability of the daily household. When the rabbis fail to map the framework of the everyday household onto the Temple house, they call attention to the cracks they "want" to see in the Temple facade. And when the rabbis decide not to map the Temple onto their own rabbinic households in the final chapter of Bavli Yoma, the very absence of that transposed template exposes the cracks they see in their own houses and in themselves as householders. They confront their weaknesses and their anxieties, not regarding the observance of Yom Kippur per se but with regard to what the prohibitions associated with Yom Kippur bring to the fore. Ironically, a rite that requires men and women to take control of their bodies unravels into a discussion for the rabbis about their lack of control and power. That Yom Kippur is about the absence of domesticity, and that quite early on in the history of Yom Kippur it comes to include both men and women equally in its observance,[4] make it a ripe analytical space for the rabbis to contemplate the realities of their own households. The household becomes framed as a codependent environment, paralleling the very nature of the Yom Kippur rite of self-denial, which is all about lack.[5] Scarcity of any sort when tied to the household always affects everyone—men and women, parents and children, masters and their disciples. In this way, the final chapter in Bavli Yoma shifts its focus away from male priests (who alone perform the Temple's domestic tasks of sacrificial food preparation and cleaning the altar). There is also a move away from the lavish materiality of the Temple rite built on an endless supply of needed resources to make it run. Instead, emphasis is placed on the stability and potential instability of the everyday house and the people who inhabit it.

In addition, for all of the rabbis' concerns over issues of knowledge transmission beyond those to whom they are blood related, as expressed in the first seven chapters, chapter eight accentuates their

Vulnerable Bodies in Vulnerable Houses   145

great anxiety over future rabbinic progeny. In this final chapter of the Bavli, the rabbis present themselves not as "confined to or defined by" the House of Study or by male-male knowledge transmission.[6] They concede that sons can go astray despite learning Torah from their fathers. They acknowledge that child rearing is also not entirely under their control, mothers and/or women being essential.[7] The rabbis also admit to being part of households as codependent men who rely on the agency of women to produce remedies for healing sickness. Women can make their own determinations of when to break fasts; that is, women have control of their own bodies in this case.[8] Women—including brides, new mothers, and, especially, pregnant women—expose the rabbis' vulnerabilities, that is, their dependencies as men who worry whether the Yom Kippur prohibitions that deny the body sustenance put their houses, and the people who live within them, in jeopardy. Moreover, entirely connected to these concerns is the rabbis' worry over whether they can serve as fair judges. They fear that poor decision making will also threaten the security and function of their own households. Reverberating here is the question: Are rabbinic houses as fragile as the Temple?

A NON-GENDERED VIEW OF THE COMMANDMENT OF INUI NEFESH

Chapter eight of the Bavli begins with a concern over how to understand the injunction of the Mishnah: "[On] Yom Kippur, it is prohibited to eat, drink, wash, anoint, wear shoes or cohabit" (M. Yoma 1:1). The Hebrew word used for "prohibited," *asur*, sets off a stammaitic discussion about whether a prohibited act carries with it the burden of the punishment of karet.[9] As biblically mandated in Leviticus 23:29 regarding inui on Yom Kippur, *karet*, the spiritual removal from the community, is the gravest punishment for transgressing a scriptural commandment decreed by God. After interweaving a baraita that speaks to this issue, the stammaim express that "there is no punishment of karet except for transgressions of eating or drinking or for performing prohibited labors on Yom Kippur" (BT Yoma 73b–74a), limiting the application of the punishment of karet to those who transgress certain prohibitions but not others. On the surface, this discussion that limits the punishment of karet seems odd, given the undifferentiated list presented by M. Yoma 8:1, not to mention the absence of any mention

146   *Bringing Down the Temple House*

of karet in the parallel tannaitic material in Tosefta Yoma. And yet the biblical verses never define what it is they mean by the commandment of inui nefesh, leaving the rabbis, beginning with the tannaim, an opening to differentiate select prohibitions from others.[10] But toward what end?

To view this textual move regarding the punishment of karet from a feminist perspective is to read against the grain, that is, to expose incoherence within texts that reveal forebodings about the cultural tensions from which these texts particularly emerge. When the rabbis create problems where none exist, that is, when they begin to "differentiate some prohibitions from others" based on protecting some transgressions from the punishment of karet and others not, one can detect something additional percolating beneath the surface, which in this case is related to gender.[11] Despite a desire for male control, the rabbis recognize that sustainable rabbinic households require more than their male selves. As such, to think about a God who follows through with the punishment of karet—which can mean anything from childlessness to a shorter life span, even receiving the death penalty—calls attention to what it is they fear. Indeed, the members (male or female) of the very households they wish to sustain confront these threats, from the failure to have children to death from an illness.[12] Recognizably, karet has a place of critical importance in relation to the integrity of the household and its inhabitants. For the rabbis, the question about how to construct secure household communities was entrenched not only in the behavior of all who made up those households but also in how God interacted with all of its members. To limit the punishment of karet, for example, linking it only to the transgressions of eating and drinking but not to the other prohibitions, reveals a desire to make allowances for potential transgressions so that the solvency of households would not be so endangered. Additional discussion on BT Yoma 78b–80a indicates that small measures of food do not violate the commandment to fast and, therefore, by implication, do not warrant karet. BT Yoma 81b examines various foodstuffs such as pepper berries, ginger, and vinegar that when eaten do not generate any liability. This contributes to the idea that the rabbis might have wished to safeguard households from the karet punishments that they believed could undo them. Thus, the rabbis not only draw fuzzier lines around the definition of what constitutes "eating" and "drinking" but restrict the category of inui as well.

Vulnerable Bodies in Vulnerable Houses

But even more concerning for the Babylonian redactors is the issue of classifying the commandment of self-denial (regarding Yom Kippur) as a clear negative commandment rather than as a positive one. This is a categorization issue that not only revives the issue of karet (BT Yoma 81a) but also raises the issue of who is required to perform bodily self-denial on Yom Kippur—men or women, or both.[13] Quite unlike the discussion about Yom Kippur in other tractates—such as in Bavli Kiddushin and Bavli Sukkah, where this distinction between positive and negative commandments specifically with respect to women is clarified—here, in chapter eight, the focus of the discussion is different. Significantly, the commandment of self-denial in Leviticus 16:29 and 23:27 and Numbers 29:7 has a positive force: "On the tenth day of the seventh month, you shall practice self-denial," rather than a restrictive tone of "do not,"[14] as BT Yoma 81a exposes. Why didn't the biblical verses say more directly, "One shall not eat on Yom Kippur?" —rendering self-denial as a negative commandment for which all men and women are required to obey, according to M. Kiddushin 1:7? The approach of the anonymous redactors on BT Yoma 81a is to explore the ramifications of rendering self-denial as a positive versus a negative commandment.[15] For example, the positive commandment of self-denial, when rendered as a negative commandment, "Do not afflict yourself," would prohibit fasting—the very opposite of self-denial.[16] A positive commandment would also mean that women are exempt. A negative commandment would include women but is punishable with karet. So where does inui nefesh belong—that is, in what category of commandments?

More specifically, Leviticus 23:29 sits at the center of the problem of categorization when it states: "Any person who does not practice self-denial throughout the day shall be cut off (נכרתה) from his kin." If one transgresses this commandment intentionally and it is considered a negative commandment, one receives the punishment of karet, that is, the punishment delineated in Leviticus 23:29 for transgressing self-denial on Yom Kippur. If this is considered a positive commandment and one transgresses it, the punishment is not karet and not as severe. This means that if, biblically, inui is rendered as a positive commandment, the explicit reference in Leviticus 23:29 to the punishment of karet would not make sense. Caught in an exegetical quandary that challenges the coherence of the commandment and its punishment of karet, in that for transgressing what looks like a positive command-

148   *Bringing Down the Temple House*

ment one receives karet (which cannot be), the Bavli works to ensure that self-denial is understood as a negative commandment.

One more exegetical move is then needed. In noting that the commandment to do no work on Yom Kippur, found in each of the verses that mention self-denial (Leviticus 16:29, 23:29–30 and Numbers 29:7), the rabbis attempt to link this commandment to the punishment of karet. Just as one receives the punishment of karet for transgressing the prohibition to do no work on Yom Kippur, so too one receives karet for transgressing the prohibitions associated with self-denial, which in this case are limited to eating and drinking.[17] In a typical rabbinic fashion, the rabbis analogize one category of law to another so that inui nefesh can be considered a negative commandment like abstaining from work on the Sabbath.[18] Visibly, in this lengthy sugya, no mention is made of women; their inclusion is taken as a matter of fact, required as they are to observe all negative commandments (M. Kiddushin 1:7). In contrast to the priests, who during their periods of service in the Temple, to include Yom Kippur, constituted a distinct gender-based, all-male group entirely separate from their wives,[19] in chapter eight of the tractate, women are in fact required to observe the prohibitions associated with Yom Kippur.

That said, the absence of any mention of women in this discussion on self-denial stands out still further.[20] In contrast to the discussions in Bavli Sukkah and Bavli Kiddushin regarding Yom Kippur, where the issue of women and the commandment of Yom Kippur is central to their discussion of positive time-bound commandments, Bavli Yoma is silent. In fact, Bavli Sukkah and Bavli Kiddushin use exegetical ingenuity to turn the commandment of sukkah into an exemption for women, but also grant Yom Kippur the force of a requirement. Sukkah emerges as a positive time-bound commandment for which women are exempt; Yom Kippur is deemed a negative commandment requiring women to observe it (BT Sukkah 28ab). In Bavli Yoma, there is no such argument. Instead, exemptions from the observance of Yom Kippur are not necessarily or clearly gendered toward more vulnerable females with domestic responsibilities in the household. The rabbinic concern is to protect the health and well-being of all people who make up the household, whether they are pregnant women or any individual who takes ill, regardless of gender.

The accomplishment is impressive: the most hierarchical rite, on the holiest of days, which requires one male high priest to conduct the

Vulnerable Bodies in Vulnerable Houses

Yom Kippur service for everyone, turns into a discussion that assumes gender parity. This one "triumph" differentiates the final chapter of Bavli Yoma from all of the first seven when viewing the tractate through a feminist lens.[21] The analysis of whether self-denial is a positive or a negative commandment is not associated with an attempt to differentiate men from women or Yom Kippur from other holiday observances as was the case in Bavli Sukkah and Kiddushin.[22] Instead, women become legal subjects like men, with the agency to protect themselves and their children from undue suffering.

Finally, to return to BT Yoma 81ab, the Babylonian redactors took a greater interest in discussing the punishment of karet for intentional sins than they did in examining the behaviors that rendered a *ḥatat* (sin offering) necessary. In so doing, they chose to push the focus of M. Yoma 8:3, which speaks only about the ḥatat and not karet, in a different direction.[23] One can sense that in commenting on this mishnah, a redactional decision has been made to steer the discussion away from the ḥatat offering mentioned in the mishnah and, instead, to raise the issue of karet. Such a redactional move may very well be connected to the fact that the ḥatat offering can only reverse an inadvertent violation of inui nefesh. An intentional breach, which indeed makes one deserving of karet, cannot be undone with this sacrifice. In addition, the punishment of karet is in God's hands alone. Tied to a requirement that is incumbent on both men and women and distinguishes the non-Temple Yom Kippur from the Temple rite, here too, Bavli Yoma conveys via its redactional decisions a desire to put distance between the Temple house and the rabbinic household. The Talmudic discourse, focused as it is on karet, pushes the act of sacrificial atonement via the ḥatat aside. Recognizably, its discussion steers toward an issue that, as the rabbis believe, remains in force without a Temple or a high priest and is entirely up to God.[24]

A COMMANDMENT WITH LENIENCIES

The Babylonian sugyot in the last chapter of Yoma try to uphold the Mishnah's prohibitions of inui nefesh—but only to a point. Recognizing that self-denial encompasses the daily acts performed on the male and female body, the rabbis underscore the need for some leniencies in cases to ease any threat to family relationships as well as personal and communal security. A tractate that began with a priest's depen-

150   *Bringing Down the Temple House*

dency on the intactness of his household in order to perform the Yom Kippur rite, that is, his marriage to one wife, leads in Bavli Yoma, in chapter eight, to the ordinary household and the ways that inui nefesh might endanger those within it. The literary constructions of familial relationships in the earlier chapters of Bavli Yoma underscore a Temple that cannot "house" functional families, or priests' children who cannot serve as honorable, effective priests. Here, however, households are recognized as vulnerable due to forces that are less controllable, necessitating exemptions. The final chapter in Yoma raises concerns and issues that run the gamut from the prohibition against bodily adornment on Yom Kippur to larger compounding fears such as suffering from a lack of food, illness, and political and natural calamities (M. Yoma 8:1; BT Yoma 78b).

Building on M. Yoma 8:1, the Bavli, by integrating additional tannaitic material and connecting it to the mishnah, underscores that kings and brides can wash their faces despite a prohibition against washing. The Bavli interestingly wishes for kings to appear in all their splendor and for brides not to repulse their husbands (BT Yoma 78b). An allowance is also made for brides to adorn themselves and new mothers to wear shoes to protect them from cold floors. Strikingly, the minority view in the mishnah, seemingly attributed to Rabbi Eliezer, is also attributed to Rabbi Ḥanina ben Teradyon. A tannaitic source on Bavli 78b recalls this rabbi martyr who is known elsewhere as willing to study Torah in an ultimate act of self-sacrifice (BT Avodah Zara 18ab).[25] Ḥanina ben Teradyon experiences extreme bodily injury at a time of Roman persecution for refusing to abandon Torah study. Strikingly, it is this rabbi (of all rabbis) who supports making allowances to relax the prohibitions associated with the body and Yom Kippur. Such allowances reflect a concern for maintaining the significant relationships of king/subject, bride/groom, and mother/child—relationships tied to protecting communal safety, building household equanimity, and supporting the well-being of new mothers needed to care for their children. Rabbi Ḥanina ben Teradyon, who dies with his wife and whose daughter is sent to a brothel by Roman decree, cannot safeguard his family through studying Torah. He therefore becomes the symbol of fragility and the need to think about how to protect familial life.

So important is the functionality of the household that the words, "My mother told me" emerge from the Babylonian amora Abaye, to undergird the infallibility of mothers. Indeed, the rabbis express the need

Vulnerable Bodies in Vulnerable Houses

to rely on their mothers for sage advice regarding the nurturing of children. Mothers, according to Abaye, teach the value of washing children in warm water, anointing them with oil, and feeding them eggs with a dish of sour milk, moldy bread, and salt from the Dead Sea (*kutaḥa*) (BT Yoma 78b).[26] Even on Yom Kippur, mothers had to perform these daily acts.[27] The health of children outweighed the commandment to fast, and leniencies to protect the well-being of children allowed mothers to wash and anoint them. According to M. Yoma 8:4, fasting is also a teachable practice that children needed to learn prior to reaching the age of majority: "We do not [require] children to practice self-denial, but we teach them [to fast] prior to a year or prior to two years [of reaching the age of majority], so that they will become accustomed to [performing] the commandments." Both mothers and fathers are responsible; both boys and girls are required.[28] However, the Bavli in a predominantly amoraic passage reflects on the welfare of children, acknowledging that not all children are the same—not all can be taught to fast in the same way at the same age. Because some are healthy and some sickly, there is an acknowledgment that the practice of fasting needs to be individualized, reflecting again the rabbis' concern with the well-being of individuals (BT Yoma 82a).

Underscoring the parent-child relationship and the significance of protecting the health and welfare of children, the rabbis emphasize what is central to the stability of a household. Feeding and not feeding children (even if connected to ritual observance) must be managed carefully if children are to survive at all. While bodily self-denial can be a threat, if it is carefully supervised by a mother (or father), a child's well-being can be maintained. Having used parent-child relationships to call attention to the dysfunctionality of priestly households in earlier chapters of the tractate, BT Yoma 78b now reverses course. The idea of nurture that surfaces in chapter eight stands in sharp contrast to earlier images of mothers who dress their sons in transparent priestly garments so that they appear naked while preforming Temple rites (BT Yoma 35b);[29] and a son who is abandoned by his father, leaving him to his mother who, in the end, eats him;[30] and the father who offers his son as an atonement for a priestly stabbing that had occurred in the Temple (BT Yoma 23a).[31]

But among the most indispensable relationships that pervade chapter eight is that of the male house member and his wife or wives. Anxiety surfaces around the fact that fasting can endanger pregnancies. While

152   *Bringing Down the Temple House*

men legislate for women and have agency over their bodies, the rabbis struggle with whether pregnant women should have authority over their own bodies to provide proper self-care, especially in the face of the commandment to fast. In fact, inui nefesh does not reduce women to objects, but neither does it raise women to the status of a unique, fully validated subject. In the case of inui nefesh, women exist at the "crossing point of subjectivity and objectification."[32] They are distinct from the high priest who is objectified and disempowered by the rabbis in earlier chapters of Bavli Yoma and who is absent from chapter eight (except in the instance of removing a priest from the altar to testify in a capital case on BT Yoma 85ab). And yet, the pregnant woman brings to the fore the rabbis' worries over procuring the next generation for their own selves. Whereas the high priest inhabits a ruined house defined by strict rules of male kinship, in chapter eight, the rabbis focus on a concern for maintaining their own households through mothers and their role in birthing children.

FASTING AND PREGNANCY

Sources in chapter eight of Bavli Yoma that refer to pregnant women and fasting on Yom Kippur encapsulate the rabbis' anxieties. M. Yoma 8:5 is clear that women who become hungry on Yom Kippur after smelling food must eat. A baraita brought to comment directly on the mishnah reflects even greater concern, not only allowing pregnant women to eat but placing them in the category of those whose lives are threatened and must therefore be saved from harm. Indeed, the concept of *pikuah nefesh* (saving a life) is taught through them:

> The Rabbis taught [in a baraita]: [If] a pregnant woman smelled consecrated meat or pig meat we insert a thin reed into the gravy [of it] and place it on her mouth. If her mind becomes settled, it is well. But if not, one feeds her the gravy itself. If her mind becomes settled, it is well. But if not, we feed her the fat itself, as there is nothing that stands in the way of saving a life except idol worship and forbidden sexual relationships and bloodshed. (BT Yoma 82a)

This sugya, after providing the sources for the three exceptions to the rules of pikuah nefesh—idol worship, forbidden sexual relationship, and bloodshed—brings two aggadic interchanges that challenge

Vulnerable Bodies in Vulnerable Houses   153

the clear-cut tannaitic exemption from fasting regarding a pregnant woman.[33] These vignettes also suggest a direct link between the decisions a pregnant woman makes regarding whether she fasts on Yom Kippur and the presumptive character of her progeny. Not surprisingly, the aggadic material functions to subvert the very premise of the larger sugya, equivocating about whether pregnant women should eat and about who has the right to make such a decision: the rabbis or the woman herself. The anxiety at the crux of rabbinic decision making comes to the fore in such an acute circumstance. Who legislates for whom when human life is at risk?

Two cases of pregnant women who smell food and presumably crave it come to the attention of a group of nameless others, who then follow the advice of Rebbe and Rabbi Hanina:

> There was a certain pregnant woman who smelled [food].[34]
>
> They [those involved (plural)] came before Rebbi [Yehudah Hanasi]. He said to them: "Go and whisper to her that today is Yom Kippur." They whispered to her, and she received the whispering.
>
> [Rebbi Yehudah HaNasi] read [this verse] on account of it [the unborn child]: "Before I formed you in the belly I knew you, [and before you came forth out of the womb, I sanctified you]" (Jeremiah 1:5).
>
> [The child that] came out of [the pregnant woman] was Rabbi Yochanan.
>
> A certain pregnant woman smelled [food]. They [those involved] came before Rabbi Hanina. He said to them: Whisper to her. But she did not receive the whispering.
>
> [Rabbi Hanina] read [this verse] on account of it [the unborn child], "The wicked are defiant from birth"[35] (Psalms 58:4). Shabetai,[36] the hoarder of fruits, came out of her (BT Yoma 82b–83a).[37]

In both of these stories women are observed to be struggling with hunger, presumably on Yom Kippur, by a group of people. These two women appear to be in public and presumably viewed by men, none of whom come forward as their husband.[38] Given the tannaitic warnings that pregnant women are not required to fast on Yom Kippur, it is surprising that a group of men approach a rabbi at all on their behalf, intimating that they need legal advice. The rabbis' advice to these men

Bringing Down the Temple House

is to whisper to the women that it is Yom Kippur. Indeed, these actions play with the boundaries of public and private space, between the community and the household, prompting the question as to why anyone is whispering. What are they trying to hide by whispering? Are they trying not to embarrass these women? Did these women not know it was Yom Kippur?

More troubling is the fact that it is unclear as to whether whispering to a woman that "it is Yom Kippur" sends the message that she can give in to her hunger cravings or is a reminder to fast. It is unclear if the second pregnant woman even heard them or simply dismissed them prior to hearing their advice when it says: "But she did not receive the whispering." That said, the decision to fast or not, to hear or not, seems to be up to her. In the first case, the woman makes the right choice, and Rebbi predicts that she will give birth to a son who will become the sage Rabbi Yohanan. In the second case, the pregnant woman makes the wrong decision, and as a result, Rabbi Ḥanina predicts she will birth a wicked son. In fact, she gives birth to the wrongdoer Shabetei. Undoubtedly, there is a lot at stake as to the decision regarding whether either woman eats or not, as this decision will have an impact on her progeny. Indeed, these women have agency, but the community has much to lose if these women legislate for themselves incorrectly.

The whispering also generates an intentional confusion in the discourse of the Bavli. It suggests that the rabbis are unsure. Is whispering a sign that they do not want their legal advice to be overheard? Do the rabbis have the authority to override the law of inui nefesh for some and not others? If those others are women, does gender dictate exemptions in the case of inui nefesh, or is it the condition of pregnancy that dictates? And if the rabbis override the law, have they done so in the name of "saving" this woman's life and therefore the life of her child? Do they have the authority to insist on the observance of a law if it might harm a woman as well as her unborn child? The redactors who insert this aggadic piece are not certain. The aggadic interchange challenges the tannaitic material that legislates quite clearly for leniency. In so doing, the rabbis express their anxiety over the power that they construct for themselves regarding an individual's health and well-being. And yet it this very power they also desire for themselves. The rabbis speak through pregnant women who are not only vulnerable in their eyes because they are pregnant but also powerful because they will bear future rabbis.[39] Their pregnant bodies are a suitable literary battleground for

Vulnerable Bodies in Vulnerable Houses   155

the rabbis' anxiety. Through them, they can admit that they do not have total control. Through them, they can also abdicate a sense of accountability, giving these women the responsibility to make a decision that will bring either reward or punishment with respect to their progeny. The rabbis concede here that they must rely on other rabbis (Rebbe and Rabbi Ḥanina) and other individuals (who witness this pregnant woman's cravings) regarding the care of these women. In addition, they might also need to relinquish their decision-making rights to women themselves to ensure their very own continuity.

In comparison to the story of Kimḥit in the Bavli, these pregnant women offer a different view of the rabbis, of women, and of the non-Temple observance of Yom Kippur. When Kimḥit argues that her actions are the reason for her sons' abilities to serve as high priests one after the other, she is mocked by the rabbis (BT Yoma 47a).[40] Her decision to be overly zealous about the requirements of female modesty, covering her head even within her own home, points to her mistaken understanding that her sons have been rewarded because of her merit. In fact, they are disqualified from serving as high priests because of their failure to uphold priestly standards of purity. Kimḥit's modest behavior is misdirected, and nothing she does transfers to them.

In the Bavli's presentation of Kimḥit, her agency functions as a critique of the priesthood and of the mothers who raise sons without priest-fathers. Similarly, these pregnant women are making decisions about their own bodies that resonate with the figure of Kimḥit; their actions are also tied to what becomes of their sons. However, in marked contrast, when contextualized in chapter eight of Bavli Yoma, outside the framework of the Temple, a shift becomes evident in the rabbis' perspective. The confidence displayed by the stammaim in the way they judge Kimḥit and critique the Temple is absent. Instead, a sense of insecurity festers. People who witness a pregnant woman craving food on Yom Kippur are insecure about how to advise her. They turn to rabbinic authorities, who recommend nothing more than whispering. The vignette reverberates with ambiguity. As arbiters of rabbinic law, Rebbe and Rabbi Ḥanina play both sides. They are authoritative in that they presume to know of the direct connection between a woman's behavior and the character of the progeny that will be born, but their recommendation for what these women should do with respect to their Yom Kippur fast is entirely unclear. It seems that the decision is hers to make. Only she knows her own body. And good decision making on the mother's part results in the reward of righteous children.

In addition, the interplay between the mishnah and lengthy explanatory tannaitic material earlier in Bavli Yoma presents priestly families who refuse to share their knowledge of Temple upkeep with those who came after them (BT Yoma 38ab). Priests of the House of Garmu, with expert knowledge on how to prepare the *panim* bread, and members of the House of Avtinas, who knew how to prepare the incense needed for Temple worship, did not transmit their knowledge. The idea of a master passing down instructions to a disciple, who is potentially outside the family circle of priest kinship, threatens the continuity of certain priestly rites and the knowledge of the tasks associated with the sancta of the Temple.[41] These references to familial relationships within the context of the Temple, as compared to those brought to the surface in the final chapter of Bavli Yoma, highlight the inability of the Temple to foster familial and master-disciple relationships so valued by the rabbinic elite. These are relationships that can be cultivated and sustained within the everyday household if both mothers and fathers, first and foremost, sustain their children's physical bodies and their own. Master-disciple types of relationships, represented here by the people who witness these pregnant women craving food, and Rebi and Rabbi Ḥanina, can also be maintained even if all that transfers between them are ambiguous whispers.

VULNERABLE RABBIS

In the continuation of the discussion about pregnant woman and the leniencies associated with fasting on Yom Kippur, the sugya on BT Yoma 83a focuses on who has the right to make determinations regarding fasting: a rabbinic authority, a medical expert, or the individual.[42] Ultimately, by the sugya's end, the Bavli highlights the opinion of the Babylonian amora Mar bar Rav Ashi, who advocates for the power of the individual (nonexpert) to "read" his or her own body and gauge the threshold of suffering. As Ayelet Libson observes, "While for the Mishnah, the experts are the ideal source of knowledge (of any type) and only if they are not accessible does one turn to the sick individual [compromised by illness], for the Talmudic redactors [of the Bavli], the individual (a nonexpert) is the ideal source of knowledge, and only if he is not accessible (due to extreme illness) does one turn to the experts,"

Vulnerable Bodies in Vulnerable Houses　　　　157

whether those experts are doctors or rabbis.[43] No doubt, the fear of making decisions that can result in sickness or even death pushes the Bavli's redactors to grant power to the individual (again, male or female), a sign that the rabbis are questioning not only their own expertise but that of medical experts as well. In this way, they lay out all avenues to save a life.

In the sugya that comments on the next mishnah (M. Yoma 8:6) about the remedies for *bulmos*, dog bites, and sore throats, the rabbis go so far as to rely on those far outside their bailiwick, including the mother of Abba bar Marta (Manyumi) and a noble woman (*matrona*), who possess the secret remedy for the disease of *tzafidna* (likely a scurvy). Case in point, Abaye relies on a traveling merchant and is cured from this ailment (BT Yoma 84a). Others include Rabbi Yehudah, who grabs bread from a shepherd to cure his bulmos, and Rabbi Yose, when suffering from the same disease, accepts foodstuffs from a city of people, depriving them of food (BT Yoma 83b).

How powerful are the rabbis and their legislative system as judges in the face of unexpected disaster, sickness, and death? Who really advocates for whom, and how? While the rabbis spend seven chapters critiquing the male-male bloodline of the priests, in Bavli Yoma, in chapter eight, they admit that even rabbinic power is constructed on precarious grounds. Recognizably, they depend on the objects of their power to provide them with the right to authority and the right to exercise it. These "objects" include women who give birth to rabbinic progeny, mothers of households who nurture their children by passing down both the knowledge of how to care for them and the cures for their illnesses, even non-Jewish women who possess secret remedies.[44] Social relations, especially within the household, fit into a spectrum of dependencies but also obligations that do not fall only on male householders or on rabbis. The rabbis admit in this chapter that such dependencies and obligations are continuously created and reorchestrated depending on the situations that arise.

Not only the legislative system but other institutional practices are seen now to have structural cracks. The transmission of Torah from father to son and from teacher to disciple is not a foolproof system. BT Yoma 86a points to individuals who cannot sustain active relationships with others—those whose business transactions are faulty or who do not speak to or act pleasantly with others. "What do people say about [this person]?" the rabbis exclaim. "Woe unto that person who

Bringing Down the Temple House

learned Torah. Woe unto his father who taught him Torah. Woe unto his teacher who taught him Torah." Torah does not ensure that one builds proper and respectful relationships, despite the accumulation of knowledge therein. And crucially, access to a system of confession and repentance (discussed toward the end of Bavli chapter eight), provoked surely by the focus on Yom Kippur, does not ensure forgiveness. Infractions between one human being and another that require that one personally request forgiveness from the other may fail and cannot always be reversed. Several aggadic vignettes speak of wrongdoers who reach out to those they have wronged, but the victims of these misdeeds are unforgiving (BT Yoma 87ab). Hence, there is no easy path to atonement; it cannot be reduced to a certainty by way of a rite. There are forces that go well beyond one's control and thwart full-fledged repentance on Yom Kippur. Such forces can be rooted in the varied nature of human relationships and the failure of Torah to militate against breaches of an interpersonal nature. In the end, such breaches destabilize the formation of rabbinic houses.

There is a prevalent thread, a thematic arc, if you will, that weaves its way through the first seven chapters of Bavli Yoma regarding the rabbis' desire to assert their authority over the priests. Condescendingly, the rabbis speak for the priests with absolute assurance, comfortably assuming complete authority in narrating the priests' ritual lives and legislating for them. However, a baraita in the final chapter on BT Yoma 86b–87a claims that this same authority that the rabbis would like to believe they possess can be abusive and "buries those who have it." This statement is aligned with reports on the behavior of the Babylonian amoraim Rav, Rava, and Rav Zutra:

> And authority buries those who have it.[45] He was naked when he entered into it [power], and he will be naked when he leaves it. And if only the going out would be like the coming in.
>
> When Rav would go out to judge cases, he [would] say this: Of his own will he goes to his death. And he does not fulfill the desires of his household and he goes [back] empty-handed to his household—and if only his coming in would be like his going out.
>
> And when he [Rava] saw a crowd (*ambuha*) [following] after him, he said: "Though he grows as high as the sky, his head reach-

Vulnerable Bodies in Vulnerable Houses　　　159

ing the clouds, he perishes forever, like his own dung; they who saw him will say: Where is he? (Job 20:6–7)"[46]

When they would carry Rav Zutra on their shoulders during the Shabbat of the Festival, he would recite [the following]: "For power does not last forever or a crown for all generations (Proverbs 27:24)."[47] (BT Yoma 86b–87a)

Bodily self-denial and the prohibitions of Yom Kippur set off more than the above-mentioned concerns about physical frailness. The rabbis also acknowledge personal, spiritual, and communal self-doubt. If the rabbis entered positions of authority "naked," that is, innocent of sin, they hope to leave these positions of privilege as upright as when they began such roles. Faced with the unforgivable threat that they could offer wrong judgments meant that the power to serve as a rabbinic judge was a dangerous one. In contrast to the high priest on Yom Kippur, who served as the ritual conduit for passing judgment and providing atonement through animal sacrifices and distinctly choreographed rites, the rabbis serve as intermediaries between people, with no set ritual formula to follow. They are judges who are judged as well.

In addition, through references to various Babylonian amoraim, the redactors insert reflections on being caught between their responsibilities as unpaid communal authorities and their roles as householders, needing to support their families. The poles of "going out" and "coming in" from their households to the court and back again repeatedly leave them hoping that they can return home as "naked" as when they left. Enmeshed within a sugya about sin and repentance, the amoraim named here put forth the idea that their work leads them closer to death than to reward, saying, "Of his own will, he goes to his death" in the pursuit of justice (BT Yoma 86b–87a).

Power is often linked to prestige, illustrated here in the last chapter of Bavli Yoma by the people who carry Rav Zutra on their shoulders, parading him around like a celebrity. Rav Zutra turns to the crowd that is lauding him and reminds them that rabbinic power is fleeting. Emerging at the end of a tractate describing a lost Temple and its leadership, the warning feels strikingly genuine: anything can be lost at any time, regardless of the value. Will the same happen to the rabbis? Is the decision on the part of the Babylonian redactors to disempower the priests in the first seven chapters connected to the desire that surfaces in chapter eight of Bavli Yoma to express their own vulnerabil-

160 *Bringing Down the Temple House*

ity? Is the stammaitic compilation of sources that generates discourse on the Temple and the priesthood a cautionary tale? Reading chapters backward from BT Yoma 86b–87a, the first seven chapters read like a discourse on failed leadership and institutional destruction, possibilities that the rabbis feared could become their reality. In the following source, linked to M. Yoma 7:4, the people flock to the early rabbinic figures, Shema'yah and Avtalyon (mentioned in chapter seven of Bavli Yoma), instead of following the high priest after he emerges from the Holy of Holies:

> [It was taught in the mishnah: They escort the High Priest to his house after the Temple Yom Kippur service in the Holy of Holies is complete.] And he would make a feast for his fellows.[48]
>
> The Sages taught [in a baraita]: There was an incident involving one high priest who exited the Holy Temple.
>
> And everyone followed him. When they saw Shema'yah and Avtalyon [heads of the Sanhedrin and predecessors of Hillel and Shammai], they left him [the high priest] and walked after Shema'yah and Avtalyon. (BT Yoma 71b)

This scene is peppered with rabbinic anxiety. If people turn away from the high priest to follow in the path of others who are not priests, would the same happen to the rabbis who are the descendants of Shema'yah and Avtalyon? For all of the power dynamics in evidence throughout tractate Yoma, the rabbis are trying to make sense of their lives and their leadership in light of shifting demands and circumstances that consistently provoke feelings of uncertainty and self-doubt. Disempowering the priests in their Temple house may be an attempt to empower themselves. However, by chapter eight, it seems that even the rabbis feel disempowered in their roles, recognizing that in the face of making difficult judgments, they do not necessarily possess the right answers. In this regard, the Babylonian stammaim are not making an argument for a replacement house or thinking of themselves as replacement priests. Rather, against the backdrop of Yom Kippur, they admit to the possibility that they can fail in the very role they have cultivated for themselves. In the end, when nothing is reliable and nothing is inevitable, on what can they count? There appears to be no protection excepting one: hope for their own survival and that of their future offspring. This is the tractate's parting message

Vulnerable Bodies in Vulnerable Houses

and the focus of the discussion in the next chapter and final chapter of this book.

CONCLUSION

Thinking literarily, chapter eight of Bavli Yoma functions as an admission on the part of the rabbis that they are fragile human beings who are no more powerful than the priests. Concerned about their daily subsistence, the list of prohibitions that define the rite of inui nefesh brings concerns about their sheer survival to the surface. Ironically, a rite that requires men and women to take control of their bodies generates thinking about the rabbis' lack of control and power. In their desire to impose their authority over the priests by marginalizing them, they admit to their own fragility with little control in the face of life's burdens. Indeed, inui nefesh becomes a ripe analytical space for the rabbis to contemplate the realities of their own households in comparison to the lavish Temple house that once stood in Jerusalem. Nothing is the same. In the final chapter in Bavli Yoma, the focus veers away from male priests, whether from the details of the Temple performance of the Yom Kippur rite or from the priests' familial relationships. Instead, emphasis is placed on the stability and potential instability of the everyday house and the people who inhabit it.

The tropes of the everyday household—food and sex, nature and nurture, health and well-being, the need for rabbinic judgments— come together in the final Bavli Yoma chapter to narrate an even larger redactional story, one that is indeed about human frailty. The images of complicated and troublesome parent-child relationships associated with the priests and the Temple in the first seven chapters of the tractate turn into discussions in the eighth chapter about the rabbis' concerns for nurturing children and maintaining their well-being. Women who were denigrated for taking on a sense of misplaced agency in the rearing of their children become in this final chapter members of households on whom the rabbis wholeheartedly depend. The most hierarchical rite orchestrated by a high priest turns into a discussion about rites that both men and women are equally required to perform, with benign exception for women and the very ill in vulnerable statuses. The formulaic quality of the role of the high priest in ensuring that the people could be cleared of their sins by a rite alone is gone. In its stead, the rabbis take on roles as caring, but also insecure, judges. Faced with

162   *Bringing Down the Temple House*

the unpredictable on a quotidian basis, they admit to being vulnerable to mistakes. Even the punishment of karet for transgressing the prohibitions associated with Yom Kippur produces textual moments that introduce rabbinic distance from the Temple and its sacrifices but also reflect deep concerns about such a punishment. Will every family member survive in spite of behavior that might be considered transgressive?

Where one might expect a line of continuity through which the memory of the most significant Temple rite, Yom Kippur, is reimagined in its non-Temple iteration, there is silence. This absence shatters the notion that the everyday household replicates the Temple house and that rabbinic Yom Kippur rites, from the liturgical to the performative, reproduce memories of a Temple past. In comparison to the eighth chapter in Yerushalmi Yoma, the tome where Temple rites are given far more attention, earlier sources in the Bavli are integrated into a redactional framework that barely mentions the Temple or the priests. Ergo, Bavli Yoma unmasks a redactional agenda that points away from the formation of a direct link between Temple Judaism and rabbinic Judaism, even though one can find evidence of this elsewhere in the Bavli.[49] The rabbis' fears reverberate through the final discourse in chapter eight: Would their own households go the way of the Temple house? Would their houses devolve into a state of chaos, dysfunction, and immorality? Bavli Yoma, which is undoubtedly about the Temple Yom Kippur and the non-Temple rite, tells another story. One who reads through its pages with the idea of the bayit and all that it conjures enables this story to surface and spotlights the rabbis' greatest hope—future offspring, a discussion that is at the center of the next chapter of this book and is the final point made before the tractate ends.[50]

Vulnerable Bodies in Vulnerable Houses   163

CHAPTER 9

THE CASE

OF PURITY AND

IMPURITY

• • •

To conclude this feminist analysis of Bavli Yoma is to call attention to one of the most significant considerations in the construction of well-regarded rabbinic houses: adherence to the laws of purity and impurity that affected those who were married. As tractate Yoma draws to a close, the Babylonian redactors reintroduce purity and impurity law. In so doing, they shift the very parameters of Temple-related purity law from the high priests on Yom Kippur to its observance in non-Temple houses. But rather than reappropriating the ascetic requirements obligated of the priests and integrating them into the non-Temple observance of Yom Kippur, a far more subtle process unfolds. Baraitan material is worked into the final sugya that treats purity and impurity as a distinct and separate category of law from its ties to the priests' role in the Temple Yom Kippur. The various types of impurity that typically disqualified the high priest on Yom Kippur, or any other priest from performing rites while serving in the Temple, do not disrupt individuals from the attainment of atonement during their observance of Yom Kippur outside the Temple. The extensive prayer rite that developed in association with Yom Kippur and that necessitated an additional service at the end of the day, called Ne'ilah, no longer required a state of bodily purity equivalent to the demands on the high priest's service in the Temple. In fact, as Bavli Yoma conveys, in observing Yom Kippur outside the Temple, one did not need to immerse before engaging in any of the five required prayer services. This allowance is striking in that rabbinic literature does not lack for instances where bodily purity is required before prayer and Torah study.[1] All males, for example, were required to immerse before saying Shema or studying Torah, both practiced presumably as a means to re-create a Temple-like "priestly" status in men's daily lives. This raises the question as to

164

why Bavli Yoma at this point communicates a position regarding purity and impurity that differentiates the Temple Yom Kippur from the non-Temple observance. Why not instead use the category of purity law to link them? Theoretically, this would represent continuity on some level between the two Yom Kippur experiences.[2]

SEXUAL PURITY LAW: THE BACKGROUND

The last mishnah of Yoma (M. Yoma 8:9) has a metaphorical reference to the mikveh (ritual bath) and conveys that for some tannaim, the focal point was shifting regarding the laws of purity and impurity. The transformative image of a mikveh to affect ritual purification and cleanse one of sins is used metaphorically to describe the ability of Yom Kippur itself to change individuals through the process of repentance rather than requiring actual immersion, as was once required to enter the Temple.[3] M. Yoma 8:9, which states, "I [God] will sprinkle clean water upon you and you shall be clean" (Ezekiel 36:25), is followed by a verse that builds on the meaning of the word *mikveh* as hope, referring to God as the "Hope of Israel" (Jeremiah 17:13). This strengthens the point that "I [God] will give you a new heart and put a new spirit into you" (Ezekiel 36:26) without requiring a physical immersion. In the final sugya of Bavli Yoma, however, actual immersion in a mikveh is reintroduced, not for the purpose of atonement, but to make a point about ritual purity law and Yom Kippur. Rather than building on the idea of spiritual purification communicated in the M. Yoma 8:9, the Bavli now incorporates material found in T. Yoma that moves the discussion in a different direction, taking up the issue of actual immersions in *mikva'ot* and whether such immersions are required or even allowed on Yom Kippur itself.

Over time and in the wake of the destruction of the Temple, the rabbis continued to struggle with how to integrate purity and impurity into their rabbinic legal system. Early on, it appears that some rabbis wished to maintain biblical purity law for men not merely as tied to sexual relations but to incorporate priest-like purity into rabbinic ritual life.[4] That said, regarding non-Temple settings, T. Berakhot 2:12, JT Berakhot 3:4, 6c, and BT Berakhot 22a (baraita) permit reading Torah and the study of Mishnah, Midrash, halakhah, and aggadah for those who are ritually impure, including the *zav* (a man who experienced a nonseminal discharge on three consecutive days or three times in one

The Case of Purity and Impurity   165

day), the *zavah* (a woman who experienced a discharge on three consecutive days during a time of month when she was not menstruating), and the *nidah* (the menstruating woman). However, the *ba'al keri* (the man who has a seminal emission) is excluded from participation in any of these Torah-study activities until he immerses.[5] This parallels the rules governing priests during their service in the Temple who were disqualified when they had seminal emissions.[6]

Beyond question, for the rabbis, there is a fundamental difference between a seminal emission and all the other fluxes that render an individual impure.[7] The discharges of the nidah, the zav, and the zavah are entirely unavoidable.[8] These fluxes do not render those who become impure by them unable to participate in Torah study and prayer, despite the fact that such impurities would have distanced them from the Temple precincts and certainly would have disqualified the priests from performing any Temple-related rites.[9] In contrast, a seminal emission is directly tied to sexual desire.[10] Therefore, only the ba'al keri must distance himself from his sexual body before engaging in Torah study or prayer.[11] These early rabbinic sources suggest that for some rabbis, Torah study was linked to a type of holiness rooted in sexual restraint.[12]

The idea of the sexless male was also connected to prayer and donning tefillin.[13] M. Berakhot 3:4 prohibits a ba'al keri from reciting the Shema prayer aloud, including the blessings before and after Shema, as well as the blessing before eating.[14] Rituals such as prayer were equated with sacrifices in some rabbinic sources, which connected the rabbis with their priestly forebearers still further.[15] Both Bavli and Yerushalmi Berakhot build on a system of purity law incumbent on the Temple priests, integrating purity law with Torah study as well as prayer.[16] To grant authority to the rabbinic idea of immersion for the ba'al keri prior to Torah study and prayer in a post-Temple era, the tannaim anachronistically attributed the decree to the biblical figure Ezra.[17] But according to the stammaitic layer in Bavli Berakhot 22a, there is evidence that for some amoraim, such as Rabbi Zeira, a proportion of Jews had already abolished the practice.[18]

For Bavli Yoma, the overall perspective is quite different from tractate Berakhot, however. Bringing up the ba'al keri, particularly in the last sugya of Bavli Yoma, and departing from the main idea of the mishnah on which it comments (M. Yoma 8:9), raises issues related to differentiating priest from rabbi and Temple house from rabbinic house. Rather than building on the idea presented in M. Yoma 8:9 of a mikveh

166   *Bringing Down the Temple House*

that spiritually purifies individuals from sin, the final sugya in Bavli Yoma brings to a fitting end point the issues that have been reverberating throughout the tractate regarding the rabbis' desire to shift away from the Temple house.[19] By raising the issue of the extent to which rabbinic piety, specifically on Yom Kippur, depended on male sexual self-control, this final sugya picks up on the extent to which purity law undergirds everyday rabbinic houses in ways that distinguish it from the Temple.[20] Did the non-priest, like the priest in the Temple, need to remain pure throughout his observance of Yom Kippur? Did a seminal emission, involuntary or otherwise, disqualify him from observing Yom Kippur as it did for the high priest? What is the relationship between purity and prayer and between purity and Yom Kippur, and how do these connect with the way in which sexuality is dealt with in the context of Bavli Yoma, as discussed in chapter six?

THE FINAL SUGYA IN BAVLI YOMA: OF MAN OR OF WOMAN BORN?[21]

BT Yoma 88a is constructed around two tannaitic sources that mention all of the following who may immerse on Yom Kippur: the ba'al keri, the zav, the zavah, the nidah, the metzora or metzora'at (a person afflicted with a type of skin disorder), a man who has cohabited with a nidah, a person who has been in contact with a corpse, and a woman who has recently given birth. For all of the apprehension over protecting the high priest from having a seminal emission on Yom Kippur, which would prevent him from performing the avodah, the final chapter in the tractate does not share the same concern regarding the non-Temple rite.[22] Sources on BT Yoma 88a that presumably represent two versions of one tannaitic tradition convey this point:[23]

> It is a dispute among tannaim, as it was taught in a baraita: All those who are obligated to immerse themselves, immerse themselves in their usual manner on Yom Kippur. A nidah and a woman who has given birth immerse themselves in their usual manner on the night of Yom Kippur. A ba'al keri [on Yom Kippur] may immerse himself at any time until Minhah (the afternoon prayer). Rabbi Yose says, anytime throughout the entire day.

> [Another] baraita raises a contradiction: A zav, zavah, metzora, metzora'at, a man who cohabits with a nidah and a person im-

The Case of Purity and Impurity   167

pure from a corpse, immerse themselves in their usual manner on Yom Kippur. A nidah and a woman who has given birth immerse themselves in their usual manner on the night of Yom Kippur. A ba'al keri [on Yom Kippur] immerses at [any time] throughout the entire day; Rabbi Yose says, from Minḥah and onward he may not immerse himself.[24]

Both baraitot require that one should immerse when the legally appropriate time for immersion arrives, even when it coincides with Yom Kippur.[25] Although the Mishnah (M. Yoma 8:1) and the Tosefta (T. Yoma 4:1) are clear that washing is prohibited, these sources emphasize that ritual immersion is a separate category of law from washing to cleanse oneself (BT Yoma 77b).[26] More to the point, these two baraitot intimate that Yom Kippur has no impact on the general practice of ritual purity law and immersion; the rituals connected to purity and impurity appear to supersede Yom Kippur. One must observe them, whether it is Yom Kippur or not. Following this line of reasoning, as the Bavli points out, the purpose of the inclusion of these two baraitot is to flesh out yet another issue of the law as it relates to prayer on Yom Kippur.

From a purely intellectual perspective, purity law is used to make sense of a prayer-related issue: Does Ne'ilah (the concluding evening prayer service of Yom Kippur) replace Ma'ariv (the daily nightly prayer service), or must the latter be said in addition to it? Capitalizing on the fact that the two baraitot (above) reverse the opinions of Rabbi Yose and the sages (*tanna kama*), the Bavli uses its analysis of these two baraitot to weigh in on the issue related to Ne'ilah in a typically stammaitic fashion. It is not unusual for the stammaim to flesh out an amoraic difficulty, in this case, Rav's position on Yoma 87b, as to whether Ma'ariv must be said in addition to Ne'ilah or not. Rav's position happens to be rooted in an earlier tannaitic quandary regarding whether Ma'ariv on any given evening is optional or required.[27] By bringing in tannaitic material, the stammaim attempt to clarify the position of Rav, and therefore the ruling about Ne'ilah and Ma'ariv. But percolating underneath this discussion is the deeper conundrum of whether immersion, and therefore purity law, is linked to repentance on Yom Kippur at all. Can prayer without immersion affect atonement? Does one need to be ritually pure to pray on Yom Kippur? Despite the larger context, which is about prayer, the answer might very well be no.

The mere mention of the ba'al keri in association with Yom Kippur

Bringing Down the Temple House

drives a wedge between priest and non-priest. Evidence of this is set off by comparing the baraitot that appear on BT Yoma 88a with the parallel version found in the Tosefta. This Toseftan baraita, as distinct from the Bavli's version, specifically includes mention of the priests and the importance of their ritual purification for eating the priestly gift of footstuffs (*terumah*) after nightfall on Yom Kippur. No priest could eat terumah unless he was ritually pure. As such, Rabbi Yossa says, "Priests immerse in their usual manner with nightfall so that they can eat terumah in the evening [after Yom Kippur ends]" (T. Yoma 4:5). Significantly, and in keeping with the pattern noted in Bavli Yoma's incorporation of other baraitot in earlier chapters of this book, the baraitot quoted on BT Yoma 88a appear to be emended to suit the redactional agenda of the Babylonian stammaim. Here in this Bavli sugya, the priests and concerns about their status as ba'alei keri do not appear. Instead, the focus of the baraitot quoted on BT Yoma 88a is only on requirements for those not serving as priests.

Compared to the priests in the Temple in earlier chapters of BT Yoma, the discussion here is quite different. Great measures were taken to ensure that the high priest did not have a seminal emission; accountability for his purity status was in sharp focus. Becoming a ba'al keri would disqualify him from conducting the Yom Kippur rite altogether.[28] As well, a seminal emission meant that he could not atone for himself, his family, or the community at large. Perhaps even after the Temple was destroyed, he continued to eat terumah, and therefore laws related to priestly purity remained in force. In contrast, in Bavli Yoma, becoming a ba'al keri on Yom Kippur does not interfere with an individual's ability to repent and receive atonement. Because eating terumah is not relevant to non-priests whether after Yom Kippur at nightfall or on any other day, it then makes sense that the piece of the Toseftan baraita mentioning the priests is left out. Its very absence reflects the agenda of the final redactors, who in crafting this final passage are not interested in the priests' purity requirements and how they affect the non-Temple observance of Yom Kippur. The stammaim are not intent on drawing a connection between the rulings associated with the priests and purity law incumbent on all.

It is also important to think about BT Yoma 88a through the lens of biblical law. Leviticus 15:16 speaks to the purification of the ba'al keri as a two-step process. There it states, "When a man has a seminal emission, he shall bathe his whole body in water and remain unclean until

The Case of Purity and Impurity 169

evening." The ba'al keri immerses and then must wait until evening before declaring himself pure. But as distinct from the process that Rabbi Yossa describes in T. Yoma 4:5, where the priest waits until nightfall to immerse and his shift to a state of purification occurs that same evening, the ba'al keri described here can begin the process of ritual purification on Yom Kippur itself by immersing. Nothing about his status of impurity affects his prayer for atonement. The process of purification, to rid himself of the impurity caused by a seminal emission, does not appear linked to making prayer on Yom Kippur permissible to him. He does not have to be in a state of ritual purity to pray for atonement, for himself or others, as these are separate categories of law.

The ba'al keri—just like the zav, the zavah, the nidah, and others who became ritually impure—immerses on Yom Kippur because he is required to do so at the earliest opportunity.[29] Despite a level of disagreement regarding the possibility that immersion can be put off to a later time than legislated (see the opinion of Rabbi Yose above),[30] the stammaim on BT Yoma 88a make the following point: "Immersion at its proper time, is a mitzvah (commandment)."[31] To support this point, the stammaim bring the following baraita and then clarify the ruling to make allowances for immersing on Yom Kippur if this is the appropriate time for the ba'al keri:

> It is taught in a baraita: If one experiences a seminal emission on Yom Kippur, he goes down and immerses himself and in the evening rubs his body.
>
> In the evening?! [How could he rub off impediments to his immersion after the fact]?!
>
> [Really?!]: What was, was.
>
> Rather say, [what the baraita meant to say was]: "From the evening [before] he should rub [away any impediments to immersion on his body]."[32]

Pushing through the redactional layer of this Talmudic passage is the point that a man must immerse on Yom Kippur if he becomes a ba'al keri, in keeping with the idea that immersion at its proper moment of time is a mitzvah. As was the practice, prior to a ritual immersion, a person was required first to wash away any impediments that might prevent the ritual waters from covering every place on his or her

170   *Bringing Down the Temple House*

body. But on Yom Kippur, washing and rubbing off dirt or debris were prohibited. Hence, one stammaitic opinion, speaking from a position of leniency, expresses that because it is a mitzvah to immerse at the right time, even on Yom Kippur, a person has permission to overlook the first stage in the process of purification. He may exempt himself from the prohibition associated with the day of Yom Kippur of washing one's body. The reason: *"mai d'hava hava"* (what was, was). Effectively, the stammaim are recommending that the ba'al keri can consider his immersion on Yom Kippur valid, despite the fact that he has not washed his body first. The stammaim, however, reject this leniency and argue instead that it is better to wash in advance of Yom Kippur, preparing for the possibility that a seminal emission could occur. In this way, an individual would be able to ritually immerse at the appropriate time without the prior step of washing to remove any impediments to a full body immersion on Yom Kippur itself, when washing is prohibited. The question, however, looms: Why are the stammaim so concerned about the ba'al keri and immersing on Yom Kippur? Why not insist that he wait until after Yom Kippur to immerse? He has to wait anyway for nightfall before he can consider himself fully pure, surely a requirement for having sexual relations.

Other passages in the Bavli favor the position that immersion needs to take place in its legally appointed time.[33] BT Ta'anit 13a, BT Beitzah 18b, and BT Shabbat 111a, for example, all quote versions of the baraita found on BT Yoma 88a: "All those who are required to immerse, do so in their usual manner, whether it is Tisha B'av or Yom Kippur." In BT Ta'anit 13a, ritual immersions not only override the prohibition against washing on fast days and concerns about the use of hot water but also the act of mourning the loss of the First and Second Temples on Tisha B'av.[34] BT Ta'anit 13a dismisses the position of Rabbi Ḥanina (deputy of the high priest) that allowing ritual immersions interferes with the goal of the fast, which is to remember the Temple. Instead, Bavli Ta'anit states that a fast day like Tisha B'av does not prevent all who need to immerse from doing so, nor does immersion weaken the ritual remembrance of the Temple.[35] BT Beitzah 17b–18b considers whether ritual immersions can be done on a Sabbath that falls right before a holiday. Given that such immersions, like the immersion of utensils, "repair" the body by enabling a person to have sexual relations following immersion, and repairing is forbidden on the Sabbath,

The Case of Purity and Impurity

this passage questions whether immersions done for the sake of purifying one's body are permissible on Shabbat and Yom Kippur at all. Does Yom Kippur parallel Shabbat in its requirements, or are there additional stringencies on this High Holy Day? BT Beitzah and BT Shabbat 111a both assert that Yom Kippur law regarding immersions is not stricter than Sabbath law; therefore, since one can immerse one's body on the Sabbath for the sake of ritual purification, one can immerse on Yom Kippur. In this way, one can hold by the requirement to immerse on the appropriate day at the appropriate time.

In BT Yoma 88a, the import is the same: some rabbis believe that the appointed time to observe purity law supersedes all. Correct timing is integral to the proper performance of purity rituals. The reasons for immersing on the Sabbath or Tisha B'av or Yom Kippur are connected to time, not to prayer.[36] This supports the idea that for the ba'al keri, as well as for the other ritually impure persons listed in BT Yoma 88a, sexual impurity is not an impediment to prayer and is not an obstacle in one's course of repentance and atonement on Yom Kippur. In fact, the rulings discussed in all three Talmudic passages serve as arguments for the continued existence of a working system regulating purity, albeit one that operates alongside festivals and fast days, without obstructing or transgressing them.[37] In separating purity law from holiday observance and from prayer, Bavli Yoma distinguishes the Temple-based Yom Kippur from the rabbinic one. But more significant to this discussion is the fact that the high priest, who needed much assistance to maintain his purity status on Yom Kippur at the risk of disqualification, is differentiated from the non-priest who can take steps to change his ritual standing even on Yom Kippur itself without disrupting his observance.

But the question still remains. Why do the stammaim push to maintain ritual purification on Yom Kippur, given the necessity of bathing before immersion and the need to wait until nightfall to be considered ritually pure anyway? Speaking just about Bavli Yoma and thinking with the degree of precariousness that the rabbis keep touching on in this final chapter of the tractate, it seems fitting that they are also concerned about obstacles to sexual relations. While the end of the sugya on BT Yoma 88a offers some clues, it seems that the rabbis are also grappling with their own longevity. Any form of impurity will delay sexual relations for citizen, priest, and rabbi alike, and abstinence of any length for any reason delays the possibility of additional progeny.

Bringing Down the Temple House

Given the detailed discussion with which the sugya ends (below), it appears that what the rabbis feared most was their inability to ensure that they would produce another generation.[38]

SEMINAL EMISSIONS ON YOM KIPPUR ARE GOOD OMENS

As tractate Yoma comes to a close, tannaitic and amoraic sources are woven together by the redactors of the Bavli, with no parallel in the Yerushalmi. A seminal emission that once disqualified priest and non-priest from the Temple surprisingly emerges as a good omen for men who experience it on Yom Kippur:

> A tanna taught a baraita before Rav Naḥman: If one has a seminal emission on Yom Kippur, his sins have been forgiven.
>
> But it has been taught in a [different] baraita [regarding a person who had a seminal emission on Yom Kippur]: His sins are arranged. What is [meant by] arranged? [It means his sins are] arranged to be forgiven.
>
> A tanna of the academy of Rabbi Yishmael taught: One who has a seminal emission on Yom Kippur should worry all year long. But if he lives out the year, he may be assured that he has a place in the World to Come.
>
> Rabbi Naḥman bar Yitzhak said: Know [that it is so] because the entire world is starved [of pleasure],[39] while he [the ba'al keri] is satisfied [sexually]. When Rav Dimi came [to Babylonia] he said: He [the ba'al keri] will live long, multiply and multiply further. (BT Yoma 88a)

Seminal emissions on Yom Kippur can be a sign that a man is cleared of sin and serves as a promise of a place in the World to Come. The Babylonian amora Rabbi Naḥman bar Yitzhak, in his description of the ba'al keri, imagines this person as a man satisfied in a world starving for sexual satisfaction. He acknowledges sexual desire as an appropriate expression of male sexuality, even on Yom Kippur. Encrypted within Rav Naḥman's comment is an attempt to propose that what distinguishes the Temple priest from the rabbinic male is sexuality, but under and by what terms? Rav Dimi follows and supports Rav Naḥman's position further. Linking seminal emissions and

The Case of Purity and Impurity

masculine virility is evidenced by having many children. Making this link is a conspicuous power move that reverses the high priest's ascetic sexual behavior with which the tractate began. The bodily experience of a seminal emission that once disqualified the priests has been over-ridden.[40]

The parallel material in Yerushalmi Yoma (JT Yoma 8:1, 44d) accentuates this position that appears in the Bavli. The Yerushalmi acknowledges the need to sort out what is meant by the category "ba'al keri," as linked to whether one could have sexual relations on Yom Kippur. Commenting on M. Yoma 8:1, which lists the Yom Kippur prohibitions, including that of sexual relations, the amora Rabbi Ya'akov bar Aḥa said in the name of Rabbi Yassa, who said in the name of Rabbi Yehoshua ben Levi, that "[a seminal emission] is not [considered] keri unless [it occurred as a result of] sexual relations."[41] Others argue that one can be considered keri if he imagines himself having sexual relations with a woman in a dream. But the more pointed distinction between BT Yoma 88a and JT Yoma 8:1, 44d emerges in a different baraita, which states, "Ba'alei keri immerse in their usual manner *privately* on Yom Kippur (JT Yerushalmi 8:1, 44d)."[42] In fact, as the Yerushalmi also notes, "It once happened with [the tanna] Rabbi Yose bar Ḥalafta that they saw him immersing privately on Yom Kippur." Of course, "seeing" a rabbi immerse "privately" generates its own set of quandaries. But putting that aside, the baraita and the vignette support the idea that immersing on Yom Kippur is required, adding one important detail absent in Bavli Yoma: that secrecy is paramount. Therefore, it seems that the Yerushalmi is trying to support the Yom Kippur prohibition found in M. Yoma 8:1 regarding sexual relations but also acknowledges that some had seminal emissions on Yom Kippur itself. The passage tries to play both sides, prohibiting a man from becoming a ba'al keri on Yom Kippur while recognizing that this occurred.

With this in mind, it is interesting that nowhere does BT Yoma 88a mention the need for privacy on Yom Kippur when immersing.[43] This is especially surprising given that the baraitan material quoted in the Bavli mentions Rabbi Yose, who is the same tanna as Rabbi Yose bar Ḥalafta named in the Yerushalmi.[44] Without the valence of someone trying to hide his need to immerse (through a private immersion) when he becomes a ba'al keri on Yom Kippur, the Bavli appears to be more open than the Yerushalmi to ridding oneself of bodily impurities on Yom Kippur itself in order to abide by the legal strictures of time. Fur-

174   *Bringing Down the Temple House*

thermore, whereas the Yerushalmi discusses immersion in conjunction with M. Yoma 8:1 and the prohibition of sexual relations, in the Bavli the discussion is connected to the final mishnah in tractate Yoma that focuses on spiritual purification from sin. This comparison brings the Bavli's agenda more clearly to the fore—the Bavli appears to be more open to the idea that a man could become a ba'al keri on Yom Kippur and that he could immerse on Yom Kippur itself without interrupting his observance of the holiday.[45] A seminal emission marks a man as impure, but it is a status he needs to and can take steps to reverse. This further accentuates the point that purity and impurity law once required of the priests on Yom Kippur in the Temple does not inform the non-Temple Yom Kippur observance. In building the rabbinic household, purity and impurity are so vital that they supersede the stringencies of Yom Kippur. There is no move here to reappropriate the Temple rites of purity and impurity associated with Yom Kippur; this category of law belongs to members of everyday households who must maintain bodily purity in an ongoing way throughout the year so that they can have sexual relations with their spouses.

Admittedly, BT Yoma 88a does not clarify or categorize the circumstances under which a seminal emission may or may not occur, leaving these details open to speculation more than in the Yerushalmi, where there is some attempt to define who can be classified as a ba'al keri. In the Bavli, however, it is not clear as to whether a man ejaculated during sexual relations on Yom Kippur, or as a result of self-arousal, or due to an involuntary nocturnal emission.[46] Rashi, discussing BT Yoma 88a, is convinced that the ba'al keri has experienced a spontaneous emission of semen in this context. Perhaps his interpretation stems from the belief that self-arousal is transgressive because it means wasted seed.[47] Hence, Rashi imagines that God has sent a direct sign through this event over which the ba'al keri has no control. Whichever definition or description of the ba'al keri one accepts, according to the Babylonian amoraim, Rav Naḥman and Rav Dimi, this is a good omen. A man who has a seminal emission on Yom Kippur, even on a day when sexual relations are, according to the Mishnah (M. Yoma 8:1), prohibited, has received a sign from God that he will have children.

Immersions on Yom Kippur for the ba'al keri presented in the two baraitot on BT Yoma 88a suggest that sexual relations might very well have been happening on Yom Kippur. This supports the more permissive stammaitic attitude toward procreative sexual relations

The Case of Purity and Impurity

that emerged on BT Yoma 77b, as discussed in chapter seven of this book. Maybe the rabbis merely wished it to be so. In their hope for future progeny, the redactors of this tractate shaped the sources available to them, even manipulated earlier sources, to make room for the idea that couples can have permissible procreative sex either during Yom Kippur, after which they can immerse. Picking up from the aggadic narrative on BT Yoma 69b, where the sexual Inclination (yetzer) was valued for the sake of populating the world with offspring, here the tractate comes to a close, making the same point. Stressing the virility of the rabbis, over and against the sexless high priest, accentuates what matters most for the continuity of the rabbinic household in this tractate.[48] In spite of all of the rabbis' discomfort with the centrality of the priestly bloodline in Bavli Yoma,[49] at the end of the tractate, they want exactly what the priests have: kin. Remarkably, the core rabbinic idea of cultivating students to pass on Torah knowledge in order to reproduce themselves, which is the rabbis' "answer" to the priests' bloodline of succession, is not mentioned. Even if Rashi is correct and Bavli Yoma ends with a reference to the uncontrolled nocturnal sexual emissions of men, seeing them as good omens, the tractate ends by signifying that the lack of male self-restraint is positive, transmuting that into progeny.[50]

CONCLUSION: INTERCONNECTING THREADS AND THE MESSIANIC BAYIT

When the rabbis look back on the priests, they imagine themselves in control of the priests' body and their sexuality, with the power and entitlement to ensure that the Temple's Yom Kippur rite will operate as they think it should (eliminating sexual activity by the priests). This and other references to instability in the Temple house emerge throughout the first seven chapters of the tractate, seeping through in multiple references to familial relationships, including that of husband-wife and parent-child. Issues related to the priestly bloodline, where ancestry supersedes merit, also surface as points of critique, setting the stage for a rabbinic meritocracy. And yet here, at the very end of the tractate, the rabbis want what the priests have: biological descendants.[51] Taking this one step further, the rabbis do not indicate on Bavli Yoma 88a whether such offspring will be male or female or whether they are the progeny of Torah-learned men. What matters is biological continuity sanctioned by God, premising the significance of the body over the mind. The making of the rabbinic household is dependent on, at a minimum, sexual relations. For this to occur, immersions must occur in [their] proper time.

While the Mishnah ends on a note of hope—one can be spiritually cleansed by God on Yom Kippur—the Bavli ends with an anxious message that encapsulates the tension between power and powerlessness in its most visceral manifestation: the seminal emission. On the one hand, the rabbis, unlike the priests, can ejaculate semen on Yom Kippur without disqualifying themselves from its observance. On the other hand, future children are predicated on either a potentially uncontrolled experience as determined by God (a nocturnal emission) or a controlled marital one with resonances of immorality (as brought to the fore on BT Yoma 69a). While sexuality reappears over and over throughout the tractate, reflecting a common trajectory in the Babylonian Talmudic material, focusing on sexuality captures that very slippery point between the insecure feeling of having no control regarding one's future and having the power to produce another generation. While anthropologists, psychologists, linguists, and metaphor theorists look for literary manifestations of gender to reveal cultural conceptualizations based on views of sexuality, it is also the case that gender and sexuality are interwoven into rabbinic literature in ways that embody the rabbis' lived experience. Their very bodies offer a way of communicating the precise point where their desire for authority as male rabbis intersects with all that challenges them—from building viable households for their families to managing the insecurities of the world at large.[52]

Bavli Yoma, it can be said, ends as it began, with a bayit signified by the sexual relationships therein. While not parallel to the Temple bayit inhabited by sexless priests as M. Yoma 1:1 points out, this bayit is dependent on ensuring that a man's "wife" becomes her husband's "house," birthing children. In the end, birthing progeny, building the future, stands out as more significant than mourning the Temple's destruction or creating a ritual means to remember it.

The significance of offspring is encapsulated further in one more source, found in the last chapter of the tractate where the messianic bayit is described. This is the juncture in the eighth chapter of Bavli Yoma that comes closest to imagining a new Temple. A larger aggadic passage, it builds on Ezekiel 47, where the prophet is led through

The Case of Purity and Impurity   177

a future Temple to witness water emerging from its interior.[53] The passage in the Bavli then textually breaks from the physicality of the Temple house and the sacrificial rites led by its male priests that are mentioned in the immediately preceding chapters of Ezekiel (BT Yoma 77b–78a). Instead, the passage brings together a more concrete legal discussion about whether one can enter a river and become wet on Yom Kippur (this to visit a rabbinic teacher or his father) and the issue of whether "barefootedness" on Yom Kippur makes this crossing permissible at all. Wedged into the middle of this discussion about prohibitions associated with self-denial (shoes being a form of prohibited physical pleasure) on Yom Kippur, BT Yoma 77b–78a depicts a flowing river that will emerge from the holiest spot of ground, where the Temple once stood. An amoraic tradition attributed to Rabbi Pinḥas in the name of Rav Huna of Tzippori states that this future stream of water will continue to widen throughout the Temple chambers and courtyards. Building partially on M. Middot 2:8, this stream in time will spread from under the threshold of the Temple and flow as far as the House of David, increasing in strength. The goal of this flowing river is to turn the space where the Temple once was (and its surroundings) into a large mikveh. In Ezekiel 47:1–12, the water enables "every living creature that swarms" to live and every kind of tree to yield fruit. In Bavli Yoma 77b, men who become impure due to abnormal discharges (zavim) and women due to discharges that are not menstrual (zavot) and women who become impure due to menstrual blood (niddot) and women who recently gave birth are automatically purified by the rush of this holy water.[54] The prophet Zechariah's vision for a future time is then cited: "On that day, there shall be a fountain opened for the House of David [beit David] and to the inhabitants of Jerusalem for purification and [for ridding themselves of] uncleanness (לְחַטָּאת וּלְנִדָּה)" (Zeḥariah 13:1). This future house purifies not by sacrifices or priests but simply by covering bodies with its bounty, that is, with an endless supply of the purest water. This flow of water ensures that impurities are reversed and that sins, which were once removed by the sin offerings that accompanied these immersions, are expunged.[55] Blood that once streamed through the Temple from the slaughter of sacrifices and ceremonies that required the sprinkling of blood are now replaced by a new paradigm—one of regeneration—signified by an unending fountain of water purifying all within its reach. The image of a future bayit with no priestly leaders and as a nongendered space becomes the model of a spiritual bayit where all bodily impurities are purged.[56]

In this final chapter of Bavli Yoma, the stammaim flesh out the tannaitic prohibitions that define self-denial. More significant, they acknowledge that the rite of self-denial has entailed denying the body of the very resources its needs to survive and acknowledging that some people are more fragile than others. The image of water bubbling up from the very core of the Holy of Holies promises the availability of a resource often scarce in life for survival and for purification: water. And while droughts can threaten the subsistence of households, they can also disallow the kind of ritual immersions needed for procreative sex and therefore the assurance of progeny, which provides the rabbis the future they so desire. In the rabbinic imagination, the purifying force of water enables individuals to engage in sexual relationships. As well, mention of the House of David serves as a reminder that the rabbis are linked to a messianic future emerging from the line of David and not from a line of priests.

Finally, Bavli Yoma rejects the more stringent understanding of asceticism exhibited by other religious groups, including Christians, for whom sexual renunciation was paramount.[57] By making the point that Yom Kippur is an ascetic rite that can still embrace a new profile, one that is partially rooted in acts of self-denial but integrally connected to sexuality and procreation, Bavli Yoma intervenes in the project of rabbinic self-definition and self-determination. For priests, as they are described in this tractate, physical purity and nonsexuality are intimately connected to atonement and Temple performance, the high priest standing out as an elite member, accountable to all. Fortunately for the non-priest, physical purity, while vital, is now not clearly linked to men or women's ability to atone. In working to balance sexuality and ascetic behaviors into a complex religious structure that can be identified as rabbinic Judaism, the redactors of Bavli Yoma choose and manipulate sources, creating a through line in tractate Yoma that shifts attention away from the Temple house and the priesthood. In the end, they express that which is most important to them: a line of children who will act as their successors. So significant are progeny that they might even be conceived on the day of Yom Kippur itself, the holiest of days.

The Case of Purity and Impurity

AFTERWORD

...

From sacrificial knives with handles of gold to expensive tunics and lamps that sparkle, splendid objects recall the Temple's lavish materiality. Implements housed in a geometric space of interlocking chambers, gates, and doors, with enough animals, incense, and water to ensure its continued operation, provide an image of a grand bayit. Gaston Bachelard has argued that the "house is one of the greatest powers of integration for the thoughts, memories and dreams of mankind," a statement that rings true for the houses of Bavli Yoma.[1] This tractate bears the signs of sustained thinking about what it means to be housed and what, at baseline, houses must possess to survive and flourish. The redactors' move from the most hierarchical of Temple rites, the service of Yom Kippur and its many components, to the non-Temple rite, defined by the absence of food, water, anointing, adornment, and sexual relations.

Yom Kippur serves as a prime locus for the rabbis to build an imagined Temple house on the embers of memories of it, but it is also where they can think about what stabilizes and destabilizes households. In so doing, they critique the Temple and think about the ordinary household not as a replacement ritual site but as a place where eating, drinking, washing, and caring for oneself and others happens. Through the choices they make regarding their sources—from the earliest rabbis, the tannaim and amoraim, to the anonymous voices—Bavli Yoma's redactors craft a literary unit that reflects what it means to be housed in Babylonia, without the Temple house.

Bavli Yoma's focus on the Temple house sets the stage for using a feminist analysis to illuminate aspects often overlooked when approaching a rabbinic document about the Temple and its male priests. Rather than considering what Bavli Yoma says about the Yom Kippur rite and its details, a feminist investigation captures the issues that often arise when thinking about houses and the people who inhabit them—marriage, motherhood, fatherhood, domesticity, sexuality (including sexual purity laws), and birthing children—issues that reach beyond the dramatization of the Yom Kippur rite. The relationships commonly associated with houses, including that of husband-wife (chapter one), father-son (chapter two), mother-son (chapters three, four, and five), and brother-brother (chapter five), function as literary tropes that unsettle the Temple house.[2] In Bavli Yoma, priests are constructed as husbands who treat their wives as if they are Temple implements without human agency, needed only for performing the Temple avodah on Yom Kippur (chapter one). The high priest, as the rabbis imagine him, held on to "one wife" "for that one day" in order to perform his priestly duties on the highest of Holy Days. Similarly, while mothers are mentioned along with their priest-sons, they are not mentioned with their husbands, even though it is husbands who grant sons priestly blood ties. When mothers exhibit appropriate rabbinic values, as Helene did, their values are not transmitted to their own sons or to the priests they try to support with Temple donations (chapter three). Sons of mothers with unsuitable, self-serving values, such as those who prepare expensive priestly tunics that are transparent, don their mothers' gifts—only to be moved aside by brothers who step up to replace them (chapter five). When mothers and fathers push their values to extreme limits, as does Kimhit, who is overly pious (chapter four), and a father who claims his son's death as capable of atoning for the sins of the people (chapter two), these mothers, fathers, and their sons are all mocked. Through presenting such relationships, the rabbis reflect a desire to take down the Temple's hierarchical structure by associating familial dysfunction with its priests, weakening the image of the priesthood.[3] In this way, a feminist analysis exposes a thread running through Bavli Yoma where the rabbis critique the priests and the Temple without communicating a sense of longing for its return.

In addition, the very structure of the Temple and its chambers, and the purity within, is shaken by a comparison to the lived-in or ancillary houses that define everyday life in chapter one of the tractate. A discussion about the mezuzah aligns the Temple with "undignified" house structures (by comparison), such as the tannery (*beit haborski*), the bathhouse (*beit hamerhatz*), the house of immersion (*beit hatevilah*), and the bathroom (*beit hakise*). Impurities that seep into the very structures of houses (nega'im) become a means to challenge whether Jerusalem, synagogues, and houses of study can ever absorb the Temple's holiness. But wedged between the least holy of houses and the Temple is the ordinary house inhabited by men and women and children and to which this journey through Bavli Yoma ultimately points. In the eighth and final chapter of the tractate, the rabbis move away from the priests to confront their own human condition in ways that distance themselves from the Temple and its priests but also call into question the strength of the rabbinic houses they wish to construct.

Building on what is amiss in the Temple house, the rabbis are making space for something different—new ideas and new relationships—all within different houses. The Temple, constructed of stone and mortar, reliant on the wealth of its constituency, rooted in hierarchy and dependent on leaders related by bloodline, is all about materiality, class, and ancestry. In a stark reversal in the eighth and final chapter of the tractate, discussions about the non-Temple Yom Kippur focus on the eating, drinking, and reproducing human being—male or female, rabbi or priest. The priestly hierarchy is moved aside. Everyone is required to practice inui nefesh on Yom Kippur—men, women, and even children are included. Any image of a substitute house to replace the holy Temple, any yearning for a Temple past or any rite that conjures memories of priests performing the Yom Kippur avodah, does not surface.

In comparison to the most hierarchical Temple rite of Yom Kippur, the practice of inui nefesh represents what threatens everyone—fathers, mothers, wives, husbands, children, pregnant women, brides, rabbis, disciples, judges, and kings, regardless of gender, class, or ancestry. The rite is connected to the hope that everyone will be, as they are on Yom Kippur, minimally sustained at the very least. The various leniencies introduced into the discussion of inui nefesh are intended to ensure that the rabbinic household, specifically its members, are poised to survive, particularly in the face of practicing a set of prohibitions. But in the rabbis' arguments for their own survival in the face of ascetic practices that can be threatening to all, what emerges at this crossroad from Bavli Yoma is the ability of its final redactors to consider what the underside of power truly looks like.[4] The rite of Yom Kippur asks human beings to look deeply to their own nature, to their human condition. Through the instrument of self-denial one is to consider that no human being is immune from human frailty, the antipole of power.[5] Like the Temple, mundane houses are equally insecure spaces, dependent as they are on the availability of resources such as food and water, on the health and well-being of their members, and on the ability of the rabbis (as leaders) to be guiding forces by making correct judgments.

Afterword

For all of that, the greatest threat communicated in the eighth chapter of Bavli Yoma is that there might be no bloodline. The rabbis look to the patriline of the priests with envy, wishing for biological progeny produced through their seed, despite the value they place on the meritocracy of the master-disciple relationship. Circling back to the beginning of the tractate, material associated with the first mishnah accentuates that a seminal emission disqualifies the high priest from performing the Yom Kippur rite, yet at the virtual end of Bavli Yoma, men have seminal emissions on Yom Kippur itself. In fact, seminal emissions on Yom Kippur have a new incarnation as signs from God that predict future progeny. The sexed body becomes a glorified rendering in comparison to the priest serving in the Temple. Additionally, by virtue of insisting that immersions for sexual impurities take place in their legally proper time, even on Yom Kippur, in the final sugya (BT Yoma 88a), the rabbis have more assurance that reproduction can and will happen. For the rabbinic household to survive, there must be future offspring.

And yet despite the fact that Yom Kippur observance falls equally on both men and women, the final word in Bavli Yoma still belongs to men. Sated sexually by seminal emissions on Yom Kippur, it is men who receive signs from God that they will produce offspring. No mention is made of the women who bear these children. This gender-biased binary social structure, it seems, is too powerful, too comforting for the rabbis, too structurally embedded in rabbinic culture to be abandoned.[6] For the rabbis, the lack of power they fear—whether political, religious, or human—prompts a desire for more control. To advance their influence, the rabbis disempower whole classes of people who might have just as much power as they do—such as women who birth children and priests who have biblically mandated rights to Jewish leadership, even without a Temple. Gendered stereotypes abound then and now, indicating that culture is powerful. But does rabbinic culture have to be determinative? Can the past point us in more than one direction, offering us a choice of different futures? Do these texts have to work even now, for us, in the ways they always have?[7] Could there be, should there be, alternate methods by which they can be studied? To follow Julia Watts Belser's call for reconstitutive ethics, I argue for the notion that a rabbinic document such as Bavli Yoma can provoke us toward new ways of thinking not actually stated in the texts themselves.[8] Like the rabbis, we too can rethink the meaning of bayit. As the rabbis look for new models of leadership and try to think about what life looks like from the view of the household, Bavli Yoma reminds us of the need to think about what turns households into spaces where human beings can flourish.

When I think about cultivating thriving households on the coattails of Bavli Yoma, Sarah Ruddick's work *Maternal Thinking: Toward a Politics of Peace* comes to mind. Like the rabbis in their relation to the priests, Ruddick finds in the mother-child relationship an interpersonal dynamic that is enviable. However, when Ruddick calls attention to this relationship, she points to it as an alternative power model that teaches us, even requires us, to give voice and agency to the less powerful, the child. Mothering is both an act of power and recognized powerlessness. Mothers nurture with the knowledge that an acknowledged powerlessness will take over where power once was as they lead their children to become independent adults.[9] To accomplish this, mothers must assert and willingly concede power at the same time, not as the rabbis, who in recognizing their own fragility override it by asserting control over others to empower themselves. Such an ideal, if taken on by mothers and non-mothers alike, resonates with me as I think about the "houses" we can construct and deconstruct today.

Enmeshed as we are in who constitutes a family, deciding who can be part of a community, who can marry whom, who is a Jew, who we call our children, and the biases associated with childlessness (either desired or not), at the end of Bavli Yoma "we" are poised to make arguments for "our" own choices. Like the rabbis who decide to ultimately distance themselves from the Temple grandeur and its priestly hierarchy, we can appeal to our strength to resist the cultural forces that have and continue to define the Jewish house.[10] What is a house or a home if not something we ourselves have the freedom to define?[11] What is a family without the right to decide who is considered part of it? We need to become people who never think about power without thinking about our own powerlessness and theirs. Adopting the mother-child relationship as a model, not as the rabbis do to critique the Temple house and priesthood but as a way to become maternal thinkers, can help us chart the course of caring for others, guiding them through life's passages. Whether we have children or not, whether we are male, female, or nonbinary, thinking about the practice of mothering will offer us new ways of living in all of the houses we inhabit, not as mothers necessarily but as people who "mother."

Afterword

Finally, as a scholar, I have used this study of Bavli Yoma to think about my own disciplinary house and to stand alongside others who value studying the tractate as a literary unit. My ability to locate a narrative thread running throughout the tractate related to the theme of the house by virtue of a feminist analysis supports the argument of viewing the Bavli's anonymous redactors as authors with redactional agendas. Like Moulie Vidas and Mira Wasserman, I have argued here that Bavli Yoma reflects a self-conscious authorial voice, that is, authors who choose which sources to include and which to exclude, which earlier sources to align with later ones, which sources to emend, and, finally, where to insert their anonymous voices in order to convey a particular message authoritatively. Indeed, the authors of Bavli Yoma produce a work of "thematic breadth," to use Wasserman's words.[12]

I know that I have challenged many who divide tractates into historical layers rooted in the belief that the Bavli is an anthology of sources. No doubt, even Bavli Yoma appears fragmented; it meanders from one topic to another, integrates subjects connected to and disconnected from Yom Kippur into its discourse, and speaks via association that runs off course.[13] However, approaching the tractate from a macro view divulges a coherent literary scope. It pushes us to see that not all rabbis mourned the loss of the Temple. Not all saw themselves and the houses they constructed as contiguous with the Temple of Jerusalem. Its materiality, its lavishness, its support of a priestly caste cared for by non-priests meant that for some rabbis, an essential break was desired. Not all wished to re-form the hierarchical priesthood by proposing a new hierarchy modeled exactly on it. And not all wished to re-create the Temple in their everyday homes or ritual lives; Yom Kippur, as discussed in the eighth chapter of Bavli Yoma, is a case in point. When it came down to it, minimal subsistence, including food, water, and sexual relations, became more central to this tractate than replacing the Temple house with the house of study. Birthing children turned out to be more significant than cultivating the master-disciple relationship, more powerful in ensuring the rabbis' succession line. Looking at the whole tractate rather than its individual parts brought me to see unexpectedly another side of the rabbis. This undertaking enabled me to witness that as powerful as the memory of the Temple is in rabbinic literature and postrabbinic literature, it was not necessarily a house to which all rabbis wanted to return. I was able to look beyond Yom Kippur and beyond the presumption that Bavli Yoma was a tractate primed

186 *Bringing Down the Temple House*

to narrate and remember a Temple Yom Kippur rite "in all its glory." It is my hope that this analysis of Bavli Yoma will encourage scholars to interact with this tractate and others in a manner that rediscovers and brings to the fore the authorial threads that might problematize still further the nature of the rabbinic house and its connection to the Temple bayit. I also hope that such an exercise will generate within each of us a desire to rethink the houses we now inhabit and those we still need to build.

ACKNOWLEDGMENTS

• • •

I look forward to Yom Kippur every year. It is the day when I am completely absorbed in an observance of a Jewish holiday without worrying about the domestic tasks that often draw my attention away from the central meaning of holiday observances. On Yom Kippur, I can focus my attention inward on my religious self; it is exceptional time. Writing this book about Bavli Yoma was, ironically, a parallel experience. This past year amid the global pandemic, every social event, every conference, every public teaching engagement that required travel, not to mention every Jewish holiday, was effectively cancelled. As frightening as the pandemic was, staying safe meant an escape from the frenetic daily routine as well as the many chores connected with living according to a Jewish calendar. Every day ensured me long blocks of time to think and to write, broken up only by meal making. Every day there was time to be alone in my thoughts, completely immersed in the solitary ritual of writing as my family continued their work in the spaces around me. Inside my house, the study of Bavli Yoma became my respite from a world that was coming apart. Lockdown felt like a never-ending period distinct from any other time I had ever experienced. Like Yom Kippur, it allowed me to turn inward and think about what mattered to me. It has been a year of exceptional time.

I gratefully acknowledge that it took a small village of people to complete this book. With much gratitude I recognize Tal Ilan who in spearheading a feminist commentary project on the Babylonian Talmud invited me to work on Bavli Yoma. Scholarly gatherings at Freie Universität Berlin organized by Tal Ilan; at Stanford's University Taube Center for Jewish Studies organized by Charlotte Fonrobert; and at the Katz Center for Advanced Judaic Studies at the University of Pennsylvania organized by Steven Weitzman (funded by the Taube Center and the Katz Center) made vital contributions to the development of my feminist approach to this tractate.

Conceptualizing the frame for this book, however, and the move from writing a feminist commentary to embarking on a monograph, occurred during the time that I was a fellow at the Katz Center for Advanced Judaic Studies at the University of Pennsylvania. The theme of the 2019–2020 fellowship year was "The Jewish Home: Dwelling on the Domestic, the Familial, and the Lived-In." Committed as I was to ensuring that my sabbatical time would be productive, I moved to Philadelphia believing that to write a book about the Jewish "home," I needed to leave home. That proved to be an excellent strategy until the spread of COVID-19 prompted the University of Pennsylvania to close its campus.

Abruptly the rules changed. I lost my scholarly cohort and my ready access to the Katz Center library. Although I had to return home far earlier than expected, it was those invaluable months at the center where I gained the momentum to work during the months at home that followed. This is a far better book because of the time I spent at the Katz Center with a cohort of remarkable colleagues. My thanks to Steven Weitzman, Natalie Dohrmann, the supportive staff, and all of the members of this fellowship year for the most productive and stimulating year of my career. Special thanks to Melissa Cradic, Federica Francesconi, Pratima Gopalakrishnan, Katherine Sorrels, and Gregg Gardner who continued to read drafts of my work in the months after we returned home, enabling me to revise and meet the deadlines set by Brandeis University Press.

Among the greatest gifts I have had in preparing this book is the great fortune of learning with and from so many students at the Jewish Theological Seminary where I am a faculty member. I cannot thank them enough — the graduate, rabbinical, and List College students, as well as participants in JTS's adult education programs in schools and synagogues across the country, together with whom I studied Bavli Yoma. You all helped me to hone my views and mold my thoughts. Each one of you inspired me with your contagious interest. Most especially, I thank the forty-five rabbis at the JTS Rabbinic Leadership Training Institute in winter 2020 who pushed me to think more deeply about Yoma while in the middle of writing this book. I hope that all of you hear your voices in these pages.

Many thanks as well to my colleagues at the Jewish Theological Seminary for their continuous support for my work. From the incredible faculty to the entire support staff, each of you have contributed to bringing this book to completion. Special thanks to the librarians, David Kraemer, Naomi Steinberger, and Ina Cohen, for enabling me to do my research at every turn. My thanks to our present chancellor and past provost, Shuly Rubin Schwartz, for all of her encouragement and commitment to my pursuit of this scholarly endeavor; our previous provost, Alan Cooper, and to our previous chancellor, Arnold Eisen; as well as esteemed members of my Department of Rabbinic Literatures and Cultures — Judith Hauptman (emeritus) and Joel Roth (emeritus), Eliezer Diamond, Richard Kalmin, David Kraemer, Jonathan Milgram, Rachel Rosenthal, Jason Rogoff, Mordechai Schwartz, Burton

Visotzky, and Sarah Wolf—and of course to my dear friend Amy Kalmanofsky. I am also grateful to Vivian Mann (z"l) for sharing her love of material Jewish culture and who with incredible charm and warmth modeled what it means to be a caring teacher and devoted scholar.

I am also grateful to so many other supportive colleagues who read drafts, came to presentations of my work, served as peer reviewers, and shared insights that helped me to write this book, including: Elizabeth Shanks Alexander, Carole Balin, Mara Benjamin, Beth Berkowitz, Aryeh Cohen, Naftali Cohn, Erez DeGolan, Charlotte Fonrobert, Gregg Gardner, Simcha Gross, Chaya Halberstam, Tal Ilan, Jane Kanarek, Sarit Kattan Gribetz, Rebecca Kobrin, Naomi Koltun-Fromm, Gail Labovitz, Luciana Lederman, Sarra Lev, Dalia Marx, Miriam Meir, Viola Alianov Rautenberg, Rachel Rosenthal, Nancy Sinkoff, Mira Wasserman, Sarah Wolf, and Dvora Weissberg.

Many thanks to the Frankel Center for Judaic Studies at the University of Michigan for awarding me a fellowship to work on Bavli Yoma within the framework of a year focused on gender in 2014. It was there that I wrote two preliminary articles that were revised and incorporated into this book. Most especially I thank Beth Wenger, the head fellow, and Deborah Dash Moore, who was the head of the center at the time, for recognizing the value of my contribution to the field and who encouraged me to focus intently despite the commute from New York City to Detroit. Deborah's words to me when I accepted the fellowship—"to invest in myself"—ring true to this day as I keep trying to balance family and the need to carve out space to do what I love, which is to contribute to the field of Talmud and Rabbinics.

Working with co-project directors—Michelle Chesner Margolis, Joshua Teplitsky, and Adam Shear—on a digital humanities project, Footprints: Jewish Books through Time and Place, about the journeys of copies of Jewish books across the globe, offered me ongoing inspiration. Our weekly meetings, whether spent writing an article or discussing next steps in expanding our database, always reminded me of the difficult process involved in articulating ideas, even for these most gifted of academics. Every Tuesday when we reach the end of our meetings, I am so thankful for the ways in which they have taught me to think and work outside my silo. Many thanks for your strong colleagueship and friendship.

I am ever so indebted to my copyeditor, Baynon McDowell, without whom I could not have put the finishing touches on the manuscript for this book. Her utter care with regard to my work has been invaluable. She can now even read Talmudic texts with a critical eye. My gratitude to Sylvia Fuks Fried for encouraging me at every turn and without whom I would not have

Acknowledgments   191

completed this manuscript. And of course many many thanks to all those at Brandeis University Press and Hadassah Brandeis who have carefully overseen every stage of the process of bringing this book into the world, including Sylvia Barack Fishman, Lisa Fishbayn Joffe, and Heather Tamarkin.

Immense gratitude to the artist Jacqueline Nicholls, whose artwork appears on the cover of this book. Thank you for adding such a significant feminist voice to the project of reading Talmud. Your work is inspirational.

In the end, though, it comes down to the love of friends and family. Mine have sustained and continue to sustain me at every turn. Thank you to devoted Wellesley friends: Carole Balin, Joanne Levine, Iris Kopeloff, Beth Notar, Carrie Goodman Pianin, Kirsten Russell, and Rahmawati Sih. I cannot begin to tell you how much I treasure your friendship. Special thanks to Abby Knopp for walking through Central Park with me every Shabbat morning (no matter the weather) during the pandemic. You listened to me talk about the contents of this book and complain about the utterly time-consuming process about which so few understand. Our walks inspired me to keep going. My thanks to Freddy Slomovic for always taking such sincere interest in my work, reading every book I write, including this one. To Rebecca Kobrin for her unending generosity and spirit, pushing me with a phone call every other day to keep me on track, and to Nancy Sinkoff, who never allowed me to lose faith in myself and promised me that I could get it done. Thank you to Marcie Cappell, Todd Chenko, Diana Heller Friedman, Laura Radensky, Rachel Seder, Sarah Sternklar, Amy Weill, Didi Wallerstein, and Ariel Zwang. All of you have seen me through this project with unconditional love and support.

No one could be more fortunate to have such loving parents as Sheila and Wallace Lehman, who believe in being passionate about an idea, utterly value and share my commitment to the field of Jewish studies, and take enormous pride in my devotion to it. They raised me to love learning and to love the Talmud, all the while instilling in me a sense of responsibility to share what I have learned. Thank you for always finding a way to enjoy the classes I teach and for finding the time to zoom in not only to my presentations but also to those given by my students. I love the way you are proud of me for teaching them. I am exceedingly fortunate to have wonderfully supportive and caring in-laws, Leah and Henry Klapholz; a fun-loving aunt and uncle, Maddy and Harvey Krauser, who constantly remind me how important it is to love living life; loving and highly devoted siblings who can always make me laugh, Nancy and Samuel Leibowitz, Daniel and Deborah Lehman, and Marc Klapholz; as well as lively and loving nieces and nephews, Alexan-

192   *Acknowledgments*

der, Doria, Joshua, Aviva, and Rachel. My cousin Lori Kass is in every way like another sister to me, and along with her husband, David, and children, Abby and Zev, always remind us of what truly matters in this life.

For the months of the pandemic, every dinner revolved around discussions about the priests in the Temple, which as my son likes to recall sarcastically, kept them "on the edge of their seats." In the beginning, there was much willingness on the part of my husband and sons to talk through my ideas and encourage me to keep going. My family humored me. Kept me laughing. By the end, however, there was much eye-rolling and an insistence that I add only two more words to the book, "The End." They were done. I was done. It was time to let go. There was much more to say, but it was time to think about the next book. It is because of my husband, Ari, and our children, Jonah and Gabriel, that my days are filled with the best that life has to offer. With every passing day, I love them more. As I bring this book to its conclusion, I feel nothing but gratitude and love for them. This book is as much theirs as it is mine. It is to them that I dedicate it.

Acknowledgments

NOTES

...

INTRODUCTION

1. The Feminist Commentary on the Babylonian Talmud project, edited by Tal Ilan, considers the tractate as a unit of analysis but premises the instances where women are mentioned as the basis for its commentary. The objective is to bring Talmudic passages to light that have often been overlooked in traditional commentaries. Authors have mined a chosen Babylonian Talmudic tractate searching for relevant passages that mention women. Its volumes differ from monographs written on tractates of the Bavli in that the focus is not on exposing the thematics that emerge or locating a narrative arc, but rather on allowing the base text to drive the analyses in commentary style. The following volumes have been completed: Tal Ilan, *Massekhet Ta'anit: A Feminist Commentary on the Babylonian Talmud* (Tübingen: Mohr Siebeck, 2008); Shulamit Valer, *Massekhet Sukkah: A Feminist Commentary on the Babylonian Talmud* (Tübingen: Mohr Siebeck, 2009); Tamara Or, *Massekhet Betsah: A Feminist Commentary on the Babylonian Talmud* (Tübingen: Mohr Siebeck, 2010); Federico Dal Bo, *Massekhet Keritot: A Feminist Commentary on the Babylonian Talmud* (Tübingen: Mohr Siebeck, 2013); Dalia Marx, *Tractates Tamid, Middot and Qinnim: A Feminist Commentary on the Babylonian Talmud* (Tübingen: Mohr Siebeck, 2013); Tal Ilan, *Massekhet Hullin: A Feminist Commentary on the Babylonian Talmud* (Tübingen: Mohr Siebeck, 2017); Dvora Weisberg, *Massekhet Menahot: A Feminist Commentary on the Babylonian Talmud* (Tübingen: Mohr Siebeck, 2020); and Gail Labovitz, *Massekhet Moed Katan: A Feminist Commentary on the Babylonian Talmud* (Tübingen: Mohr Siebeck, 2021).

2. Building on the work of Charlotte Fonrobert in her feminist analysis of the Babylonian tractate Nidah, I recognized that for the redactors of tractate Yoma, spatial metaphors were also key to a discourse related to power and control. As Fonrobert argues, metaphors related to the house turn women's bodies into architectural constructs in an attempt to both understand and control them. See Charlotte Elisheva Fonrobert, *Menstrual Purity: Rabbinic and Christian Reconstructions of Biblical Gender* (Stanford: Stanford University Press, 2000), 40–68. Also see Cynthia M. Baker's book, *Rebuilding the House of Israel: Architectures of Gender in Jewish Antiquity* (Stanford: Stanford University Press, 2002), where she also makes the argument that a house is

not only "where" a woman/wife is, but is also part of "who" and "what" she is (35). My argument expands on their observations, noting how the rabbis use the relationships of the household, building on the equation of "wife" and "house," to deconstruct the Temple house. Women stabilize the house, according to Fonrobert. However, the breakdown of the relationships associated with houses, such as that of the husband-wife and parent-child, bring the instability of the house, especially the Temple house, to the fore. Whereas Hayim Lapin, in his exploration of the mishnaic household, looks at houses as sites of domestic, economic, and ritual behavior, my study here, in contrast, focuses singularly on the familial relationships of husband-wife, mother-son, father-son, and brother-brother and how they help shape the disparate sources in the Bavli into an argument that runs throughout the tractate. See Hayim Lapin, "The Construction of Households in the Mishnah," in *The Mishnah in Contemporary Perspective*, ed. Alan J. Avery-Peck and Jacob Neusner (Leiden: Brill, 2006), 55–80.

3. The texts of Bavli Yoma at the center of this feminist analysis are those where the bodies of women and men intersect with the Temple bayit and the everyday house. For this reason, the women who appear in these texts are not found in the market, on the street, in the *beit midrash* (house of study), in the *beit din* (court), or inside the Temple courtyards. I align myself in part methodologically with Ishay Rosen-Zvi, who in his work on Mishnah Sotah suggests the need to produce more narrowly focused studies of the rabbis' use of gender, analyzing specific cases (mine being Bavli Yoma). In doing so, we are able to resist generalizing about the rabbis' process of gendering and its purposes. With that, we can become more nuanced readers who better detect the different processes of marginalization and mechanisms of exclusion on the part of the rabbis. As Ishay Rosen-Zvi correctly illuminates, at the root of every exclusion, every act of differentiation, is a different problem. *The Mishnaic Sotah Ritual: Temple, Gender and Midrash* (Leiden: Brill, 2012), 11. See my article "Feet in the Rabbinic Imagination and the Prohibition against Wearing Shoes on Yom Kippur," *AJS Review* 43, no. 2 (2019): 321, where I offer another example of Rosen-Zvi's approach.

4. Shelly Matthews, "Thinking of Thecla: Issues in Feminist Historiography," *Journal of Feminist Studies in Religion* 17, no. 2 (2001): 46–54; Elizabeth Clark "The Lady Vanishes: Dilemmas of a Feminist Historian after the 'Linguistic Turn,'" *Church History* 67 (1998): 12–13.

5. Kate Cooper, "Apostles, Ascetic Women, and Questions of Audience: New Reflections on the Rhetoric of Gender in the Apocryphal Acts," *Society of Biblical Literature Seminar Papers* 31 (Atlanta: Scholars Press, 1992), 147–

153, and her *The Virgin and the Bride: Idealized Womanhood in Late Antiquity* (Cambridge, MA: Harvard University Press, 1996).

6. Indeed, what we see here is not only a contest of authority among men, as Kate Cooper points out, but one taking place between men and men as well as between men and women, rooted in the rabbis' insecurities. See Cooper, *Virgin and the Bride*, 55.

7. See Mieke Bal, *Death and Dissymmetry: The Politics of Coherence in the Book of Judges* (Chicago: University of Chicago Press, 1988), 7.

8. In speaking about the relationships that define the households of Jewish late antiquity, I am reading rabbinic texts and gathering the rabbis' perceptions of the individuals who make up their households. In this book, I make no claims that such households inform or shape those of the present day. See Kath Weston, *Families We Choose: Lesbians, Gays, Kinship* (New York: Columbia University Press, 1991).

9. Baker, *Rebuilding the House of Israel*, 55–66, 192, n. 67, argues that the term *bayit* connects persons, institutions, and locations and signifies a whole complex of intersecting routines and relations. Whereas Baker argues that the meanings of bayit resonate with one another, I argue that in Bavli Yoma, the rabbis use a particular and more limited conceptualization of the household and its inhabitants to critique the Temple bayit.

10. The narrative that has dominated Jewish historiography for most of the twentieth century describes the post–Second Temple period (post-70 CE) as marked by the rapid decline of a priestly hierarchy, making room for the swift rise of a rabbinic elite. This historical perspective is challenged not only by epigraphic and archaeological remains, but also by Jewish literature from the period, which supports the idea that priests continued to identify as priests, maintained their economic standing by continuing to receive tithes, and played a role in the religious and political affairs affecting the Jewish community after the Temple was destroyed. For a discussion of the role of the priests in the aftermath of the destruction of the Temple, see Matthew Grey, "Jewish Priests and the Social History of Post-70 Palestine" (PhD diss., University of North Carolina, 2011), 6–12, 84; Seth Schwartz, *Josephus and Judean Politics* (Leiden: Brill, 1990), 58–109; Stuart A. Cohen, *The Three Crowns: Structure of Communal Politics in Early Rabbinic Jewry* (Cambridge: Cambridge University Press, 1990), 158–171; Catherine Hezser, *The Social Structure of the Rabbinic Movement* (Tübingen: Mohr Siebeck, 1997), 487; and Geoffrey Herman, "Priests and Amoraic Leadership in Sassanian Babylonia," *Proceedings of the Twelfth World Congress of Jewish Studies* (Jerusalem: World Union of Jewish Studies, 2000), 65–66.

Notes to Introduction

11. This is distinct from what I argue elsewhere regarding the Temple bayit. I have noted that the concept of bayit, which is used to define many institutions, places, and people in rabbinic culture, conjures up a pervading desire for all that the Temple connotes. I have not found that to be the case in Bavli Yoma. See my chapter "Reimagining Home, Rethinking Sukkah: Rabbinic Discourse and its Contemporary Implications," in *Jews at Home: The Domestication of Identity*, ed. Simon J. Bronner (Oxford: Littman Library of Jewish Civilization, 2009), 110–111.

12. See Moshe Simon-Shoshan, "Talmud as Novel: Dialogic Discourse and the Feminine Voice in the Babylonian Talmud," *Poetics Today* 40, no. 1 (2019): 218, who argues that these ideological perspectives are often driven by giving voice to the "other"—common people, non-Jews, women, and heretics. As he sees it, these voices are "social and ideologically distinct from the dominant voice of the stam and the rabbinic establishment in general."

13. Like Fonrobert in *Menstrual Purity*, 9, I also look for a counter-discourse in rabbinic literature, that is, moments of rupture in the androcentric fabric. Also see Daniel Boyarin's discussion regarding approaches to reading rabbinic texts in "Rabbinic Resistance to Male Domination: A Case Study in Talmudic Cultural Poetics," in *Interpreting Judaism in a Postmodern Age*, ed. Steven Kepnes (New York: New York University Press, 1995), 119; Jana Sawicki, *Disciplining Foucault: Feminism, Power, and the Body: Thinking Gender* (New York: Routledge, 1991), 14; Boyarin, *Carnal Israel: Reading Sex in Talmudic Culture* (Berkeley: University of California Press, 1993), 227–228; and Boyarin, "Reading Androcentrism against the Grain: Women, Sex, and Torah-Study, *Poetics Today*, 12, no. 1 (1991): 29–30.

14. Goce Naumov, "Embodied Houses: The Social and Symbolic Agency of Neolithic Architecture in the Republic of Macedonia," in *Tracking the Neolithic House in Europe: Sedentism, Architecture, and Practice*, ed. Daniela Hofmann and Jessica Smyth (New York: Springer, 2013), 66. Claude Levi-Strauss, *Structural Anthropology* (New York: Basic Books, 1963), 61, argues that women are always more than signs in texts. He writes, "Words do not speak, while women do; as producers of signs, women can never be reduced to the status of symbols or tokens."

15. Renato Rosaldo, "Notes toward a Critique of Patriarchy from a Male Position," *Anthropological Quarterly* 66, no. 2 (1993): 81, 86, argues that the mistreatment of men by other men of a different class or race has received far less attention than the male mistreatment of women. See Michael G. Peletz, "Neither Reasonable nor Responsible: Contrasting Representations of Masculinity in a Malay Society," *Cultural Anthropology*, 9, no. 2 (1994): 137;

and David Gilmore, *Manhood in the Making: Cultural Conceptions of Masculinity* (New Haven: Yale University Press, 1990). Scholars such as Dalia Marx and Natan Margalit see the male priests as exhibiting feminine behaviors. See Marx, *Tractates Tamid, Middot and Qinnim*, 11–12, and Natan Margalit, "Priestly Men and Invisible Women: Male Appropriation of the Feminine and the Exemption of Women from Positive Time-Bound Commandments," *AJS Review* 28, no. 2 (2004): 303–304.

16. Marx, *Tractates Tamid, Middot and Qinnim*, 11–14, argues that the priests represent a "a gender unto themselves" as well as a "nonmasculine manhood." They are a distinct class whose gender is always relative.

17. For an example of scholarly discussions about the rabbis' attempts to define themselves in contrast to "others," including women, gentiles, and non-rabbinic Jews, see Mira Balberg, "The Emperor's Daughter's New Skin: Bodily Otherness and Self-Identity in the Dialogues of Rabbi Yehoshua ben Hanania and the Emperor's Daughter," *Jewish Studies Quarterly* 19 (2012): 182; and *Purity, Body, and Self in Early Rabbinic Literature* (Berkeley: University of California Press, 2014).

18. M. Yoma 1:3; BT Yoma 18a. Due to the lack of knowledge of the priests, the rabbis instruct them how to perform the Yom Kippur rite.

19. BT Yoma 29b, where priests who did not arrange *panim* (bread) properly are compared to monkeys.

20. BT Yoma 35b, where priests appear naked in tunics made for them by their mothers. I discuss this in chapter five.

21. BT Yoma 9a notes that most high priests served less than a year. See the parallel in JT Yoma 1:1, 38c. Joshua ben Gamala was appointed as high priest when his wife paid off the king (BT Yoma 18ab). Jonathan Klawans, *Purity, Sacrifice, and the Temple* (Oxford: Oxford University Press, 2006), 179–187, discusses rabbinic sources revealing that the position of high priest was bought and sold. Also see his discussion and references to other places in rabbinic literature where the priests are described negatively.

22. See BT 23ab; JT 2:2, 39d where one priest stabs another. I discuss these sources in chapter two.

23. BT Yoma 29b–30a. See Lehman, "Feet in the Rabbinic Imagination and the Prohibition against Wearing Shoes on Yom Kippur," 319–338. For example, see BT Yoma 47a regarding the semen from which the priest Yishmael ben Kimhit was born. I discuss this in chapter four.

24. BT Yoma 47a.

25. BT Yoma 6ab, 13a–14a. I discuss this material in chapter one.

26. See M. Yoma 5:7 about the necessity for performing the priestly rite

in order. Performing an action out of sequence was tantamount to "ritual failure" and was as if the high priest had done nothing. See Naftali S. Cohn's discussion in *The Memory of the Temple and the Making of the Rabbis* (Philadelphia: University of Pennsylvania Press, 2013), 67. See BT Yoma 54a, where two priests with disqualifying blemishes were doing work on the wood needed for the altar but were disqualified from offering sacrifices. Also see Julia Watts Belser's theoretical treatment of the disqualification of priests from serving in the Temple: "Reading Talmudic Bodies: Disability, Narrative, and the Gaze in Rabbinic Judaism," in *Disability in Judaism, Christianity, and Islam: Sacred Texts, Historical Traditions, and Social Analysis*, ed. Darla Schumm and Michael Stolzfus (New York: Palgrave Macmillan, 2011), 12–18.

27. BT Yoma 2a–6a; 8ab; 14ab.

28. Baker, *Rebuilding the House of Israel*, 35.

29. Sarah Franklin and Susan McKinnon, "Relative Values: Reconfiguring Kinship Studies," in *Relative Values: Reconfiguring Kinship Studies*, ed. Sarah Franklin and Susan McKinnon (Durham: Duke University Press, 2001), 18–19.

30. See Elizabeth Shanks Alexander's extensive discussion of generating cultural reproduction via Torah study (in the context of discussing women and Torah study): *Gender and Timebound Commandments in Judaism* (Cambridge: Cambridge University Press, 2013), 178, 184–188. In addition to shaping disciples, Torah would then shape practice beyond the rabbis' elite circles of masters and their disciples, ensuring the future of Jewish tradition. Furthermore, fathers were responsible for teaching their sons Torah, and while biological reproduction was necessary, it was not enough to ensure that a father's identity would endure beyond him. That depended on ensuring that his son studied Torah.

31. See BT Sanhedrin 99b, where Reish Lakish highlights the idea of spiritual parenthood: "Everyone who teaches Torah to his friend's son, Scripture accounts him as though he made him." Also see Moshe Lavee's discussion of BT Sanhedrin 99b in *The Rabbinic Conversion of Judaism: The Unique Perspective of the Bavli on Conversion and the Construction of Jewish Identity* (Leiden: Brill, 2018), 104–106; and Franklin and McKinnon, "Relative Values," 13.

32. Franklin and McKinnon, "Relative Values," 4, 15.

33. Relations of power and weakness are central to the articulation of classificatory boundaries that distinguish priest from rabbi; kinship frames these boundaries in nature, in biology. Franklin and McKinnon, "Relative Values," 1–3. Also see Natalie Kampen, "Houses, Paintings, Family and

Emotion," in *Family in the Greco-Roman World*, ed. Ray Laurence and Agnata Strömberg (London: Continuum I, 2012), 167.

34. This word can mean "followers" or "family members/loved ones." Here I think it is best translated as "fellows."

35. BT Yoma 71b intimates that Shema'yah and Avtalyon were descended from the "nations" and did not have Israelite lineage. BT Gittin 57b conveys that Shema'yah and Avtalyon were the teachers of Hillel and Shammai and descended from the Assyrian Senaḥeriv (as referred to by Rashi, *D"H yaytun benai ammamin*, BT Yoma 71b).

36. Paul Frederick Lerner, Benjamin Maria Baader, and Sharon Gillerman reflect on the need for more analyses focusing on masculinities in Jewish gender studies in the introduction to their edited volume, *Jewish Masculinities: German Jews, Gender, and History* (Bloomington: Indiana University Press, 2012), 9. As well, see Björn Krondorfer, Introduction to *Men and Masculinities in Christianity and Judaism: A Critical Reader*, ed. Björn Krondorfer (London: SCM Press, 2009), xi–xxi, where he notes that critical studies of men in religion are lacking given the vast number of roles that men assumed in antiquity, from priests, to rabbis, monks, prophets, disciples, patriarchs, elders, and bishops.

37. See Naftali S. Cohn's discussion in *Memory of the Temple*, 3–4, 13, regarding the Mishnah's inclusion of many Temple narratives. He points out that because the rabbis recognized the many overlapping subgroups of Judeans who continued to see the Temple as central even after its destruction, the rabbis seized on the Temple, claiming to have precise knowledge of its workings, as a way to argue for their own significance.

38. Cohn, *Memory of the Temple*, 13–15, although Cohn focuses on the tannaitic period.

39. See Klawans's *Purity, Sacrifice, and the Temple*, 145–174, for a detailed analysis of non-rabbinic sources (Dead Sea literature) that pinpoint the lax standards and incorrect practices believed to have defiled the Temple, not to mention the notion that the Temple was morally defiled by sin. Klawans argues that rabbinic sources are not as severe in their treatment of the Temple as he argues, "[For the rabbis] there was nothing particularly wrong with the Temple that was destroyed . . . they simply want back what they lost" (175–211, esp. 210).

40. See Jonathan Z. Smith, *Map Is Not Territory: Studies in the History of Religions* (Leiden: Brill, 1978), xiii–xiv, 130–142, 160–166, 185–189, who argues that the rabbis replaced "locative" Temple ritual overseen by the priests with a newer "utopian" pattern that was not dependent on a central holy place.

Notes to Introduction

Smith also claims that such a transition was not unique to the rabbis and was a common development among religions during the Greco-Roman period. See Baruch Bokser, "Approaching Sacred Space," *Harvard Theological Review* 78, no. 3 (1985): 287–288, 298–299. And see Klawans's larger discussion and critique of this view in *Purity, Sacrifice, and the Temple*, 145–211, esp. 202.

41. BT Yoma 6ab.

42. BT Yoma 35b.

43. BT Yoma 23a.

44. BT Yoma 47a.

45. Others have argued for the significance of reading Talmudic material within a larger literary frame, as exemplified by the works of Jeffrey Rubenstein, *Talmudic Stories: Narrative Art, Composition, and Culture* (Baltimore: Johns Hopkins University Press, 1999) and *Stories of the Babylonian Talmud* (Baltimore: Johns Hopkins University Press, 2003); Barry Scott Wimpfheimer, *Narrating the Law: A Poetics of Talmudic Legal Stories* (Philadelphia: University of Pennsylvania Press, 2011); and Julia Watts Belser, *Power, Ethics, and Ecology in Jewish Late Antiquity: Rabbinic Responses to Drought and Disaster* (New York: Cambridge University Press, 2015) and *Rabbinic Tales of Destruction: Gender, Sex, and Disability in the Ruins of Jerusalem* (New York: Oxford University Press, 2018). I advance this approach of studying larger topical consolidations of Talmud-related text using an entire Babylonian tractate as a unit of analysis.

46. See Avraham Weiss, *Hithavut hatalmud bishlemuto* [The Talmud Bavli as a literary unit] (New York: Hamosad lezikhron Aleksander, 1943). For an overview of the history of Talmud scholarship in the twentieth century, see Aryeh Cohen, *Rereading Talmud: Gender, Law and the Poetics of Sugyot* (Atlanta: Scholars Press, 1998), and Mira Beth Wasserman, *Jews, Gentiles, and Other Animals* (Philadelphia: University of Pennsylvania Press, 2017), 17–24. For an overview of the Wissenschaft movement in its historical context, see Michael Meyer, *Response to Modernity: A History of the Reform Movement in Judaism* (Detroit: Wayne State University Press, 1995), 75–99. See also Ismar Schorsch, "From Wolfenbüttel to Wissenschaft: The Divergent Paths of Isaak Markus Jost and Leopold Zunz," in *The Leo Baeck Institute Year Book* 22, no. 1 (1977): 109–128.

47. Wasserman, *Jews, Gentiles, and Other Animals*, 18.

48. Moulie Vidas, *Tradition and the Formation of the Talmud* (Princeton: Princeton University Press, 2014), 1, and Richard Kalmin, "The Formation and Character of the Babylonian Talmud," in *The Cambridge History of Juda-*

ism IV: The Late Roman-Rabbinic Period, ed. Steven T. Katz (Cambridge: Cambridge University Press, 2006), 840.

49. Shamma Friedman, *Talmudic Studies: Investigating the Sugya, Variant Readings, and Aggada* (New York: Jewish Theological Seminary, 2010), 30, argued that "the collation of Amoraic formulations *apart* from the words of the anonymous layer of the Talmud shall place before scholars of Talmudic law, Jewish history and rabbinic language a *reliable* corpus, as opposed to the anonymous layer of the Talmud, in which many of the formulations, being the 'give and take,' are necessarily rejections and conjectures." And see Moulie Vidas's discussion of this point in *Tradition and the Formation of the Talmuds*, 9, in his excellent overview of scholarship on the Talmud's formation.

50. Vidas, *Tradition and the Formation of the Talmud*, 9–10.

51. See David Weiss Halivni's seminal work in English describing his theory of the stam in *Midrash, Mishnah, and Gemara: The Jewish Predilection for Justified Law* (Cambridge, MA: Harvard University Press, 1986), 76–92. In fact, Halivni coined the term *stammaim* to refer to the anonymous redactors, a word that has become central to the vocabulary Talmud scholars use to describe the anonymous layer. Also see Jeffrey L. Rubenstein's translation of Halivni's introduction to *Mekorot umesorot: Bava batra* (Jerusalem: Magnes Press, 2007) in *The Formation of the Babylonian Talmud: David Weiss Halivni* (Oxford: Oxford University Press, 2013). See Shamma Friedman, "Perek ha'ishah rabah babavli: Betzeruf mavo klali al derekh ḥeker hasugya" [A critical study of Yevamot X with a methodological introduction], in *Meḥkarim umekorot: Me'asef lemada'ei hayahadut* [Texts and studies: Analecta Judaica I], ed. Ḥayim Zalman Dimitrovsky (New York: Jewish Theological Seminary of America, 1978), 275–441. For an example of a contemporary approach to stammaitic activity, see Vidas, *Tradition and the Formation of the Talmud*, as well as his summary of the earlier approaches of Halivni, Friedman, and Yaakov Sussman, 4–5, n. 7, 8, 9; Wasserman, *Jews, Gentiles, and Other Animals*, 18.

52. Halivni, *Midrash, Mishnah, and Gemara*; Vidas, *Tradition and the Formation of the Talmud*, 4.

53. Wasserman, *Jews, Gentiles, and Other Animals*, 21.

54. Vidas, *Tradition and the Formation of the Talmud*, 13–14; 45–80, esp. 76–80, where Vidas discusses his "new appreciation of the stam."

55. Vidas, *Tradition and the Formation of the Talmud*, 81; Yaakov Elman, "Babylonian Baraitot in the Tosefta and the 'Dialectology' of Middle Hebrew," *AJS Review* 6 (1991): 2, points out that additions were made to the

Notes to Introduction   203

baraitot found in the Tosefta until the geonic period. See also Vered Noam's study of the addition of the cruse of oil into Bavli Shabbat 21b, "Nes pakh hashemen: Ha'umnam makor leverur yaḥasam shel ḥazal laḥashmona'im" [The miracle of the cruse of oil: Questioning its use as a source for assessing the sages' attitude toward the Hasmoneans], *Zion* 67 (2002), 396–400.

56. Wasserman, *Jews, Gentiles, and Other Animals*, 22.

57. Jacob Neusner, *The Reader's Guide to the Talmud* (Leiden: Brill, 2001), and *The Documentary Foundation of Rabbinic Culture: Mopping Up after the Debates with Gerald L. Bruns, S. J. D. Cohen, Arnold Maria Goldberg, Susan Handelman, Christine Hayes, James Kugel, Peter Schäfer, Eliezer Segal, E. P. Sanders, and Lawrence Schiffman* (Atlanta: Scholars Press, 1995), xvi–xx, xxii–xxv. Also see Neusner, *Judaism: Evidence of the Mishnah* (Chicago: University of Chicago Press, 1981), 1–24, and Christine Elizabeth Hayes, *Between the Babylonian and Palestinian Talmuds* (New York: Oxford University Press, 1997), 10–11.

58. Vidas, *Tradition and the Formation of the Talmud*, 12–13.

59. Wasserman, *Jews, Gentiles, and Other Animals*, 19. For example, see Watts Belser, *Rabbinic Tales of Destruction: Sex, Gender, and Disability in the Ruins of Jerusalem*, and *Power, Ethics, and Ecology in Jewish Late Antiquity: Rabbinic Responses to Drought and Disaster*); Daniel Boyarin, *Socrates and the Fat Rabbis* (Chicago: University of Chicago Press, 2009); and Wimpfheimer, *Narrating the Law: A Poetics of Talmudic Legal Studies*, 9–13, 31–37. Jeffrey Rubenstein's work looks at the literary features found in Talmudic stories and considers how these features work with adjacent dialectical material. See Jeffrey L. Rubenstein, *Talmudic Stories: Narrative Art, Composition, and Culture* (Baltimore: Johns Hopkins University Press, 1999), and *Stories of the Babylonian Talmud* (Baltimore: Johns Hopkins University Press, 2010). Rubenstein and Wimpheimer contributed valuable instruction on reading aggadic material in their larger literary frames. Other scholars, such as Daniel Boyarin in *Carnal Israel: Reading Sex in Talmudic Culture*, have pointed to the larger cultural context in which talmudic material was redacted as significant to understanding differences between, for example, Talmudic passages in the Yerushalmi versus the Bavli.

60. Wasserman, *Jews, Gentiles, and Other Animals*, 19. Jeffrey Rubenstein's *A History of Sukkot in the Second Temple and Rabbinic Periods* (Atlanta: Scholars Press, 1995) considers the entire tractate of Sukkah but is centered on using all of the corpora that deal with the holiday for the purposes of generating a history of its development and not Bavli Sukkah alone as one literary unit.

61. Wasserman, *Jews, Gentiles, and Other Animals*, 21–23. It is, of course,

possible to overread for thematic unity and force a tractate into a preconceived notion of unity that it does not possess. Nevertheless, it would be valuable to investigate more systematically whether and why some tractates possess a greater thematic unity than others. In addition, approaching the tractate as a unit of discourse also aims to challenge modes of reading, made easier by the Internet, that encourage selective and noncontextual readings of specific passages.

62. Wasserman, *Jews, Gentiles, and Other Animals*, 20. Yerushalmi Yoma, as compared to Bavli Yoma, embraces Temple ritual and the priesthood in a more positive vein. It also lacks the coherence in evidence apparent in the Bavli, appearing more as a collection of discrete sources that are not as well integrated into sugyot as in the Bavli. Many of the sources in Yerushalmi Yoma have parallels in the Bavli, but it seems that the Bavli tampered with them and built on them, as I will show. In addition, sources that appear in Yerushalmi Yoma do not necessarily appear aligned with the same mishnah or in the same chapter when they appear in the Bavli.

63. See Wimpfheimer's examples in *Narrating the Law* (e.g., 116). For a scholarly engagement with Wimpfheimer and Boyarin, see Simon-Shoshan, "Talmud as Novel," 105–112.

64. See Fonrobert, *Menstrual Purity*; Christine Elizabeth Hayes, *Between the Babylonian and Palestinian Talmuds: Accounting for Halakhic Difference in Selected Sugyot from Tractate Avodah Zarah* (New York: Oxford University Press, 1997); Alyssa M. Gray, *A Talmud in Exile: The Influence of Yerushalmi Avodah Zarah on the Formation of Bavli Avodah Zarah* (Providence: Brown University, 2005); Belser, *Rabbinic Tales of Destruction*, and Belser, *Power, Ethics, and Ecology in Jewish Late Antiquity*. Regarding studies of tractates of the Mishnah, see Baruch Bokser (on Mishnah Pesaḥim), *The Origins of the Seder: The Passover Rite and Early Rabbinic Judaism* (Berkeley: University of California Press, 1984), and Rosen-Zvi (re: Mishnah Sotah), *The Mishnaic Sotah Ritual: Temple, Gender and Midrash*.

65. BT Yoma 21a; 54a. Regarding BT Yoma 54a, see especially Rachel Neis, *The Sense of Sight in Rabbinic Culture: Jewish Ways of Seeing in Late Antiquity* (Cambridge: Cambridge University Press, 2013), 102–104. Also see Mishnah Avot 5:5, which is quoted in BT Yoma 21a, and a discussion of it in Mira Balberg, *Blood for Thought: The Reinvention of Sacrifice in Early Rabbinic Literature* (Berkeley: University of California Press, 2017), 183–184; see her discussion of the ways in which the rabbis glorify the role of sacrifices, pointing to the ways in which sacrifices are used to create an "affective portrayal of the Temple's 'golden age.'" Balberg's argument that the Yom

Notes to Introduction   205

Kippur sacrificial rite at the center of Mishnah Yoma is elided with the daily sacrificial rite holds true for Bavli Yoma as well. The final redactors wished to ground the exceptional Yom Kippur day into a seamlessly operating institution that ultimately would return (188–219). That said, where Balberg sees a heightened emphasis in Mishnah Yoma on Temple offerings as manifestations of perfect procedure, I see the pejorative attitude toward the priests (in the Mishnah and in the Bavli). I view the rabbis' constant supervision of the priests as a means of critique, distancing themselves from the Temple and making room for themselves.

66. Jacob Milgrom, *Leviticus 1–16: A New Translation with Introduction and Commentary* (New Haven: Yale University Press, 1998), 1066–1070, where he argues that inui (self-denial) was not initially part of the ten-day New Year's festival that culminated on the 10th day of Tishrei with jubilation and merriment. Inui was associated with rites undertaken during times of emergency when the people needed to purge themselves of their sinful behavior in order to reverse the calamity. Priests could enact this rite whenever needed. But when the high priest could no longer declare such an emergency fast day, then the penitential aspects of the rite were transferred to the 10th day of Tishrei, and the two rites were combined into one.

67. See Rubenstein's discussion in *History of Sukkot in the Second Temple and Rabbinic Periods*, 4–6, where he distinguishes between Passover and Shavuot. The meaning of the Paschal lamb was transferred to unleavened bread and turned into a Passover seder symbol, whereas Shavuot lost its Temple origins in that nothing replaced the two loaves of bread or the sacrifices. Eventually Shavuot came to be associated with the giving of the Torah at Mount Sinai, but this connection was not apparent in the Bible. Also see Baruch Bokser, *The Origins of the Seder and Early Rabbinic Judaism* (Berkeley: University of California Press, 1984), and "Ritualizing the Seder," *Journal of the American Academy of Religion* 56, no. 3 (1988): 443–471.

68. Note that this reference to the priestly blessing is an insertion on BT Yoma 87b of a mishnah from M. Ta'anit 4:1. This mishnah refers to the priests' performance of the priestly blessing brought merely to flesh out a point about the structure of the final central prayer service of Yom Kippur (the Ne'ilah amidah) and is not directly connected to making a point about the introduction of Temple practice into the rite of Yom Kippur. Also consider that M. Yoma 8:3 and 8:8 make reference to the *ḥatat* offering. M. Yoma 8:8 also references the *asham* offering. However, only in the case of M. Yoma 8:8 does the Bavli add a brief comment and, in so doing, reminds us that these offerings are to atone for inadvertent sins. They can also be brought

after Yom Kippur because asking for atonement is not limited to Yom Kippur (BT Yoma 85b). Parallel sugyot in the Yerushalmi focus in a more extensive way on discussing these offerings.

69. Note that sources such as M. Ma'aser Sheini 5:2, M. Ta'anit 4:8, and M. Ta'anit 7:3 express a hope explicitly for the rebuilding of the Temple, absent from Mishnah and Bavli Yoma. M. Keilim 1:6–9 considers the Temple's Holy of Holies as the holiest place on earth. See Klawans, *Purity, Sacrifice, and the Temple*, 202, where he notes that no rabbinic source questions, much less refutes, the claim made in Mishnah Keilim that the Holy of Holies is the holiest place on earth.

70. Ezekiel 8.

71. Daniel 10:20.

72. In chapter six, I discuss the fact that in the middle of this midrashic piece, women are mentioned as receiving the reward of the World to Come for waiting up all night for their husbands who study Torah.

73. Michael D. Swartz, "Ritual Is with the People: Sacrifice and Society in Palestinian Yoma Traditions," in *The Actuality of Sacrifice: Past and Present*, ed. Alberdina Houtman, Marcel Poothius, Joshua Schwartz, and Joseph Turner (Leiden: Brill, 2014), 206–227; "Liturgy, Poetry, and the Persistence of Sacrifice," in *Was 70 CE a Watershed in Jewish History? On Jews and Judaism before and after the Destruction of the Second Temple*, ed. Daniel R. Schwartz, Zeev Weiss, and Ruth A. Clements (Leiden: Brill, 2012), 393–412; and "The Choreography of Blood in Mishnah Yoma," in *Jewish Blood: Reality and Metaphor in History, Religion, and Culture*, ed. Mitchell B. Hart (London: Routledge, 2009), 70–82. See also BT Yoma 87b below for one version of the *vidui* (confession) that did not appear in the first seven chapters of the tractate but appears in the eighth chapter:

Rav Hamnuna said: My God, before I was formed, I was unworthy. Now that I have been formed, it is as if I had not been formed. I am dust while alive, how much more so when I am dead. See, I am before You like a vessel filled with shame and disgrace. May it be Your will that I may sin no more, and as for the sins I have committed before You, erase them in Your compassion, but not by suffering. [The Gemara adds]: This is the confession that Rava used all year long; and [it was the confession] that Rav Hamnuna Zuta used on Yom Kippur. [But the rabbis admit further down on the *amud* (Talmudic page) that the most important part of the confession is to say, "I have sinned."]

Also note that BT Yoma 87b mentions the five prayer services in which one confesses on Yom Kippur without making any connection to Temple

Notes to Introduction   207

rites. The five immersions (BT Yoma 71a) before each of the five Temple services in which the high priest changed his garments and the seven sprinklings of blood have no equivalent in the post-Temple Yom Kippur rite. Also see BT Yoma 53b, where the rabbis instruct the high priest regarding his prayers. In fact, the sugya intimates that the prayers of Rabbi Ḥanina ben Dosa were more powerful than those of the high priest.

74. Scholars have argued that the priest was replaced by a householder (often a woman) who oversaw the inner workings of home-based rituals, bringing the symbol of the Temple into the household. See Sharon Koren, *Forsaken: The Menstruant in Medieval Jewish Mysticism* (Waltham, MA: Brandeis University Press, 2011), 6; Cecilia Haendler, "Women and Priests in Tractate Hallah: Gender Readings in Rabbinic Literature," *Melilah Manchester Journal of Jewish Studies* 13 (2019); and Christiane Tzuberi, "'And the Woman Is a High-Priest': From the Temple to the Kitchen, from the Laws of Ritual Im/Purity to the Laws of Kashrut (Toharot)," in *Introduction to Seder Qodashim*, ed. Tal Ilan, Monika Brockhaus, Tanja Hidde (Tübingen: Mohr Siebeck, 2012), 93. See Bokser, *Origins of the Seder*, for a discussion on the move from a Temple-based Passover to one that took place at home with symbols that represented the Passover sacrifice. Jonathan Z. Smith argues that sacrifice shifted into the home and was replaced by discourse: "Trading Places," *Relating Religion: Essays in the Study of Religion* (Chicago: University of Chicago Press, 2004), 223.

75. There is, however, one exception on BT Yoma 13b. See note 77.

76. BT Yoma 20b, 35b, 36ab, 37a, 39b, 40ab (goat sent to Azazel): 43b, 61a, 66a.

77. Note that there is one exception on BT Yoma 13b where the requirement of the high priest to eat sacrificial meat is complicated by his status as an *onein* (the period of time after a family member has died and prior to the burial). During this period of *aninut*, a priest would not be able to eat any sacred foods (see Deuteronomy 26:14, BT Zevaḥim 101a). This leaves us with the question: Would a priest be able to serve as an onein on Yom Kippur? Rava concludes that Yom Kippur is an exception. The high priest can serve as an onein because no one is eating. Had it been an ordinary day, the priest would not have been able to serve, because in that case he would have had to eat the meat of the sacrifice. Alternatively, M. Yoma 7:4, referred to above, when presented along with a parallel baraita on BT Yoma 71b, relays that after the high priest exited the Holy of Holies, he would make a feast for his "fellows." It is not clear that the day of Yom Kippur had passed. M. Yoma 7:4 specifically states that it was still the holiday (*yom tov*) itself.

78. Daniel Stökl Ben Ezra, *The Impact of Yom Kippur on Early Christianity: The Day of Atonement from Second Temple Judaism to the End of the Fifth Century* (Tübingen: Mohr Siebeck, 2003), 19–28. Also see Israel Knoll and Shlomo Naeh, "Milu'im vekipurim," *Tarbitz* 62 (1993): 18–44. Dalia Marx, in *Tractates Tamid, Middot and Qinnim* (11), writes that the Temple is a "description of a fantasized reality that has ceased to exist (and maybe never actually existed [as the rabbis describe it])." She argues that it is "a literary or reflective device to help the rabbis contemplate their status as a defined leading group." Also see Yonatan Feintuch, "Bein kohanim laḥakhamim: Al aggadah aḥat beheksherah haraḥav bevavli Yoma" [Between priests and rabbis: An analysis of an Aggadah and its wider context in Bavli Yoma], *Meḥkerei Yerushalayim besifrut ivrit* 23 (2010): 1–14, and Peter Schäfer, "Rabbis and Priests, or: How to Do Away with the Glorious Past of the Sons of Aaron," in *Antiquity in Antiquity: Jewish and Christian Pasts in the Greco-Roman World*, ed. Gregg Gardner and Kevin Osterloh (Tübingen: Mohr Siebeck, 2008), 155–72.

79. Ishay Rosen Zvi's discussion on the issue of ritual narratives is in *The Mishnaic Sotah Ritual*, 240–241 (see note 5). Also see Ishay Rosen-Zvi, "Orality, Narrative, Rhetoric: New Directions in Mishnah Research," *AJS Review* 32, no. 2 (2008): 243–249.

80. Marx, *Tractates Tamid, Middot and Qinnim*, 15. See also BT Ta'anit 27a.

81. Cohn, *Memory of the Temple* 6–11. See also William Scott Green's "What's in a Name? The Problematic of Rabbinic 'Biography,'" in *Approaches to Ancient Judaism: Theory and Practice*, ed. William Scott Green (Missoula: Scholars' Press for Brown University, 1978), 77–96, regarding the extent to which, as a scholar, one can rely on rabbinic texts for the reconstruction of a historical past—in the case here of the Temple. I am arguing for the idea that we receive a better view of the approach of the redactors of the Bavli than we do of the individuals whose opinions appear in its sugyot.

82. Wasserman, *Jews, Gentiles, and Other Animals*; Philippe Buc, *The Dangers of Ritual: Between Early Medieval Texts and Social Scientific Theory* (Princeton: Princeton University Press, 2001), 4.

83. For example, Klawans, in *Purity, Sacrifice, and the Temple*, 175–211, argues that ancient Jews extended the boundaries of the Temple by "sacrificializing" and "templisizing" food, prayer, and purity rites, even before the Temple was destroyed. Surely, he adds, this was true in the aftermath of its destruction in 70 CE. For another significant argument about the Temple, the cult, and the priesthood, see Balberg, *Blood for Thought*, 4–5, 225–229, who argues that we should not transform the destruction of the Temple into "one of the most cataclysmic events in world history," thinking that it

Notes to Introduction   209

caused Jews and Christians as well as inhabitants of the entire Roman Empire to ban sacrifice and replace the priests. It is an overstatement to view the "interiorization and privatization of worship" as the invention of the Jews in response to the Temple's destruction. She wishes to move us away from thinking that the rabbinic project was to create "a sustained and durable nonsacrificial version of Judaism," that is, to fill the empty slots with a new religious vision. While offering sacrifices in the Temple ended after the fall of the Temple, the rabbis continued to produce texts as if the sacrificial cult remained active (229). While Klawans and Balberg make important arguments for all of rabbinic literature and the rabbis' relationship to the Temple, I am making an argument just for Bavli Yoma. I see Bavli Yoma as one perspective among others.

84. Undeniably, the main theme of Bavli Yoma is Yom Kippur, and as such, this tractate serves as a significant contributive text to the history of the development of the holiday. References to Yom Kippur appear also throughout rabbinic literature, addressing issues that are not mentioned in Bavli Yoma, such as the idea that fasting replaces sacrifice. Together with documents such as those from the collections Sifra, Tosefta Yoma, and Yerushalmi Yoma, as well as the gamut of non-rabbinic sources such as those from Qumran, Philo, and Josephus, there is large body of material from which to engage in a diachronic approach to the study of Yom Kippur. However, this is not a book about Yom Kippur along the lines of Rubenstein's *History of Sukkot*.

85. See Lapin, "The Construction of Households in the Mishnah," 58–61.

86. Alexei M. Siverstev, *Households, Sects, and the Origins of Rabbinic Judaism* (Leiden: Brill, 2005), 213–215, 255. Siverstev suggests that household-based halakhah developed within the house during the tannaitic period after the destruction of the Temple. However, in later years, the debates surrounding legal matters affecting the family were transferred to master-disciple circles and the house of study. I have not observed this pattern in Bavli Yoma. Instead, the rabbinic household and the householders—including women—became central to concerns about navigating daily survival. Fasting and refraining from sexual relations, for example, evoked cause for concern among Babylonian rabbis and turned the household into a place where legal decisions were made by individuals experiencing, for example, sickness on Yom Kippur or raising children who needed to be fed in spite of the requirement to fast, as I discuss in chapters 7 to 9. Also see Ayelet Hoffman Libson, *Law and Self-Knowledge in the Talmud* (Cambridge: Cambridge University Press, 2018), 126–152.

210   *Notes to Introduction*

87. See Siverstev, *Households*, 214. Siverstev points out that a household's everyday functioning had to be monitored carefully in order to ensure that Jews lived a religiously meaningful life. Again, this is not the discourse of Bavli Yoma.

88. See Maurice Halbwachs, *On Collective Memory*, ed. and trans. Lewis A. Coser (Chicago: University of Chicago Press, 1992), 86, and Elizabeth A. Castelli's use of Halbwach's theory to think about the development of Christianity and the construction of its identity through the memory of past suffering in *Martyrdom and Memory: Early Christian Culture Making* (New York: Columbia University Press, 2004), 12–19.

89. Halbwachs, *On Collective Memory*, 86.

90. Martha Nussbaum, *Hiding from Humanity* (Princeton: Princeton University Press, 2004), 17–18. Also see Belser, *Rabbinic Tales of Destruction*, xxii–xxiii, where she argues that rabbinic Babylonia is a fruitful site to deal with Roman conquest and feelings of powerlessness, because historical events are not bound to a particular historical moment and geographical place. Catastrophes can "overspill clear boundaries" for centuries. The Roman conquest of Judea, as Belser argues, is an "attritional catastrophe" shaped by temporal and geographic displacements and stretches past the confines of time and territory.

91. BT Yoma 86a.

92. BT Yoma 88a.

93. See Daniel Boyarin, *Carnal Israel: Reading Sex in Talmudic Culture*; Ishay Rosen-Zvi's discussion in *Demonic Desires: "Yetzer Hara" and the Problem of Evil in Late Antiquity* (Philadelphia: University of Pennsylvania Press, 2011) 113–114, and his *Demonic Desires*, where he argues that sexuality is the locus of the Bavli's interests and that sources in the Bavli "see sex all around them" in a manner unparalleled in Palestinian literature (113–114). See also Rosen-Zvi's expansion of Michael L. Satlow's argument in *Tasting the Dish: Rabbinic Rhetorics of Sexuality* (Atlanta: Scholars Press, 1995): 319.

94. See Shlomo Naeh, "Freedom and Celibacy: A Talmudic Variation on Tales of Temptation and Fall in Genesis and Its Syrian Background," in *The Book of Genesis in Jewish and Oriental Christian Interpretation: A Collection of Essays*, ed. Judith Frishman and Lucas van Rompay (Lovanii [Leuven]: In Aedibus Peeters, 1997), 73–89. Also see Haleh Emrani, "'Who Would Be Mine for the Day!' Irano-Judaic Marriage Customs in Late Antiquity," *Iranian Studies* 49, no. 2 (2016), 217–231.

95. Yishai Kiel, "Study versus Sustenance: A Rabbinic Dilemma in Its Zoroastrian and Manichaean Context," *AJS Review* 38, no. 2 (2014): 280–281,

Notes to Introduction   211

290. Also see Peter Brown, *The Body and Society: Men, Women, and Sexual Renunciation in Early Christianity* (New York: Columbia University Press, 1989), 83–102.

96. The translations of sources from BT Yoma are my own and are based on the standard printed edition of the Babylonian Talmud (Vilnius: Romm, 1880–1886). Where I find relevant discrepancies in textual witnesses, I point them out in the notes. For Talmud variants, see the Friedberg Jewish Manuscript Society (https://fjms.genizah.org) and the Sol and Evelyn Henkind Text Data Bank of Talmudic manuscripts collected by the Saul Lieberman Institute for Talmudic Research at the Jewish Theological Seminary in New York.

CHAPTER 1. UNSETTLING THE TEMPLE BAYIT

1. Bavli Yoma not only speaks of the Temple-based Yom Kippur but also the daily sacrifices. Sometimes there is slippage, and it is difficult to determine whether it is speaking of the Temple service of Yom Kippur or the sacrifices offered daily. See, for example, BT Yoma 23a, where a dramatization of priests racing up a ramp to participate in the Temple service may or may not be taking place on Yom Kippur. I discuss this text in detail in chapter two.

2. Timothy Wardle, "Who Is Sacrificing? Assessing the Early Christian Reticence to Transfer the Idea of the Priesthood to the Community," in *Ritual and Metaphor: Sacrifice in the Bible*, ed. Christian A. Eberhart (Atlanta: Society of Biblical Literature, 2011), 100–101, discusses the way that the Temple, the sacrificial cult, and the priesthood were reinterpreted by other groups of Jews and early Christians. For a larger discussion about whether to refer to this process as one of spritu_alization, transference, borrowing, or templization (*initatio Temple*), see Georg Klinzing, *Die Umdeutung des Kultus in der Qumrangemeinde und im Neuen Testament* (Göttingen: Vanderhook and Ruprecht, 1971); Elisabeth Schüssler Fiorenza, "Cultic Language in Qumran and the New Testament," *CBQ* 38 (1976): 161; Klawans, *Purity, Sacrifice, and the Temple*, 220, 251; Jonathan Z. Smith, "The Temple and the Magician," in *Map Is Not Territory: Studies in the History of Religions* (Leiden: Brill, 1976), 187–189; and Steven Fine, *This Holy Place: On the Sanctity of the Synagogue during the Greco-Roman Period* (Notre Dame, IN: University of Notre Dame Press, 1997), 32, 55.

3. Mieke Bal, *Death and Dissymetry: The Politics of Coherence in the Book of Judges* (Chicago: University of Chicago Press, 1988), 5, 17.

4. Gaston Bachelard, *The Poetics of Space*, trans. Maria Jolas (Boston: Beacon Press, 1994), xxxvii.

5. Susan D. Gillespie, "Beyond Kinship: An Introduction," in *Beyond Kinship: Social and Material Reproduction in House Societies*, ed. Rosemary A. Joyce and Susan D. Gillepsie (Philadelphia: University of Pennsylvania Press, 2000), 3, 8–10; and Janet Carsten and Stephen Hugh-Jones, Introduction to *About the House: Lévi-Strauss and Beyond*, ed. Janet Carsten and Stephen Hugh-Jones (Cambridge: Cambridge University Press, 1995), 1–46.

6. See BT Yoma, chapter eight, and chapters seven, eight, and nine of this book.

7. Carsten and Hugh-Jones, Introduction to *About the House*, 3. The authors argue that anthropologists have focused more on the body than on the house. As a result, there is a gap in studies that explore the interrelationship between the body and the house that they attempt to fill.

8. Pierre Bourdieu, *Outline of the Theory of Practice* (Cambridge: Cambridge University Press, 1977), 89, and "The Kabyle House or the World Reversed," in *The Logic of Practice*, trans. Richard Nice (Cambridge: Polity Press, 1990 [1970]), as discussed by Carsten and High-Jones, Introduction to *About the House*, 2. Adrienne Rich, *Of Women Born: Motherhood as Experience and Institution* (New York: Norton, 1995), 42–43, points to sociologists of the early twentieth century who argued that women were the "embodied home." Women not only were viewed as the "basis of all institutions" but also the "buttress of society." Indeed, the rabbis' understanding of home, referring to their wives as their homes, as I point out below, was an image many embraced for centuries.

9. I am influenced here by feminist scholars who in the past two decades have looked at "women" as a trope used to "think with." See Dina Stein, "A Maidservant and Her Master's Voice: Discourse, Identity, and Eros in Rabbinic Texts," *Journal of History of Sexuality* 10, no. 3 and 4 (2001): 375–397, where she views the slave/maidservant references in aggadic texts as a trope. For an excellent overview of this approach, see Elizabeth Clark, "The Lady Vanishes: Dilemmas of a Feminist Historian after the 'Linguistic Turn,'" 12–13, and Shelly Matthews, "Thinking of Thecla: Issues in Feminist Historiography," 39–55, esp. 46–55, including her reference to Lévi-Strauss, *Structural Anthropology*, 61. Also note Peter Brown's work where he points out that women who play a central role in the *Apocryphal Acts*, for example, should not be read as "evidence for the actual role of women in Christianity. Rather, they reflect the manner in which Christian males of that period partook in the deeply ingrained tendency of men in the ancient world to use women 'to think with.'" Brown, *Body and Society: Men, Women, and Sexual Renunciation in Early Christianity*, 153.

Notes to Chapter 1

10. The Hebrew word *bayit*, meaning "home" or "house," is similar to the Greek words *oikos* and *oikia* and the Latin word *domus* that refer to a physical building as well as a "home" or "household." See Carolyn Osiek and David L. Balch, *Families in the New Testament World: Households and House Churches* (Louisville, KY: Westminster John Knox Press, 1997), 6.

11. For example, the Holy of Holies is *beit kodesh hakodashim* (M. Middot 4:5, 4:7, 5:4) or *beit hakaporet* (M. Middot 1:1, 5:1), and the area containing the altar, the *heikhal*, is referred to as *habayit* (M. Middot 4:1). Indeed, the priest responsible for watching over all of the Temple is the *ish har habayit* (literally, the man of the mount of the house) (M. Middot 1:2).

12. Baker, *Rebuilding the House of Israel*, 56–59.

13. Baker, *Rebuilding the House of Israel*, 55–56, 192, n. 67, where she argues that while the term *bayit* must be read within a broad matrix of meanings, one cannot divorce one meaning from another, as the rabbis choose their language carefully. Also see my article regarding the *sukkah* where I make an argument more closely aligned with Baker, in "Reimagining Home, Rethinking Sukkah: Rabbinic Discourse and Its Contemporary Implications," 107–139. I would argue that the rabbis' use of the word is more nuanced in Bavli Yoma and that each use must be examined individually and in its literary context.

14. The Temple chambers are referred to as *beit avtinas* (Mishnah Yoma 1:5), *beit hamoked* (BT Yoma 15b), and *beit haparvah* (Mishnah Yoma 3:3). The Holy of Holies is *beit kodeshei hakodashim* (BT Yoma 52a) and *beit hakaparot* (BT Yoma 21a). The place where sacrificial animals are prepared is *beit hamitbaḥim* (M. Middot 3:5).

15. In the semantic universe of both the Bavli and Yerushalmi, a wife is often referred to as "his [her husband's] house." See Gail Labovitz's discussion of this process of metaphorization and examples such as BT Shabbat 118b, where the following statement is attributed to Rabbi Yose: "In [all] my days, I have not called my wife, 'my wife,' nor my ox, 'my ox,' but rather my wife [I called] 'my house' and my ox [I called] 'my field.'" See also Bereishit Rabbah (Theodor-Albeck, ed.), 17:2: BT Gittin 52a, BT Sukkah 27b, and BT Megillah 13a. See also Gail Labovitz, *Marriage and Metaphor: Constructions of Gender in Rabbinic Literature* (Lanham, MD: Rowman & Littlefield, 2009), 97–146; Fonrobert, *Menstrual Purity*, 40–67, esp. 41, where she states that the rabbis metaphorize the woman's body and compare it to the inanimate house; and Baker, *Rebuilding the House of Israel*, 48–53, who challenges Fonrobert's "woman-as-house" metaphor, seeing the equation as more complex, rather than static and inert, 192, n. 66. Bachelard, *Poetics of Space*, 7,

speaks of the "material features of the house" in its ability to offer protection. The fact that he uses characteristics commonly associated with the "house" as an instrument for analyzing the human soul points to the fact that even in the early twentieth century (when he wrote), women were thought to be interchangeable with "house."

16. Baker, *Rebuilding the House of Israel*, 35.

17. See Baker, *Rebuilding the House of Israel*, 48–49, where she discusses M. Yoma 1:1 and T. Yoma 1:1 but not the extensive discussions in the Bavli and Yerushalmi. Also see BT Yoma 6a, *Tosafot D"H mibeito lamah peresh*. Also note that all references to the Tosefta are drawn from Saul Lieberman, ed., *Tosefta* (New York: Jewish Theological Seminary of America, 1955), except where otherwise indicated.

18. Note that M. Yoma 1:1 refers to this chamber as the Palhedrin chamber, but T. Yoma 1:1 has the "Parhedrin" chamber resulting in some slippage in manuscripts, and even here in the Bavli; see BT Yoma 8b. See Bavli manuscripts Munich 6 and Enelow 270 that have "Palhedrin." I will refer to this chamber as the Parhedrin chamber throughout.

19. Individuals who were ritually impure were not allowed to enter the holy precincts of the Temple, touch the sacred vessels, or eat any portion of the sacrifices until they underwent the ritual of purification. Experiencing a bodily flux or a skin disease prevented them from interacting with the holiness of the Temple. M. Yoma 3:3 warns, "No person enters the [Temple] Courtyard for service, even if he is pure, until he immerses"; this is in case he might have forgotten to immerse after a seminal emission (JT Yoma 3:3, 40b and BT Yoma 30a). In discussing how important it was for the priests, in particular, to maintain a status of purity while serving in the Temple, M. Sanhedrin 9:6 asserts that priests punished fellow priests for performing sacrificial rites while impure by taking them outside the Temple Court and "split[ting their] brain[s] open with logs." A baraita found in the Bavli's discussion of this mishnah indicates that impure priests who performed the Temple service were at risk of death (BT Sanhedrin 83a). T. Yoma 1:18 supports this point as well. Further expansion of the baraita found on BT Sanhedrin 83a indicates that even priests who had immersed during the day but had performed a priestly rite before nightfall were subject to the same punishment.

20. Elizabeth Shanks Alexander, "Ritual on the Threshold: Mezuzah and the Crafting of Domestic and Civic Space," *Jewish Social Studies* 20, no. 3 (2014): 121–122 and her discussion of the designation of the priest as a "family man," in M. Yoma 1:1. That said, the priest's sequestration in connection with performing Temple rites couches him as sexless, even if married.

Notes to Chapter 1

21. See BT Yoma 2ab and JT Yoma 1:1, where the rabbis discuss the basis for the idea of a seven-day sequestration prior to Yom Kippur using biblical material. This period of separation, however, is not biblical. Comparisons are made to Moses's sojourn at Sinai, to the inauguration of Aaron and his sons into the priesthood, and to the *parah adumah* (the rite of the red heifer).

22. M. Yoma 1:1 does not explicitly mention that the reason for sequestering the high priest is due to the fear that he might become impure due to having sexual relations with his menstruant wife, but T. Yoma 1:1, BT Yoma 6a, and JT Yoma 1:1, 38d are explicit about it.

23. Leviticus 15:16 commands priests to immerse themselves immediately following a seminal emission, thus remaining unclean until evening. This meant that priests could not perform cultic practices in the Temple unless they had immersed, distancing sexuality from their roles in the sacred Temple. See Deborah W. Rooke, "Breeches of the Covenant: Gender, Garments, and the Priesthood," in *Embroidered Garments: Priests and Gender in Biblical Israel*, ed. Deborah Rooke (Sheffield: Sheffield Phoenix Press, 2009), 28. Arguably, the high priest would have enough time to immerse before the start of Yom Kippur if he had a seminal emission, but not if he experienced a seminal emission on Yom Kippur itself. Sexual relations with a women in nidah, a zav, or a zavah required a seven-day waiting period before the priest became pure and could perform Temple rites. The significance of maintaining ritual purity before Yom Kippur is also communicated on BT Yoma 18a regarding the need to control a high priest's food intake. Certain foods were thought to cause seminal emissions.

24. See BT Yoma 13a–14a and JT Yoma 1:1 38d. Yerushalmi Yoma differs from the Bavli and resolves the problem generated by Rabbi Yehudah's requirement of a substitute wife in M. Yoma 1:1 by simply allowing the high priest to marry again on Yom Kippur. The Yerushalmi is more concerned about whether a high priest, who cannot become betrothed on the Sabbath, can marry on Yom Kippur, which for legal purposes parallels the Sabbath. If he cannot remarry on the Sabbath, preparing a substitute wife would not be possible. However, the Yerushalmi is clear to differentiate a rabbinic injunction forbidding marriages on the Sabbath and holidays from what was permitted in the Temple. This difference between the Yerushalmi and the Bavli is suggestive. In the end, the framers of the Yerushalmi did not see the marital status of the high priest as a challenge to the execution of the avodah. In their minds, the avodah could be perfectly executed in the event of the death of the high priest's first wife. Furthermore, the Yerushalmi is also completely comfortable with the replacement of the high priest in the

event of his disqualification, inserting a passage praising the mother who sees two of her sons in the role of high priest, one to replace the other. Found here as a comment on M. Yoma 1:1 instead of where the Bavli positions it, far later in the tractate, generates a different interpretive spin (see chapter 4). Possibly this is connected to the status of the framers of the Yerushalmi as rabbis in the land of Israel, which may have resulted in greater allegiances to or nostalgia for a Temple-based Judaism than felt by their contemporaries in the diasporic regions of Babylonia.

25. Also see JT Yoma 1:1, 38d, where the Yerushalmi, unlike the Bavli, is clear to note that the concern for the death of a high priest's wife affects the entire community and therefore should be treated as a matter of great concern.

26. Aside from a concern mentioned on BT Yoma 6b that replacements of high priests be made from the same priestly family when corpse impurity disqualifies a priest, the rules of substitution are strikingly absent. It would seem that replacing the high priest means that a brother or son (maybe a cousin) would have to be available, in keeping with the patrilineal structure of the priesthood. Indeed, when the Bavli briefly discusses the high priest's replacement in the first chapter of Bavli Yoma, the focus is only on whether he can ever return to his original role as high priest after being disqualified. Worry over competition and enmity developing between the original high priest and his substitute renders the replacement high priest—when he completes the duties of filling in—unable to continue to wear the attire of the high priest, perform any duties of the high priest in the future, or abide by any laws commanded of the high priest. He cannot even perform the duties of an ordinary priest because of the principle that "in sacred matters we elevate but do not lower" (BT Yoma 12b–13a).

27. BT Yoma 14a, Rashi *D"H mi lo miterid* pinpoints the midrashic derivation from Numbers 18:8 in BT Hullin 132b, where the notion that priests were supposed to feel like kings when they ate the sacrificial offerings is expressed. A status as an onein would negate that sense of majesty.

28. See the context on BT Yoma 14a. "[Rava said] to him [Rav Adda bar Ahavah]: How can these cases be compared? There, [in the mishnah,] since it is Yom Kippur, when everyone does not eat, he too will not come to eat. [Therefore, the priest can serve]. However, here, during the rest of the year, when everyone eats, he too will come to eat [and therefore he cannot serve in the Temple as an onein]." Oddly, the first seven chapters of Bavli Yoma do not discuss high priests and the requirement of fasting on Yom Kippur to fulfill the requirement of self-denial (Leviticus 16), even though it is so

Notes to Chapter 1

217

central to Yom Kippur (see BT Yoma, chapter eight). See also M. Yoma 7:4 and BT Yoma 71b, where the high priest makes a feast for his "fellows" after exiting from the Holy of Holies. It is not clear that Yom Kippur has ended with sunset.

29. For example, see BT Yoma 12b–13a, where a replacement high priest can generate enmity between himself and the first high priest he needed to replace. In fact, the replacement high priest is referred to as a high priest's *tzarah* (rival), as if the two priests are two wives married to one husband. In the end, the stammaim deflect this, arguing that there is no need for concern. See also T. Yoma 1:4; 1:6.

30. Jonathan Z. Smith, *Imagining Religion: From Babylon to Jonestown* (Chicago: University of Chicago Press, 2004), 63–65.

31. Note that this sugya is lengthy and complicated. Space constraints have limited my ability to work through every logical unit in this chapter or to explain the ways that the Bavli introduces and then reformulates its cases.

32. For a more extensive discussion of the requirement of mezuzah, see Alexander, *Gender and Timebound Commandments in Judaism*, 229–233. With respect to the fact that women are required to place a mezuzah on their doorposts, Alexander argues that this is because "women, slaves, and minors reflect the fullness of the Jewish household . . . they help constitute its very existence." Placing the mezuzah on a doorpost is, for the rabbis, a boundary that distinguishes a Jewish home from a non-Jewish one.

33. Gaston Bachelard, *The Poetics of Space* (Boston: Beacon Press, 1994): xxxii, xxxi, xiv, as discussed in Carsten and Hugh-Jones, Introduction to *About the House*, 3.

34. See T. Yoma 1:2:

> The Rabbis taught: All of the chambers in the Temple are exempt from [the commandment] of mezuzah except the Parhedrin (chamber): because it is the house of residence of the high priest for seven days [before Yom Kippur].

> Rabbi Yehudah said: Was it that this was the only house of residence there [in the Temple]? Rather, all [structures] that were houses of residence are required [to fulfill the commandment of] mezuzah. Any [structures] that are not houses of residence are exempt.

35. At times, there is some slippage between the role of the high priest on Yom Kippur and his role in daily service. See, for example, BT Yoma 19a.

36. See BT Yoma 8b where a baraita is quoted in the name of Rabbi Yehudah: "Was it the Parhedrin chamber [where they sent the high priest]? Was it not the chamber of Balvatai [where the high priest was sent]? Rather, at

218   *Notes to Chapter 1*

first they called it the chamber of Balvatai [signifying a place for aristocrats]. However, [later] when money was given [to obtain] the priesthood [as a bribe, the chamber was renamed the Parhedrin chamber]." This new name signified a group referred to as the "Parhedrin." Like these non-Israelite aristocrats who were replaced every twelve months, the high priests were also removed every year due to inappropriate behavior, such as bribery.

37. It is not absolutely clear that this lengthy narrative about the high priest in the Parhedrin chamber is describing the seven-day period before Yom Kippur, but in the context of commenting on the mishnah's narration of the actions of the high priest prior to Yom Kippur, it seems that the Bavli understands it that way.

38. Sources from as early as the tannaitic period offer a negative picture of the priests. For example, someone other than the high priest had to ensure that his bowel movements were controlled (BT Yoma 18a). The *zekeinim* (possibly rabbinic sages) familiarized the high priest with the procedures necessary for performing the "order of the day." This included the need to parade bulls in front of the high priest so that he would know which animals to sacrifice. See M. Yoma 1:3 (BT Yoma 18a): "On Yom Kippur eve [in the] morning, they stand him at the eastern gate and pass before him bulls and rams and sheep so that he will be familiar [with the animals] and [grow] accustomed to the service." For fear that the high priest would have a seminal emission while asleep, he was not allowed food, as food induces sleep (M. Yoma 1:4 and BT Yoma 18a). M. Yoma 1:3, 1:6 and T. Yoma 1:8 intimate that the high priest was illiterate and needed someone to read the Torah portion containing the Yom Kippur avodah to him during these seven days of sequestration. M. Yoma 1:6 states that the high priest turned to the rabbis (*talmidei hakhamim*) to study with him during this weeklong period if the high priest was not himself a sage. A baraita (tannaitic source) on BT Yoma 4a describes the high priest as requiring "two talmidei hakhamim of the disciples of Moses, to the exclusion of the Sadducees, to [transmit the laws of the Yom Kippur service]" during the seven-day sequestration. Additional material found in both Talmuds, in response to M. Yoma 1:1, suggests that placing the high priest in a separate chamber before Yom Kippur was necessary in order to instruct him regarding his duties, relying on a midrashic interpretation of Leviticus 16:3 that claims a presumed period of preparation required of Aaron, the biblical high priest. The Yerushalmi is more forthright in interweaving the idea that sequestering the high priest was linked to both maintaining his sexual purity and his need for instruction. According to JT Yoma 1:1, 38c and BT Yoma 4a, after this period of instruction, the high

Notes to Chapter 1   219

priest could not return home at night, in order to protect him from having relations with his wife, so that he would remain ritually pure. For a historical analysis of this seven-day period of separation, see Israel Knohl and Shlomo Naeh, "Milu'im vekipurim," *Tarbitz* 62 (1993): 17–18.

39. There is a disagreement between the rabbis and Rabbi Yehudah regarding this point that is constructed by the stammaim. See BT Yoma 10b.

40. As the sugya unfolds, it becomes clearer that the biblical commandment requires a person to be "housed" in a space in order to require a mezuzah, irrespective of whether a ritual action is performed there, as BT Yoma 11b states: "[And you shall write them on the doorposts of your] house—Just as a house that is specifically [used for one] to reside [requires a mezuzah, so too any structure where one resides requires a mezuzah]. This excludes [structures] not specifically [used for one] to reside." This also seems to exclude the Parhedrin chamber because the high priest is there for just seven days, hence the need for Rabbi Yehudah's rabbinic exception and the Bavli's explanation of it, as noted above. Rabbi Yehudah argues that the Parhedrin chamber needs a mezuzah by rabbinic decree. Biblically, it is exempt because the priests are there temporarily.

41. Note that BT Yoma 10b specifically states, "It is only on a rabbinic level that [the mezuzah requirement] was enacted regarding the chamber, in order that one would not say that a high priest is imprisoned in jail."

42. Alexander, "Ritual on the Threshold," 121–122, argues that spaces that require mezuzot are households of men, women, children, and servants. The Parhedrin chamber may seem like an exception, in that the high priest does not dwell there with his wife. However, as Alexander argues, this Temple space evoked the husband-wife relationship despite her absence; he was there, after all, to protect himself from impurities that might result because of their relationship. Therefore, it needs a mezuzah. This is not the reasoning of Rabbi Yehudah as understood by BT Yoma 10b.

43. See BT Yoma 11a, Rashi *D"H mai ne'ototroḥatzot*, where he notes that these spaces are derogatory because women are present within them naked, rendering them as spaces undignified for the placement of mezuzot. Also note that the Bavli is quite distinct from its brief parallel in Yerushalmi Yoma 1:1, 38c, where no mention is made of women's spaces in conjunction with the mezuzah.

44. This discussion in BT Yoma is not only more inventive and expansive than its parallel in the Yerushalmi; it is also distinct from the legal discussion in evidence in BT Menachot 33b, where the protective function of the mezuzah is noted. These issues are not mentioned here, engaged as the

Bavli is in an analysis that reflects on the Temple and the priesthood rather than on the purpose of the mezuzah. BT Menachot reads as follows:

Rava says: It is a mitzvah to place [the mezuzah] in the handbreadth adjacent to the public domain. What is the reason for this? The Rabbis say that it is in order that one encounter the mezuzah immediately [upon one's entrance to the house]. Rav Ḥanina from Sura says: So that the mezuzah protects [the house].

Also see BT Yoma 10a where the Bavli discusses whether a sukkah must have a mezuzah; also see other discussions on BT Sukkah 3a, 10a. See Lehman, "Reimagining Home, Rethinking Sukkah," 122–123, for a discussion of BT Yoma 10a.

45. According to BT Yoma 11a, Nikanor's gate was the only other place in the Temple that had a mezuzah because of its location. Right beyond it was the Parhedrin chamber.

46. BT Yoma 11a has two versions of this baraita. One includes the storehouses that women make use of, and the other does not.

47. Edward Jay Watts, *The Final Pagan Generation: Transformation of the Classical Heritage* (Oakland: University of California Press, 2015), 46, writes, "Romans felt that odors exercised incredible power. Foul air was thought to be a cause of disease, and odorous substances that masked it were used for pest control, fumigation, cleaning, and medicine." Many thanks to Erez DeGolan for leading me to this source.

48. JT Yoma 1:1, 38c, the parallel sugya, is strongly influenced by the word *gates*, בשאריך, in the commandment found in Deuteronomy 6:9 and 11:20. The discussion revolves around whether the "gates" of the Temple Mount and its courtyards need mezuzot. The Yerushalmi concludes that the Temple gates need mezuzot because through them one enters a *beit dirah*, that is, a house where God resides. This offers a different perspective from Bavli Yoma, which stops short of suggesting that mezuzot signify God's presence in space.

49. *Nega'im* is a wider category of impurity that affects bodies and objects as well as houses. BT Yoma 11b–12a focuses on the issue of house impurity. For a larger discussion, see Mira Balberg, "Rabbinic Authority, Medical Rhetoric, and Body Hermeneutics in Mishnah Nega'im," *AJS Review* 35, no. 2 (2011): 323–346.

50. Biblically, it was the priests who oversaw every step of the process in reversing house leprosy. They had the authority to deem a house pure or uninhabitable (Leviticus 14:34–53). The priest also performed the final purification ritual of slaughtering a bird, then dipping a live bird into the blood of

Notes to Chapter 1

the dead bird, and finally sprinkling the affected house with this blood seven times (Leviticus 14:51). Bavli Yoma, however, does not describe this process. The priest seems to have been written out, appearing to have no power over the purity of the house spaces he was biblically mandated to oversee. See specifically M. Nega'im 12:5 regarding the tensions between the rabbis' role and that of the priests in declaring houses pure or impure. See also Balberg, "Rabbinic Authority," 339, where she discusses how the rabbis move the priests aside, turning their biblical role as overseers of house leprosy into an "atrophied" one.

51. Leviticus 14:34–36 states, "When you enter the Land of Israel that I gave you as a possession, and I inflict an eruptive plague upon a house in the land you possess, and [when] the one whom the house is his shall come and tell the priest . . . the priest shall then . . ." This means that leprosy can only infiltrate into the walls of houses that a person owns, that is, to the exclusion of synagogues and houses of study that are not specifically "his" (BT Yoma 11b–12a). Adding another level of complexity to this sugya, a baraita is introduced where the tannaim debate the issue of which Israelite tribe owned what part of the Temple and Jerusalem (BT Yoma 12a).

52. Specifically, with respect to the synagogue the rabbis clearly state that synagogues have mezuzot because of a *ḥazan* who resides there (BT **Yoma** 11b).

53. Carsten and Hugh-Jones, Introduction to *About the House*, 3.

54. She must watch over the purity of her own body, as even her sexual organs are called bayit, and also over the domestic demands of an operative household. See M. Nidah 2:1 and 2:5 and M. Mikva'ot 8:4 and Baker's discussion in *Rebuilding the House of Israel*, 53, as well as Fonrobert, *Menstrual Purity*, 50.

55. See M. Nidah 2:1 and 2:5 and M. Mikva'ot 8:4 and Baker's discussion in *Rebuilding the House of Israel*, 53, as well as Fonrobert, *Menstrual Purity*.

CHAPTER 2. VIOLENCE IN THE TEMPLE

1. Thanks to Naomi Koltun-Fromm for her constructive advice regarding this chapter. This is a much-expanded version of my article "Imagining the Priesthood in Tractate Yoma 2:1–2 and BT Yoma 23a," *Nashim: A Journal of Jewish Women's Studies and Gender Issues* 28 (2015): 88–105.

2. Versions of this source appear in T. Yoma 1:12; T. Shevu'ot (Zuckermandel, ed.) 1:4; Sifrei Bamidbar (Kahana, ed), Mas'ei 161; JT Yoma 2:1, 39d; and BT Tamid 28a. For another discussion of this text, see Shmuel Ze'ev Safrai and Chana Safrai, *Mishnat Eretz Yisrael: Masekhet Yoma* (Jerusalem:

E. M. Liphshitz, 2010), 61–67; and Yonah Fraenkel, *Sipur ha'agadah: Aḥdut shel tokhen vetzurah* [The aggadic narrative: Harmony of form and content] (Tel Aviv: Hakibbutz Hameuḥad, 2001), 34–39. See also Amram Tropper, *Keḥomer beyad hayotzer* [Like clay in the hands of the potter] (Jerusalem: Zalman Shazar Center, 2011), 27–45, for an in-depth source-critical analysis of all the sources mentioned above. Also see Sarra Lev, "Talmud That Works Your Heart: New Approaches to Reading," in *Learning to Read Talmud: What It Looks Like and How It Happens*, ed. Jane L. Kanarek and Marjorie Lehman (Boston: Academic Studies Press, 2016), 183–189.

3. Martha Himmelfarb, *A Kingdom of Priests: Ancestry and Merit in Ancient Judaism* (Philadelphia: University of Pennsylvania Press, 2006), 164–170. While the arguments that I make in this chapter seem to challenge Himmelfarb's claims regarding the relationship of the rabbis to issues of ancestry and the Temple, I speak only from the perspective of Bavli Yoma here. I am not arguing that this tractate represents the only perspective communicated in rabbinic literature.

4. Charlotte Elisheva Fonrobert, "Education as Filiation: BT *'Eruvin* 72b–73a," *Nashim: A Journal of Jewish Women's Studies and Gender Issues* 28 (2015): 9–29. Fonrobert, in her discussion of the *eruv* and the definition of the rabbinic household, calls attention to the desire of rabbis to see themselves as father figures to their students (20). Also see Daniel Boyarin, *Carnal Israel: Reading Sex in Talmudic Culture*, where he notes that the rabbis worried consistently about their own ability to reproduce themselves (207), and Elizabeth Shanks Alexander, *Gender and Timebound Commandments in Judaism* (Cambridge: Cambridge University Press, 2013), 184–188.

5. See M. Yoma 1:1; BT Shabbat 118b; BT Gittin 52a; Tamara Or, *Massekhet Betsah: A Feminist Commentary on the Babylonian Talmud*, 20; Tal Ilan, *Massekhet Ta'anit: A Feminist Commentary on the Babylonian Talmud*, 26–28; Baker, *Rebuilding the House of Israel*, 35, 58–59; and Fonrobert, *Menstrual Purity*, 40–67.

6. See Michael G. Peletz, "Neither Reasonable nor Responsible: Contrasting Representations of Masculinity in a Malay Society," *Cultural Anthropology* 9, no. 2 (1994): 137, and David Gilmore, *Manhood in the Making: Cultural Conceptions of Masculinity* (New Haven: Yale University Press, 1990). Peletz points out that in masculinity studies, some scholars introduce the "dialectically related domain of femininity." Thus, scholars such as Dalia Marx and Natan Margalit see the male priests as exhibiting feminine behaviors. See Dalia Marx, *Tractates Tamid, Middot and Qinnim*, 11–12, and Margalit, "Priestly Men and Invisible Women: Male Appropriation of the Feminine

Notes to Chapter 2

and the Exemption of Women from Positive Time-Bound Commandments," *AJS Review* 28, no. 2 (2004): 303–304. See also Daniel Boyarin, *Unheroic Conduct: The Rise of Heterosexuality and the Invention of the Jewish* (Berkeley: University of California Press, 1997), where he argues that Torah study was the "quintessential performance of rabbinic Jewish maleness" (143).

7. For example, compare M. Ketubot 5:5 and T. Kiddushin 5:15. See also Miriam Peskowitz, *Spinning Fantasies: Rabbis, Gender, and History* (Berkeley: University of California Press, 1997), 60–66.

8. Miriam Peskowitz, *Spinning Fantasies: Rabbis, Gender, and History*, 53.

9. Scholars have made attempts to link "women" and "priests" in different ways. Dalia Marx, in *Tractates Tamid, Middot and Qinnim*, 13, suggests that for the rabbis, the priests are a "gender unto themselves," 11–12. Christiane (Hannah) Tzuberi has proposed that women take over the role of the priests, moving ritual from the Temple house into the rabbinic household, in "'And the Woman Is a High-Priest': From the Temple to the Kitchen, from the Laws of Ritual Im/Purity to the Laws of Kashrut (Toharot)," in *Introduction to Seder Qodashim (FCBT V)*, ed. Tal Ilan, Monika Brockhaus, and Tanje Hidde (Tübingen: Mohr Siebeck, 2013), 19. Cecilia Haendler, "Women and Priests in Tractate Hallah: Gender Readings in Rabbinic Literature," *Melilah Manchester Journal of Jewish Studies* 13 (2019): 87, 92–93, makes note of the fact that initially priests and then women were responsible for the ritual of *hallah* separation, as they are both connected to the domestic task of dough preparation. That said, in rabbinic literature, women ultimately outweigh the priests regarding this rite because they continue to perform it, whereas in the absence of the Temple, the priests no longer do so. Haendler thus poses the question as to whether the rabbis drew on feminine images when they constructed the priests, as Marx suggests, or whether they viewed women as replacement priests, as Tzuberi suggests, transferring sancta into the home via their domestic work in the kitchen.

10. Interestingly, BT Yoma 71a points to the idea that men were feminine in the way they studied Torah. However, Torah study is not linked to domesticity. The tasks associated with the upkeep of the rabbinic household, while required of women and often performed by men, bore no religious significance. To some extent, they promoted a male/female labor division, binding women to the household tasks of grinding flour, baking bread, laundering clothing, and making beds, at the risk of providing their husbands with grounds for divorce if they failed to take on these responsibilities (M. Ketubot 5:5). See Peskowitz's discussion in *Spinning Fantasies*, 60–66, and Tamara Or, *Massekhet Betsah: A Feminist Commentary on the Babylonian Tal-*

mud, 25–27. Paralleling several ancient cultures, domesticity was associated with women. Or, for example, refers to the Euripidean drama *Captive Melanippe* for the notion that in the absence of a woman, the house is never tidy. See Christopher Collard, Martin J. Cropp, and Kevin H. Lee, *Euripides: Selected Fragmentary Plays with Introductions, Translations and Commentaries*, vol. 1 (Warminster: Aris & Phillips, 1995): 240–280.

11. Priests served in the Temple for only brief periods each year, on a rotation basis. They were divided into twenty-four shifts (*mishmarot*), each serving for a two-week period. It is unclear to what extent they maintained daily rites connected with their status as priests during the time that they were not serving in the Temple.

12. Regarding the introduction of competition and aggressiveness in the performance of the Passover sacrifice, see M. Pesaḥim 8:3.

13. See Marx, *Tractates Tamid, Middot and Qinnim*, 13–14, and Tzuberi, "'And the Woman Is a High-Priest,'" 174. Tzuberi argues that, post-destruction, housewives took over the role of the priests and became concerned with the uncleanness of everyday objects. One "house," overseen by male priests, became another "house," overseen by women. I do not see evidence of this in Bavli Yoma and discuss this further in chapters six, seven, and eight.

14. See Deuteronomy 17:9, 19:17, and 21:5; M. Middot 5:4; T. Hagigah 2:9.

15. As both Ishay Rosen-Zvi and Mira Balberg noted, the rabbis viewed the priests as being at the top of the religious hierarchy but subordinated them to the "ethos of Torah study," which was entirely the domain of the rabbis. Balberg argues that with respect to skin afflictions, the rabbis made determinations expecting the priests to depend on rabbinic knowledge. The rabbis also wished to see themselves as controlling the courts, even when their decision making revolved around issues connected with the cult and the priesthood. See Balberg, "Rabbinic Authority, Medical Rhetoric, and Body Hermeneutics in Mishnah Nega'im," *AJS Review* 35, no. 2 (2011): 337–339, esp. 337, n. 54 (about M. Nega'im 3:1), and Rosen-Zvi, "Haguf vehamik-dash: Reshimat mumei hakohanim bemishnah vemekomo shel hamikdash beveit hamidrash hatana'i" [Temple and the body: The list of priestly blemishes in the Mishnah and the place of the Temple in the Tannaitic house of study], *Mada'ei hayahadut* 43 (2005–2006): 66; and Himmelfarb, *Kingdom of Priests*, 165–170.

16. See also T. Yoma 1:8.

17. The midrashic play on 1 Samuel 11:8 and 15:4 runs far deeper than I am addressing here. According to the literal sense of these verses, Saul

Notes to Chapter 2   225

was merely gathering troops. The midrashim incorporated here present the word *bezek* in 1 Samuel 11:8 as pottery shards and the word *tela'im* in 1 Samuel 15:4 as lambs, each of which they presume Saul used for counting the people he sent out into battle. Furthermore, there is additional amoraic material incorporated here that builds on Hosea 2:1, "The number of people shall be like that of the sands of the sea, which cannot be measured or counted," problematizing the notion that the Israelites can be counted.

18. This might be a statement made by the amora Rabbi Mani, although it is not entirely clear. See BT Yoma 22b.

19. I discuss the eglah arufah in greater detail below when Rabbi Tzadok uses the rite to instruct the people.

20. See BT Yoma 22b: "Rav Yehudah said in the name of Shmuel: 'Why did the monarchy of the House of Saul not endure when there was no flaw in [Saul's family]?'" As Rabbi Yoḥanan said in the name of Rabbi Shim'on ben Yehotzadak, "We do not appoint a leader over the community unless he has a box of creeping creatures hanging behind him [that is, some flaw in his family ancestry], so that if he becomes arrogant, we can say, 'Turn around [to look at what is behind you].'" Rav Yehudah's statement functions to explain why kingship passed from Saul to David's line. The sugya, however, highlights Saul's sins as well.

21. Regarding whether Rabbi Shim'on ben Yehotzadak was a priest, see Semaḥot 4:7. There, Rabbi Yoḥanan is referred to as his brother and was willing to contract impurity when he visited Rabbi Shim'on ben Yehotzadak's grave. Corpse impurity indicates that they were from a priestly family. I thank Matthew Grey for pointing me to this source.

22. One manuscript version of BT Yoma 22b–23a (Enelow 270) includes the word איבה, which means "enmity" and clarifies what the word נוטר means, which is to harbor (as in to harbor enmity).

23. Although this point is not necessarily related to forgiving people on Yom Kippur, M. Yoma 8:9 does discuss the significance of reaching out to someone you have wronged. When BT Yoma 87a–87b comments on this, M. Yoma 8:9 includes vignettes that challenge this process of appeasement and forgiveness.

24. Indeed, rabbinic masculinity centers on intellectual prowess, developed and sustained by a competitive male study partner who, according to Bereishit Rabbah 69:2, "sharpens" the mind of his fellow "as a knife is sharpened against another." In the same vein, BT Ta'anit 7a points out, in the name of Rabbi Ḥanina, that Torah scholars sharpen each other through their discussions of legal matters in the course of arguments conducted "for

the sake of Heaven." As Dalia Marx notes in *Tractates Tamid, Middot and Qinnim*, 10, many sources describe the house of study as an intellectually tense place of scholarly interaction and where the rabbis encourage intellectual competitiveness. But that too can be fatal. In the famous story of "the oven of Akhnai," a dispute in the Beit Midrash resulted in the death of Rabban Gamliel (BT Bava Metzia 59a–b), and in another well-known tale, the jealousy between the amoraim Rabbi Yoḥanan and Reish Lakish resulted in the undoing of their close teacher-student relationship and the death of both of them (Bava Metzia 84a). The rabbis in both stories do not physically kill each other; they die of emotional wounds triggered by overly intense debates. Rabbi Yoḥanan and Reish Lakish argue about the purity of a sword, a knife, a dagger, a spear, a hand sickle, and a harvesting sickle, but they never actually take up arms. In BT Ketubot 62b, the amora Rava does pick up a weapon to discipline his son Rav Yosef for leaving the Beit Midrash before the end of an agreed-on six-year period, to return to his wife on the eve of Yom Kippur. In the end, however, Rava never uses the weapon. Father and son argue verbally, missing the opportunity to eat before the Yom Kippur fast. The difference is palpable. See also Boyarin's in-depth analysis of the relationship between Rabbi Yoḥanan and Reish Lakish in *Unheroic Conduct*, 129–144.

25. At the end of the tractate, BT Yoma 86b refers to David as well. However, in contrast to the way that David is depicted here, he is referred to there as "a good leader [along with Moses who] arose from the Jewish people." David asks that his sins not be made public. BT Yoma 86b then quotes Psalms 32:1, attributing the verse to David saying, "Fortunate is he whose transgression is forgiven, whose sin is hidden." The distinctive nature of these two depictions of David correlates with the difference in the way the rabbis present the Temple and the priesthood in the first seven chapters of the tractate, as compared to the final chapter of the tractate that focuses on the non-Temple Yom Kippur.

26. According to the baraita, priests who cheat the system receive lashes from the priest appointed to oversee the peki'a. Abaye clarifies that the peki'a refers to a whip. See BT Yoma 23a.

27. Arguably, the rabbis were recalling the image of the Greco-Roman male, imposing characteristics onto the priests as a way to both denigrate such behaviors and, at the same time, construct a different type of masculinity for themselves. See Boyarin, *Unheroic Conduct*, 11. In a world where gladiatorial combat and public executions in stadiums were popular entertainment, the tannaim could imagine themselves differently from the dominant Greco-Roman ideals of manliness. See Beth A. Berkowitz, *Execution*

Notes to Chapter 2

and Invention: Death Penalty Discourse in Early Rabbinic and Christian Cultures* (New York: Oxford University Press, 2006), 153–158; and Boyarin, *Unheroic Conduct*, 142–143.

28. See T. Yoma 1:12.

29. See T. Shevu'ot (Zuckermandel, ed.), 1:4.

30. JT Yoma 2:1, 39d has "my brothers," as do MSS London, BL Harl. 5508 (400); New York, JTS Rab. 108 (EMC 319); and Wien, Oesterreichische Nationalbibliothek Cod hebr. A 39.

31. This statement should be read rhetorically, as the stammaim point out later in the sugya on BT Yoma 23a.

32. The printed editions, including the Venice edition of 1520, have *ga'u kol ha'am bivkhiyah*, "all of the people burst out weeping," suggesting that both priests and non-priests wept. However, the manuscripts of BT Yoma 23a, including London, BL. Harl. 5508 (400); Munich 6 and 95; New York, JTS Rab. 108 (EMC 319); St. Petersburg, RNL Evr. II A 293/1; Vatican 134; and Bologna, Archivio di Stato Fr. Ebr. 29 have *ga'u kulam bivkhiyah*, "and everyone burst out weeping," suggesting that only the priests reacted to Rabbi Tzadok's words. According to the version in the printed editions of BT Yoma 23a, that includes "our brothers" and "all of the people"; it seems that Rabbi Tzadok brought the entire community, priests and non-priests, to tears.

33. All of the manuscripts call him "Rabbi" Tzadok, but it is possible that he was once a priest. See Saul Lieberman, *Tosefta Kifshuta* (New York: Jewish Theological Seminary, 1992), *Seder Mo'ed*, IV, 735–736, nn. 56–57. The readings that record Rabbi Tzadok as calling out to "my brothers" rather than "our brothers" might suggest a familial relationship with the priests he was addressing. At the very least, he seems to have had strong connections to the Temple; he is described as having fasted for forty days in the hope of preventing its destruction (BT Gittin 56a). See also M. Menachot 9:2, M. Meilah 1:6, M. Sanhedrin 7:2, M. Shekalim 8:5, T. Beitzah 3:6, and BT Berakhot 36a, which make reference to Rabbi Tzadok in conjunction with priestly issues. See also Fraenkel, *Sipur ha'agadah: aḥdut shel tokhen vetzurah*, 35–36, for a discussion of the identity of Rabbi Tzadok in this source. Also see Matthew Grey, "Jewish Priests and the Social History of Post-70 Palestine" (PhD diss., University of North Carolina, 2011), 6–12, 84, 92–98, regarding priests who were active in the rabbinic movement, 44. Richard Kalmin, in *Jewish Babylonia between Persia and Roman Palestine* (New York: Oxford University Press, 2006), 43, argues that sources included in the Bavli, in particular, reflect an investment in anachronistically describing rabbis as dominating the institutions of the past, like the Temple.

228 *Notes to Chapter 2*

34. Aharon Lichtenstein cites the passage on Bavli Yoma 23a in "On the Assassination of Prime Minister Yitzchak Rabin, zl," accessed June 2020 at https://www.etzion.org.il/en/assassination-prime-minister-yitzchak-rabin -zl.

35. See BT Yoma 12b; Rashi to BT Yoma 23b, *D"H einah mevi'ah eglah arufah*; and Tosafot to BT Yoma 23a, *D"H virushalayim einah mevi'ah*. And see Roger De Verteuil, "The Scapegoat Archetype," *Journal of Religion and Health* 5, no. 3 (1966): 211.

36. In rabbinic literature, weeping is not necessarily considered something that women do or that marks them as more emotional. Notwithstanding the amora Rav's comment that "[a woman's] tears are frequent," which serves as a warning against offending one's wife (BT Bava Metzia 59a), male rabbis also weep in Talmudic literature. In the words of Charlotte Fonrobert, they are often represented as "emotionally overcharged." Their weeping has specific causes and brings deep-seated and painful emotions to the surface. For example, Rabbi Yoḥanan cries over the death of his colleague and former student Resh Lakish (BT Bava Metzia 84a), and when he reflects on Psalms 33:7, he recalls the irreverent behavior of the people in the Temple (BT Yoma 9b). Rabbi Pinḥas ben Yair weeps on seeing the wounds of his father-in-law, Rabbi Shim'on bar Yoḥai (BT Shabbat 33b). Rabbi Eliezer's eyes "stream with tears" because he has been banned from the Beit Midrash and his possessions have been deemed ritually impure and burned (BT Bava Metzia 59b). The rabbis believe that tears prompt God to listen (BT Bava Metzia 59a, quoting Psalms 39:13). The fact that all of "the house of Israel" joins in crying with the priests on BT Yoma 23a intimates that the rabbis saw weeping as an acceptable male reaction. It also can be a sign that the priests have shed their more aggressive, even violent, behaviors, thereby connecting them to the larger Jewish community in what appears to be a collective process of atonement. This image stands in direct contrast to sources authored in the Greco-Roman world that characterize women as crying more easily than men and men who weep as being "like" women. The weeping of the House of Israel noted in this baraita is textual evidence for Daniel Boyarin's observation that "those practices and performances that defined the rabbi as feminized from the point of view of the dominant [Greco-Roman] culture were those that constituted masculinity within the dominant [rabbinic] culture." See Charlotte Elisheva Fonrobert, "When the Rabbi Weeps: On Reading Gender in Talmudic Aggadah," *Nashim* 4 (2001): 60–65, 70, specifically with reference to BT Bava Metzia 59a–b, and Boyarin, *Unheroic Conduct*, 70, 142.

Notes to Chapter 2

37. See the discussion above regarding the definition of the beit din.

38. See Rashi, BT Yoma 18b, *D"H leziknei kehunah*, where he refers to the idea that the priests were preparing incense.

39. See Moshe Halbertal, *On Sacrifice* (Princeton: Princeton University Press, 2012), 121–122, n. 23, where he points out that if the substitute for a sacrifice is not found, sacrifice leads to murder, death, and the destruction of love.

40. See Daniel R. Schwartz, "Two Pauline Allusions to the Redemptive Mechanism of the Crucifixion," *Journal of Biblical Literature* 102, no. 2 (1983): 259–268; and Stökl Ben Ezra, *Impact of Yom Kippur on Early Christianity*, 173–174. While this Christian imagery arguably is driven by biblical notions of a scapegoat emerging from the story of the binding of Isaac in Genesis 22 and from the image in Leviticus 16 of the scapegoat used on Yom Kippur to clear the people of their sins, it is also possible that the image of God's son, Jesus, bearing the brunt of sin, had an impact on the rabbis who constructed the tannaitic source found in BT Yoma 23a. However, the baraita completely rejects the image of the suffering servant of God and the notion that the death of a human being can be the source of another's redemption. This image of a human sacrifice may be part of a rabbinic polemic not only against the priesthood but also against Jewish Christians.

41. Naomi Koltun-Fromm, "Non-Jewish Sources for Late Ancient Jewish History," in *A Companion to Late Ancient Jews and Judaism, Third Century BCE–Seventh Century CE*, ed. Naomi Koltun-Fromm and Gwynn Kessler (Hoboken, NJ: Wiley, 2020), 167.

42. Also see Romans 6:10 and 1 Peter 3:18, which led Martin Hengel to conclude that Jesus's death was believed to bring about universal atonement for all people. See Eyal Regev, *The Temple in Early Christianity: Experiencing the Sacred* (New Haven: Yale University Press, 2019), 4, 319–320, n. 7, and Martin Hengel, *The Atonement: The Origins of the Doctrine in the New Testament* (Minneapolis: Fortress, 1981), 47, 53. Note that Daniel Boyarin in *Dying for God: Martyrdom and the Making of Christianity and Judaism* (Stanford: Stanford University Press, 1999) argues that the rabbis were not engaged in an outright polemic against Christianity and that they had more sympathy for Christians and Christianity than we might presume. See page 28 regarding his discussion of Rabbi Eliezer.

43. Equally so, Richard Kalmin joins Boyarin and others in warning against oversimplifying the relationship between Judaism and Christianity by thinking that Jews and Christians were hostile to one another. Arguably there are sources that reflect hostility, but there are also instances where

permeable boundaries are evident. Kalmin, *Migrating Tales: The Talmud's Narratives in their Historical Contexts* (Berkeley: University of California Press, 2014), 10.

44. All the available manuscripts of BT Yoma 23a have the words *harei hu kaparatkhem*, "Behold, he is your atonement," while other versions of the story, including T. Yoma 1:12, T. Shevu'ot 1:4, Sifrei Bamidbar, Mas'ei 161, and JT Yoma 2:1, 39d, have *ani* (or *hareini*) *kaparatkhem*: "I am your atonement." The image in the Bavli's version of the son as an atonement most strongly parallels that of a Temple offering.

45. As noted above, see the parallel version of the Temple incident in JT Yoma 2:1, 39d (and see T. Yoma 1:12). The Toseftan version ends differently, asserting that God has left the Temple because of the spilling of blood, leaving it impure. See Kalmin, *Jewish Babylonia*, 47, 60.

46. Tropper, *Keḥomer beyad hayotzer*, 32, refers to M. Sanhedrin 2:1 in the version of MS Kaufmann to explain this alternative reading.

47. Mira Balberg, "Artifact," in *Late Ancient Knowing: Explorations in Intellectual History*, ed. Moulie Vidas and Catherine Michael Chin (Berkeley: University of California Press, 2015), 20–24.

48. In JT Yoma 2:1, 39d, King Menasseh is absent, and no reference is made to the First Temple.

49. Note that T. Yoma 1:12 and T. She'vuot 1:4 have one additional comment after the quotation of the verse from 2 Kings 21:16, stating that because of the murder in the Temple, the Shekhinah departed and the Temple became impure. Yerushalmi Yoma does not have this passage. On some level, it seems that the redactors of the Bavli material, who drew on the Toseftan material, did not want to go so far as to say that God had abandoned the Temple house altogether. Rather, it is the priests with whom they have more difficulty.

50. The first version of the baraita above on BT Yoma 23b does not have the word קיים, although this word paraphrases the father's comment that his son is still writhing.

51. See JT Yoma 2:1, 39d, which does not include the reference to Menasseh.

52. Note that 2 Chronicles 33:9–20, which is the parallel biblical description of the events narrated in 2 Kings 21, not only describes how King Menasseh led the people astray and was captured by the Assyrians, but it also presents him as a king who entreats God and reverses his sinful behavior. God hears his prayers and returns him to Jerusalem where he cleanses the Temple and restores the altar dedicated to God. Repentance through prayer

Notes to Chapter 2

is possible. Rebuilding the Temple is a reasonable hope. Echoes of more positive attitudes toward the Temple reverberate here. However, BT Yoma 23a fails to articulate this point explicitly. The reference to Chronicles is strikingly absent. In admittedly an argument from silence, one cannot help but notice this absence and how it suits the redactors of Yoma to rely on the image of King Menasseh in Kings rather than from Chronicles. See JT Sanhedrin 10:2, 28c, where the narrative found in 2 Chronicles is cited. See also Betsy Amaru, "The Killing of the Prophets: Unraveling a Midrash," *Hebrew Union College Annual* 54 (1983): 171.

53. It is also important to acknowledge that a larger narrative tradition is represented in Mishnah Sanhedrin 10:2, JT Sanhedrin 10:2, 28c, BT Sanhedrin 103b and BT Yevamot 49b–50a (see baraita) that informs the tannaitic version of this story in the Bavli, specifically the decision to add on the quote from 2 Kings. Its addition reveals an underlying struggle that is more pronounced in Bavli Yoma's version of the story than in Yerushalmi Yoma's version, where the verse from 2 Kings is absent. In these additional sources, Menasseh is thought to be responsible for the death of the prophet Isaiah, despite the fact that neither this king or prophet is mentioned together in the Bible. According to various versions of the story, Isaiah rebuked Menasseh, and Menasseh in turn killed him by sawing through a tree in which the prophet was hiding. For a discussion of the Talmudic sources about King Menasseh's killing of Isaiah, see Kalmin, *Migrating Tales: The Talmud's Narratives in Their Historical Contexts*, where he argues that the trope was circulating throughout the Roman East. Also note that ancient Christians quoted Isaiah's prophecies more than those of any other prophet, seeing in them the prefigurement of Jesus's coming, 29–44. See also Amaru, "The Killing of the Prophets," 170, and Gabriel Said Reynolds, "On the Quran and the Theme of Jews as Killers of the Prophets," *Al-Bayān Journal* 10, no. 2 (2012): 12–14. Resonances of Isaiah, arguably a stand-in for Jesus, disclose that there are threats to a developing rabbinic theology percolating among the Jews. New prophets, Jesus among them, with no patrilineal connections, either biblically mandated or externally imposed, are threatening.

54. Carol Delaney discusses this idea of cutting oneself off from family members in order to assert power and authority in her discussion of the binding of Isaac in Genesis, "Cutting the Ties That Bind: The Sacrifice of Abraham and Patriarchal Kinship," in Sarah Franklin and Susan McKinnon, ed., *Relative Values: Reconfiguring Kinship Studies* (Durham: Duke University Press, 2001), 448. She notes that "Abraham's position as apical ancestor, as father of many nations, was constituted by a series of ruptures, referred to

in biblical commentary as his 'trials' in which he cuts the ties that bind—to his father, his kin, other peoples, his wife, his concubine—and, ultimately, the closest tie of all, to his sons."

55. See Naftali S. Cohn, *The Memory of the Temple and the Making of the Rabbis* (Philadelphia: University of Pennsylvania Press, 2013), 13. Cohn builds on Beth Berkowitz's use of postcolonial theory in *Execution and Invention* and on Sara Mills's *Discourse* (London: Routledge, 2004), 69–115. Mills bases herself on Michel Foucault's discussion of the concept of "discourse" in *The History of Sexuality: An Introduction*, vol. 1 (New York: Random House, 1978), 11.

56. Cohn, *Memory of the Temple*, 13.

57. On the rabbis' self-definition by identifying themselves against "others," including women, gentiles, and non-rabbinic Jews, see Mira Balberg, "The Emperor's Daughter's New Skin: Bodily Otherness and Self-Identity in the Dialogues of Rabbi Yehoshua ben Hanania and the Emperor's Daughter," *Jewish Studies Quarterly* 19 (2012): 182, and *Purity, Body, and Self in Early Rabbinic Literature* (Berkeley: University of California Press, 2014).

58. According to Boyarin, *Unheroic Conduct*, 143.

59. Catherine M. Chin and Moulie Vidas, Introduction to *Late Ancient Knowing: Explorations in Intellectual History*, ed. Moulie Vidas and Catherine Michael Chin (Berkeley: University of California Press, 2015): 2–3.

CHAPTER 3. MOTHERS AND SONS

1. See Gregg E. Gardner, "Competitive Giving in the Third Century CE: Early Rabbinic Approaches to Greco-Roman Civic Benefaction," in *Religious Competition in the Third Century C.E.: Jews, Christians, and the Greco-Roman World*, ed. D. Rosenblum, L. C. Vuong, and N. P. DesRosiers (Göttingen: Vandenhoeck & Ruprecht, 2014), 81–92, about rabbinic parallels to Greek benefaction. On women as benefactors, see Gillian Ramsey, "The Queen and the City: Royal Female Intervention and Patronage in Hellenistic Civic Communities," *Gender and History* 23, no. 3 (2011): 511, where she points to a growing tide beginning in the third century BCE of female euergetism, or doing good deeds, that extended through the late Hellenistic and Roman periods. Gifts and charity were nonthreatening ways for women to connect themselves to public life. Also see Rebecca Stephens Falcasantos, "Wandering Wombs, Inspired Intellects: Christian Religious Travel in Late Antiquity," *Journal of Early Christian Studies* 25, no. 1 (2017): 115, regarding women in the third to fifth century CE who supported building projects such as temples and, later, churches.

Notes to Chapter 3

2. Sherri Ortner, "Is Female to Male as Nature Is to Culture?," *Feminist Studies* 1 (1972): 15. Also see Marjorie Lehman, Jane L. Kanarek, and Simon J. Bronner, Introduction to *Mothers in the Jewish Cultural Imagination*, ed. Marjorie Lehman, Jane L. Kanarek, and Simon J. Bronner (Liverpool: Liverpool University Press, 2017), 1–20.

3. Cynthia Chapman, *The House of the Mother: The Social Roles of Maternal Kin in Biblical Hebrew Narrative and Poetry* (New Haven: Yale University Press, 2019), 1–3, articulates a pattern that often occurs in biblical patrilineal genealogies (*toledot*) similar to what I am seeing here in Bavli Yoma. Such genealogies introduce households that contain not only fathers but also mothers, wives, concubines, slave wives, sons, daughters, foreigners, and slaves. But by introducing maternal kin groups, biblical narratives disrupt the neatness of the patriline. The rabbis wish to do the same in Yoma through mothers.

4. More than a lack of control over women and their reproduction, as Mary Douglas, Nancy Jay, and Judith Romney-Wegner discuss in other contexts, is how men express anxiety around the role of women who also have strong cultural influence. For the rabbis, this engenders concerns about the master-disciple relationship and their wishes for greater control in that arena. See Nicole J. Ruane, *Sacrifice and Gender in Biblical Law* (New York: Cambridge University Press, 2013), 161–162, where she discusses Mary Douglas, *Purity and Danger: An Analysis of the Concepts of Pollution and Taboo* (London: Routledge & Kegan Paul, 1966), 24–28; Judith Romney-Wegner, *Chattel or Person? The Status of Women in the Mishnah* (New York: Oxford University Press, 1988), vi; and Nancy Jay, *Throughout Your Generations Forever: Sacrifice, Religion, and Paternity* (Chicago: University of Chicago Press, 1992).

5. According to Richard Kalmin and Daniel Boyarin, Babylonian rabbinic Jewish culture was porous. Physically located in Sassanian Babylonia, the rabbis drew from the cultures of both the Sassanian and Roman empires and the intellectual currents of Roman Hellenism, Syriac Christianity, and Sassanian Zoroastrianism. See Daniel Boyarin, "Hellenism in Jewish Babylonia," in *The Cambridge Companion to the Talmud and Rabbinic Literature*, ed. Charlotte Elisheva Fonrobert and Martin S. Jaffee (Cambridge: Cambridge University Press, 2007), 336–363; Richard Kalmin, *Jewish Babylonia between Persia and Roman Palestine*; and Julia Watts Belser, *Rabbinic Tales of Destruction*, xvii–xviii. For a recent critique of approaches to the study of the impact of Persian culture on the rabbis, see Simcha Gross, "Rethinking Babylonian Rabbinic Acculturation in the Sassanian Empire," *Journal of Ancient Judaism* 9, no. 2 (2018): 280–310, and his analysis of BT Kiddushin 70ab.

6. Belser, *Rabbinic Tales of Destruction*, xvii, xix.

7. Joyce Antler, *You Never Call! You Never Write! A History of the Jewish Mother* (New York: Oxford University Press, 2007), 3, 8–9. Also see Serene Jones, *Feminist Theory and Christian Theology: Cartographies of Grace* (Minneapolis: Fortress, 2000), 36–37, who argues in a far broader context that mothers are often the vessel through which cultural constructs move and settle. Such constructs are frequently contested and change depending on the context. And see F. Scott Spencer's reflections on Jones's work in *Salty Wives, Spirited Mothers, and Savvy Widows: Capable Women of Purpose and Persistence in Luke's Gospel* (Grand Rapids, MI: Eerdmans, 2012), 59; and Lehman et al., Introduction to *Mothers in the Jewish Cultural Imagination*, 1–20.

8. Galit Hasan-Rokem, *Web of Life: Folklore and Midrash in Rabbinic Literature*, trans. Batya Stein (Stanford: Stanford University Press, 2000), 109, 119–125, 143, argues that this story, as well as other stories about mothers and their sons, has antecedents and parallels in rabbinic and non-rabbinic sources, attesting to a wide circulation of them. As Hasan-Rokem points out in her discussion of aggadic stories that appear in rabbinic literature, "Folk literature is the result of a living process engaging its authors in verbal and artistic negotiations with their social and cultural surroundings." Different versions of the story about the mother of Doeg, who consumes him, recall Leviticus 26:29, Deuteronomy 28:57, and 2 Kings 7:24–30, pointing to the curse that befalls those who sin: they must eat their children. It also refers to a tradition that was circulating orally even before the tannaitic era among Jews and early Christians. Rather than reading the story intertextually, as Hasan-Rokem does, I focus on this material in its context in the third chapter of Bavli Yoma. I thank Mira Wasserman for sharing her discussion of this story in her unpublished article, "Mothers and Martyrs in Lamentations Rabbah," 2011.

9. See BT Yoma 38b–39a, where in making a point about one leader replacing another, Rabbi Ḥiya bar Abba says in the name of Rabbi Yoḥanan that the prophet Samuel replaced the priest Eli, referring to 1 Samuel 3–4.

10. For parallel versions of this story, see Eikhah Rabbah (Vilna, ed.), 1:51; 2:23; (Buber, ed.), parashah 1 and 2; Sifra *Beḥukotai* 2 (Weiss ed., 6:3, 1862); Josephus, *Jewish War*, trans. H. St. J. Thackery (Cambridge, MA: Harvard University Press, 1957–1961), 6:201–219. For an excellent comparison of all of the versions of this story, see Jane Kanarek, "Memorializing the Temple through the Maternal Practice of Arakhin," http://thegemara.com/memorializing-the-Temple-through-the-maternal-practice-of-arakhin/, accessed June 2020. Also see Tal Ilan, "Ha'em she'akhlah et benah" [The

Notes to Chapter 3

mother who ate her son], in *Bein Yosephus leḥazal*, vol. 2, ed. Tal Ilan, Vered Noam, et al. (Jerusalem: Yad Ben Zvi, 2017).

11. See M. Sanhedrin 10:1 and BT Berakhot 17b. Doeg the Edomite is one of seven individuals who are listed by name in the Mishnah and are denied a portion in the World to Come.

12. See Sifra, *Beḥukotai* 2,6:3, where Doeg's father is recorded as having died. His mother made a donation of gold equivalent to Doeg's weight once a year.

13. Compare this also to the story of Marta bat Boethus in Eikhah Rabbah (Vilna ed.), 1:50; (Buber ed.), parashah 1; and BT Gittin 56a. See Belser's discussion in *Rabbinic Tales of Destruction*, 186–193, about the equation between women's bodies and disaster. Women like Marta become paradigms for the suffering that ensued in conjunction with the destruction of the Temple. Marta is also mentioned in BT Yoma 18a. She uses her gold *dinarim* to bribe King Yannai to appoint her husband as the high priest, highlighting the corruption evident in priestly leadership.

14. See Jane Kanarek, "Pilgrimage and Piety: Rabbinic Women and Vows of Valuation," *Nashim* 28 (2015): 61–74, regarding *mishkal* in M. Arakhin 5:1, T. Arakhin 3:1, and BT Arakhin 19a.

15. Leviticus 27:1–8 records the number of shekels based on one's age and sex that could be dedicated to the Temple. See Kanarek, "Pilgrimage and Piety," 61–74, and "Rewriting Arakhin: Women and Tannaitic Vows of Valuation," *AJS Review* 40, no. 2 (2016): 261–277.

16. Baruch A. Levine, *The JPS Torah Commentary: Leviticus* (Philadelphia: Jewish Publication Society, 2003), 193. See also Jacob Milgrom, who points to vowing a person's worth as a way to prevent an instance such as Jephthah's dedication of his daughter, as well as to dissuade individuals from taking the vow to become nazirites. *Leviticus 23–27: A New Translation with Introduction and Commentary* (New York: Doubleday, 2001), 2410–2411. Kanarek disagrees with Milgrom as she notes in "Pilgrimage and Piety," 71, n. 15. See Kanarek, "Memorializing the Temple." Also see Krista Dalton for another perspective on donations made by women, in which they expect something from the rabbis in return. Writing about material in Yerushalmi Sotah, Dalton discusses the case of a wealthy woman who in giving tithes wants to be taught Torah. See "Teaching for the Tithe: Donor Expectations and the Matrona's Tithe," *AJS Review* 44, no. 1 (2020): 49–73.

17. See Sifra, *Beḥukotai* 2:6, 3, where Doeg's father is recorded as having died. His mother made a donation of gold equivalent to his weight once a year.

18. See Dalton, "Teaching for the Tithe," 51, regarding women patrons donating to rabbinic scholars for the ability to learn Torah, and Ramsey, "Queen and the City," 511.

19. Belser, *Rabbinic Tales of Destruction* (185–193), points to Marta bat Boethus along with the mother of Doeg as paradigmatic examples of rich widows facing the crisis of the destruction of the Temple. Believing that they could rely on their wealth, they are fallible in the face of disaster.

20. I thank Beth Berkowitz, Sarah Wolf, and Erez DeGolan for reading early drafts of this section and Gregg Gardner, Sarit Kattan Gribetz, and Daniel Schwartz for their feedback in a session on Helene of Adiabene at the Association for Jewish Studies in 2020.

21. Helene is referred to with the title "queen" in far fewer instances in rabbinic literature than she is referred to as "mother." In M. Nazir 3:6 and BT Sukkah 2b, she is referred to as a queen. In T. Sukkah 1:1, M. Yoma 3:10, T. Yoma 2:3, and JT Yoma 3:8, 40b, and BT Yoma 37a, Helene is "mother." Every manuscript mentions that she is the mother of Munbaz, but not every manuscript tells us that she is a queen. Also see Sarit Kattan Gribetz, "The Mothers in the Manuscripts: Gender, Motherhood and Power in the Toledot Yeshu Narratives," in *Toledot Yeshu in Context: The Jewish "Life of Jesus" in Ancient, Medieval, and Modern History*, ed. Daniel Barbu and Yaacov Deutsch (Tübingen: Mohr Siebeck, 2019), 119–120, and Galit Hasan-Rokem, "Polymorphic Helena: *Toledot Yeshu* as a Palimpsest of Religious Narratives and Identities," in *Toledot Yeshu* (The life story of Jesus) *Revisited: A Princeton Conference*, ed. Peter Schäfer, Michael Meerson, and Yaacov Deutsch (Tübingen: Mohr Siebeck, 2011), 264–268.

22. Sources such as Josephus, *Jewish Antiquities*, trans. Louis H. Feldman (Cambridge, MA: Harvard University Press, 1926–1965), 20:49–53; 20:101; T. Peah 4:18; JT Peah 1:1, 15b; and BT Bava Batra 11a point to the generosity of the house of Adiabene, specifically to Helene and her sons. Amid famine, they provided relief to the Jews in Jerusalem. See Gregg E. Gardner, *The Origins of Organized Charity in Rabbinic Judaism* (New York: Cambridge University Press, 2015), 13, including n. 48. For other references to Helene in Josephus, see *Antiquities*, 20:15-56; and see *Jewish War*, 5:55, 5:119, 5:147, 5:253; 6:355 (referring to her tomb in Jerusalem, to a monument built to honor her, and to her palace in Jerusalem).

23. Katharina Galor, "Domestic Architecture," in *The Oxford Handbook of Jewish Daily Life in Roman Palestine*, ed. Catherine Hezser (Oxford: Oxford University Press, 2010).

24. Ishay Rosen-Zvi observes in *The Mishnaic Sotah Ritual*, 158, that He-

Notes to Chapter 3

lene's donation of a tablet, or plaque, with the sotah passage does not appear in any rabbinic source as one of the vessels or implements used in Temple worship—not even in Mishnah Sotah. See his discussion of the development of the sotah rite from a magical act that required the priest's recitation of the passage from memory to the need for an educational device in tannaitic literature (160). Also see Sarit Kattan Gribetz, "Consuming Texts: Women as Recipients and Transmitters of Ancient Texts," in *Rethinking 'Authority' in Late Antiquity: Authorship, Law, and Transmission in Jewish and Christian Tradition*, ed. A. J. Berkovitz and Mark Letteney (New York: Routledge, 2018), 183–184, and Tal Ilan, *Jewish Women in Greco-Roman Palestine* (Tübingen: Mohr Siebeck, 2006), 137.

25. See BT Yoma 37ab, Rashi, *D"H vidot sekinin* (on 37b).

26. See the baraita on BT Yoma 37b.

27. See Gardner, *Origins of Organized Charity*, 137, 151, where he mentions how T. Peah 4:18 presents Munbaz as an exemplar of charitable giving. He is a king willing to give up his fortune for immaterial reward in the World to Come.

28. See T. Yoma 2:3: "Munbaz as king made the handles of the knives used on Yom Kippur out of gold, and he was remembered with praise. Helene, his mother, made a nivreshet of gold and placed it on the entrance to the heikhal."

29. Compare M. Yoma 3:10 and T. Yoma 2:3. Also see the Kaufmann manuscript of the mishnah MSA 50, fol. 63r, which reflects the same reading as most other manuscripts of the Talmud. More specifically, when the mishnah refers to Nikanor's doors, the correct reading is, "[Regarding] Nikanor, miracles occurred to his doors, and they remembered him with praise." The correct Hebrew word is אותו, not אותן. Had the mishnah used the plural form of the word אותן, one could argue that the mishnah was praising Munbaz, Helene, and Nikanor for their gifts. That is not the case here. Only Nikanor is praised. The details of the miracles mentioned in this mishnah are fleshed out in a baraita quoted on BT Yoma 38a, where Nikanor's doors are referred to as the only ones used in the gates of the Temple that were not covered in gold. Some, however, as the baraita notes, argue that they were made of copper and shone like gold.

30. I am imagining this as Sarit Kattan Gribetz has suggested to me—that the nivreshet functioned as a sundial.

31. See T. Yoma 2:3, BT Yoma 37b, and Yerushalmi Yoma 3:8, 41a. It seems that the Bavli reworked this material to highlight the fact that the

nivreshet was what shone when the sun hit it and signaled the proper time for reciting Shema. Shema is not mentioned in T. Yoma 2:3.

32. BT Yoma 37b.

33. *Mishmar* refers to priests who served in the Temple on a rotating basis, and *ma'amad* refers to non-priests who accompanied the priests to Jerusalem. See BT Ta'anit 26a for a more detailed description of *anshei hama'amad* and BT Yoma 37b, Rashi *D"H anshei hama'amad*.

34. See BT Berakhot, beginning with 2a, where the rabbis discuss the issue of when to say Shema. See Sarit Kattan Gribetz, *Time and Difference in Rabbinic Judaism* (Princeton: Princeton University Press, 2020) with respect to rabbinic conceptualizations of time.

35. See Richard Kalmin, "The Adiabenian Royal Family in Rabbinic Literature of Late Antiquity," in *Tif'eret leyisrael: Jubilee Volume in Honor of Israel Francus* (New York: Jewish Theological Seminary of America, 2010): 74–75, where he uses this interpolation in the Bavli as an example to support the idea that the Bavli subjected its sources more freely to editorial tampering. This is also the case when the Bavli reincorporates the tannaitic story about Kimhit and her sons into Bavli Yoma (see chapter four). See Shamma Friedman, "Habaraitot batalmud habavli veyachasan lemakbiloteihen shebatosefta" [The Bariatot in the Babylonian Talmud and their relationship to parallels in the Tosefta], in *Atara lehayim: Mekhkarim basifrut hatalmudit veharabanit likhvod professor Hayyim Zalman Dimitrovski* [Atara lehayim: Studies in the Talmud and medieval rabbinic literature in honor of Professor Hayyim Zalmon Dimitrovsky], ed. Daniel Boyarin Marc G. Hirshman, Menahem Schmelzer, Shamma Friedman, and Israel Ta-Shma (Jerusalem: Magnes Press, 2000), 163–201, 183–201.

36. So laden is the prayer with personal covenantal loyalty that martyrs recite verses from Shema at the moment of death, as mentioned in the martyrdom narratives found in Bavli Gittin 57b, also involving a mother and her sons. I discuss these narratives when I discuss Kimhit in chapter four.

37. Deuteronomy 6:5–9, 11:13–21; Numbers 15:37–41.

38. I thank Gregg Gardner for suggesting that M. Shabbat 2:6 may inform Helene's gifts in that women were responsible for ensuring that the lamp was lit before the Sabbath. In this regard, the daily household informs the Temple. This also raises the issue of how material objects serve as memory tools to remember the Temple house. It is curious that many of the objects mentioned in Yoma associated with Temple rites never become part of the rabbinic house.

Notes to Chapter 3   239

39. See M. Berakhot 3:3, BT Berakhot 20ab, M. Kiddushin 1:7, and BT Kiddushin 34a.

40. Josephus suggests that Helene brought Judaism to her entire province, leading them to conversion, although rabbinic tradition is not clear about her origins. Depicted positively throughout rabbinic literature, she also uses her monarchical advantage to assist the Jews, even aiding them in a time of famine. See *Jewish Antiquities*, 20:15–56. Also see Daniel R. Schwartz, "God, Gentiles, and Jewish Law: On Acts 15 and Josephus's Adiabene Narrative," in *Geschichte—Tradition—Reflexion: Festschrift für Martin Hengel zum 70*, ed. H. Cancik, H. Lichtenberger, and Peter Schäfer (Tübingen: Mohr Siebeck, 1996), 265–272; Shulamit Valler, *Massekhet Sukkah: A Feminist Commentary on the Babylonian Talmud* (Tübingen: Mohr Siebeck, 2009), 49; Ilan, *Jewish Women in Greco-Roman Palestine*, 31; Ilan, *Integrating Women into Second Temple History* (Peabody, MA: Hendrickson, 2001), 25–26; Lawrence Schiffman, "The Conversion of the Royal House of Adiabene in Josephus and Rabbinic Sources," in *Josephus, Judaism, and Christianity*, ed. Louis H. Feldman and Gohei Hata (Leiden: Brill, 1987), 293–312; Kalmin, "Adiabenian Royal Family," 61–77; Galit Hasan-Rokem, "Material Mobility vs. Concentric Cosmology in the Sukkah: The House of the Wandering Jew or a Ubiquitous Temple?," in *Things: Religion and the Question of Materiality*, ed. Dick Houtman and Birgit Meyer (New York: Fordham University Press, 2012): 160–164; Etka Liebowitz, "A New Perspective on Two Jewish Queens in the Second Temple Period: Alexandra of Judaea and Helene of Adiabene," in *Sources and Interpretation in Ancient Judaism: Studies for Tal Ilan at Sixty*, ed. Meron M. Piotrkowski, Saskia Dönitz, Geoffrey Herman, and Tal Ilan (Leiden: Brill, 2018), 41–65. Also see T. Megillah 3(4):30, JT Megillah 4:12, 75c, and BT Menachot 32b, where the Adiabenian royal family is described as observing Jewish law, referring specifically to the "House of Munbaz," although Helene is not named. A more specific reference to the conversion of Helene's sons appears in Beraishit Rabbah 46:11. Bereishit Rabbah refers to the circumcision of the sons of Ptolemaios, who are Munbaz and Izates. Helene is not mentioned by name in this source as Ptolemaios's wife, although reference is made to the mother of Munbaz and Izates. For the most comprehensive discussion of both rabbinic and non-rabbinic sources that mention Helene, see Michal Marciak, "Izates and Helena of Adiabene: A Study on Literary Traditions and History" (PhD diss., Leiden University, 2012), and for the treatment of Helene in the anti-Christian polemical work *Toledot Yeshu*, see Gribetz, "Mothers in the Manuscripts," 118–120.

41. Possibly she is widowed.

42. Shulamit Valler, *Massekhet Sukkah* (Tübingen: Mohr Siebeck, 2009), 49; Cynthia M. Baker, "The Queen, the Apostate, and the Women Between: (Dis)Placement of Women in Tosefta *Sukka*," in *A Feminist Commentary on the Babylonian Talmud: Introduction and Studies*, ed. Tal Ilan, Tamara Or, Dorothea M. Salzer, Christiane Steuer, Irina Wandrey (Tübingen: Mohr Siebeck. 2007), 169–173.

43. See JT Sukkah 1:1, 51d and Kalmin's discussion in "The Adiabenian Royal Family" on the difference between the baraita about Helene's sukkah in the Bavli as compared to the Yerushalmi, 62–64.

44. Note that Mishnah Sotah contains no mention of this golden tablet. T. Sotah 2:1, however, notes that a tablet was set into the sanctuary wall so that the priest could copy the sotah curses and then expound the pericope. In this way, the wife who was accused might be better able to understand the details of the trial by ordeal as the priests would serve as her mediators. Sarit Kattan points out that in Mishnah Yoma, the rabbis turn Helene into the ideal transmitter of the text of the sotah. As such, an accused woman has a text written and available to her; she then hears it, understands it, and ingests it, participating in all stages of the process. See "Consuming Texts," 184. Also see Rosen-Zvi, *Mishnaic Sotah Ritual*, 158–160.

45. See the parallel sugya in Bavli Gittin 58b–60a that is constructed to respond to a mishnah about priests reading Torah before the Levites and Levites before the Israelites, in the interest of maintaining peace between people (*darkhei shalom*). While Helene is not named in BT Gittin 60a, the baraita quoted there references her through mention made of her gift of the sotah tablet.

46. Miriam B. Peskowitz, *Spinning Fantasies: Rabbis, Gender, and History*, 139, argues that in donating this tablet, Helene grants women more information about the laws that affected them. She also created an opportunity to gather protestations on the part of women against one of the most subversive rites taking place in the Temple. See also Lynne Walker and Vron Ware, "Political Pincushions: Decorating the Abolitionist Interior 1787–1865," in *Domestic Space: Reading the Nineteenth-Century Interior*, ed. Inga Bryden and Janet Floyd (Manchester: Manchester University Press, 1999), 58–83, who make this argument in the case of British women who decorated their homes with material objects that reflected their opposition to slavery.

47. If we rely on M. Nazir 3:6 and its claim that Helene took on the status of a nazirite in fulfillment of a vow premised on the return of her son from battle safely, this source would indicate that Helene went to Jerusalem to make the offerings associated with the vow. Upon learning that such a dec-

laration cannot be made unless one lives in the Land of Israel, she relocates there from Adiabene and observes another seven years as a nazirite after her arrival. The rabbis therefore construct her as someone who is familiar with Temple practice and the priesthood. M. Nazir 3:6; BT Nazir 19b–20; JT Nazir 3:6, 52b. Therefore, Helene seems, in the rabbis' construction of her, to be knowledgeable enough to instruct the priests regarding matters other than the sotah.

48. Intriguingly, women who survive the sotah rite unharmed are promised progeny according to Numbers 5:28. Among the reasons that scholars have put forth to explain the interest of the tannaim in the sotah rite is its connection to the theme of fertility. See BT Berakhot 31b, where Hannah desperately asks God for a child, threatening that she will hide from Elkhanah, her husband, leading him to think that she is a sotah. Because of her ability to prove her innocence, Hannah believes, according to the Bavli, that God will grant her a child. Rosen-Zvi, *Mishnaic Sotah Ritual*, 171. Also see Ishay Rosen-Zvi, "Haishah hanitzevet: Tefilat Hannah bidrashot hazal" [The standing woman: Hannah's prayer in rabbinic exegesis], in *Tarbut yehudit be'ein hasearah: Sefer hayovel leYosef Ahituv* [Jewish culture in the eye of the storm: A Jubilee book in honor of Yosef Ahituv], ed. Avi Sagi and Nahem Iman (Ein Tzurim: Hakibbutz Hameuhad, 2002), 675–698.

49. Compare this discussion of Helene to the treatment of her in T. Sukkah 1:1, BT Sukkah 2b–3a, and JT Sukkah 1:1, 51d. Tosefta and Yerushalmi Sukkah mention that her sons were sages. See Kalmin, "Adiabenian Royal Family," 62–63.

50. See Schwartz, "God, Gentiles, and Jewish Law," 266–269, on the instruction of Helene and her son Izates as described by Josephus.

51. While Ishay Rosen-Zvi argues that the sotah rite was practiced during Helene's time, by the time of the redaction of tannaitic sources into the Bavli's discussion the practice had fallen by the wayside. Rosen-Zvi also points out that we cannot know what the practice looked like during the second Temple period, but he seems convinced that its appearance in tannaitic literature, not to mention references to it in Josephus and Qumran literature, indicate that it was practiced. Rosen-Zvi, *Mishnaic Sotah Ritual*, 161.

52. Peskowitz, *Spinning Fantasies*, 139.

53. Peskowitz, *Spinning Fantasies*, 136–139, argues that women's gossip about sotah women was a method of disciplining themselves. See Rosen-Zvi, *Mishnaic Sotah Ritual*, 159, and Lisa Gruchcow, *Writing the Wayward Wife: Rabbinic Interpretations of Sotah* (Leiden: Brill, 2006), 105, n. 61.

54. Note that in M. Sotah 3:4 Ben Azzai says, "A man is obligated to teach

Torah to his daughter so that if she drinks, she would know that merit is what suspends [the punishment] for her." R. Eliezer says, "Whoever teaches Torah to his daughter, it is as if he teaches her sexual lasciviousness." See Kattan Gribetz, "Consuming Texts: Women as Recipients and Transmitters of Ancient Texts,", 178–183, and Dalton, "Teaching for the Tithe," 52–54. Also see Sarah Wolf's analysis of Rabbi Yirmiyah: "'Haven't I Told You Not to Take Yourself Outside of the Law?' Rabbi Yirmiyah and the Characterization of a Scholastic," *AJS Review* 44, no. 2 (2020): 1–27. And see Devorah Steinmetz, "Agada Unbound: Inter-Agadic Characterization of Sages in the Bavli and Implications for Reading Agada," in *Creation and Composition: The Contribution of the Bavli Redactors (Stammaim) to the Aggada*, ed. Peter Shäfer and Jeffrey L. Rubenstein (Tübingen: Mohr Siebeck, 2005), 295, and her argument regarding the ways that specific character traits or values—in this case regarding Rabbi Eliezer—are assigned to specific rabbis. I sense that the interchange between Rabbi Eliezer and the "wise woman" reflects a trope about this rabbi that is rooted in Mishnah Sotah dismissing the value of women's Torah knowledge. That Helene does not appear in Bavli or Yerushalmi Sotah remains a curiosity.

55. I discuss BT Yoma 66b in greater length in chapter four.

56. Dalton, "Teaching for the Tithe," 49–73.

57. Peskowitz, *Spinning Fantasies*, 91–108, 131–139. Also note Peskowitz's references to Proverbs 31 regarding the definition of a woman of valor that resonates through the Bavli's discussion of Kimhit below.

58. Daniel Boyarin, in *Socrates and the Fat Rabbis*, 32, argues that the rabbis mock their own intellectual enterprise, as I have noted here in Bavli Yoma through the figure of Rabbi Eliezer. The Talmud's legal enterprise, Boyarin argues, is complicated by the Talmud's inclusion of rabbinic self-doubt. See also Wolf's analysis of this phenomenon in the Bavli through an examination of Rabbi Yirmiyah: "'Haven't I Told You Not to Take Yourself Outside of the Law?,'" 4.

CHAPTER 4. FROM INSIDE OUT

1. T. Yoma 3:20.

2. JT Yoma 1:1, 38d.

3. BT Yoma 47a.

4. Vayikra Rabbah (Margoliot, ed.), Aharei mot, 20:11.

5. See Avot derabi Natan, A (Schechter, ed.), 35, *D"H Asarah Nisim*, where a later version of the baraita records miracles that happened in the Temple (BT Yoma 21a). One of the miracles was that the high priest never had

a seminal emission on Yom Kippur. Avot derabi Natan points out that the one exception was Yishmael, the son of Kimḥit. In this version of the story of Kimḥit, the saliva is conflated with *keri*, which is a seminal emission, another reason for disqualification.

6. Tanḥuma (Buber, ed.), Aharei mot, 9; Tanḥuma (Warsaw, ed.), Aharei mot, 7.

7. Pesikta derav Kahana (Mandelbaum, ed.), Aharei mot, 26:10.

8. Bamidbar Rabbah (Midrash Rabbah, Jerusalem, ed.), Bamidbar 2:26.

9. All of these sources that contain the Kimḥit story are similar and follow the tradition found in the Tosefta and Yerushalmi, as I note below. The Bavli is the only source where we find a different ending to the Kimḥit story, which I also discuss.

10. Daniel Stökl Ben Ezra uses this terminology in his discussion of the role of Yom Kippur in the religious lives and literature of early Christians: "Fasting with Jews, Thinking with Scapegoats: Some Remarks on Yom Kippur in Early Judaism and Christianity, in Particular 4Q541, Barnabas 7, Matthew 27 and Acts 27," in *The Day of Atonement: Its Interpretations in Early Jewish and Christian Traditions*, ed. Thomas Hieke and Tobias Nicklas (Leiden: Brill, 2012), 168.

11. See Shmuel Eliezer Edels (Maharsha): *Ḥidushei Aggadot*, Yoma 47a, where he argues that Kimḥit's son, Yishmael, mentioned in the Bavli version, had a father who was Pabi. Clearly bothered that Yishmael did not have lineage back to his father, he conflated Yishmael ben Pabi with this priest named Yishmael ben Kimḥit. Also see JT Yoma 3:6 (40b), BT Yoma 9a, and BT Yoma 35b.

12. See, for example, BT Berakhot 16a, BT Shabbat 88b, BT Ta'anit 24b, BT Gittin 36b, and BT Bava Metzia 110a, where Rav Mari is referred to as the son of Shmuel's daughter. In other instances, Rav Mari is also referred to as the son of Rachel: see BT Shabbat 124b, 154a, BT Yevamot 45b, 92b, BT Gittin 36b, and BT Bava Metzia 73b. Rashi notes in his comment to BT Berakhot 16a (*D"H Berah devat Shemu'el*) that the daughter of Shmuel, Rachel, was abducted and raped by a non-Jewish man named Issur. She became pregnant from that encounter. Although Issur converted before Rav Mari was born, the rape of Rachel by Issur was not considered a holy union. For this reason, Rav Mari was referred to in the name of his mother, that is, in the name of the parent who had a Jewish lineage. Also see BT Yoma 84a, Abba bar Marta.

13. Nonbiblical mothers often are not named in rabbinic literature. In Bavli Yoma, for example, Abaye's mother (BT Yoma 78b) and Eleazar ben Ḥarsom's mother (BT Yoma 35b) are nameless. See material in BT Kiddu-

244   *Notes to Chapter 4*

shin 31b, also in the Bavli, where Rabbi Tarfon's mother is discussed but not named.

14. Ilana Pardes, *Countertraditions in the Bible: A Feminist Approach* (Cambridge, MA: Harvard University Press, 1992), 156.

15. Chapman, *The House of the Mother: The Social Roles of Maternal Kin in Biblical Hebrew Narrative and Poetry* (New Haven: Yale University Press, 201), 201–206. Although it is the case that Jacob will marry into his mother's family; see Genesis 28.

16. Kate Cooper, *The Virgin and the Bride: Idealized Womanhood in Late Antiquity* (Cambridge, MA: Harvard University Press, 1996), 19. See also Peter Hatlie, "Images of Motherhood and Self in Byzantine Literature," *Dumbarton Oaks Papers* 63 (2009): 44; Claudia Rapp, "Figures of Female Sanctity: Byzantine Edifying Manuscripts and Their Audience," *Dumbarton Oaks Papers* 50 (1996): 329; and Rosen-Zvi, *Mishnaic Sotah Ritual*, 7, where he discusses the importance of examining places in rabbinic literature where gender-related knowledge is generated and maintained.

17. Also see parallel sources in JT Megillah 1:10, 72a; JT Horayot 3:2, 47d, and Vayikra Rabbah, Aharei mot 20:11. See Baker, *Rebuilding the House of Israel*, 64–70.

18. In looking for the contexts where Kimhit is found in midrashic collections such as Vayikra Rabbah, Aharei mot, 20:11–12, and in the later collections, including Pesikta derav Kahana (Mandelbaum, ed.), Aharei mot, 26:10–11, and *Tanhuma* (Buber, ed.), Aharei mot, 9–10; (Warsaw, ed.), 7, Kimhit is mentioned alongside Miriam. The death of Miriam signifies that the righteous atone for all of Israel, pointing to a possible connection between Kimhit and Miriam. By the thirteenth century, Kimhit became the righteous model of modesty, even a symbol for appropriate conduct during sexual relations that therefore grants those who follow in her footsteps the reward of great sons—see Menahem Recanati (1250–1310), Harekanati al hatorah (Deuteronomy), in *Sifrei Halevushim*, ed. Mordekhai ben Abraham Jaffee, 7 vols. (Jerusalem: Zikhron Aharon), 1999–2000, Ki Teize 24:1. She is still a topic of analysis in the Talmudic commentary of Shmuel Eliezer Halevi Edels (Maharsha, 1555–1631), *Hidushei Aggadot*, Yoma 47a, as late as the early seventeenth century, as well as in the Torah commentary by Hayim Joseph David Azulai (1724–1806), *Sefer Torat hahidah: Al hatorah* (Jerusalem: Oz vehadar, 1994). See Azulai's comment on Vayikra Tazri'a, n. 11, where he refers to the question posed by Maharsha as to why the rabbis did not question the father of the seven high priests regarding what he did to deserve the reward of high-priest-sons. The reply, according to Maharsha, is

Notes to Chapter 4   245

"because the essence of everything is dependent on the mother and whether she is righteous [and not the father]." Menaḥem ben Shlomo Meiri, in *Beit Habeḥirah*, Yoma 47a, *D"H Kevar Biarnu*, indicates that the tradition, or story, from the Land of Israel was more praiseworthy than the tradition in the Bavli, recognizing the distinction made in the tannaitic baraitot found in the Talmudim. Most of these later sources see Kimḥit as meritorious, relying on Psalms 45:14, "Every honorable king's daughter is within," as well as the play on Kimḥit's name, pointing to the power she had in raising admirable sons.

19. Kimḥit emerges as an inspiration for religious women because she connects raising seven sons who are high priests with a commitment to modesty, covering her hair even in her house. Here are the words of an Orthodox Jewish woman invoking Kimḥit: "I try to cover my hair at all times so that even the four walls will not see my hair. If I adhere closely to the laws regarding head-covering, I hope that I will be privileged to give birth to sons who are God-fearing and knowledgeable in Torah." From as early as the tannaitic period, women who entered the bridal canopy without head coverings were presumed to be virgins, with marriage contracts (*ketubot*) valued at 200 zuz. Women who walked out in public with their hair exposed created grounds for their husbands to divorce them (M. Ketubot 7:6; BT Ketubot 74ab). Female demons in later rabbinic sources, such as Lilith, have long, uncovered hair, suggesting that a woman who does not cover her hair spreads evil (BT Eruvin 100b). According to BT Berakhot 24a, a woman's hair is considered an enticement to men (*ervah*). Susan Weiss, "Under Cover: Demystification of Women's Head Covering in Jewish Law," *Nashim* 17 (2009): 94, 97.

20. The tannaitic version of the Kimḥit narrative in the Bavli appears nowhere else in rabbinic or post-rabbinic collections. Rashi, as I noted above (BT Yoma 47a), in *D"H lo ra'u korot beiti*, cites the verse (found in JT Yoma 1:1; 38d) from Psalms 45:15, which is missing in the Bavli's baraita. Rashi, however, by referring to the verse from Psalms, narrows the glaring difference between the two versions. My interpretation does not reflect Rashi or the translation found in Sefaria, https://www.sefaria.org/Yoma.47a?lang=bi.

21. See Baruch Bokser, "*Ma'al* and Blessings over Food: Rabbinic Transformation of Cultic Terminology and Alternative Modes of Piety," *Journal of Biblical Literature* 100, no. 4 (1981): 563–572 for a careful look at the development of the biblical concept of *ma'al* associated with the Temple that then takes on a new form in later rabbinic literature. The development, while gradual, can be seen when comparing amoraic and stammaitic Babylonian material to the way this concept is treated in the Mishnah.

22. Sources such as ones that appear in the third chapter of tractate Kiddu-

shin and the seventh chapter of tractate Yevamot carefully construct Jewish lineage within the context of valid marriages and prompt the question as to why a similar discussion of the rules for determining a replacement priest does not appear in rabbinic literature. Other rabbinic sources are not helpful. The tannaitic collection Sifra comments directly on the biblical injunction in Leviticus 16:32: "The priest who has been anointed and ordained to serve as priest in place of his father shall make expiation." This instruction unequivocally states that a son takes precedence over all others in "making atonement," that is, if he is fit to perform the role to replace his father (Sifra Aharei mot 5, 8:5). That said, there is little additional information or guidance if there are no sons. The fifth-century midrashic collection Vayikra Rabbah, in commenting on Leviticus 16, goes only so far in supporting the notion that a high priest had to be replaced if he became impure or died, relating that Aaron's sons replaced him specifically because of impurity and then again following his death. See Vayikra Rabbah, Aharei mot, 20:11, where Rabbi Hiya bar Abba states that after Aaron died, his son Eleazar took over for him, and after Eleazar's death, Eleazar's brother took over for him, setting up a hereditary framework regarding the priesthood. Building on Exodus 29:29–30 and its mention of the garments that are passed down from priest-father to priest-son, BT Yoma 72b makes mention of the fact that sons succeed their fathers as high priests in a discussion to determine whether the sons of priests anointed for war also follow their fathers. The goal of the passage, however, is not to delineate specifics about who takes over from whom.

23. See also JT Yoma 1:1; 38d; BT Yoma 35b.

24. See specifically M. Kiddushin 3:12 and the Talmudic material that follows on BT Kiddushin 66ab. In the case of two Jews married to one another, progeny follow the status of the father. If he is a priest, the child is also a priest. If one parent is Jewish and the other is not, the status of the child follows the mother. M. Yevamot 7:5 and the Talmudic material that comments on this situation grapple with the issue of whether the offspring of a Jewish mother and a non-Jewish father is a *mamzer*, a child born from a forbidden union. See Shaye J. D. Cohen, "The Matrilineal Principle in Historical Perspective," *Judaism* 34, no. 1 (1985): 5–13.

25. Mishnah Yoma 3:9 describes the choreography of the Yom Kippur avodah vividly, positioning the deputy high priest on the high priest's right-hand side and the head of the priestly family on his left, without any mention of their specific relationship to the high priest in terms of responsibilities, even in the event of disqualification having happened. Whether they function as the backup priests, ready to step in should a problem arise, is not de-

Notes to Chapter 4 247

lineated. The Babylonian amora Rav Yehudah suggests that this deputy high priest is a fool (*bor*): one who lacks any knowledge of appropriate priestly behavior, that is, before the Bavli's editors step in to claim that students always stand to the right of their teachers (BT Yoma 37a). Clearly the Bavli imposes its own rabbinic values onto the relationship of the high priest and the deputy high priest, suggesting that they are teacher-student. Here we can see that their blood relationship matters less than the hierarchy formed in the name of transferring knowledge to the next generation.

26. Priests buy and sell the high priesthood, even killing other priests through sorcery, bypassing heredity as the main "legitimate" factor in determining who would be the next priest in line for this role (JT Yoma 1:1, 38c; BT Yoma 8b–9a, 18a).

27. See the version of this text in T. Yoma 1:4 and its parallel on BT Yoma 12a.

28. M. Avot 5:5 and BT Yoma 21a indicate that one of the miracles that occurred in the Temple on Yom Kippur was that no priest had a seminal emission. And yet here the high priest needed to be replaced on Yom Kippur due to a seminal emission. *Tosafot Yeshanim D"H velo eira keri* (see BT Yoma 21a) notes that the event could have been another type of impurity, such as saliva landing on one's robes. In addition, as the comment in *Tosafot Yeshanim* notes, the tannaitic source indicating that the high priest never had an emission refers to the First Temple period only. During the Second Temple period, there were high priests who were disqualified for seminal emissions, requiring other men similar to Ben Ilas/Ilam to assume the role.

29. Note the parallel: T. Yoma 3:15 reads as follows:

And he made a day of festivity for his fellows [for other priests לאוהביו] (see Mishnah Yoma 7:4 for larger context).

There is a story about Shim'on, the son of Kimḥit, who went out to speak to the Arab king and spittle sprayed [out] from his [the king's] mouth and fell on his [the high priest's] garment. And his brother entered and took his place [serving] in the [position of] the high priest. The mother of these two [priests] saw two of her sons [serving] as high priests in one day.

30. The parallel version, BT Yoma 47a, does not include a reference to Yom Kippur. Still, most commentators, including Rashi, assume that the day was Yom Kippur, probably reading the Yerushalmi source into the Bavli. See also Meiri, *Beit Habeḥirah*, Yoma 47a, *D"H Kevar be'arnu*.

31. JT Ḥagigah 3:8, 79d tells the story of priests who went out to speak to a woman about her nest offering brought after giving birth and spittle

emerged from her mouth, defiling him. See Dalia Marx, *Tractates Tamid, Middot and Qinnim: A Feminist Commentary on the Babylonian Talmud*), 189–191, who compares this text to the one in Yoma.

32. Note that on BT Shabbat 118b, the same is said about Rabbi Yose: "In all my days, the beams of my house have never seen the seams of my undergarment." This, according to Rashi, was a way of describing the extreme modesty of Rabbi Yose. He would never simply undress and appear naked in his house. Rather, he would sit on the edge of his bed with the sheets around him before lifting up his undergarment. See Rashi, Shabbat 118b, *D"H lo ra'u korot*.

33. The JPS translation of Psalms 45:14-15 reads as follows: "The royal princess, her dress embroidered with golden mountings, is led inside to the king."

34. See BT Yoma 49a, where the question is posed as to what occurs if the high priest scoops up incense into his hands and then immediately dies. The question arises, "Can the substitute high priest take the incense from the first high priest, or must he scoop anew?"

35. Note that versions of this story indicate that this son of Kimḥit meets an Arab, a king, and/or a hegemon. While versions differ as to the title of the person, he is non-Jewish and of some rank.

36. See, for example, BT Nidah 33b, where an *am ha'aretz* was considered a zav such that if his saliva landed on another person, it rendered that person impure.

37. See Meiri, *Beit Habeḥirah*, Yoma 47a, *D"H Kevar be'arnu*, where in the context of commenting on the Kimḥit story, Meiri states the law of non-Jews becoming zavim.

38. Parallel sources in JT Megillah 1:10, 72a and in JT Horayot 3:2, 47d use the word לטייל, and not לדבר or סיפר, which suggests that Shim'on went walking "with the king." In the Bavli, they appear to be talking.

39. The passive form of the verb for spraying suggests that the act was not one of malice. The king does not spit at Shim'on; he merely sprays saliva on him accidentally while trying to talk to him. M. Yoma 6:6–7 conveys that a high priest's clothes become impure from the moment he goes outside the walls of the Temple courtyard or beyond the walls of Jerusalem.

40. Baker, *Rebuilding the House of Israel*, 68, notes the following in her analysis of Kimḥit: "The house is, of course, the site of married sex. . . . In Kimḥit's story, as in countless places in rabbinic writings, head hair is linked to sex, and the habits of hair are integral to the regimes of ordering and purification that attend sexual (genital) intimacy." I am not convinced that the

Notes to Chapter 4

versions of the Kimḥit story intend for us to imagine that there is a husband-father figure with whom she is having marital relations. After all, her sons are mentioned in her name without any mention of a father. As such, her modesty is extreme in that she is hiding herself from "no one." If no one sees the seams of her undergarment, she remains clothed and is sexless.

41. Note that Kimḥit is a Hebrew name, etymologically linked to the Hebrew word *kemaḥ*. Helene is a non-Jewish name, distinguishing her heritage from that of Kimḥit.

42. The Yerushalmi associates Kimḥit with the "modest" royal princess of Psalms 45:14, "whose glory is within her" and who dons an exquisite dress "embroidered with golden mountings" (ממשבצות זהב לבושה). See other places where this verse appears in JT Megillah 1:10, 72a; BT Yevamot 77a; BT Gittin 12a; and BT Shevu'ot 30a. See Fonrobert, *Menstrual Purity*, 68, for her reference to this verse and Aryeh Cohen, *Rereading Talmud: Gender, Law, and the Poetics of Sugyot* (Atlanta: Scholars Press, 1998): 205–206. BT Shevu'ot 30a uses Psalms 45:15 to explain why women are excluded from serving as witnesses: "It is not the way [אורחה] of woman [to appear in court] because 'the entire honor of a king's daughter is inside." In other words, a woman who acts honorably never ventures outside her home.

43. The Yerushalmi version continued to have a profound impact on later commentaries. See Rashi on BT Yoma 47a and Meiri, *Beit Habeḥirah*, Yoma 47a, where in their comments on the Bavli passage (47a) they highlight the lesson of Kimḥit's modesty by referring to Psalms 45:15, which is quoted in the Yerushalmi tradition and not in the Bavli version, further contributing to this stereotype.

44. In the chapter where Yom Kippur is mentioned, Leviticus 16:11–13 states: "Aaron shall then offer his bull of sin offering to make expiation for himself and his household. He shall slaughter his bull of sin offering and he shall take a panful of glowing coals scooped from the altar before the Lord, and two handfuls of finely ground aromatic incense, and bring this behind the curtain. He shall put that incense on the fire before the Lord, so that the cloud from the incense screens the cover that is over [the Ark of] the Pact, lest he die."

45. Note the context of BT Yoma 47a where the Bavli describes the difficulties of holding the hot coal pan in the right hand, suggesting that Yishmael ben Kimḥit needed strength for this. The spoon of incense, which is cold, needed less care and was carried in his left hand.

46. Almost all of the available early textual witnesses do not include the title of "rabbi" before Yishmael's name, including British Library 400; Vene-

250   *Notes to Chapter 4*

zia (Bomberg/printed edition, 1520); Munich 6; Enelow 270, 271; and Pirko-vitz 293. Some versions do have the title of "rabbi," including the Vilna Shas, in order to signify that some of the priests were "rabbinized" following the destruction of the Temple. References to Kimḥit's sons in the Yerushalmi (JT Yoma 1:1, 38d) do not include "rabbi." Richard Kalmin, *Jewish Babylonia between Persia and Roman Palestine* (New York: Oxford University Press, 2006), 43, argues that the Bavli anachronistically describes the rabbis as dominating institutions such as the Temple. He points out that there was an inclination "to visualize rabbis virtually everywhere, controlling most of what mattered in the world" (47).

47. The word זרד can mean strength or valor. In the verb form, it means "to act valiantly." Jastrow notes that the metaphor is based on the image in Proverbs 31:29, although the word זרד is not used there.

48. The root of this word is זרה, which means to select or winnow.

49. This should be ותאזרני, in accordance with Psalms 18:40. The root of this word is אזר, which means strength.

50. See Bavli Yoma 47a, manuscript, Enelow 271 כל העולם כולו נברא מברור ואני מברור שבברור. Note that Munch 6 of Bavli Yoma has the following version, which printed editions of the Bavli (Vilna and Bomberg 1520–1523) do not have: כל העולם כלו מברור ואני מברור שבברור

51. See Proverbs 31:29, where the woman of valor is praised above all: רבות בנות עשו חיל ואת עלית על כלנה

52. See BT Nedarim 41b, where the connection between eating arsan and good health is evident. Also see BT Yoma 47b, Rashi, *D"H ika de'amri*, where Rashi defines the terms arsan and zariz. See BT Berakhot 37a and BT Moed Katan 13b (and Rashi there). Although the terms are not fleshed out in any of these Talmudic sources, Rashi adds that pregnant women prepared arsan and zariz so that they and their fetuses would remain well. Kimḥit's son Yishmael points out that his mother was better than them all, presumably because of what she chose to eat.

53. Fonrobert, *Menstrual Purity*, 40–68, regarding women's bodies and the "house" metaphor.

54. On BT Yoma 47a Rashi quotes Ruth 3:2 to call attention to Boaz's act of winnowing the barley on the threshing floor, building on the Hebrew word זָרֶה—to winnow—in that verse. In an effort to explain למלחמה [חיל] ותזרני in 2 Samuel 22:40 and המאזרני חיל למלחמה in Psalms 18:33 mentioned in the sugya, Rashi points out that God winnowed or chose the choicest seed from Yishmael's father and ensured that it impregnated Kimḥit. Therefore, Yishmael, a priest with large hands, could be most effective in his role as high

Notes to Chapter 4   251

priest. For a contemporary discussion highlighting the continued impact of biology on gender differentiation, see Susan Franklin, "The Anthropology of Biology: A Lesson from the New Kinship Studies," in *The Cambridge Handbook of Kinship*, ed. Sandra Bamford (Cambridge: Cambridge University Press, 2019), 113–115.

55. Janet Carsten, *After Kinship* (Cambridge: Cambridge University Press, 2004), 6. Carsten raises questions about the nature of kinship, which the rabbis raise as well. To what extent is kinship a pregiven, natural order of things, and to what extent is it shaped by human engagement? What is "natural" and what is "cultural"? No doubt, kinship can be viewed as given by birth and therefore unchangeable, or maybe it is shaped by the ordinary, everyday activities of family life, like feeding children, and is not biological. Anthropologists for the most part distinguished between biological and social kinship, which, in Carsten's work, is the subject of greater scrutiny.

56. Gwynn Kessler, *Conceiving Israel: The Fetus in Rabbinic Narrative* (Philadelphia: University of Pennsylvania Press, 2009), 114–126, points out that post-biblical Jewish texts emphasize the male seed as primary in creating the embryo/fetus, along with God. In this rare exception, Rabbah bar Yonatan makes the argument that Kimhit is solely responsible for her son's strength and readiness for the high priesthood because of the food she eats "while sick," that is, while pregnant.

57. Yaakov Elman, "Babylonian Baraitot in the Tosefta and the 'Dialectology' of Middle Hebrew," *AJS Review* 16, no. 1–2 (1991): 2, points out that additions were made to the baraitot found in the Tosefta until the geonic period.

58. Note that the parallel version of this source found in JT Megillah 1:10, 72a and JT Horayot 3:2, 47d claims the high priest to have been Shim'on, the son of Kimhit and not Yishmael. The brother who replaces Shim'on is Yehudah and not Yosef or Yesheivav.

59. Although the outline of this story is similar to the Yerushalmi version, the Bavli contains several telling differences, including two versions of the events in which Kimhit's son Yishmael ventures outside the Temple. In the first instance he is replaced by his brother Yesheivav, and the second time by his brother Yosef.

60. Instead of a king, as in the Yerushalmi's version, Kimhit's son Yishmael meets with an "Arab" and then a "hegemon."

61. None of the textual witnesses mention that it is Yom Kippur. This occurs in the Yerushalmi's version.

62. See Samuel Krauss, *Talmudische Archaologie*, vol. 1 (Leipzig: G. Fock,

1910–1912), 195, 651, for a description of the fact that women wore their hair in braids or plaits on the top of their heads. Loose hair was considered "uncovered" hair. Also see Numbers 5:18 and Rashi's comment there regarding the priest, who, during the sotah rite, "uncovers" the suspected woman's head, and BT Sotah 8a. For a comprehensive record of the legal sources related to women's head coverings and more specifically sources that point to the possibility that braiding one's hair might constitute a "head covering," see Michael J. Broyde, "A Special Supplement: Hair Covering and Jewish Law; Biblical and Objective (*Dat Moshe*) or Rabbinic and Subjective (Dat Yehudit)," *Tradition: A Journal of Orthodox Jewish Thought* 42, no. 3 (2009): 165–167; Baker, *Rebuilding the House of Israel*, 69.

63. Indeed, according to M. Ketubot 7:6, if she ventures out in public and her head is not covered (ויצאה וראשה פרוע), this is grounds for divorce, and she "goes out [is divorced] without collecting her *ketubah* money."

64. The Hebrew word הועילו conjures up the valorous description of women in Proverbs 31:29, on one level, but also the notion that women cannot be "offered up," as a sacrifice might be. This resonates with the idea that women who are overzealous in their performance of commandments might intend to "offer up" themselves, as if to sacrifice themselves to God. The point here is that God does not accept their offering. For covering their hair, women are not "raised up" and rewarded by God with successful sons.

65. This is based on Carsten's argument in *After Kinship*, 9.

66. If the body is a symbol of society and reflects a desired social structure, as Mary Douglas argues, then Kimḥit's failure to guarantee that her sons uphold standards of bodily purity necessary for maintaining the high priesthood signifies that for the rabbis, something is awry in the social fabric represented by the Temple. See Mary Douglas, *Purity and Danger*, 142, and *Natural Symbols: Explorations in Cosmology* (London: Routledge, 1996), 69–87, where she equates body symbolism and social structures. Also see Ruane, *Sacrifice and Gender in Biblical Law*, 157.

67. Helene is a mother of seven sons in tractate Sukkah (BT Sukkah 2b) and not anywhere in Yoma.

68. The trope of the religious martyr is a prevailing one in non-rabbinic sources such as the books of Maccabees, Josephus, and Christian sources, as well as in rabbinic literature. As Elizabeth Castelli points out, for early Christians, "martyrdom was a form of culture making, whereby Christian identity was indelibly marked by the collective memory of the suffering of others." Dying for the sake of one's religious beliefs granted meaning to suffering and death. Out of chaos, martyrdom generated a feeling of order; it

drew attention to itself in the moment and generated penetrating and riveting memories for later generations. Martyrs aligned themselves with power by simultaneously repudiating self and weakening their victimizers. They turned themselves into heroes and heroines and their oppressors into victims. Elizabeth A. Castelli, *Martyrdom and Memory: Early Christian Culture Making* (New York: Columbia University Press, 2004), 4, 36, 199. See also where Castelli quotes Søren Kierkegaard, noting that when tyrants die, their rule is over, but when martyrs die, their rule begins (200). See Kierkegaard, *Papers and Journals*, 352, in *Religion and Violence: Philosophical Perspectives from Kant to Derrida*, ed. Hent DeVries (Baltimore: Johns Hopkins University Press, 2002), 169.

69. See Galit Hasan-Rokem, *Web of Life: Folklore and Midrash in Rabbinic Literature*, 114–125. Note also that the story of Doeg, the son of Yosef (BT Yoma 38b), can be found encapsulated in rabbinic narratives as tied to martyrdom; see Eikhah Rabbah (Buber, ed.), parashah 1. Here, however, in Bavli Yoma, mothers are not linked to martyrdom. See Wasserman, "Mothers and Martyrs in Lamentations Rabbah," 18.

70. Daniel Joslyn-Siemiatkoski, "The Mother and Seven Sons in Late Antique and Medieval Ashkenazi Judaism: Narrative Transformations and Communal Identity," in *Dying for the Faith, Killing for the Faith: Old-Testament Faith-Warriors (1 and 2 Maccabees) in Historical Perspective*, ed. Gabriela Signori (Leiden: Brill, 2012), 128–129. According to Hasan-Rokem, who makes her argument from the perspective of folk narratives, similarities in martyrdom narratives develop in early Christian and rabbinic culture simultaneously and in mutual communication. She indicates that stories of martyrdom, such as that of the mother Miriam bat Tanḥum in Eikhah Rabbah (Buber, ed.), parashah 1, and Saint Perpetua, a young woman martyred in Carthage in the early third century, are in dialogue with one another. This makes it difficult to determine which rabbinic sources were earlier or later or to chart the exact development of the narratives. See Hasan-Rokem, *Web of Life*, 121–125.

71. See BT Gittin 57b, where the Bavli accentuates that God saw this mother (who became childless) as one who was joyful in her household, quoting Psalms 113:9. She is praised for raising her sons as she did. See parallels in Eikhah Rabbah, parashah 1, and Pesikta Rabbati (Margoliot, ed.), 43.

72. Belser, *Rabbinic Tales of Destruction*, 123–125.

73. Belser, *Rabbinic Tales of Destruction*, 125; Hasan-Rokem, *Web of Life*, 125.

74. There is a long history of communities that constituted and sustained

themselves through the memory of mothers who martyred both themselves and their sons. In a world where different communities vied for legitimacy and competed with one another, whether it be Jews and Jews, or Jews and Christians, or Christians and Romans, martyrdom surfaced as a means of spiritual and political legitimization. Mothers who emerge as the main figure in many martyrdom narratives often signify desired shifts in relationships of power among men. See Castelli, *Martyrdom and Memory*, 5, and Joan Wallach Scott, *Gender and the Politics of History* (New York: Columbia University Press, 1988), 28–50, specifically, 42.

75. As Julia Watts Belser points out, "Jewish law and literature has long engaged the question of whether death is preferable to enslavement, idolatry, or sexual violation." See *Rabbinic Tales of Destruction*, 53, as well as Joslyn-Siemiatkoski, "Mother and Seven Sons," 127–132; Gerson D. Cohen, "Hannah and Her Seven Sons in Hebrew Literature," in *Studies in the Variety of Rabbinic Literature*, ed. Gerson D. Cohen (Philadelphia: Jewish Publication Society, 1991), 420–429.

76. Castelli, *Martyrdom and Memory*, 199.

77. See the passage immediately before the mother and her seven sons are discussed in BT Gittin 57b. Indeed, the boys who martyred themselves after being taken captive and believed they were doomed to prostitution thought that they would receive the reward of the World to Come. Instead, the sons are described, based on the image in Psalms 44:23, as men choosing to drown like sheep prepared for slaughter.

78. Hasan-Rokem, *Web of Life*, 114; Ephraim E. Urbach, *The Sages: Their Concepts and Beliefs*, trans. Israel Abrahams (Jerusalem: Magnes Press, 1975), 444–448. Aaron Oppenheimer, "Kedushat haḥayim veḥeruf hanefesh be'ikvot mered bar-kokhba [Sanctity of Life and Martyrdom following the Bar Kochba Revolt]," in *Kedushat hahayim veḥeruf hanefesh: Kovetz ma'amarim shel Amir Yekutiel* [Sanctity of life and martyrdom: Studies in memory of Amir Yekutiel], ed. Isaiah M. Gafni and Aviezer Ravitzky (Jerusalem: Zalman Shazar Center for Jewish History, 1992).

79. More to the point, in a tannaitic source found in BT Bava Batra 11a, a mother and her seven sons appear to teach the lesson that anyone who saves one life has preserved the entire world. The story focuses on an impoverished mother who turns to Benjamin the Righteous, in need of funds from the charity plate. Claiming he has nothing left for her, she responds, "My master, if you do not sustain me, a woman and her seven sons will die." Sensing her dire circumstances, Benjamin gives her money from his own funds, and the family survives. On Benjamin's deathbed, the ministering

Notes to Chapter 4   255

angels convince God to restore him to health as a reward for saving a woman and her seven sons. In contrast to the mother who joins her sons, martyring herself rather than worshipping idols, this mother begs for assistance for her own survival and that of her sons. Promoting the rabbinic ideal of saving a life to save the world, the rabbis laud Benjamin the Righteous. This mother's persistence in ensuring the survival of her sons is significant not only because through her actions, particular values such as providing for the needy are brought to the fore, but also because her sons are the recipients of her protective actions. By comparison, they are not like the seven sons of Bavli Gittin, who live and die willingly for a rabbinic ideal passed on to them from a heroic mother. They are also not the seven sons of the Kimḥit narrative, each of whom becomes disqualified from the priesthood.

80. Janet Carsten and Stephen Hugh-Jones, "Introduction: About the House: Lévi-Strauss and Beyond," in *About the House*, ed. Janet Carsten and Stephen Hugh-Jones (Cambridge: Cambridge University Press, 1995), 20. See their larger discussion regarding the role of Lévi-Strauss's anthropological approach to conceptualizing the house at the intersection of the built structure, the people who reside inside it, and the ideas a house represents, depending on the context in which we find them (1–21).

CHAPTER 5. INTERGENERATIONAL TRANSMISSION AND THE PROBLEM OF MOTHERS

1. An earlier version of this chapter appeared as Marjorie Lehman, "Dressing and Undressing the High Priest: A View of Talmudic Mothers," *Nashim* 26 (2014): 52–74. This article has been revised extensively.

2. According to Numbers 20:25–29, when Aaron was about to die, Moses marked the transfer of leadership by stripping off his priestly vestments and putting them on his son Eleazar. This image may have played a role in the later construction of the mother who prepares her son for the priesthood by weaving his vestments. Dvora Weisberg discusses these verses in "Clothes (un)Make the Man: *bMenaḥot* 109b," in *Introduction to Seder Qodashim (FCBT V)*, ed. Tal Ilan, Monika Brockhaus, and Tanja Hidde (Tübingen: Mohr Siebeck, 2012), 207. Also see Dafna Shlezinger-Katsman, "Clothing," in *The Oxford Handbook of Jewish Daily Life in Roman Palestine*, ed. Catherine Hezser (Oxford: Oxford University Press, 2010).

3. BT Yoma 25a quotes the same baraita as that quoted in BT Yoma 35b. Rashi to BT Yoma 25a, *D"H kidetani Rav Yehudah . . . Rav Shemu'el bar Yehudah*, explains that the mothers of priests would craft priestly garments for their sons to show off the greatness of their wealth as well as the beauty of

the garments they made. They were also interested in beautifying the objects used in the Temple.

4. Terry Arendell, "Conceiving and Investigating Motherhood," *Journal of Marriage and Family* 62 (2000): 1201, proposes that references to mothers are sites of exploration for understanding various cultures.

5. Kate Cooper, *The Virgin and the Bride: Idealized Womanhood in Late Antiquity*, 19; see also Hatlie, "Images of Motherhood and Self in Byzantine Literature," 44, and Rapp, "Figures of Female Sanctity: Byzantine Edifying Manuscripts and their Audience," 329.

6. Miriam B. Peskowitz, *Spinning Fantasies: Rabbis, Gender, and History*, 13. While spinning and weaving were feminized in tannaitic literature, as Peskowitz notes (see M. Ketubot 5:5 and 5:9), Gail Labovitz discusses instances where men engage in "thigh" spinning (M. Moed Kattan 3:4). See "A Man Spinning on His Thigh: Gender, Positive Time-Bound Commandments and Ritual Fringes; Mishnah Mo'ed Katan 3:4," *Nashim* 28 (2015): 77. Also see Laura Gawlinski, "Theorizing Religious Dress," *What Shall I Say of Clothes? Theoretical and Methodological Approaches to the Study of Dress in Antiquity*, ed. Megan Cifarelli and Laura Gawlinski (Boston: Archaeological Institute of America, 2017), 172, and Alicia J. Batten, Carly Daniel-Hughes, and Kristi Upson-Saia, "Introduction: What Shall We Wear," in *Dressing Judeans and Christians in Antiquity* (Surrey: Ashgate, 2014): 7–8, who argue that dress is a way to control a social group and maintain group values and boundaries. As such, an exploration of instances where women weave garments for their priest-sons invites investigation into the social boundaries the rabbis wish to construct and deconstruct.

7. Joyce Antler, *You Never Call! You Never Write!: A History of the Jewish Mother*, 3.

8. Deborah W. Rooke, "Breeches of the Covenant: Gender, Garments and the Priesthood," in *Embroidered Garments: Priests and Gender in Biblical Israel*, ed. Deborah W. Rooke (Sheffield: Sheffield Phoenix Press, 2009), 20–21, and Diana Crane, *Fashion and Its Social Agendas: Class, Gender, and Identity in Clothing* (Chicago: University of Chicago Press, 2000).

9. See Exodus 28:34–35. Aaron is instructed to intersperse golden bells between the pomegranates woven into the hem of his priestly robe and to wear the robe while officiating. Linen breeches intended to "cover [the priests'] nakedness" were to be worn so that priests would not "incur punishment and die" (Exodus 28:43). Priestly garments were protective, inasmuch as they were necessary for proper service.

10. See Weisberg, "Clothes (un)Make the Man," 207.

Notes to Chapter 5

11. Exodus 28; Rooke, "Breeches of the Covenant," 20–21.

12. Marx, *Tractates Tamid, Middot and Qinnim*, 12–13.

13. The parokhet, described in Exodus 26:31–34 and 36:8, was a curtain made of colorful yarns and fine-twisted linen. Its function was to hide the Ark in the area designated as the Holy of Holies. Later, it was depicted in rabbinic sources as being so large that it required 300 priests to immerse it for purification purposes and was significant enough for two new veils to be made every year. See M. Shekalim 8:5 and Avi Kahana, "Asiyat haparokhet leveit hamikdash" [The making of the Temple's parokhet], *Ketoret Shiloh* (2009): 206–207. See also T. Shekalim 2:6, which associates women with the task of weaving the parokhet; Josephus, *Jewish War*, 5:213, and the Letter of Aristeas, 86. See also Marx, *Tractates Tamid, Middot and Qinnim*, 36–39. Marx refers to Matthew Dillon, *Girls and Women in Classical Greek Religion* (New York: Routledge, 2002), 57–60, arguing that women were connected with weaving in surrounding cultures as well. Miriam Peskowitz, in *Spinning Fantasies*, 1–10, also discusses the linkage between women and weaving in Greco-Roman literature.

14. See the imagery found in the Apocalypse of Baruch (2 Baruch 10:6–19), a lamentation over the destruction of the First Temple, composed shortly after the destruction of the Second Temple, which offers another example of clothing spun from expensive materials. During the construction of the First Temple, virgin women were said to be spinning cloth of fine linen and silk using a high-quality gold from Ophir procured by Solomon. Also see 1 Kings 10:10–13. See Peskowitz, "Spinning Fantasies," 162, and Marx, *Tractates Tamid, Middot and Qinnim*, 41–42, both of whom discuss this source in relation to women's contributions to the preparation of Temple objects.

15. For more background on the significance of the priestly wardrobe, see BT Yoma 73a, which asks whether the priest anointed for the purpose of being present with the people when they go out to battle, based on Deuteronomy 20:1–9, should don four garments, as an ordinary priest would; possibly he should wear eight, like the high priest. A baraita suggesting that the priest who goes out to battle should not wear any priestly garments is quickly rejected by the amora Abaye, who fears that the absence of a proper priestly wardrobe might call this priest's identity into question. The amora Rabbi Adda bar Ahavah even suggests that a high priest may be distinguished from a regular priest by his linen belt (*avnet*; BT Yoma 12a). According to M. Tamid 1:1, priests remove their vestments at night because they have no priestly ceremonies to perform. They sleep in everyday clothing, placing their vestments under their heads to signify their connection to

them. The color of a priest's clothing communicated something about his purity status. If he had a blemish of defect or conduct, he clothed himself in black; otherwise he wore white clothing (M. Middot 5:4). Clothing thus carried with it important symbolism, distinguishing priests from non-priests and pure from impure priests. For an overview of the interconnection between dress and group identity in the daily life of classical Greece and Rome, from texts to ritual practices, see Batten et al., "Introduction: What Shall We Wear?," 1–18. Relevant for the discussion here is their point that studying dress illuminates the social dynamics and structures of communities.

16. Note that JT Yoma 7:3, 44b and Vayikra Rabbah 10:6 present the high priest's tunic as atoning for a person wearing a mixture of wool and linen, forbidden by biblical law. Vayikra Rabbah, in particular, makes reference to Joseph's tunic, presumably made from these two materials and given to him by his father in an inappropriate display of favoritism (Genesis 37:3). According to JT Yoma 7:3, 44b, the tunic enabled a priest to atone for the sin of bloodshed committed by another person. Also see BT Zevaḥim 88b.

17. See BT Yoma 72b and its reference to Exodus 35:19. The passage uses the phrase "enemies of Israel" as a euphemism for Israel, fearing that mention made of no survivorship might invite harm. Also note that JT Yoma 7:3, 44b states clearly that just as sacrifices atone, so too do the priests' garments. Also see BT Arakhin 16a.

18. Mary Ellen Roach and Joanne Bubolz Eicher, "The Language of Personal Adornment," in *The Fabrics of Culture: The Anthropology of Clothing and Adornment*, ed. Justine M. Cordwell and Ronald A. Schwarz (New York: Mouton, 1979), 10, make the argument that clothing can function as an act of speaking in its ability to distinguish "the powerful from the weak, the rich from the poor . . . the leader from the follower." See also Michael L. Satlow's reference to Roach and Eicher and his discussion of T. Yoma 1:22 in "Jewish Constructions of Nakedness in Late Antiquity," *Journal of Biblical Literature* 116, no. 3 (1997): 430–432.

19. The women mentioned in Bavli Yoma 35b and 66b illustrate that women who spin belong to a textual tradition that recognizes women as weaving sacred objects, such as the parokhet, indispensable to the Temple cult. These acts of weaving position women as connected to the performance of Temple rites within the context of a daily labor typically gendered female. Making veils is paid work, and women receive wages for making the parokhet. According to the Yerushalmi (JT Shekalim 4:3, 48a), such payments are drawn either from monies designated for Temple upkeep or from contributions to the Temple chamber, suggesting that women are contrib-

Notes to Chapter 5

utors to the daily maintenance of the Temple and played a role in Temple rites. Although extra-rabbinic sources stress that the veil is woven by virgins, rabbinic texts attribute this work to women who desire to use their skills to contribute to the Temple's sanctity. See Marx, *Tractates Tamid, Middot and Qinnim*, 38–40. BT Yoma 54a points to an additional seven veils made for the Temple to sanctify it with beautiful accoutrements. See also Marx, *Tractates Tamid, Middot and Qinnim*, 38, and Kahana, "Making of the Temple's Parokhet," 202–203.

20. Peskowitz, *Spinning Fantasies*, 103–105.

21. M. Ketubot 5:5 states: "These are the works that a wife must perform for her husband: . . . working in wool. . . . Rabbi Eliezer says: Even if she brought in a hundred bondwomen, he compels her to work in wool, for idleness leads to dull-mindedness."

22. Peskowitz, *Spinning Fantasies*, 106–107. It is not clear how to define the word שעמום in M. Ketubot 5:5. It has been translated as everything from "dull-minded" to "unchaste."

23. See M. Ketubot 7:6; BT Ketubot 72b, and Rashi, *D"H, vetoveh verad keneged paneiha*. See also Peskowitz, *Spinning Fantasies*, 22–23.

24. M. Sotah 6:1. Peskowitz discusses this mishnah in *Spinning Fantasies*, 107–112.

25. M. Sotah 6:1 states that even if her husband heard about his wife's seclusion with another man from a "flying bird," he must divorce her.

26. This statement by Rabbi Eliezer appears along with the verse from Exodus 35:25: "And all of the skilled women spun with their own hands." In referring to the construction of the Tabernacle and labor that engaged the skills of both women and men, women are specifically referred to as possessing חכמת לב when described as having the skill to spin yarns and fine linen.

27. Wimpfheimer, *Narrating the Law: A Poetics of Talmudic Legal Stories*, 124, points to the ways in which stories, such as the one I mention here where questions are posed to Rabbi Eliezer, draw in the themes of the larger passage.

28. See Sarit Kattan Gribetz, "Consuming Texts: Women as Recipients and Transmitters of Ancient Texts," 178–183.

29. See T. Yoma 1:23, where the link between what mothers make for their sons and the notion of transferring it to the Temple is mentioned. The discussion in the Bavli builds on T. Yoma 1:23, embedding it in a sugya that is also concerned about the transference of what is privately owned to the Temple. JT Yoma 3:6, 40cd discusses whether utensils and garments created for Temple use can be used for non-Temple purposes by non-priests, but

does not directly connect this idea to mothers making garments for their priest-sons.

30. The Bavli refers to this high priest as Yishmael ben Pabi, while the Tosefta and the Yerushalmi call him Yishmael ben Piabi. They are the same figure, and the discrepancy between the manuscripts is unremarkable.

31. For a larger discussion of the absence of women from the beit midrash, see David Levine, "Why No Women in the Beit Midrash?" in *Introduction to Seder Qodashim (FCBT V)*, ed. Tal Ilan, Monika Brockhausm and Tanja Hidde (Tübingen: Mohr Siebeck, 2012), 179–180. See also Boyarin, *Unheroic Conduct*, 152–154.

32. M. Menaḥot 5:6 points to women waving their offerings; Sifra, Vakiyra 2, 2:2 and BT Ḥagigah 16b make allowances for women to perform the rite of "laying the hands" on sacrifices. M. Zevaḥim 3:1 allows women to slaughter sacrifices, although they were not encouraged to do so. T. Arakhin 2:1, in remarking that women were not seen in the Temple court except when they needed to bring offerings, indicates that women were not excluded from the Temple. See Marx, *Tractates Tamid, Middot and Qinnim*, 98–118, and "Tractate 'Qinnim': Marginality or Horizons," in *Introduction to Seder Qodashim (FCBT V)*, ed. Tal Ilan, Monika Brockhaus, and Tanja Hidde (Tübingen: Mohr Siebeck, 2012): 260; and Susan Grossman, "Women and the Jerusalem Temple," in *Daughters of the King*, ed. Susan Grossman and Rivkah Haut (Philadelphia: Jewish Publication Society, 1992), 15–37. Chana Safrai and Avital Campbell Hochstein, *Nashim baḥutz — nashim bifnim: Mekoman shel nashim bamidrash* [Women out — women in: The place of women in the beit midrash] (Tel Aviv: Miskal-Yediot Aḥronot and Ḥemed Books, 2008) 47–55, analyze references in midreshei halakhah (collections of midrashic comments on biblical verses with legal content) to women's involvement in offering sacrifices.

33. See Leviticus 12; M. Qinnim 1:4.

34. According to BT Yoma 9a, women brought nest offerings to Shiloh, and the sons of Eli sinned, either by having sexual relations with these women or by delaying their offerings from being offered. See Marx's discussion in *Tractates Tamid, Middot and Qinnim*, 192–193.

35. Marx, *Tractates Tamid, Middot and Qinnim*, 117–119.

36. BT Yoma 35b, Rashi, *D"H Sheyimserenah latzibur* has difficulty understanding why the tunic must be transferred to the Temple when M. Yoma 7:1, BT Yoma 68b suggest that the high priest can wear his own white robe while reading from the Torah on Yom Kippur rather than his sacred garments, if he chooses.

Notes to Chapter 5

37. I draw here from Ann Snitow, "Feminism and Motherhood: An American Reading," *Feminist Review* 40 (1992): 49. See also Arendell, "Conceiving and Investigating Motherhood," 1201. I agree with Lynne Hume that "religious dress is a visible signifier of difference. The message communicated is that the wearer chooses to follow a certain set of ideological or religious principles and practices. Dress distinctions function to set one religious community apart from other religious communities, and they also operate within religion to distinguish hierarchies, power structures, gender distinctions, ideas of modesty, roles, mores, group identity, belief, and ideology." In other words, dress is a "visible signifier of difference." Hume, *The Religious Life of Dress: Global Fashion and Faith* (London: Bloomsbury, 2013): 1.

38. See Moses Maimonides (Rambam), *Mishneh Torah* (Jersualem: Shivtei Frankel, 2007, Hilkhot klei hamikdash, 8:7, for an explanation of the transferring garments from private to public ownership.

39. JT Yoma 3:6, 40d is numbered JT Yoma 3:7 in Talmud Yerushalmi, ed. Yaakov Sussmann (Jerusalem: Academy of the Hebrew Language, 2001), a transcription of the Leiden manuscript of the Yerushalmi. However, the Vilna and Venice printed editions of the Yerushalmi record it as 3:6, 40d.

40. See BT Yoma 25a, where the amora Rav Yehudah (or possibly Rav Shmuel bar Yehudah) also states that a priest whose mother made a tunic for him that was not intended for communal atonement can perform an individual Temple service with it.

41. It is difficult to reconstruct the historical development of the tradition in the Bavli about mothers crafting priestly tunics for their sons, except to say that it parallels the material found in the Tosefta, though the Tosefta, like the Yerushalmi, uses the word *ma'aseh* to report the stories involving Yishmael ben Piabi/Pabi and Eleazar ben Harsom, while the Bavli uses the phrase *amru alav*, "they said of him." It seems that the Bavli's redactors conflated an earlier tradition in the Yerushalmi about these priests' expensive garb with a tannaitic tradition reflected in the Tosefta that mentions their mothers. The Bavli then changed the word "ma'aseh" to "amru alav." See Yaakov Elman, "Babylonian Baraitot in the Tosefta and the 'Dialectology' of Middle Hebrew," *AJS Review* 16 (1991): 2, where he points out that additions were made to the baraitot of the Tosefta until the geonic period.

42. According to BT Yoma 9a, both Yishmael ben Pabi and Eleazar ben Harsom served as high priests for longer periods than other high priests, who often did not last a year.

43. Many thanks to Steven Fine of Yeshiva University and Vivian Mann of

the Jewish Theological Seminary for helping me to understand this point about wet clothing.

44. T. Yoma 1:21–22 reads as follows: "There is a story about the mother of Ishmael ben Piabi who made him a tunic worth one hundred maneh. And he would stand and make offerings on the altar wearing it. There is another story about the mother of Rabbi Eleazar ben Ḥarsom who made him a tunic worth twenty thousand [maneh]. And he would stand and [make offerings] on the altar [while wearing it]. [But] his brothers, the priests, removed him, because he appeared naked [while wearing the tunic]." T. Yoma 1:23 refers to a woman who transfers (תמסרנה) ownership of a garment that she made to the Temple, whereas the Bavli indicates that it is, specifically, a mother's priest-son who does the transfer (ימסרנה).

45. Also see T. Yoma 1:23.

46. The high priests appear with the title "rabbi" here in BT Yoma 35b. Textual evidence, however, is mixed, sometimes having "rabbi" before one priest's name and not the other (British Library 400 and Munich 6) and sometimes with "rabbi" before both priests' names (Munich 95 and Oxford Opp. Add. fol. 23, and the printed edition, Venice 1520–1523, as well as the manuscript evidence of JT Yoma 3:6, 40d). In some manuscripts and printed editions, such as MSS Munich 6 and 95, MS Oxford Opp. Add. fol. 23, and the Venice printed edition of the Bavli, Eleazar ben Ḥarsom appears with the title "rabbi," while Ishmael ben Piabi/Pabi (referred to as Shim'on ben Piabi in MS Munich 95) does not. In JTS Rabb. 1623/2 (EMC 271), neither high priest appears with that title. That priests appeared in the Bavli with the moniker "rabbi" reflects a desire on the part of the rabbis to "rabbinize" the priests in order to imagine the priestly caste as wedded to a developing rabbinic Judaism. Richard Kalmin argues in *Jewish Babylonia*, 43, that it is not surprising, especially for the Bavli, to describe the rabbis anachronistically as dominating the institutions of the past, like the Temple. Kalmin argues that there is an inclination in rabbinic literature "to visualize rabbis virtually everywhere and controlling most of what truly mattered in the world" (47). That Eleazar ben Ḥarsom is referred to as "rabbi" even in Palestinian sources suggests a common textual desire to see the priests through a rabbinic lens. In BT Yoma 9a (Vilna edition), Eleazar ben Ḥarsom appears in a list of only four Second Temple high priests who served in that role for more than one year (the others were Shim'on Hatzadik, Yoḥanan, and Yishmael ben Pabi). He is also the only one there referred to as "rabbi." In BT Yoma 35b, both Yishmael ben Pabi and Eleazar ben Ḥarsom carry the title "rabbi."

Notes to Chapter 5

47. See BT Yoma 71b–72a, where the thickness of the priestly tunics is discussed in detail.

48. See Rashi, Yoma 35b, *D"H kehamra bemizgah*, who argues that despite the thickness of glass, one could see through to the wine within the glass. So too could one see the body of the high priest; that is, the thickness of a material does not necessarily hide what is covered by it.

49. Furthermore, they are mothers with incredible means and the independence to spend monies as they wish. If Mishnah Ketubot considers one maneh to be the compensation designated in the *ketubah* when marrying a widow and enough to sustain her for a period of time following her husband's death, then a sum of 20,000 maneh to make one priestly garment seems unfathomable (M. Ketubot 1:2, 10:4). According to M. Yoma 3:7 and T. Yoma 1:21, the amount of money that the high priest could draw from the Temple treasury to spend on his clothing did not exceed 30 maneh, again calling attention to the amount spent or allowable. That husbands own the proceeds of their wives' handiwork and the usufruct from property they bring into their marriages (M. Ketubot 5:5, 8:1–2, BT Ketubot 59b), not to mention that women with children do not inherit their husbands' estates, draws attention to the extent to which mothers had their own monies (BT Bava Batra 115ab). Therefore, the women depicted here suggest that women in certain cases had money and could make decisions about how to use it. See Naftali S. Cohn, "When Women Confer with Rabbis: On Male Authority and Female Agency in the Mishnah," *Journal of the Society of Textual Reasoning* 6, no. 2 (March 2011), 6/number2/TR06_02_Cohn.html/. See also Peskowitz, *Spinning Fantasies*, 27–48.

50. Exodus 28:42–43 warns that priests who do not cover their bodies appropriately with the correct garments will incur punishment and die.

51. Both T. Yoma 1:22 and its parallel, JT Yoma 3:6, 40d, use the term *horid/horiduhu* (they removed him). Based on the use of the same word in JT Berakhot 4:1, 7d, referring to Rabban Gamliel and his post as head of the academy, I argue here that the verb is used similarly and that the brothers did remove Eleazar ben Harsom from his position as high priest. Alternatively, Saul Lieberman notes that Eleazar was prevented from performing his cultic duties while wearing the transparent tunic and that once he donned a more appropriate priestly garment, he was able to resume them. See Lieberman, *Tosefta kifeshuta* (New York: Jewish Theological Seminary, 1992), 4:726. See also Yonatan Feintuch, "Bein kohanim lahakhamim: Al aggadah ahat behekhsherah harahav bevavli Yoma" [Between priests and rabbis: An analysis of an Aggada and its wider context in Bavli Yoma], *Mehkerei Yerushalayim*

besifrut ivrit 23 (2010): 8, and his discussion of the way the Bavli tampered with an earlier tannaitic tradition.

52. Here, the Bavli reworked traditions found in the Yerushalmi and used the Tosefta to mold the tannaitic tradition into one that suited the rabbis' own agenda in the Bavli. This lends support to Kalmin's claim in *Jewish Babylonia*, 37, that the Bavli emends available traditions from the Land of Israel to suit its own concerns.

53. In Greco-Roman culture, the naked body was seen as the highest form of beauty. Greek art and athletics glorified the naked male athlete; gods and goddesses were sculpted naked; initiation rituals for boys and girls and even priestly sacrifices were performed naked. The rabbis, influenced by the biblical association of nakedness with shame and immodesty, did not share this view. See Kenneth Clark, *The Nude: A Study in Ideal Form* (Princeton: Princeton University Press, 1953), 23–24, 30–34; Larissa Bonfante, "Nudity as a Costume in Classical Art," *American Journal of Archaeology* 93 (1989): 543–546; and for pictures on vases of naked men receiving Olympic prizes: Judith Swadding, *The Ancient Olympic Games* (London: British Museum, 1999), 74–75. For Jewish attitudes, see Nahum Ben-Yehuda, "Jewish Dress and Religious Identity in the Land of Israel during the Roman Era: The Talmudic Dress Code" (master's thesis, Bar-Ilan University, 2012). I thank Steven Fine for pointing this work out to me and Nahum Ben-Yehuda for sharing his thesis with me. For a more nuanced discussion of Greco-Roman perspectives on nakedness, see Satlow, "Jewish Constructions of Nakedness in Late Antiquity," 429–454.

54. See M. Ketubot 7:6; BT Ketubot 72b; Peskowitz, "Spinning Fantasies," 22–23.

55. Michael Satlow, "Jewish Constructions of Nakedness in Late Antiquity," 450, argues that an aversion to nakedness in the sancta was unique to Israelites and Jews. From the ancient Near East to Greek and Roman cultures in late antiquity, exposing the naked body, including the phallus, in sacred contexts was not problematic. In addition, male divinities were commonly depicted as naked in Greco-Roman art (450–451). See Nanette Salomon, "Making a World of Difference: Gender, Asymmetry, and the Greek Nude," in *Naked Truths: Women, Sexuality, and Gender in Classical Art and Archaeology,"* ed. Ann Olga Koloski-Ostrow and Claire L. Lyons (London: Routledge, 1997), 203. Also see Mary Beard, "Priesthood in the Roman Republic," in *Pagan Priests: Religion and Power in the Ancient World*, ed. Mary Beard and John North (London: Duckworth, 1990), 17–48. Regarding Babylonian culture, see Yishai Kiel, "Confessing Incest to a Rabbi: A Talmu-

Notes to Chapter 5   265

dic Story in Its Zoroastrain Context," *Harvard Theological Review* 107, no. 4 (2014): 403, 419–420, who discusses an instance of a mother's admission of incestual relations with her son to Rav Ḥisda, situating the vignette within the Zoroastrian context where incest was considered a pious act (BT Avodah Zarah 17a). Zoroastrians believed incestual relations, such as those between a mother and her son, could prevent the effects of a crime worthy of death. In contrast, for the rabbis of BT Avodah Zarah, a mother's incestuous act makes her deserving of punishment. Also see Yaakov Elman, "'He in His Cloak and She in Her Cloak': Conflicting Images of Sexuality in Sassanian Mesopotamia," in *Discussing Cultural Influences: Text, Context, and Non-Text in Rabbinic Judaism*, ed. Rivka Ulmer (Lanham, MD: University Press of America, 2007), 131, 133, 135.

56. Regarding rabbis from the Land of Israel and their relationship with Rome, see Seth Schwartz, *Were the Jews a Mediterranean Society? Reciprocity and Solidarity in Ancient Judaism* (Princeton: Princeton University Press, 2010): 112–118, esp. 117. Although the Babylonian rabbis lived hundreds of miles from the Land of Israel, there is much evidence to suggest that there was frequent interchange, specifically by traveling back and forth. Moreover, despite cultural divides, there was some degree of porousness. See Yaron Z. Eliav, "The Material World of Babylonia as Seen from Roman Palestine: Some Preliminary Observations," in *The Archaeology and Material Culture of the Babylonian Talmud*, ed. Markham J. Geller (Leiden: Brill, 2015), 155–159, and Getzel Cohen, "Travel between Palestine and Mesopotamia during the Hellenistic and Roman Periods: A Preliminary Study," in *The Archaeology and Material Culture of the Babylonian Talmud*, ed. Markham J. Geller (Leiden: Brill, 2015), 186–208.

57. See Anat Israeli and Inbar Raveh, "'He Did Not Embarrass Her': Motherhood and Shame in Talmudic Literature," *Nashim* 33, no. 1 (2018): 20–37, who discuss Tosefta 1:21–22 in the context of material about mothers in JT Kiddushin 1:7, 61b and BT Kiddushin 31ab.

58. For a collection of rabbinic sources that present this perspective on the rabbis' attitudes toward nakedness, see Satlow, "Jewish Constructions of Nakedness in Late Antiquity," 431–440.

59. See Mary R. Lefkowitz, "The Motivations for St. Perpetua's Martyrdom," *Journal of the American Academy of Religion*, 44, no. 3 (1976): 419. Lefkowitz discusses the phenomenon of an incestuous emotional pairing of a father and his daughter so as to keep a disintegrating family together.

60. Adrienne Rich points to the underlying contradiction in patriarchal societies "between the laws and sanctions designed to keep women es-

sentially powerless and the attribution to mothers of almost superhuman power." See *On Lies, Secrets, and Silence: Selected Prose, 1966–1978* (New York: Norton, 1980), 263.

61. Lisa Jean Moore and Mary Kosut, "Bodies as Mediums," in *The Body Reader* (New York: New York University Press, 2010), 141, and Linda B. Arthur, ed., Introduction to *Religion, Dress and the Body* (Oxford: Berg, Oxford International, 1999), 2, 6. Mary Douglas, in *Purity and Danger: An Analysis of the Concepts of Pollution and Taboo* (London: Routledge and Keegan Paul, 1966), 163–164, argues that the body is a symbol of a society's social order. See also Douglas, *Natural Symbols: Explorations of Cosmology* (London: Routledge, 1996), 69–87, and "Social Preconditions of Enthusiasm and Heterodoxy," in *Forms of Symbolic Action: Proceedings of the 1969 Annual Meeting of the American Ethnological Society* (Seattle: American Ethnographical Society, 1969), 71. For a larger discussion on looking at the body as a social construct, analyzing it as a text for the embedded messages of culture, see John G. Gager, "Body-Symbols and Social Reality: Resurrection, Incarnation, and Asceticism in Early Christianity," *Religion* 12 (1892): 347; Pierre Bourdieu, "Cultural Reproduction and Social Reproduction," *Knowledge, Education, and Social Change*, ed. Robert Brown (London: Tavistock, 1973); and Catherine B. Burroughs and Jeffrey David Erenreich, Introduction to *Reading the Social Body* (Iowa City: University of Iowa Press, 1993), 1–12.

62. See Sherry B. Ortner's discussion of relative gender status in "Gender Hegemonies," *Cultural Critique* 14 (1989–1990): 37–38.

63. See T. Kiddushin 1:11 and BT Kiddushin 29a, where fathers but not mothers are required to fulfill various religious obligations, including circumcision, redemption of the firstborn son, Torah study, teaching a child a craft, teaching him to swim, and finding him a wife.

64. Margalit, "Priestly Men and Invisible Women," 310–311, points out that a father is commanded to pass down to his son the responsibility to perform a set of "covenantal" or religious obligations as a way to continue his line. While this, as Margalit argues, is akin to the priesthood in its male-male transference from father to son, bloodline is not a requirement. See Elizabeth Shanks Alexander, *Gender and Timebound Commandments in Judaism* (Cambridge: Cambridge University Press, 2013), 178. 184–188, regarding the rabbis' commitment to cultural reproduction via Torah study. Fathers were responsible for teaching their sons Torah. However, biological reproduction was not enough to ensure that a father's identity would endure beyond him. That depended on ensuring that his son studied Torah, even if he needed to relinquish this role to a master teacher. For a discussion of the

Notes to Chapter 5

master-disciple relationship within the context of a discussion of the rabbinic household and the requirement of an *eruv*, see Fonrobert, "Education as Filiation," 9–21, who highlights the tension between "genetic" and "pedagogical replicability." See as well Catherine Heszer, *The Social Structure of the Rabbinic Movement* (Tübingen: Mohr Siebeck, 1997), and Boyarin, *Carnal Israel*, 207–211.

65. Only a few rabbinic sources support the idea that women should study Torah, while other sources oppose it. See Jane Kanarek, "All Are Obligated: Sacrifice, Sight and Study," in Ilan et al., *Introduction to Seder Qodashim (FCBT V)*, 220–221; Boyarin, *Carnal Israel*, 177; Tal Ilan, *Silencing the Queen: The Literary Histories of Shelamzion and Other Jewish Women* (Tübingen: Mohr Siebeck, 2006), 94; and Marjorie Lehman, "Rereading Beruriah through the Lens of Isaac Bashevis Singer's Yentl," *Nashim* 31 (2017): 123–145.

66. Dalia Marx, in *Tractates Tamid, Middot and Qinnim*, 8–10, argues that "brothers" in rabbinic literature may not denote actual brothers but rather the members of the priestly caste, who were blood related. I understand the word *eḥav* as "brothers," referring to actual brothers of the high priest.

67. See BT Menaḥot 109b and its parallel, JT Yoma 6:3, 43cd, where a priest's embarrassment at donning feminine clothing forces him to flee the Temple and the position of the high priesthood, which had been turned over to him after the death of his father, Shim'on Hatzadik. The failure of a priest to clothe himself appropriately leads to removal from his post. See Weisberg, "Clothes (un)Make the Man," 193–211, and Kalmin, *Jewish Babylonia*, 75–80, who discuss this story.

68. See Hatlie, "Images of Motherhood," 45.

69. The presence of mothers in the Bavli and their absence in the Yerushalmi reflect different perspectives on the priesthood and, indeed, different sets of concerns. Richard Kalmin has argued that Jews in the Land of Israel were more comfortable with living alongside non-rabbis, even those in leadership roles such as priests and kings. This may explain Eleazar ben Ḥarsom's refusal, in the Yerushalmi, to abdicate his priestly position. It also explains Eleazar ben Ḥarsom's ritual circumambulations, surely a sign of maintaining "the house" and its rituals at all costs after his nakedness was revealed. The brother-brother relationship in evidence in the Yerushalmi also encapsulates through its imagery a functional priestly kinship. Closer in time and place to the Temple, the redactors of Yerushalmi Yoma identify more closely with the priesthood and seem to have less desire to distance themselves from it. In contrast to the Bavli's more problematic rendering of

268   *Notes to Chapter 5*

Eleazar ben Ḥarsom and his relationship to his mother, the Yerushalmi is less interested in challenging the foundations of this relationship. Kalmin, *Jewish Babylonia*, 60.

70. While Eleazar ben Ḥarsom is mentioned in other places in rabbinic literature, BT Yoma 35b is the only place he is mentioned along with his father. JT Taʾanit 4:5, 69a and Eikhah Rabbah (Vilna ed.) 2:4 describe Eleazar ben Ḥarsom as owning one thousand cities as well as one thousand ships, but they do not mention his father or his commitment to Torah study. See Yonatan Feintuch's extensive literary analysis of this baraita in BT Yoma 35b, "Ben Kohanim," 1–14, and his discussion of its connection to the clothing of the high priest.

71. The Torah has the most profound influence on Eleazar ben Ḥarsom and transforms him into a model for others, as conveyed in a final statement at the end of the baraita on BT Yoma 35b: "Eleazar ben Ḥarsom obligates the wealthy people [to study Torah]." Moreover, the story about his ambitious acquisition of Torah knowledge transforms this priest into a rabbi, making him worthy of the title. See note above about the Bavli's reference to him as "Rabbi."

72. Peskowitz, *Spinning Fantasies*, 23.

73. I am making no claim as to the historical dating of the change from patrilineal to matrilineal descent. Tannaitic literature seems to point to a rabbinic commitment to matrilineality, although the change could have taken hold earlier or later. See Cohen, "Matrilineal Principle in Historical Perspective," 5–13.

74. Cooper, *The Virgin and the Bride: Idealized Womanhood in Late Antiquity*, 19; see also Hatlie, "Images of Motherhood and Self in Byzantine Literature," 44, and Rapp, "Figures of Female Sanctity: Byzantine Edifying Manuscripts and their Audience," 329.

CHAPTER 6. SEXUALITY INSIDE AND OUTSIDE THE TEMPLE HOUSE

1. Michael D. Swartz, "Ritual Is with People: Sacrifice and Society in Palestinian Yoma Traditions," in *The Actuality of Sacrifice: Past and Present*, ed. Alberdina Houtman, Marcel Poothius, Joshua Schwartz, and Joseph Turner (Leiden: Brill, 2014), 207–208, discusses the different ways that M. Yoma, T. Yoma, JT Yoma, and various liturgical poems (*avodah piyutim*) describe the Temple service of Yom Kippur. He argues that M. Yoma was one of the only tractates to be recited in the synagogue because of the way it narrates the Avodah service, 207–208.

Notes to Chapter 6

2. Mieke Bal, *Death and Dissymmetry: The Politics of Coherence in the Book of Judges* (Chicago: University of Chicago Press, 1988), 2.

3. Baker, *Rebuilding the House of Israel*, 54–59.

4. For a discussion about the Mesopotamian cultural orbit and its porousness as reflected in the Babylonian Talmud, see Daniel Boyarin, "Hellenism in Jewish Babylonia," in *Cambridge Companion to the Talmud and Rabbinic Literature*, ed. Charlotte Elisheva Fonrobert and Martin S. Jaffee (Cambridge: Cambridge University Press, 2007), 336–363. For some pushback regarding the way we read Babylonian sources due to the presence of the Babylonian Jewish community between two rival empires, Sassania and the eastern Roman empire, see Julia Watts Belser, *Rabbinic Tales of Destruction*, xvii–xix. Yishai Kiel, in "Study versus Sustenance: A Rabbinic Dilemma in Its Zoroastrian and Manichaean Context," *AJS Review* 38:2 (2014): 282, offers an excellent example of possible cross-cultural influences. Shai Secunda points out in *The Talmud's Red Fence: Menstrual Impurity and Difference in Babylonian Judaism and Its Sasanian Context* (Oxford: Oxford University Press, 2020), 68, that as a minority, Jews did not suffer significant persecution while living under the Sassanians.

5. For a discussion of the role of the priests in the aftermath of the destruction of the Temple, see Matthew Grey, "Jewish Priests and the Social History of Post-70 Palestine" (PhD diss., University of North Carolina, 2011), 6–12, 84; Seth Schwartz, *Josephus and Judean Politics*, 58–109; and Catherine Hezser, *The Social Structure of the Rabbinic Movement* (Tübingen: Mohr Siebeck, 1997), 487. Regarding the continued activities of priests in Babylonia, see Geoffrey Herman, "Priests and Amoraic Leadership in Sassanian Babylonia," 65–66.

6. See Shlomo Naeh, "Freedom and Celibacy: A Talmudic Variation on Tales of Temptation and Fall in Genesis and Its Syrian Background," in *The Book of Genesis in Jewish and Oriental Christian Interpretation: A Collection of Essays*, ed. Judith Frishman and Lucas van Rompay (Lovanii: In aedibus Peeters, 1997), 73–89. Also see Haleh Emrani, "'Who Would Be Mine for the Day!': Irano-Judaic Marriage Customs in Late Antiquity," 217–231.

7. Kiel, "Study versus Sustenance," 280–281, 290. Also see Brown, *The Body and Society: Men, Women, and Sexual Renunciation in Early Christianity*, 83–102.

8. See Eithne Lubhéid, *Pregnant on Arrival: Making the Illegal Immigrant* (Minneapolis: University of Minnesota Press, 2013), 19–20. In a discussion about the boundaries between "legal" and "illegal" migrants to Ireland, Lubhéid points out how enmeshed issues related to sexuality are in con-

structing a culture of Irish attitudes toward this issue. He correctly leads us, including those of us in fields far from his own, to factor in sexuality as a lens for understanding the construction of political, religious, or economic perspectives on a given topic.

9. Lubhéid, *Pregnant on Arrival*, 29.

10. Daniel Boyarin, *Carnal Israel; Reading Sex in Talmudic Culture* (Berkeley: University of California Press, 1993). Ishay Rosen-Zvi, in *Demonic Desires: "Yetzer Hara" and the Problem of Evil in Late Antiquity* (Philadelphia: University of Pennsylvania Press, 2011), 113–114, argues that sexuality is the locus of the Bavli's interests and that sources in the Bavli "see sex all around them," in a manner unparalleled in Palestinian literature (113–114), and he expands on Michael L. Satlow's argument in *Tasting the Dish: Rabbinic Rhetorics of Sexuality*, 319. Also see Rachel (Rafe) Neis, *The Sense of Sight in Rabbinic Culture: Jewish Ways of Seeing in Late Antiquity* (New York: Cambridge University Press, 2013), 90–112, 117–169.

11. It is not clear when the prohibition against sexual relations emerges, as it is not specifically delineated in the biblical material regarding the commandment of self-denial on Yom Kippur. Stökl Ben Ezra, *The Impact of Yom Kippur on Early Christianity*, 36–37, notes that the prohibition against sexual relations was part of most religious abstention rites. Whereas one might have expected stricter rules of self-denial following the destruction of the Temple, this did not occur.

12. Daniel Boyarin, "Internal Opposition in Talmudic Literature: The Case of the Married Monk," *Representations* 36 (Autumn 1991): 88, argues that the activities of the reproductive body were considered as important as those of the speaking body, and yet the rabbis express that "sex" and "text" are in conflict. As Boyarin argues, keeping our eyes on both poles of this tension and on whether the tension was accentuated or resolved will enable us to account for many features of rabbinic culture.

13. See Marjorie Lehman, "Reading the Gendered Rhetoric of Yom Kippur," in *Introduction to Seder Qodashim (FCBT V)*, ed. Tal Ilan, Monika Brockhaus and Tanja Hidde (Tübingen: Mohr Siebeck, 2012), 33–56, for a discussion on the treatment of sexuality and asceticism in tractate Yoma.

14. Bal, *Death and Dissymmetry*, 5, argues that the Book of Judges is about a social revolution related to a change in the institution of marriage, procreation, and kinship.

15. Steven Fraade, "Ascetical Aspects of Ancient Judaism," in *Jewish Spirituality from the Bible through the Middle Ages*, ed. Art Green (New York: Crossroad, 1987), 256–257.

Notes to Chapter 6

16. David Biale, *Eros and the Jews: From Biblical Israel to Contemporary America* (New York: Basic Books, 1992), 34; Brown, *Body and Society*, 67.

17. Fraade, "Ascetical Aspects of Ancient Judaism," 257.

18. As Fraade points out in "Ascetical Aspects of Ancient Judaism," 254, 257, 260, ascetic behavior was continually associated with patterns of self-abnegation when in fact there were a variety of definitions circulating in the late antique world.

19. Elizabeth Castelli, "'I Will Make Mary Male': Pieties of the Body and Gender Transformation of Christian Women in Late Antiquity," in *Body Guards: The Cultural Politics of Gender Ambiguity*, ed. Julia Epstein and Kristina Staub (New York: Routledge, 1991), 29. Brown, "Body and Society," 5–32.

20. Kiel, "Study versus Sustenance," 280–282, 290, esp. n. 55.

21. Judith Perkins points out in *The Suffering Self: Pain and Narrative Representation in the Early Christian Era* (London: Routledge, 1995), 124, that societies are characterized by competing relations of power and as a result are quite complex. But, she says, when distanced by history, cultures often appear "univocal."

22. Michal Bar-Asher Siegal argues in *Early Christian Monastic Literature and the Babylonian Talmud* (New York: Cambridge University Press, 2013) that the most effective comparisons are those that can define which Christians we are dealing with and which Jews. Often scholars do not define what kinds of Christian sources they are relying on and therefore cannot evaluate whether the sources they are reading offer an accurate picture of the Persian Empire that is productive for making such comparisons (13). She also points out that the model proposed regarding Jews in the Land of Israel should not be imposed automatically on the Jews living in Babylonia. See also Adam H. Becker, "Beyond the Spatial and Temporal Limes: Questioning the 'Parting of the Ways' Outside the Roman Empire," in *The Ways That Never Parted: Jews and Christians in Late Antiquity and the Early Middle Ages*, ed. Adam H. Becker and Annette Yoshiko Reed (Tübingen: Mohr Siebeck, 2003), 392, and Bar-Asher Siegal's discussion of Becker, 18–19.

23. Kiel, in "Study versus Sustenance," 281, argues that cultural and religious expressions were rarely generated in cultural isolation. Communities were penetrable, and Jewish Babylonia was no different. Yaakov Elman has offered many examples that point to the fact that the Babylonian rabbis were particularly susceptible to acculturation. See his "Acculturation to Elite Persian Norms and Modes of Thought in the Babylonian Jewish Community of Late Antiquity," in *Neti'ot leDavid: Sefer hayovel leDavid Halivni* [A Jubilee volume in honor of David Halivni], ed. Yaakov Elman, Ephraim B. Halivni,

and Zvi Steinfeld (Jerusalem: Orhot, 2004), 31–56, and his "Middle Persian Culture and Babylonian Sages: Accommodation and Resistance in the Shaping of Rabbinic Legal Tradition," in *Cambridge Companion to Rabbinic Literature*, ed. Charlotte Elisheva Fonrobert and Martin S. Jaffee (Cambridge: Cambridge University Press, 2007), 165–197.

24. Fraade, "Ascetical Aspects of Ancient Judaism," 256–257. Fraade also offers a definition of asceticism: "A definition of religious asceticism, therefore, should be specific enough to include its two main components: (1) the exercise of disciplined effort toward the goal of spiritual perfection (however understood), which requires (2) abstention (whether total or partial, permanent or temporary, individualist or communalistic) from the satisfaction of otherwise permitted earthly, creaturely desires" (257). Fraade points to a continuous struggle in evidence in rabbinic literature as the Jews navigate the tension between a desire for transcendent ideals and the reality of worldly obstacles such as eating and sexuality. See Eliezer Diamond, *Holy Men and Hunger Artists: Fasting and Asceticism in Rabbinic Culture* (Oxford: Oxford University Press, 2004), 9, where he discusses Fraade's claim.

25. According to the Babylonian amora Ravina (BT Yoma 6a), it was more common to contract impurity through sexual contact with one's wife than through an outside source of impurity, such as contact with a corpse prior to Yom Kippur.

26. The word used in M. Yoma 1:1 is מפרישין, which refers to someone other than the high priest who takes responsibility to separate him.

27. See M. Yoma 1:4, M. Yoma 1:7, and BT Yoma 19b, which discuss how to keep the high priest awake on the "eve of Yom Kippur toward nightfall." Particular foods were believed to cause arousal, increasing the risk of a seminal emission. While M. Avot 5:5, quoted on BT Yoma 21a, nostalgically records the belief that one of the ten miracles to occur in the Temple was that the high priest never experienced a seminal emission on Yom Kippur, JT Yoma 1:1, 38cd and BT Yoma 12a present a case where a high priest was in fact removed from his position as a result of a seminal emission on the holiday.

28. BT Yoma 32a.

29. This is rooted in commandments placed on Aaron and his sons in Numbers, where non-priests are warned, on punishment of death, against encroaching on the space and responsibilities of the priests (Numbers 1:51; 3:10, 38; 18:7). Dalia Marx, *Tractates Tamid, Middot and Qinnim* (Tübingen: Mohr Siebeck, 2013), 11.

30. M. Kelim 1:6–9.

Notes to Chapter 6

31. For a discussion of the history of the rabbinic linkage between holiness and sexual restraint, see Naomi Koltun-Fromm, *Hermeneutics of Holiness: Ancient Jewish and Christian Notions of Sexuality and Religious Community* (New York: Oxford University Press, 2010), 231–236.

32. See Neis, *Sense of Sight*, 90–112, where she discusses this text at length, comparing sections of it to parallels in the Tosefta (T. Yoma 2:15) and JT Shekalim 6:1, 49c.

33. This is a midrashic comment on Song of Songs 1:13: "My beloved to me is a bag of myrrh lodged between my breasts." This verse in the context of BT Yoma 54a is intended to invoke the intense emotion of love between God and the people. Also see 1 Kings 8:8.

34. See Steven D. Fraade, "Facing the Holy Ark, in Words and in Images," *Near Eastern Archaeology* 82, no. 3 (2019): 156. Also note that Cecilia Haendler has argued that the water spigots mentioned in M. Yoma 3:10 were designed to look like breasts based on the Hebrew word used for spigot, *dad*, which means breast. Paper delivered at the AJS, San Diego, 2019.

35. Note the play on the word *ervah*, which can mean "nakedness" from the Hebrew root ערי, to expose or bare. For an extensive analysis of this word see Neis, *Sense of Sight*, 91, no. 43.

36. To accentuate the longevity of the image, Rav Acha bar Ya'akov notes that while the actual keruvim were gone from the time of the First Temple, an image of them in the Second Temple was carved onto the Temple walls. Note that the sugya quotes 1 Kings 6:29: "And he carved all the walls of the house roundabout with carved figures of keruvim and palm trees and open flowers, within and without."

37. 1 Kings 6:35, 7:36 also mention the keruvim. In Exodus 25:20, keruvim are linked to the Ark. Also see Raanan Eichler, "Cherub: A History of Interpretation," *Biblica* 96, no. 1 (2015): 28–30.

38. In BT Yoma 54ab, the Babylonian amora Rav Shila interprets 1 Kings 7:36 as referring to a man who clings to his partner (*levayah*) in describing the keruvim. The JPS translation, however, is as follows: "On its surface—on its sides—and on its insets, [Hiram] engraved keruvim, lions and palms, as the clear space on each allowed, with spirals roundabout."

39. See Marx, *Tractates Tamid, Middot and Qinnim*, 122–123, and her reference to Raphael Patai's discussion of the keruvim in *The Hebrew Goddess* (New York: Ktav Publishing 1968), 136, and Admiel Kosman and Avraham Ofek, *Masekhet nashim: Ḥokhmah, ahavah, ne'emanut, teshuḳah, yofi, min, kedushah: keri'ah besipurim talmudiyim verabaniyim ushenei midrashei shir* [Tractate Nashim: Wisdom, love, faithfulness, passion, beauty, sex, holi-

ness: Readings in talmudic and rabbinic stories and two midrashic poems] (Jerusalem: Keter, 2007), 147–152.

40. Many thanks to Erez DeGolan for pointing this out. Also see Neis, *Sense of Sight*, 93–94.

41. Neis, *Sense of Sight*, 93–94. Fraade, "Facing the Holy Ark," 156, argues that from biblical to First Temple times, the Ark was invisible to all except to a few priests, and during the Second Temple, there was no Ark at all.

42. Neis, *Sense of Sight*, 93, discusses how a woman moves from modesty to the total exposure of her body when she moves from fiancé to spouse.

43. Bal, *Death and Dissymetry*, 27.

44. Neis, *Sense of Sight*, 94–95, calls attention here to the way that gender is unsettled in this passage.

45. BT Bava Batra 99a discusses that when the Temple was destroyed, the keruvim faced away from one another. Also note that the word מעורין is used again here, suggesting that the embrace of the keruvim is indeed a sexual one. See Neis's discussion on p. 91, no. 43, in *Sense of Sight*.

46. See 1 Kings 6:29.

47. Neis, *Sense of Sight*, 90–112.

48. Ruth Mazo Karras, *Unmarriages: Women, Men, and Sexual Unions in the Middle Ages* (Philadelphia: University of Pennsylvania Press, 2020), 2.

49. BT Yoma 9b has no parallel in the Yerushalmi, again supporting Kalmin's observations that Babylonian sources reflect a desire on the part of the rabbis to assert their authority over the priests and the Temple, in this case claiming that they understand the reasons for the destruction of the First Temple. See Richard L. Kalmin, *Jewish Babylonia between Persia and Roman Palestine* (Oxford: Oxford University Press, 2006), 38, 87.

50. See the parallel text in BT Shabbat 62b, where the exegesis of Isaiah 3:16 is contextualized within a discussion about wives cursing their husbands for not gifting them with acceptable adornments. The exegesis of Isaiah 3:16 is brought in as an example of a gendered depiction of women who show off their beauty, enticing men. Nothing is said about the destruction of the Temple in tractate Shabbat, only that cursing one's husband brings about the punishment of poverty. It seems, therefore, that the context into which this exegetical statement is made reflects the overarching themes of the tractate where it is found.

51. Note the comparison to Luke 7:36–39:

Now one of the Pharisees was requesting Him [Jesus] to dine with him, and He entered the Pharisee's house and reclined at the table. And there was a woman in the city who was a sinner; and when she

Notes to Chapter 6

learned that He was reclining at the table in the Pharisee's house, she brought an alabaster vial of perfume, and standing behind Him at His feet, weeping, she began to wet His feet with her tears, and kept wiping them with the hair of her head, and kissing His feet and anointing them with the perfume. Now when the Pharisee who had invited Him saw this, he said to himself, "If this man were a prophet He would know who and what sort of person this woman is who is touching Him, that she is a sinner."

52. See Deborah A. Green, *The Aroma of Righteousness* (University Park: Pennsylvania State University Press, 2011), 20–63, regarding the historical, archaeological, and textual evidence related to aromatics, and Satlow, *Tasting the Dish*, 158–159, and his discussion of seductresses. For a more contemporary point about the stereotypes surrounding the sexual allure of women, see Susan Bordo, *Unbearable Weight: Feminism, Western Culture and the Body* (Berkeley: University of California Press, 1993), 6. For the Bavli parallel, see BT Shabbat 62b.

53. Attributed to the Babylonian amoraim, this passage relates back to earlier tannaitic material on BT Yoma 38a (including the mishnah), where incense production is attributed to the priestly family referred to as "the house of Avtinas." They are remembered unfavorably for their refusal to teach others this art of making incense. However, because the incense they prepared was so sweet smelling, they were careful to behave in a way that was beyond reproach, never allowing their own wives to wear this or other perfumes. They were fearful that their wives would be suspected of stealing it from that which they prepared for the Temple. See Green, *Aroma of Righteousness*, 144. Leviticus 16:12–13 offers a description of the incense sacrifice offered twice daily by the priests as well the incense cloud that emerged on Yom Kippur specifically. Green argues that the pleasant scent of the incense on Yom Kippur was not for the high priest but rather to effect some change in God through its smell. The idea was to get God's attention and prepare for atonement (73–76).

54. See BT Yoma 39b: "Goats that were in Jericho would sneeze from the fragrance of incense."

55. Edward Jay Watts's discussion in *The Final Pagan Generation: Transformation of the Classical Heritage* (Berkeley: University of California Press, 2015), 46–49, points to the fact that the Romans also believed odor to have great power. Holding on to the notion that foul air could cause disease, ancient households took steps to mask awful smells; Romans also perfumed their baths as well as the walls of their homes. They wore fragrances on their

bodies, decorated their homes with pleasant-smelling objects such as flowers and wreaths, and burned incense.

56. A passage that highlights the relationship between David and Batsheva serves as an opportunity for the rabbis to grapple with David's sinful behavior in response to Batsheva's sexuality. Intent on understanding David's sins and his punishments, the Bavli differentiates between punishments exacted on David individually and those exacted on the whole people (BT Yoma 22b).

57. Bal, *Death and Dissymmetry*, 27.

58. In BT Yom 9ab, the destruction of Shiloh is tied to the sexually immoral behaviors of Eli's priest-sons (1 Samuel 2:22).

59. See, for example, M. Yoma 3:4–5:

The high priest undressed, descended and immersed, ascended and dried himself. They brought him the golden vestments, and he put them on and then he sanctified his hands and feet. They brought him the *tamid* offering. He made an incision in [its throat] and another [priest] completed the slaughter for him. He received the blood and threw it. . . . If the high priest was old or of a delicate nature they warmed the water for him and poured it into the cold water [of the mikveh (ritual bath)] so that [the water] would lose its chill.

60. In Exodus 30:19–21, God commands Aaron and his sons to wash their hands and feet before serving in the Tent of Meeting so "that they may not die." But the rabbis in Bavli Yoma struggle to find the scriptural locus for this rite of washing one's hand and feet that was to occur between each change of vestments on Yom Kippur (BT Yoma 31b–32b). While the latter is clearly delineated in T. Yoma 1:17–18, which relies on Exodus 30:20 for teaching this rite, instructions for the rite of cleansing one's hands and feet for Yom Kippur do not appear anywhere in BT Yoma. In the Bavli, Exodus 30:19–21 serves only to discuss whether the second sanctification or washing of the high priest's hands and feet between each of the five Yom Kippur services occurs while he is dressed in his new vestments or not (BT Yoma 32b). Leviticus 16:23–24 plays a far larger role in the discussion but is used to discuss the high priests' required full-body immersion. Also compare the Bavli with JT Yoma 3:6, 40c, where Rabbi Yoḥanan argues that the sanctification of the hands and feet is not essential to the Yom Kippur rite of the high priest. And see BT Zevaḥim 20a–21b for another extensive discussion on hand and foot washing. Also see JT Yoma 3:3, 40b for the Yerushalmi's discussion about full-body immersions.

61. See John 13:1–17, where Jesus washes his disciples' feet and com-

Notes to Chapter 6

mands his disciples to wash the feet of one another. In fact, foot washing remains a church rite in some traditions. Note that hand and foot washing is also a requirement stated in the Quran 5:6. See Ahmed Achrati, "Hand and Foot Symbolisms: From Rock Art to the Qur'an," *Arabia* 50, no. 4 (2003): 488.

62. See 1 Samuel 24:4, where Saul enters a cave, להסך את רגליו, to relieve himself.

63. See Deuteronomy 23:2, where anyone who "has his member cut off" cannot be admitted into "the congregation of the Lord."

64. Note the following parallel found in a baraita quoted on BT Nidah 13a, where the context is one of preventing seminal ejaculation that wastes seed:

Rabbi Eliezer says: Whoever grasps the penis and urinates, it is as if he brings a flood upon the world. The rabbis said to Rabbi Eliezer: But [if he does not hold his penis] will not droplets [of urine] splash on his feet and [because of this] he will appear like one who has a crushed penis, and it will be found out that he casts aspersions on his children, that they are mamzerim?

Although the context in Bavli Nidah is unrelated to priests, it reflects a larger rabbinic fear regarding questionable kinship. When quoted in Bavli Yoma, the source takes on a different valence in its reference to priests. In Yoma, the issue of urine droplets is tied to the Temple rite of hand and foot washing and, more specifically, to the priests.

65. Note that on BT Yoma 30a, after discussing the need for hand and foot washing, the rabbis discuss the issue of what occurs when one defecates and excrement remains on one's body at a time when he needs to recite Shema. Interestingly, there is no reference to washing one's hands and feet in a way that parallels priestly requirements. The Bavli focuses on whether one can recite the Shema or not in the wake of the vileness of excrement that might be visible on one's body and then moves on to discuss washing one's hands after urinating as related to cleanliness.

66. Catherine Hezser, "The Halitzah Shoe: Between Female Subjugation and Symbolic Emasculation," in *Jews and Shoes*, ed. Edna Nahshon (New York: Berg, 2008), 50, discusses the sexual symbolism of the foot and the shoe.

67. Much sexual innuendo in rabbinic literature was associated with feet and most especially heels (specifically the use of the word עקב). For example, see BT Nedarim 20a, where looking at the "heel" of a woman would lead one to beget degenerate children. See Admiel Kosman's discussion about Mar Ukba and the references to "heel" in BT Ketubot 67b, *Gender and the Dialogue in the Rabbinic Prism* (Berlin: Walter De Gruyter, 2012), 47–48.

68. See M. Yoma 3:5 and the baraita quoted on BT Yoma 34b about fastidious priests who needed hot water to temper the water used for their immersions.

69. Mieke Bal, *Lethal Love: Feminist Literary Readings of Biblical Love Stories* (Bloomington: Indiana University Press, 1987), 3.

70. The narrative that dominated Jewish historiography for most of the twentieth century describes the post–Second Temple period as marked by the rapid decline of a priestly hierarchy, making room for the swift rise of a rabbinic elite. This historical perspective is challenged not only by epigraphic and archaeological remains but also by Jewish literature from the period, which supports the idea that priests continued to identify as priests, maintained their economic standing by continuing to receive tithes, and played a role in the religious and political affairs affecting the Jewish community after the destruction of the Temple. See Grey, "Jewish Priests and the Social History of Post-70 Palestine," 6–12, 84; Schwartz, *Josephus and Judean Politics*, 58–109; and Hezser, *Social Structure of the Rabbinic Movement*, 487. Regarding the continued activities of priests in Babylonia, see Herman, "Priests and Amoraic Leadership in Sassanian Babylonia," 65–66.

71. Kalmin, in *Jewish Babylonia between Persia and Roman Palestine*, discusses Babylonian anxiety about their authority, as compared to Palestinian rabbis, 37–60. Elizabeth Shanks Alexander, in *Gender and Timebound Commandments in Judaism* (Cambridge: Cambridge University Press, 2013), 179–185, writes on cultural reproduction through teaching Torah to one's disciples. Also see Lehman, "Dressing and Undressing the High Priest," 58–60.

72. Bal, *Death and Dissymetry*, 5–6.

73. Bal, *Death and Dissymmetry*, 179, 229–230.

74. See Boyarin, "Hellenism in Jewish Babylonia," and Rosen-Zvi, *Demonic Desires*.

75. Both manuscripts, British Library 400 and Munich 95, mention concern about fathers mistakenly marrying their daughters. Biblically, fathers could have sex with daughters without concern for incest, but generally did not in an attempt to preserve their daughters' virginal status: Johanna Stiebert, *First-Degree Incest and the Hebrew Bible: Sex in the Family* (London: Bloomsbury T&T Clark, 2016), 71–72.

76. The concern here is that the visiting rabbi might be gone within a week and therefore lose the opportunity that he created for himself to marry temporarily. If the woman was a nidah, they would not be able to have sex until she counted seven days after her menstrual period had ended.

Notes to Chapter 6

77. BT Yevamot 37b. See as well the larger scholarly discussion about men marrying provisional wives believed to protect them from being unable to control their sexual passions in Boyarin, *Carnal Israel*, 134–146; Isaiah Gafni, "The Institution of Marriage in Rabbinic Times," in *The Jewish Family: Metaphor and Memory*, ed. David Kraemer (Oxford: Oxford University Press, 1989), 24–25; Ishay Rosen-Zvi, "Yetzer hara, miniyut, ve'isurei yiḥud: Perek be'antropologiya talmudit" [Yetzer hara, sexuality and yihud: A chapter of talmudic anthropology], *Theory and Criticism* 14 (1999): 64–65; Michael L. Satlow, *Jewish Marriage in Antiquity* (Princeton: Princeton University Press, 2001), 26–30; Emrani, "'Who Would Be Mine for the Day!,'" 217–231.

78. Note that this passage joins tannaitic material and reports about amoraim together into one passage. I discuss here the overall impression it leaves. I do not discount the fact that asking the question, "Who will be mine for a day?" in and of itself, may have been a request for sexual relations outside the context of a formal marital union. For example, BT Berakhot 57b notes that sexual relations bring pleasure to the body. See Tal Ilan, *Massekhet Ta'anit: A Feminist Commentary on the Babylonian Talmud* (Tübingen: Mohr Siebeck, 2008), 23. Boyarin discusses this passage in *Carnal Israel*, 62–76. Also see Emrani, "'Who Would Be Mine for the Day!,'" 225, who notes that temporary marriages were common among the Jews' Zoroastrian neighbors. In this regard, Emrani argues, Babylonian Jews had more in common with their non-Jewish neighbors than with Jews in the Land of Israel, who had not recorded that such a practice existed among them.

79. See BT Yoma 18b. Rashi and especially Tosafot, *D"H yeḥudei bealma* discuss the difficulties this passage raises.

80. See Mishnah Yoma 1:1 and the sugyot that comment on this mishnah, including BT Yoma 13a: "And this one [woman, designated for him in case of his wife's death] cannot be considered a house [that is, suitable for him to marry]." See also BT Gittin 52a and its parallel, BT Shabat 118b, where the following statement is attributed to R. Yose: "In [all] my days, I have not called my wife 'my wife' nor my ox, 'my ox,' but rather my wife [I called] 'my house' and my ox [I called] 'my field.'" For other examples of the equation between "wife" and "house," see Bereishit Rabbah 17:1; 95:30; BT Sukkah 27b; BT Megillah 13a.

81. Boyarin, *Carnal Israel*, 46–57, 141, and Satlow, *Tasting the Dish*, 314, where he, like Boyarin, notes that Palestinian rabbis were more ambivalent about sexual relations for pleasure than Babylonian rabbis. In his *Jewish Marriage in Antiquity*, 26–34, Satlow discusses Babylonian attitudes toward marriage, noting that Babylonian rabbis viewed marriage as a legitimate

means for channeling male sexual desire. See also Diamond, *Holy Men and Hunger Artists*, 127, and his discussion of the rabbis' "restricted" sex lives, which were defined by a rabbi's commitment to fulfilling his conjugal duties and procreation. In BT Nedarim 20ab, the rabbis place certain limitations on sexual behaviors in the name of producing more perfect offspring.

82. Menahem H. Schmelzer, "How Was the High Priest Kept Awake on the Night of Yom Ha-Kipurim?" in *Studies in Jewish Bibliography and Medieval Hebrew Poetry: Collected Essays* (New York: Jewish Theological Seminary of America, 2006), 218, discusses M. Yoma 1:7 and BT Yoma 19b. These sources highlight the practice of keeping the high priest awake all night on Yom Kippur. The Tosefta and the Bavli report that some of the nobility in Jerusalem, who also remained awake during all of Yom Kippur, would generate some type of noise during the night, called a *kol havarah*. Although it is unclear exactly what the nature of the noise was, Abba Shaul in BT Yoma 19b suggests that the practice had to be abandoned because it led to sinful behavior following the destruction of the Temple. Rashi, commenting on Abba Shaul's statement (*D"H elu shehayu hote'in*) seems to suggest that there was some sort of merrymaking that took place on Yom Kippur that led to lewd behavior.

83. Tal Ilan, *Massekhet Ta'anit*, 49–60. Also see BT Yoma 19b–20a, where Elijah connects the fact that the Messiah had not yet come with the fact that virgins were being defiled in Nehardea on Yom Kippur. See Paul Mandel, "'Lo hayu yamim tovim leyisrael kahamishah asar be'av ukheyom hakipurim': Al hamishnah ha'aharonah shel masekhet ta'anit vegilguleiha" ["There were no happier days for Israel than the Fifteenth of Av and the Day of Atonement": On the final mishnah of Tractate Ta'anit and its transmission], *Te'udah* 11, no. 5 (1996): 148–149, 168, 172. Stökl ben Ezra, *Impact of Yom Kippur on Early Christianity*, 36, notes that some communities celebrated Yom Kippur with an "ambivalent mix of afflictions and joy," while others observed Yom Kippur as a day of active ascetic behavior.

84. Gribetz, *Time and Difference in Rabbinic Judaism*, 22, quotes from John Chrysostom's Yom Kippur sermon in which he warns people against joining the Jews during their festivals.

85. See Rosen-Zvi, *Demonic Desires*, 74–84, for a discussion about the yetzer and his discussion of the personification of the yetzer in its ability to argue (89). Note that he also cautions against assuming that the yetzer is synonymous only with sexuality as it is here on BT Yoma 69b (102, esp. 198–199, n. 1).

86. Regarding BT Yoma 69b, see also Boyarin, *Carnal Israel*, 62–63. Boyarin translates this as "female" relatives; other translations use the term

Notes to Chapter 6

"forbidden" relatives. The underlying point is to make reference to incestual relations.

87. Boyarin, *Carnal Israel*, 62–75. Also see my articles: "Reading the Gendered Rhetoric of Yom Kippur," 33–56, and "Rabbinic Masculinities: Reading the Ba'al Keri in Tractate Yoma," *Jewish Studies Quarterly* 22 (2015): 109–136.

88. Michael L. Satlow, "'And on Earth You Shall Sleep': 'Talmud Torah' and Rabbinic Asceticism," *Journal of Religion* 83 (2003): 205, 215–216, discusses the nature of Torah study as a disciplined type of behavior tantamount to *askisis* in late antiquity, albeit in a more pronounced way in the context of the Jews in the Land of Israel. Satlow also refers to Susan Ashbrook Harvey, "'Asceticism,' in Late Antiquity: Guide to the Postclassical World," ed. G. W. Bowersock, Peter Brown, and Oleg Grabar (Cambridge, MA: Harvard University Press, 1999), 317–318, esp. 317, for a definition of asceticism, noting that it "is the practice of a disciplined life in pursuit of a spiritual condition. In late antiquity, this discipline was exercised through a physical and mental process of ordering the self in relation to the divine." In Satlow's understanding, the pursuit of Torah fits this definition. Also see Boyarin, *Carnal Israel*, 134–146.

89. Boyarin, *Carnal Israel*, 134–166.

90. This is the translation if one presumes that the root of the word is ‏נ.ד.ד‎.

91. In BT Yoma 35b, when a "wicked person" is asked why he did not engage in Torah study and he answers that his handsome nature fueled his evil inclination, that is, his desire for sex, the Bavli seems confident that he could have resisted this inclination. Citing the power of Joseph, who was also handsome and fended off the advances of Potiphar's wife, the source conveys that men have the power to control their sexual passions, even in the face of women who entice them.

92. Boyarin, *Carnal Israel*, 134–166. Also see Boyarin, "Internal Opposition in Talmudic Literature: The Case of the Married Monk," 87–113.

93. Bavli Ketubot, in commenting on M. Ketubot 5:6, pinpoints the frequency with which husbands need to fulfill their conjugal duties to their wives and correlates the frequency with their husbands' chosen livelihoods. More relevant here is the fact that Bavli Ketubot mentions husbands who return home to their wives immediately prior to Yom Kippur after long periods of absence studying Torah in order to fulfill their conjugal duties. Rabbis like Rav Reḥumi, a disciple of Rava in Maḥoza, who failed to return home to his wife, met an untimely demise (BT Ketubot 62b). BT Ketubot 63a also makes note of Rava's decision to send his married son to study in the Baby-

lonian academy of Rav Yosef for six years. After three years, Rava's son chose to come home right before the onset of Yom Kippur. BT Shabbat 127b narrates the story of a worker who asks his master for the wages owed to him so that he can return home in time for Yom Kippur, also highlighting some connection between Yom Kippur and at-homeness; and Bavli Pesachim 109a makes mention of husbands who left the Beit Midrash and returned home for this holiday as well. Finally, see T. Yoma 4:2, which does not appear in the Bavli, where Rabbi Akiva leaves the Beit Midrash so as to feed his children before Yom Kippur. While, quite remarkably, none of these stories surface in Bavli Yoma, their association with Yom Kippur calls attention to the degree to which the rabbis pushed against the ascetic nature of the holiday, supporting, to some degree, the trajectory in evidence among the Nehardean men who have sex on the eve of Yom Kippur. Satlow, *Tasting the Dish*, 269–278, compares the Bavli's discussion of M. Ketubot 5:6 to the Yerushalmi's discussion of the same mishnah (JT Ketubot 5:8, 30ab). There he notes that the overall perspective of the Bavli is to express the tension that marital sexual life raises for the Torah scholar, which, as I observe, does not surface in Bavli Yoma. In "'And on Earth You Shall Sleep,'" 205, 215–216, Satlow argues that Torah study was "the ascetic practice par excellence" for the rabbis and functioned to replace the dominance of the sacrificial cult.

94. Karras, *Unmarriages*, 2.

CHAPTER 7. SUSTAINING THE RABBINIC HOUSEHOLD

1. See Bal, *Death and Dissymmetry: The Politics of Coherence in the Book of Judges*, 2. This is another example of what Mieke Bal argues for when she examines the Book of Judges: focusing on themes that are often considered marginal to a work and instead viewing them as more central.

2. Note that a sugya on BT Yoma 74a that mentions *piggul* (invalidated sacrifices), *notar* (leftover parts of the sacrifices), and *tevel* (produce from which tithes had not been removed for religious contribution and are forbidden to be eaten) examines the idea of eating on Yom Kippur and whether transgressing with these foodstuffs warrants the punishment of karet. However, these tannaitic references are not discussed for the purposes of examining a connection between inui nefesh and the Temple rite of Yom Kippur.

3. The only exception is *nesi'at kapayim* (BT Yoma 87b), the priestly blessing, which is not mentioned in the first seven chapters of Bavli Yoma.

4. This is unlike the way in which Passover is reenacted during a Seder at-home meal. See Bokser, *Origins of the Seder: The Passover Rite and Early Rabbinic Judaism* (Berkeley: University of California Press, 1984). Mira Bal-

Notes to Chapter 7   283

berg and Simeon Chavel's "The Polymorphous Pesah: Ritual between Origins and Reenactment," *Journal of Ancient Judaism* 8, no. 3 (2017): 292–343, offers a very different critical analysis of sources regarding Passover that challenges Bokser's conclusions.

5. See Michael D. Swartz, "Ritual Is with the People: Sacrifice and Society in Palestinian Yoma Traditions," in *The Actuality of Sacrifice: Past and Present*, ed. Alberdina Houtman, Marcel Poothius, Joshua Schwartz, and Joseph Turner (Leiden: Brill, 206–227); "Liturgy, Poetry, and the Persistence of Sacrifice," in *Was 70 CE a Watershed in Jewish History? On Jews and Judaism before and after the Destruction of the Second Temple*, ed. Daniel R. Schwartz, Zeev Weiss, and Ruth A. Clements (Leiden: Brill, 2012), 393–412; and "Yoma from Babylonia to Egypt: Ritual Function, Textual Transmission, and Sacrifice," *AJS Review* 43, no. 2 (2019): 339–353, esp. 341, n. 10, and 345, where Swartz argues for sources in the Bavli that describe prayer leaders who recite passages from the Mishnah (M. Yoma 3:8). See also BT Yoma 87b for one version of the *vidui*, or confession, that did not appear in the first seven chapters of the tractate (including in the Mishnah), but appears in the eighth chapter:

> Rav Hamnuna said: My God, before I was formed, I was unworthy. Now that I have been formed, it is as if I had not been formed. I am dust while alive, how much more so when I am dead. See, I am before You like a vessel filled with shame and disgrace. May it be Your will that I may sin no more, and as for the sins I have committed before You, erase them in Your compassion, but not by suffering.
>
> [The Gemara adds]: This is the confession that Rava used all year long; and [it was the confession] that Rav Hamnuna Zuta used on Yom Kippur.

The rabbis admit further down on BT Yoma 87b that the most important part of the confession is to say, "I have sinned."

6. The fragility of life in the ancient world and its connection to expectations to beget and rear children is discussed in Brown, *The Body and Society: Men, Women, and Sexual Renunciation in Early Christianity*, 6.

7. Eliezer Diamond, *Holy Men and Hunger Artists: Fasting and Asceticism in Rabbinic Culture* (Oxford: Oxford University Press, 2004), 134, argues that more than their Babylonian counterparts, rabbis in the Land of Israel embraced ascetic behaviors. Bavli and Yerushalmi Yoma support this observation. While the Bavli will question the Mishnah's requirement of sexual abstinence, the Yerushalmi supports it. Regarding asceticism in the broader cultural orbit, see, for example, Michal Bar-Asher Siegal, *Early Christian Monastic Literature and the Babylonian Talmud* (New York: Cambridge Univer-

sity Press, 2013). Also see Steven D. Fraade, "Ascetical Aspects of Ancient Judaism," in *Jewish Spirituality: From the Bible through the Middle Ages*, ed. Art Green (New York: Crossroad Publishing, 1987); Peter Brown, *Society and the Holy in Late Antiquity* (Berkeley: University of California Press, 1982); Naomi Koltun-Fromm, *Hermeneutics of Holiness* (Oxford: Oxford University Press, 2010); Jennifer Barry, *Bishops in Flight: Exile and Displacement in Late Antiquity* (Berkeley: University of California Press, 2019); Yishai Kiel, "Al ta'anit umeni'at mazon batalmud habavli le'or ha'ideologiya hazoroasterit" [Fasting and self-deprivation in the Babylonian Talmud in light of Zoroastrian ideology], *Jewish Studies, an Internet Journal* 12 (2013).

8. See Libson, *Law and Self-Knowledge in the Talmud*, 126–152, where she discusses how a pregnant woman can listen to signs from her own body and protect it by nourishing it without needing to turn to a male expert. In the amoraic layers of Bavli Yoma, power is given over to individuals, with the understanding that they know their own bodies better than the rabbis.

9. See Julia Watts Belser, "Disability and the Social Politics of 'Natural' Disaster: Toward a Jewish Feminist Ethics of Disaster Tales," *Worldviews* 19 (2015): 53–58. Belser makes an important point when she argues that rabbinic narratives about the fall of Jerusalem often position women as symbols of the decline and reversal of Jewish fortune, building on their wealth and privilege or their sheer vulnerability. The fact that the requirements of self-denial fall on both men and women in the context of the prohibitions of Yom Kippur suggests that women are not necessarily treated as more naturally vulnerable than men. Indeed, they can take agency to safeguard themselves and their children, reversing the image of them seen elsewhere in rabbinic literature.

10. Yonatan Feintuch discusses the Bavli's focus on manna in "Uncovering Covert Links between Halakhah and Aggadah in the Babylonian Talmud: The Talmudic Discussion of Yom Kippur Afflictions in B. Yoma," *AJS Review* 40, no. 1 (2016): 17–32, as a way to explore the intersection between halakhic material (about inui nefesh) and aggadic material (about manna). His goal is to expose the Bavli's alternate understanding of the prohibition of fasting. While I agree with this reading, I focus more on the way women are brought into this lengthy aggadic passage. Note also that Feintuch, along with Daniel Stökl Ben Ezra, argues that a long-standing tradition, dating back to Second Temple literature, connects manna with Yom Kippur, including in prayers cited by Philo that mention the journeys through the desert and God's miraculous nourishment of the Israelites. See Daniel Stökl Ben Ezra, *The Impact of Yom Kippur on Early Christianity: The Day of Atonement*

from Second Temple Judaism to the Fifth Century (Tübingen: Mohr Siebeck, 2003), 47.

11. In using the word *ritual* here and throughout this discussion of Bavli Yoma, chapter eight, I emphasize, as does Mira Balberg in her discussion of tractate Pesaḥim, that "texts about rituals are texts and not rituals." The Bavli is a discourse of multiple interconnecting layers of sources that are woven together often to convey differing ideological perspectives through a discussion of particular rituals. The redactors of this final chapter in Yoma are trying to make sense of it in light of everyday experience and the cultural world around them. See Balberg and Chavel, "Polymorphous Pesah," 343.

12. Libson, *Law and Self-Knowledge in the Talmud*, 187–188.

13. I thank Pratima Gopalakrishnan for pointing this out to me at the April 2020 Fellowship Seminar.

14. BT Yoma 75a–76a.

15. Leviticus 16:29 states: תעַנּוּ את-נפשתיכם. Leviticus 16:31, 23:32, and Numbers 29:7 have ועיניתם את-נפשתיכם; Leviticus 23:29 has תענה.

16. Oddly, the exact verse is not quoted here but is referenced by the word *inui*. See the Yerushalmi's version of this baraita, JT Yoma 8:1, 44d, which refers to Leviticus 16:29.

17. See also Sifra Aḥarei Mot, 5, 7:4.

18. Note that several manuscripts, including Munich Manuscript 6, British Library 400, and Enelow 270 and 271, all have the opinion of Abaye after that of Rabbi Zeira. This reading makes more sense in that Rabbi Zeira would be bringing the verse to support Rav Yosef, and then Reish Lakish would be bringing the same verse to support Abaye.

19. I agree with the observations of Jeffrey L. Rubenstein that the stammaim play a role as redactors in collecting the amoraic traditions they inherited, and that they were also authors insofar as they place amoraic traditions in larger sugyot of their own composition. See Jeffrey L. Rubenstein, *The Culture of the Babylonian Talmud* (Baltimore: Johns Hopkins University Press, 2003), 3–4.

20. See Feintuch's analysis of this passage in "Uncovering Covert Links," 24–25.

21. Feintuch, "Uncovering Covert Links," 27.

22. Michele Emanatian, "Metaphor and the Expression of Emotion: The Value of Cross-Cultural Perspectives," *Metaphor and Symbolic Activity* 10, no. 3 (1995): 164–166, where she argues that often metaphors are used to expand on the constraints of human conceptualization. See her references to Mark Johnson, *The Body in the Mind: The Bodily Basis of Meaning, Reason*

and Imagination (Chicago: Chicago University Press, 1987), and George Lakoff and Mark Johnson, *The Metaphors We Live By* (Chicago: University of Chicago Press, 1980). See also Gail Labovitz, "Is Rav's Wife 'a Dish'? Food and Eating Metaphors in Rabbinic Discourse of Sexuality and Gender Relations," in *Love—Ideal and Real—in the Jewish Tradition from the Hebrew Bible to Modern Times*, edited by Leonard J. Greenspoon, Ronald A. Simkins, and Jean A. Cahan (Omaha: Creighton University Press, 2008), 147–148.

23. Labovitz, "Is Rav's Wife 'a Dish'?," 148.

24. Labovitz, "Is Rav's Wife 'a Dish'?," 147–149. Men do the "sexual seeing," while women's bodies are conceptualized as food.

25. Mary Kosut and Lisa Jean Moore, "Introduction: Not Just the Reflexive Reflex; Flesh and Bone in the Social Sciences," in *The Body Reader*, ed. Lisa Jean Moore and Mary Kosut (New York: New York University Press, 2010), 11, and see their discussion of Michel Foucault, *Discipline and Punish: The Birth of the Prison* (Harmondsworth: Penguin, 1979), 25.

26. Emanatian, "Metaphor and the Expression of Emotion," 166.

27. See Julia Watts Belser, "Returning to the Flesh: A Jewish Reflection on Feminist Disability Theory," *Journal of Feminist Studies in Religion* 26, no. 2 (2010): 129–130, about the importance of recognizing ableism as connected to feminist concerns. For feminist readers, she charts an important course in prompting us to expose not only the disturbing cultural norms embedded in rabbinic texts but also our own. She reminds us that just as the rabbis turned to the bodies of women and the physically disabled to differentiate themselves from whatever weaknesses and vulnerabilities they were experiencing, many of us continue to do the same today.

28. Certain amounts of food are allowable. For example, eating less than an olive's measurement is not considered eating because it does not remove the feeling of hunger that one should feel on Yom Kippur. It is too small to put "one's mind at ease." However, a large date (with the pit) is a measurement capable of putting "one's mind at ease" on Yom Kippur. Therefore, this is the amount that is prohibited. See BT Yoma 79a and BT Berakhot 45a.

29. Supporting this shift in the image of inui nefesh, amoraic material in Bavli Yoma also makes allowances for shoe wearing and washing in certain instances, relaxing what looks like a stricter approach to ascetic behavior found in Mishnah Yoma. Indeed, the amoraim make allowances for an experience that is better described as self-denial than as affliction, as "affliction" by association brings up the notion of physical suffering. Note that some biblical translations translate *inui* as an "affliction," and not as a commandment of self-denial.

Notes to Chapter 7

30. The one exception on BT Yoma 75a is an interpretive remark regarding Proverbs 12:25, which speaks to ridding individuals of human anxiety. All of the other comments in this passage are about food.

31. This equation between women's bodies, their sexuality, and wine/food also emerges elsewhere in this chapter of Yoma on BT Yoma 76b. The rabbis use the metaphors of the virgin female and promiscuous women to conceptualize whether the biblical word *tirosh* means wine.

32. Daniel Boyarin, "Hellenism in Jewish Babylonia," in *The Cambridge Companion to the Talmud*, ed. Martin S. Jaffee and Charlotte Elisheva Fonrobert (New York: Cambridge University Press, 2007), 338. Also see Bar-Asher Siegal, *Early Christian Monastic Literature and the Babylonian Talmud*, 138–166, where she recognizes influences of monastic traditions in Babylonian versions of stories found originally in the Yerushalmi. Bar-Asher Siegal's findings lead her to conclude that there were literary connections between Jews in Babylonia and their Christian neighbors. Without delving deeply into the cross-cultural influences that had an impact on Babylonian sugyot, I see here in the eighth chapter of Bavli Yoma a desire to define rabbinic asceticism differently from that of their neighbors. I agree that this material should not be read as polemical, in keeping with Bar-Asher Siegal's careful observations of the rabbinic material she discusses (167). That the rabbis are after something new and different is not necessarily a polemic. Also see Bar-Asher Siegal's discussion of BT Avodah Zarah 17a for the ways in which the rabbis were not polemicizing against Christian monastic literature but were participating in a conversation, each drawing from the other. See Simcha M. Gross, "Rethinking Babylonian Acculturation in the Sassanian Empire," *Journal of Ancient Judaism* 9 (2018): 280–310, and "Irano-Talmudica and Beyond: Next Steps in the Contextualization of the Babylonian Talmud," *Jewish Quarterly Review* 106, no. 2 (2016): 248–255, for his argument that the Babylonian rabbinic community was not as insular as some have thought.

33. Rashi, BT Yoma 75a, in his comment *D"H arayot*, claims that דגה is the root of the word וידגו, as mentioned in Genesis 48:16. When Jacob blesses Joseph, he says, "And may they [Ephraim and Menasseh] be[come] teeming multitudes upon the earth."

34. BT Yoma 75a. See Rashi, *D"H hanakh deasirin*.

35. Presumably, underlying this interpretation of the word *fish/dagah* is the notion that the Israelites "increased," in spite of Pharaoh's attempts to oppress them, although the passage above makes no mention of it (Exodus 1:19).

36. See Stiebert, *First-Degree Incest and the Hebrew Bible*, 1–18, esp. 2. She points out that what is considered incestuous in one cultural context, for example, in Egypt, can be illegal in the rabbis' own context, differentiating themselves not only from a pre-Toraitic past but also from a pre-rabbinic life.

37. Leviticus 18, which prohibits incestuous relationships and eventually serves as the central portion read from the Torah on the holiday of Yom Kippur, has accustomed us to think about incest as unlawful.

38. As Stiebert argues in *First-Degree Incest and the Hebrew Bible*, biblical incest laws, inasmuch as there is no consistent perspective offered, represent a desire to distance individuals from being too close to their own being. Intimate contact with family members introduces a level of "discomforting proximity" that needs to be monitored in households that were probably extended, and not made up of nuclear families. To enhance social stability, minimizing sexual competition among men became desirable. Authority is easier to maintain when sexual rivalries within a household do not exist, that is, when men are not sexually drawn to the same women (73–79). Interestingly, incest law protects women from men who are not their husbands, ensuring that women are more than their bodies, more than a basic currency or commodity available to any man living within her household (81).

39. Regarding Babylonian culture, see Yishai Kiel, "Confessing Incest to a Rabbi: A Talmudic Story in Its Zoroastrain Context," *Harvard Theological Review* 107, no. 4 (2014): 403, 419–420, where he argues that Zoroastrians believed that incestual relations, such as those between a mother and her son, could prevent the effects of a crime worthy of the punishment of death. Also see Yaakov Elman, "'He in His Cloak and She in Her Cloak': Conflicting Images of Sexuality in Sassanian Mesopotamia," in *Discussing Cultural Influences: Text, Context and Non-Text in Rabbinic Judaism*, ed. Rivka Ulmer (Lanham, MD: University Press of America, 2007), 131, 133, 135.

40. In a world where sickness, blight, and drought were often very real experiences and life expectancies were short, defining the commandment of self-denial was far from simple.

41. See Stiebert, *First-Degree Incest and the Hebrew Bible*, 48, on the tensions that arose among scholars regarding incest. Some connected incest prohibitions to stances on morality, and others saw it as a needed law to prohibit what was in fact happening in multigenerational households.

42. Libson, *Law and Self-Knowledge in the Talmud*, 126–147.

43. See BT Bava Metzia 28a about caravans traveling to the Temple on pilgrimage holidays. Fasting was often associated with simple dress, such as

Notes to Chapter 7 289

sackcloth (Esther 4:3 and Jonah 3:5), whereas the priests on Yom Kippur in the Temple wore lavish garments.

44. In saying this, Bavli Yoma BT Yoma 75a negotiates the contradiction in Numbers 11:9, Exodus 16:4, and Numbers 11:8 regarding the location of where manna fell.

45. This is markedly different from the material that Julia Watts Belser discusses with respect to Bavli Gittin linking food and feasting with disaster and discussions of class and social privilege. The narrative forces that undergird this material in Gittin are entirely different from Yoma. See her *Rabbinic Tales of Destruction*, and "Opulence and Oblivion: Talmudic Feasting, Famine, and the Social Politics of Disaster," *AJS Review* 38, no. 1 (2014): 89–107.

46. Indeed, for Daniel Boyarin, feminist analysis encourages reading rabbinic texts "against the grain" in search of proto-feminist strains. He compels us to reexamine the past and seek illustrations of female power rather than weakness in the sources. The goal is to pay attention to the ruptures, discontinuities, and cracks in the systems of power so that we can develop "multiple strategies for resisting their dangerous implications without either collaborating in domination or total rejection" of the texts we study. See Boyarin, "Rabbinic Resistance to Male Domination: A Case Study in Talmudic Cultural Poetics,", 119. Also see Jana Sawicki, *Disciplining Foucault: Feminism, Power, and the Body* (New York: Routledge, 1991), 14, and Daniel Boyarin, *Carnal Israel: Reading Sex in Talmudic Culture* (Berkeley: University of California Press, 227–228; Fonrobert, *Menstrual Purity*, 9, addresses the significance of finding lapses or disturbances in the ideological coherence regarding women.

47. See BT Yoma 75b, where the idea that eating manna creates no waste, as it is absorbed into one's limbs.

48. See Genesis 34:2, where forms of the word ענה mean rape. Also see Deuteronomy 22:23, the rape of a betrothed virgin woman who fails to cry out for help; Judges 19–20, where the concubine of Gibeah is raped; 2 Samuel 13:12–14, the story of Amnon and Tamar; and Lamentations 5:11, referring to the rape of women at the time of the destruction of Jerusalem.

49. See Genesis 16:6, 9, where Sarah mistreats Hagar, and Genesis 15:13 and Exodus 1:11–13, where God treats Israel harshly. For a good summary of the use of this verb form in biblical material see Tikvah Frymer-Kensky, *Studies in Bible and Feminist Criticism* (Philadelphia: Jewish Publication Society, 2005), 243–244, 251–252.

50. Tal Ilan, *Massekhet Ta'anit: A Feminist Commentary on the Babylonian*

Talmud (Tübingen: Mohr Siebeck, 2008), 23, makes note of the fact that the word *onah* in Exodus 21:10, taken by the rabbis to refer to a husband's conjugal duty, is also derived from the same root as the word *inui*, although Bavli Yoma does not mention this marital requirement in its exploration of the term. The absence of any mention of this duty of a husband to his wife for nonprocreative sexual relations is most interesting given the push in the Bavli to suggest that only procreative relations are allowed on Yom Kippur and fall outside the definition of inui.

51. BT Yoma 77b, Rashi, *D"H mebe'ot aherot* where he argues for the possibility that Dinah was "afflicted" because Shekhem refused to have further sexual encounters with her after the first encounter, despite her desire for him. Rashi also suggests that we understand this in another way: Shekhem afflicted Dinah with sexual intercourse of an unnatural type, such as anal intercourse.

52. See the medieval commentator *Ritba* on BT Yoma 77b, *D"H mebe'ot aherot*, who argues that natural sexual relations cannot be classified as inui. Shekhem and Dinah had "unnatural sexual relations."

53. See Federico Dal Bo, *Massekhet Keritot: A Feminist Commentary on the Babylonian Talmud* (Tübingen: Mohr Siebeck, 2013), 322–323, for the Talmud's use of terms to refer to licit versus illicit intercourse. *Lo kedarkhah*, for example, used in Rashi's commentary on BT Yoma 77b, means "not according to its way." *Kedarkhah* means "in its natural way" and is semantically linked to the phrase *derekh eretz* (see BT 74b), which, according to Dal Bo, means sexual relations performed in accordance with the "way of the world," that is, practiced "decently." He adds that in having sexual relations in accordance "with the way of the world" implies sexual relations that are modest and honest and which the rabbis expect of everyone. As much as I would like to believe Dal Bo is correct here, I can only go so far as to say that "natural sexual relations" are licit relations, according to the rabbis. Sex "kedarkhah" is heterosexual intercourse between a man and a woman and can produce progeny.

54. Further support for this reading emerges when looking at the allowance in M. Yoma 8:1 and BT Yoma 78b of brides to wash their faces, despite the prohibition against washing on Yom Kippur. This is so that brides will remain attractive to their husbands and not lose their sexual appeal. In fact, the Babylonian amora Rav Ḥiyya informed Rav that men were not to withhold *taḥshitin* (adornments) of any sort from their wives for a full thirty days after their weddings, so that newly married wives could adorn themselves for their husbands even on Yom Kippur.

Notes to Chapter 7

55. Naomi Kolton-Fromm, *Hermeneutics of Holiness: Ancient Jewish and Christian Notions of Sexuality and Religious Community* (New York: Oxford University Press, 2010), 215–216, states, "While fasting clearly was practiced by the rabbis, it is not rhetoricized within a hermeneutic of holiness in the same way that sexuality is." While fasting might substitute for a sacrificial offering, eating in ritual purity at the rabbinic table, where the table becomes an altar, also occurs. Also note that passages in the eighth chapter of Yerushalmi Yoma focus far more than the Bavli on comparing Yom Kippur and its prohibitions to other fast days, suggesting that for the Bavli, Yom Kippur is more distinctive. Additionally, the Yerushalmi focuses far more so than the Bavli on wearing shoes, wading through water, and the prohibition of anointing rather than on sexual relations and eating.

56. M. Ta'anit 2:1, in describing public fasts, refers to the people of Nineveh, quoting Jonah 3:5. It also quotes Joel 2:13. In the Bible, fasting was a means of expressing submission and devotion to God as, for example, when Saul decrees a fast in 1 Samuel 14:24. David fasts when Saul dies (2 Samuel 1:12) and when his children are ill (2 Samuel 12:16). Moses fasts when receiving the Ten Commandments (Exodus 34:28) and Daniel does so when awaiting revelation (Daniel 10:3). According to the personal supplication attributed to the tanna Rav Sheshet on BT Berakhot 17a, he asks that God accept his fast as a replacement for his sacrifice on the altar, a point that is not made in Bavli Yoma. Elisheva Baumgarten argues that despite a desire on the part of Babylonian rabbis to curtail fasting, in medieval Ashkenaz it emerged as a practice with renewed rigor. By the medieval period fasting practices were linked to the Jewish calendar and included a two-day fast for Yom Kippur and fasting throughout the Ten Days of Repentance. Arguably, fasting was "food for God," recalling the idea that fasting replaced sacrifice. See Elisheva Baumgarten, *Practicing Piety in Medieval Ashkenaz: Men, Women, and Everyday Religious Observance* (Philadelphia: University of Pennsylvania Press, 2016), 54–61; see also Belser, *Power, Ethics, and Ecology in Jewish Late Antiquity*, 116–148; and Stökl Ben Ezra, *Impact of Yom Kippur*, 47–48, regarding the developing connection between prayer and self-affliction.

57. Diamond, *Holy Men*, 121–132.

58. Belser, *Power, Ethics, and Ecology in Jewish Late Antiquity*, 116–148, discusses that as early as the Mishnah, a communal ritual procedure was outlined for dealing with droughts. Also see her "Crying Out for Rain: The Human, the Holy, and the Earth in the Ritual Fasts of Rabbinic Literature," *Worldviews* 13 (2009): 234–236.

59. See T. Yoma 4:9; a version that appears on BT Yoma 86a is not a ref-

erence to self-induced suffering through fasting. In other words, suffering may be a sign of transgression, but it is not a requirement for achieving God's forgiveness. Moshe Halbertal, *On Sacrifice* (Princeton: Princeton University Press, 2012), 41–47, and Libson, *Law and Self-Knowledge in the Temple*, 147–151, broaden this discussion. They highlight just how complicated the role of fasting was among the rabbis of the late antique world. As Libson correctly notes, the rabbis were preoccupied with the theological and cultural meanings of suffering. Indeed, the eighth chapter of BT Yoma presents aspects of this struggle. See also the stories told of sages from the end of the tannaitic period who intentionally invited suffering on themselves out of fear that they unknowingly transgressed one of the commandments of the law (BT Bava Metzia 84b–85a). Interestingly, BT Yoma does not include similar cases about rabbis and does not convey that inui nefesh on Yom Kippur is for the purpose of creating the suffering body.

60. That said regarding Bavli Yoma, mention of atonement in Leviticus 16:30, which is enveloped within the commandment of self-denial on Yom Kippur in Leviticus 16:29 and 16:31, does prompt a direct association between inui and repentance that becomes deeply embedded in Yom Kippur practice and liturgy for generations. See Baumgarten, *Practicing Piety*, 54–70.

61. It is possible that the Bavli's redactors were merely following the structure of the Mishnah, which does not mention repentance until M. Yoma 8:8–9, but the absence of a clear-cut equation between inui nefesh, bodily suffering, repentance, and atonement is curious. Why are the prohibitions associated with inui nefesh disconnected from the idea of bringing about a ritually required experience of suffering in order to repent before God and be forgiven? Again, the rabbis' position is not straightforward. Although M. Yoma 8:8 states that Yom Kippur, death, and repentance together bring about forgiveness for sin, it is not clear whether "Yom Kippur" refers to the specific practice of inui nefesh or merely the passage of the day. The link is not made explicit. As well see Siegal, *Early Christian Monastic Literature*, 177–179.

62. Baumgarten, *Practicing Piety*, 56; Moshe Beer, "Al ma'asei kaparah shel ba'alei teshuvah besifrut ḥazal" [On penances of penitents in the literature of "ḥazal"], *Zion* (1981): 159–181, esp. n. 15.

63. Baumgarten, *Practicing Piety*, 56, and Beer, "Al ma'asei kaparah," 159–181.

64. Rabbi Yirmiyah comments here that Torah scholars should not fast because it weakens their ability to study. BT Ta'anit 11b.

Notes to Chapter 7

65. Note that there is debate among medieval Talmudic commentators as to whether the prohibitions of Yom Kippur (no eating or drinking, no washing, no anointing, and no wearing shoes or having sexual relations) are biblical (BT Yoma 73b). Some connect the prohibitions to the number of times that inui is mentioned in the Torah, concluding that all of the prohibitions are biblical (see BT Yoma 76a, Rashi, *D"H uve'asur*, and Rambam, *Mishneh Torah*, Shvitat Asur, 1:5). The fact that only eating and drinking are punishable by karet led some Rishonim (medieval Talmudic commentators) to distinguish eating and drinking categorically from the other four prohibitions. Some have therefore categorized washing, anointing, wearing shoes, and sexual relations as merely derived from or rooted in Scripture but not actually stated there (an *asmakhta*), distinguishing them from eating and drinking, which are considered biblical and punishable by karet. See BT Yoma 77a, Tosafot, *D"H ditnan*; Rosh Yoma 8:1.

66. BT Berakhot 45a.

67. Oddly, the sugya, despite commenting directly on a mishnah that mentions the acceptable amounts of food one can eat before eating too much and transgressing, does not use the same terminology as the Mishnah. The Bavli uses words such as שעור and חצי שעור, which are vague and open to interpretation. Later in the tractate, we find Rav Pappa's question as to whether the Mishnah's measure of a "large date" contains the pit or not as a trigger for homing in on a more precise measurement (BT Yoma 79a). Eventually the rabbis make allowances for the greatest volume of food possible, while still considering what it means to fast, debating whether "large dates" are bigger than the volume of an egg.

68. See BT Yoma 78b regarding allowances for wearing shoes and BT Yoma 77b regarding exceptions to the prohibitions of washing. See Marjorie Lehman, "Feet in the Rabbinic Imagination and the Prohibition against Wearing Shoes on Yom Kippur," *AJS Review* 43, no. 2 (2019): 336–337.

69. See note 59.

70. Klawans, *Purity, Sacrifice, and the Temple*, 201.

71. Kristina Milnor, *Gender, Domesticity, and the Age of Augustus: Inventing Private Life* (New York: Oxford University Press, 2005), 9–10. See Milnor's discussion of Augustus's simple private home built on the Palatine that was distinct from the opulence of the public spaces surrounding it. Augustus had restored eighty-two temples and the Forum Augustum, contributing to the beautification of the city of Rome. Benjamin D. Gordon, "Sightseeing and Spectacle at the Jewish Temple," *AJS Review* 43, no. 2 (2019): 271–292, discusses the grandness of the Herodian Temple built to rival Augustus's

building campaign. As a result, the Temple became an international attraction, and many made pilgrimages to visit it.

72. Mary Kosut and Lisa Jean Moore, "Introduction," 1–2.

CHAPTER 8. VULNERABLE BODIES IN
VULNERABLE HOUSES

1. See Fonrobert, *Menstrual Purity*, 40–68, regarding metaphors related to the house that turn women's bodies into architectural constructs in an attempt both to understand and control them. See also Baker, *Rebuilding the House of Israel*, 35.

2. Mary Kosut and Lisa Jean Moore, "Vulnerable Bodies," in *The Body Reader*, ed. Lisa Jean Moore and Mary Kosut (New York: New York University Press, 2010), 27, offer a contemporary reading of the interplay between power and fragility when thinking about the vulnerable body that is significant here in thinking about Bavli Yoma.

3. Klawans, *Purity, Sacrifice, and the Temple*, 20.

4. See Sifra Aharei mot, 5, 7:9 and BT Sukkah 28ab. See also Elizabeth Shanks Alexander, *Gender and Timebound Commandments in Judaism* (Cambridge: Cambridge University Press, 2013), 224.

5. Interestingly, the absence of any food preparation, including the lack of food consumption on Yom Kippur, makes it easier for women to take on the prohibitions associated with inui nefesh.

6. Dina Stein, "Collapsing Structures: Discourse and the Destruction of the Temple in the Babylonian Talmud," *Jewish Quarterly Review* 98, no. 1 (2008): 19.

7. Baker, *Rebuilding the House of Israel*, 58–59, argues that the Hebrew term *ba'al habayit* (master of the house) is specific to describing a husband who "masters" the house, while a wife is a *ba'alat habayit* (mistress of the house): she sets the house in order, overseeing its daily functioning. Therefore, while the relationship is asymmetrical, they are codependent.

8. Judith Hauptman argues that women intervened in laws related to household issues, specifically food preparation, that made husbands and wives codependent in the daily house. She argues that the domestic responsibilities of women in the household meant that they knew and transmitted legal decisions, even advising their husbands on matters pertaining to food preparation. See Hauptman's articles: "A New View of Women and Torah Study in the Talmudic Period," *Jewish Studies, an Internet Journal* 9 (2010): 249–292, https://www.biu.ac.il/JS/JSIJ/9-2010/Hauptman.pdf; "From the Kitchen to the Dining Room: Women and Ritual Activities in Tractate

Pesachim," in *A Feminist Commentary on the Babylonian Talmud: Introduction and Studies*, ed. Tal Ilan, Tamara Or, Dorothea M. Salzer, Christine Steuer, and Irina Wandrey (Tübingen: Mohr Siebeck, 2007), 109–126; "Hadavar masur lenashim: Nashim vetiksei dat beitiyim" [The matter is turned over to women: Women and domestic religious ritual], *Sidra* 24–25 (2010): 83–111; and "The Talmud's Women in Law and Narrative," *Nashim* 28 (2015): 30–50. Also see Sarit Kattan Gribetz, "Consuming Texts: Women as Recipients and Transmitters of Ancient Texts," 183–185, and Ilan, *Jewish Women in Greco-Roman Palestine*, 184.

9. Israel Moses Ta-Shma, "Karet," in *Encyclopaedia Judaica*, 2nd ed., ed. Michael Berenbaum and Fred Skolnik (New York: Macmillan Reference USA, 2007), 806–807.

10. See T. Yoma 4:3, which refers to foods that constitute a transgression on Yom Kippur. This baraita uses the words *hayav* and *patur*. No mention is made of karet. The Bavli might be building on Sifra, which, in commenting on the verse where the punishment of karet is mentioned (Leviticus 16:29), links self-denial to eating and drinking specifically (Sifra, Aharei mot 5, 7:3), mentioning karet in Aharei mot 5, 7:1.

11. Fonrobert, "Education as Filiation," 10, and *Menstrual Purity*, 9.

12. See Federico Dal Bo, *Massekhet Keritot: A Feminist Commentary on the Babylonian Talmud* (Tübingen: Mohr Siebeck, 2013), where he notes that karet is a punishment for transgressions committed intentionally and for which punishment is meted out by God. That said, the tractate *Keritot* does not delineate the legal procedure for this divine punishment. There is no description of what it means to be spiritually excised from the community and what form this takes. Other than a list of the types of sins that make one liable for karet, the tractate focuses far more intently on inadvertent or doubtful transgressions. This aligns with M. Yoma 8:3, which discusses the requirement to bring a *hatat* offering (sin offering) for inadvertent transgressions on Yom Kippur with no mention of karet. Bavli Yoma, however, in commenting on this mishnah, spends a lot of time trying to prove that self-denial is a negative commandment for which karet is the punishment but, similar to tractate Keritot, does not explicitly delineate the punishments.

13. Compare this discussion to the treatment of the *parah adumah*, where a lengthy discussion ensues as to whether a woman can perform the rites associated with it. BT Yoma 42b–43a.

14. Because women are exempt from commandments related to time, one might presume that in this case too, women are exempt. See M. Kiddushin 1:7.

296   *Notes to Chapter 8*

15. See Elizabeth Shanks Alexander, *Gender and Timebound Commandments in Judaism* (Cambridge: Cambridge University Press, 2013), on defining positive and negative commandments as the difference between "thou shalt" and "thou shalt not." See also Judith Hauptman, *Rereading the Rabbis: A Woman's Voice* (Boulder, CO: Westview Press, 1998), 226; Sacha Stern, *Time and Process in Ancient Judaism* (Portland: Littman Library of Jewish Civilization, 2004), 28; Moshe Benovitz, "Time-Triggered Positive Mitzvot as Conversation Pieces," *Hebrew Union College Annual* 78 (2007): 45, n. 1; and Marjorie Lehman, "The Gendered Rhetoric of Sukkah Observance," *Jewish Quarterly Review* 96 (2006): 309–335.

16. BT Yoma 81a. Arguably, it would be like saying, "Get up and eat." Note also that since the prohibitions that define inui nefesh are not delineated in the biblical verses, the tannaim exegetically derive them as a way to show that the prohibitions have biblical authority.

17. See M. Keritot 1:1 for the list of when one is guilty of karet. There it states that one is liable for karet if one eats or performs forbidden labor on Yom Kippur. Transgressing the other prohibitions are not listed as those for which one receives this punishment.

18. The sugya beginning on BT Yoma 81a extends to BT Yoma 82b with complex argumentation that supports and challenges the association to the prohibition against work on Shabbat and Yom Kippur. I have oversimplified the complexity of the argument presented in this sugya.

19. Marx, *Tractates Tamid, Middot and Qinnim*, 11–13.

20. A positive time-bound categorization would render women exempt, with choices regarding whether to observe Yom Kippur. A negative commandment, for which women are required, possesses a greater sense of clarity, pushing all ambiguities regarding the commandment to the wayside. In fact, it is not unusual for the Bavli to juxtapose a negative commandment with a positive one, turning the positive commandment into one that functions as a negative commandment, for which women are then required to perform. For example, drinking wine (kiddush) on the Sabbath, which appears to be a positive time-bound commandment, is analogized to not working on the Sabbath (BT Berakhot 20b). The sugya on BT Berakhot 20b juxtaposes Exodus 20:8 and Deuteronomy 5:12 as follows: "Rather, Rava said: [In the Ten Commandments in the book of Exodus], the verse said: 'Remember [Shabbat and sanctify it]' (Exodus 20:8): [while in the Ten Commandments in the book of Deuteronomy, it says]: 'Observe [Shabbat and sanctify it]' (Deuteronomy 5:12). [From these two verses, we deduce that] anyone included in [the obligation to] observe [Shabbat by

Notes to Chapter 8

refraining from working on this day], is [also] included in [the mitzvah to] remember [Shabbat by reciting kiddush]. Since these women are included in [the mitzvah] to observe [Shabbat, as there is no distinction between men and women in the obligation to observe prohibitions in general and to refrain from working on Shabbat in particular, so too] they are included in [the mitzvah of] remembering [Shabbat, which is done through drinking the wine of kiddush]." In addition, eating matzah on Passover, which also looks like a positive time-bound commandment, is linked to the negative commandment of not eating leaven on Passover due to the juxtaposition of these two commandments in Deuteronomy 16:3. These textual juxtapositions then render kiddush and matzah as commandments, for which women are required. See BT Pesachim 43b and 91b and JT Pesaḥim 8:1, 35d. I thank Elizabeth Shanks Alexander for her insights on this matter and her argument that there is no tannaitic material that links inui nefesh with the category of positive time-bound commandments. Therefore, as she argues, the sugya here in Bavli Yoma has little to build its case on regarding women. While Alexander makes a strong case, as I see it, the redactors of Bavli Yoma are making choices regarding the direction in which they wish to push this discussion. The fact that women are required, like men, to observe the prohibitions associated with Yom Kippur fits with the larger redactional trajectory present in the eighth chapter regarding the household as distinct from the Temple house. Also see Aharon Shemesh, "Letoledot mashma'am shel hamusagim 'mitzvat ase umitzvat lo ta'aseh'" [Toward a history of the terms "positive and negative commandment"], *Tarbitz* 72, no. 1 (1993): 133–150.

21. See M. Kiddushin 1:8. In T. Bikkurim 2:5, women are excluded from the priesthood. See Alexander, *Gender and Timebound Commandments in Judaism*, 59.

22. Alexander, in *Gender and Timebound Commandments in Judaism*, 46–56, notes that while the four-part ruling found in M. Kiddushin 1:7 is seen by the Bavli as generating a comprehensive statement differentiating the nature of men and women in Jewish law, earlier sources in the Tosefta and the Yerushalmi are not as convinced. See Natan Margalit, "Priestly Men and Invisible Women: Male Appropriation of the Feminine and the Exemption of Women from Positive, Time-Bound Commandments," *AJS Review* 28, no. 2 (2004). Also see Hauptman, *Rereading the Rabbis*, 222–228. Margalit and Hauptman argue that M. Kiddushin 1:7 confirms women's second-class status.

23. At the end of the sugya, the Bavli returns to explore the foods that

make one "ḥayav." That said, it is not clear from the word *ḥayav* whether this is a reference to an intentional transgression or an unintentional one; therefore, it is unclear which punishment the offender should receive. See BT Yoma 81b.

24. The issues of concern to the Yerushalmi (JT Yoma 8:3, 45a) are different from those of the Bavli with regard to M. Yoma 8:3. The issue of whether inui is a positive or negative commandment and how that relates to the punishment of karet is not expounded on.

25. The parallel source in JT Yoma 8:1, 44d does not attribute the opinion of Rabbi Eliezer in M. Yoma 1:1 to Rabbi Ḥanina ben Teradyon, but all manuscripts available to me of Bavli Yoma 78b attribute the mishnaic dictum to the opinion of this rabbi.

26. On BT Yoma 78b it says: "My mother told me: A child [requires] hot water and oil . . . he must eat egg with *kutaḥa*." See BT Pesachim 42a for a description of kutaḥa. See BT Kiddushin 31b for a reference to the fact that Abaye's "mother" was the woman who nursed him, given that his mother had died.

27. John David Penniman, *Raised on Christian Milk: Food and the Formation of the Soul in Early Christianity* (New Haven: Yale University Press, 2017), 8–9, argues that during antiquity, the proper education and rearing of children was wrapped up in issues of food and the ways in which food was both "theorized and regulated." In order to be "well-born and well-bred and well-formed, one first and foremost had to be well-fed." The idea that children were nourished as infants through the milk of Christian mothers meant that nourishment and nurture were intimately tied together (*lacte Christiano educatus*) (9). Mara H. Benjamin, *The Obligated Self: Maternal Subjectivity and Jewish Thought* (Bloomington: Indiana University Press, 2018), 63–64, likens the rabbis teaching their students to mothers nurturing their children.

28. M. Yoma 8:4 uses the Hebrew word מחנכין to stress the significance of "educating" children in the practice of fasting.

29. See my discussion in chapter five.

30. See my discussion in chapter three.

31. See my discussion in chapter two.

32. Holt Parker, "Loyal Slaves and Loyal Wives: The Crisis of the Outside-Within and Roman *Exemplum* Literature," in *Women and Slaves in Greco-Roman Culture*, ed. Sandra R. Joshel and Sheila Murnaghan (London: Routledge, 1998), 154; Dina Stein, "A Maidservant and Her Master's Voice: Discourse, Identity, and Eros in Rabbinic Texts," *Journal of the History of Sexuality* 10, no. 3, 4 (2001): 377.

Notes to Chapter 8

33. BT Yoma 82a mentions the three cases in which one cannot save themselves if endangered: idol worship, illicit relations, and murder.

34. The manuscript of Bavli Yoma, Munich 6, has ההיא עוברה דאתאי קמיה דרבי and does not suggest that this pregnant woman was smelling food and therefore craving it; rather, she merely "came before Rebbe." Other manuscripts, including the Vilna printed version, connect this vignette to the mishnah where the pregnant woman is indeed "smelling" (הריחה). However, one could translate דארחא as "by the way, incidentally," rather than as connected to the Hebrew root ריח, "smelling."

35. Literally, "womb." See JPS translation—Psalms 58:4.

36. See BT Bava Batra 90b, which states in the name of Rabbi Yochanan that Shabetai hoarded produce and then sold it at high prices.

37. See JT Yoma 8:4, 45a. In the Yerushalmi, two pregnant women come before the tanna, Rabbi Tarfon. The Bavli's version is probably a later version of the story that includes the amora Rabbi Ḥanina. Note that Ayelet Libson reads this source in the Bavli differently and assumes that the first woman was appeased when reminded that it was Yom Kippur and fasted. The second woman did not fast and gave in to her cravings. Their decisions affected their progeny, and so, for Libson, "eating on Yom Kippur, even under justified circumstances, is a risky business that should preferably be avoided." I would argue that the decisions made by these women are unclear. We only know that one was rewarded and the other was not. We cannot presume that the reward was for fasting. Possibly this pregnant woman was rewarded because she ate to care for her unborn child. See Ayelet Hoffman Libson, *Law and Self-Knowledge in the Talmud* (Cambridge: Cambridge University Press, 2018), 144.

38. Kristina Milnor, *Gender, Domesticity and the Age of Augustus: Inventing Private Life* (Oxford: Oxford University Press, 2005), 4–5, and her discussion of public versus private.

39. Just as William Fitzgerald notes that there is no surviving literature from antiquity regarding the domestic sphere inhabited by slave owners and slaves, there is no women's rabbinic literature that is written by them from the perspective of their own experience. We therefore must rely on what we can glean from these male accounts. See Fitzgerald's, *Slavery and the Roman Literary Imagination* (New York: Cambridge University Press, 2000), 2–3.

40. See my discussion in chapter four.

41. This included the Levite Hugras, who was unwilling to share a special musical method, and Ben Kamtzar, who did not want to teach his family's special way of writing (BT Yoma 38ab). Also see Kattan Gribetz, who

discusses this source in light of an exploration of textual transmission, exposing sources reflective of the refusal of some to pass down knowledge, "Consuming Texts: Women as Recipients and Transmitters of Ancient Texts," 194, n. 28. The individuals happen to be priests in Yoma.

42. The Hebrew word בקי in tannaitic literature can mean rabbinic expert or someone with legal expertise rather than a medical expert. In the Bavli here (BT Yoma 83a), the reference to an "expert" suggests a medical expert, but the use of the term בקי is not clear. See Libson, *Law and Self-Knowledge*, 145.

43. See Libson's detailed discussion of this sugya in *Law and Self-Knowledge*, 141–147.

44. Stein, "Maidservant and Her Master's Voice," 375–377. See Libson, *Law and Self-Knowledge*, where she discusses the growing interest in the individual in late antiquity. She also conveys that the Babylonian rabbis recognized that certain kinds of knowledge could only be mediated through an individual's own experience (189), which granted individuals such as women more agency. See also Parker, "Loyal Slaves and Loyal Wives," 161. Note that Fitzgerald, in *Slavery and the Roman Literary Imagination*, 1–8, explores the paradoxical nature of slavery, reminding us that it has been equated with "'social death,' insofar as the essential feature of slavery in any culture is not the legal status of the slave but his or her position as a 'socially dead' outsider. However, in other respects, the slave is quite clearly alive, and although it may seem that slavery operates only by de-humanizing slaves, a slave is useful precisely because he or she has the human attributes of knowledge, judgment, and reasoning," and therefore is an individual utterly significant to the operation of the household. Also see Mary Beard, *Women and Power: A Manifesto* (New York: Liveright, 2017), 87.

45. See Rashi, *D"H, hareshut* and *mekaberet et ba'alah*, who interprets this more literally, referring to Exodus 1:6, where Joseph, the leader, dies before his brothers.

46. See the continuation of Job 20:8–29, which predicts the future of those who are haughty.

47. I have translated the word חסן differently from the JPS translation of the Tanakh, which translates it as "property." Given other meanings of the word noted in Marcus Jastrow's *Dictionary of the Targumim, the Talmud Bavli and Yerushalmi, and the Midrashic Literature* (New York, 1926), this word can also be translated as "strength" or "power." See also Proverbs 27:24.

48. This word can mean "followers" or "family members/loved ones." Here I think it is best translated as "fellows."

Notes to Chapter 8

49. For a different view regarding the rabbis and their relationship to the Temple in the Bavli, see Stein, "Collapsing Structures," 1–28. She writes that the rabbinic corpus is replete with direct accounts of the Temple and with various transformations of and substitutions for its cult practices in the present. Stein sees the destruction of the Temple as a paradigmatic discursive event in rabbinic Babylonian discourse, arguing that rabbinic identity embodies that event, "reproducing the image of the ruined house as a complex, multifaced and *generative* model in its discursive practices." As a paradoxical image, as Stein continues, "The ruined house thus points to the fine line between structure and collapse" (27–28). I do not see the same tension regarding the Temple in Bavli Yoma or the same attempt to balance its presence and its absence. That said, her analysis focuses on BT Ketubot 61b–63a and not on Bavli Yoma, thereby supporting the idea that different tractates convey different perspectives regarding the Temple.

50. Mieke Bal, *Death and Dissymmetry: The Politics of Coherence in the Book of Judges*, 7, points to the great many details that open up the Book of Judges to another reading different from the one narrated by exegetes for centuries.

CHAPTER 9. THE CASE OF PURITY AND IMPURITY

1. I discuss the approach to the ba'al keri in BT Berakhot, below.

2. See my article, Marjorie Lehman, "Rabbinic Masculinities: Reading the *Ba'al Keri* in Tractate Yoma," *Jewish Studies Quarterly* 22, no. 2 (2015): 109–136.

3. Note that Leviticus 16:30, which is quoted in M. Yoma 8:9, says, "For on this day atonement shall be made for you to cleanse you of all your sins." This also appears in Mishnah Yoma 4:2 and 6:2, as well as in T. Yoma 2:1 but not in Bavli Yoma. Discussions in Bavli Yoma about repentance do not quote this verse.

4. See Exodus 19:6. Martha Himmelfarb, in *A Kingdom of Priests: Ancestry and Merit in Ancient Judaism* (Philadelphia: University of Pennsylvania Press, 2006), 1–10, discusses the tensions involved in becoming "a kingdom of priests" in Second Temple literature and for the rabbis in the aftermath of the destruction of the Temple. Looking at Bavli Yoma through the lens of purity and impurity points to the struggle the rabbis were having regarding their relationship to the priesthood. Bavli Yoma represents one perspective that does not entirely align with Himmelfarb's view.

5. Although *ba'al keri* is not a biblical term, it is possible that the term *keri* is derived from Deuteronomy 23:11, where a nocturnal seminal emission is referred to as a *mikre leilah*. This does not suggest that the ba'al keri, as un-

derstood by the rabbis, is a man who becomes impure only as a result of a nocturnal emission. A man also becomes a ba'al keri when he emits semen during sexual relations, as a result of self-arousal, or involuntarily. In an Amoraic statement recorded on JT Yoma 8:1, 44d, however, the definition of a ba'al keri is limited to someone who had a seminal emission as a result of sexual relations.

6. Shaye J. D. Cohen, "Purity and Piety," in *Daughters of the King*, ed. Susan Grossman and Rivka Haut (Philadelphia: Jewish Publication Society Press, 1992), 107. According to Leviticus 15:16–18, a man who has a *shikhvat zera* (a seminal emission) must immerse in water afterward, whether or not his seminal emission resulted from sexual relations. Following immersion, this man must wait until evening before considering himself pure. The duration of his impure status is the shortest of all of the four categories of impurity detailed in Leviticus 15, shorter than that of the zav, zavah, and nidah. The zav and the zavah need to wait seven days before immersing, while the nidah, despite needing to wait seven days, seems not to require immersion, according to Leviticus. Like the others, the status of the man who had a seminal flux is connected to concerns that God's sanctuary (*mishkan*) will be defiled, as noted in Leviticus 15:31. In another closely related passage, Deuteronomy 23:10–12, the male warrior who has a nocturnal seminal emission (*mikre leilah*) is required to leave the camp until he has bathed. This is stated in the same context where men are warned to urinate and defecate outside the camp, suggesting that there is something unholy about what issues from one's body (Deuteronomy 23:13–14). The overall goal is to keep the camp (and later the Temple), where God's presence resides, pure so that God will be a source of protection. In this regard, seminal impurity is linked to sancta and, more specifically, to protecting a holy space from contamination. See Shaye J. D. Cohen, "Menstruants and the Sacred in Judaism and Christianity," in *Women's History and Ancient History*, ed. Sarah B. Pomeroy (Chapel Hill: University of North Carolina Press, 1991) 274–275. See Satlow, "'And on Earth You Shall Sleep': 'Talmud Torah' and Rabbinic Asceticism,'", 215–216. Also see BT Berkahot 21b, where an argument is made for a link between God's revelation to Moses at Mount Sinai and ritual purity. There is a midrashic tradition claiming that Moses was celibate when he received the Torah and commanded the people to separate from their wives (see Exodus 19:10–11). See Naomi Koltun-Fromm's discussion in *Hermeneutics of Holiness: Ancient Jewish and Christian Notions of Sexuality and Religious Community* (Oxford: Oxford University Press, 2010), 179–194.

7. See BT Berakhot 22a and JT Berakhot 3:4, 6c. There, the Bavli and

Yerushalmi suggest that the distinction between the ba'al keri and other types of impurity may be linked to a desire to control male sexuality. The concern surfaces in discussing a legal leniency regarding male impurity, suggesting that men do not have to immerse at all. Without a requirement for the ba'al keri to immerse, some thought Torah scholars would have sexual relations with their wives "as often as roosters."

8. Sharon Faye Koren, *Forsaken: The Menstruant in Medieval Jewish Mysticism* (Waltham, MA: Brandeis University Press, 2011): 10. Koren says that seminal emissions can be controlled, while menstrual blood cannot. See also Michael L. Satlow, "'Try to Be a Man': The Rabbinic Construction of Masculinity," *Harvard Theological Review* 89, no. 1 (1996): 19–40.

9. The rabbis continue to struggle with the reasons for upholding an extensive system of purity law. For example, *Pesikta derav Kahana* 40ab attributes the following statement to Rabbi Yohanan ben Zakkai: "By your lives! The corpse does not cause impurity, nor do the waters purify; it is a decree of the Supreme King of Kings." Questioning the reasonability of purity law, he claims that one simply needs to accept God's commandments without questioning the reason for them. See Christine Hayes, "Purity and Impurity, Ritual," in *Encyclopedia Judaica*, 2nd ed., ed. Michael Berenbaum and Fred Skolnik.

10. According to Tannaitic material found in both JT Berakhot 3:4, 6c and BT Berakhot 22a, the ba'al keri is unique in his impurity. BT Niddah 35b stresses that the zav's flux is natural, while the flux of the ba'al keri emerges because of a stimulus. Nevertheless, BT Pesaḥim 67b recognizes that a ba'al keri can ejaculate against his will and that at times he cannot control it. Also see Rashi on BT Yoma 88a.

11. Alexander, *Gender and Timebound Commandments in Judaism*, 192.

12. JT Yoma 8:1 44d notes that there were "places" where ba'alei keri traditionally did not immerse. See Boyarin, *Carnal Israel: Reading Sex in Talmudic Culture*, 156–166, who compares Babylonian sources where leaving one's wife for long periods of time to study Torah was encouraged, while sources authored in the Land of Israel reflect opposition to the idea.

13. It is interesting to note that the rabbis struggle with whether ba'alei keri needed to immerse, and the practice eventually falls by the wayside. For example, see BT Sukkah 26a, where the rabbis are struggling with whether men need to immerse before wearing tefillin, grappling with the necessity for immersion as connected to the involuntary seminal emission and sexual relations. See also BT Berakhot 22a.

14. The ba'al keri could recite Shema in his heart; he simply could not

pray aloud (BT Berakhot 20a–22a). Both Talmuds indicate that the ba'al keri should merely pour nine kavim of water over his head rather than immerse fully in a mikveh, so as to make it easier and quicker to purify himself, returning to Torah study faster (M. Berakhot 3:4; BT Berakhot 20b). Yerushalmi Berakhot records that the Babylonian rabbi Ḥanina ridicules the "morning bathers" who go out to bathe before praying, as if to question the necessity of their purificatory immersions, probably following sexual relations (JT Berakhot 3:4, 6c).

15. T. Terumot 3:2 notes that the ba'al keri was not allowed to make the terumah donation of his produce to the priests because he could not recite the blessing before offering it. Also see M. Kelim 1:5 for the source forbidding the priest from eating terumah if he was a ba'al keri.

16. See JT Ta'anit 4:2, 68a.

17. See BT Bava Kamma 82a and, especially, the larger discussion in BT Berakhot 22b, where the amoraic rabbis are arguing over the details of Ezra's law, pushing for leniencies. See Aaron D. Panken, *The Rhetoric of Innovation: Self-Conscious Legal Change in Rabbinic Literature* (Lanham, MD: University Press of America, 2005), 153, 158–165, 216, where he argues that the rabbis retrojected the creation of new laws onto prior biblical authorities, who, like Ezra, were described in the Bible as being legal innovators. Also see Cohen, "Purity and Piety," 107. Note that while some geonim, possibly influenced by parallel Islamic customs, continued to require some type of immersion in water although not necessarily a full immersion in a mikveh, Maimonides overruled the practice, claiming that it had already fallen by the wayside. He reinvokes the position of Rabbi Yehudah ben Betaira (BT Berakhot 22a) that the words of Torah cannot contract impurity (*Mishneh Torah*, Hilkhot Keriat Shema, 4:8; Hilkhot Tefillah, 4:4). See Koren, *Forsaken*, 180, n. 55. Maimonides also writes: "Whatever is written in the Torah and in traditional teaching about relating to things impure and pure is relevant only to the Temple and its hallowed things" (*Mishneh Torah*, Tum'at Okhelim 16:8–9; Hayes, "Purity and Impurity, Ritual," 755). Nidah law seems to develop in the opposite direction, becoming more stringent over time. Also see Cohen, "Purity and Piety," 103–113. Interestingly, Brakke observes a different approach to impurity for Christians focused upon men and not women. See David Brakke, "The Problematization of Nocturnal Emissions in the Early Christian Church," in *Man and Masculinities in Christianity and Judaism: A Critical Reader*, ed. Björn Krondorfer (London: SCM Press, 2009), 350.

18. On BT Nidah 43a, amoraic material reduces the instances in which a ba'al keri is considered impure. For example, the Babylonian amora Shmuel

Notes to Chapter 9   305

states, "Any semen, the emission of which is not felt throughout one's body, causes no uncleanness." Additionally, he insisted that semen had "to shoot forth like an arrow" for a man to become impure, because only this type of emission results in progeny. Some rabbis wished to loosen rules surrounding the purity and impurity of the ba'al keri and were not comfortable with the biblical stringencies.

19. See R. W. Connelly, *Masculinities* (Berkeley: University of California Press, 1995), 11, who argues that masculinity is not solely constructed on the basis of a male/female binary, where women are subordinated in the name of claiming power but rather by comparing men to men.

20. Koltun-Fromm, *Hermeneutics of Holiness*, 179–209.

21. Adrienne Rich, *Of Woman Born: Motherhood as Experience and Institution* (New York: Norton and Company, 1986).

22. JT Yoma 1:1, 38d notes that a seminal emission was a common occurrence.

23. These two baraitot quoted in BT Yoma 88a were probably reworked and then integrated into the larger Talmudic passage, as I discuss later in this chapter. The earlier version (T. Yoma 4:5) clearly distinguishes between priests and the non-priests:

> The zavim and zavot immerse in their usual manner on the night of Yom Kippur. Niddot, and women who have given birth immerse in their usual manner on the night of Yom Kippur. Men who are ba'alei keri immerse in their usual manner on the night of Yom Kippur. Rabbi Yosa said: From Minḥah and onward he [the ba'al keri] may not immerse himself until it gets dark. Rabbi Yosa said: Priests immerse in their usual manner with nightfall so that they can eat terumah in the evening [after Yom Kippur ends].

24. In the second baraita on BT Yoma 88a, which deals with immersion on Yom Kippur, the rabbis and Rabbi Yose hold opposing opinions, such that the second baraita appears to contradict the first. The Talmudic passage explains away this apparent contradiction by claiming that each baraita represents a different case.

25. Reuven Kiperwasser argues that we need to consider the Greco-Roman context as having an impact on the desire of rabbis in the Land of Israel to require ritual immersion, rather than relying entirely on the influence of biblical law. Indeed, in Greco-Roman society sexual activity made one unfit to participate in religious rituals. Immersion after sexual relations was widespread in the ancient Mediterranean world among Greeks and non-Greeks alike and may explain why rabbis in the Land of Israel considered the possi-

bility that immersions following seminal emissions were necessary before praying on Yom Kippur. See Reuven Kiperwasser, "The Immersion of Ba'alei Qerain," *Jewish Studies Quarterly* 19 (2012): 325–326.

26. JT Yoma 8:1, 44d suggests that listing washing and sexual relations as separate prohibitions in the list of Yom Kippur prohibitions found in M. Yoma 8:1 is unnecessary, since the prohibition against washing would automatically preclude sexual relations, as a seminal emission would require washing prior to immersion and then a ritual immersion afterward. However, as the Yerushalmi indicates, there were places "where *ba'alei keri* [did] not immerse" at all, and, thus, since men were not required to immerse following sexual relations, the concern about washing and immersing on Yom Kippur following a seminal emission might not have been an issue. In the end, according to JT Yoma 8:1, 44d, this is the reason M. Yoma 8:1 needed to list sexual relations as a separate prohibition, in addition to washing. One would not be able to learn anything about the prohibition of sexual relations on Yom Kippur from the prohibition against washing because immersing after sexual relations was not an accepted practice.

27. BT Berakhot 27b expands on this legal issue regarding Ma'ariv.

28. Efforts were taken to ensure that the high priest did not have a seminal emission on the night of Yom Kippur. See BT Yoma 18a.

29. See Gribetz, *Time and Difference in Rabbinic Judaism*, 160–161, where she points to the integral relationship between impurity and time. Counting days and waiting periods were as important as immersion and structured time for both men and women.

30. See BT Yoma 88a and the stammaitic decision to differentiate between two tannaim named Rabbi Yose, Rabbi Yose bar Yehudah and Rabbi Yose bar Ḥalafta. These two tannaim do not hold the same position regarding the necessity for immersing "in the proper time."

31. Certainly a larger debate ensued in the Bavli around the issue of whether immersions could be delayed, and BT Yoma 88a contributes to this debate. BT Nidah 29b–30a, the Talmudic passage on which BT Yoma 88a relies, focuses on a pregnant woman who left her community and returned after having a miscarriage. Because she cannot remember when her pregnancy ended, the issue of her purification after childbirth is in question. Debate ensued in BT Nidah as to whether this woman should immerse at the first opportunity, submerging as many as 95 times in the evenings after her return to ensure that she did not make any errors and fulfilled the commandment of immersion in its proper time. Rabbi Yose bar Yehudah held the opinion, also referred to in BT Yoma 88a, that this woman should have

Notes to Chapter 9   307

only one immersion at the last possible moment when no doubt remained as to whether she was immersing too soon. Undergirding Rabbi Yose's position is the belief that immersion in its time is not a commandment and that this woman's immersion can be deferred. This would suggest that some tannaim held that one could delay immersion until after Yom Kippur. See also the parallel passage on BT Shabbat 121a.

32. See BT Yoma 88a Rashi, *D"H eimah mebaerev*, where he states that one should always remove all impediments on one's body before Yom Kippur to make sure that water would reach everywhere without interpositions. Since rubbing is not allowed on Yom Kippur, Rashi clarifies the Gemara's statement by suggesting that preparing for the possibility that one could have a seminal emission on Yom Kippur was necessary. Doing so meant that there would be nothing to impede a full immersion should a person need to immerse on Yom Kippur itself.

33. See BT Yoma 8a, a parallel source that discusses the issue of "immersion in its proper time" for high priests who experienced corpse impurity.

34. See M. Yoma 8:1, T. Yoma 8:1, and BT Yoma 77b regarding the prohibition of washing.

35. BT Ta'anit 13a makes allowances for washing in cold water only for the purpose of purification on a public fast day, although the laws are stricter with regard to mourners, who cannot immerse in cold or hot water, according to Rav Ḥisda. Also see BT Yoma 88a, Tosafot, *D"H i d'tzalei mai ta'amah derabbanan*, where a distinction is made between washing for the purposes of comfort, which is prohibited, and immersion for ritual purposes, which is allowed.

36. This is more complicated for the menstruant. See BT Nidah 29b–30a.

37. See BT Beitzah 17b–18b, noting that the purification of impure utensils would need to be done before a festival or the Sabbath. Bodily impurities are different, and there is more latitude given to performing ritual immersions on the Sabbath or on a festival.

38. The fragility of life in the ancient world and its connection to expectations to beget and rear children is discussed in Brown, *The Body and Society: Men, Women, and Sexual Renunciation in Early Christianity*, 6.

39. See Rashi, *D"H teida shekol ha'olam kulo ra'ev*, who interprets the Hebrew word *ra'ev* as referring to a world starved for sexual relations.

40. See Brakke, "Problematization," 338, where he points out that "when early Christian men discussed the significance of their nocturnal emissions, they engaged in a process of personal and communal self-definition, em-

bodying different perspectives on the church's identity in the world." Similarly, for the rabbis, their discussions about the ba'al keri reflect their desire for communal self-definition, which includes an attempt to understand their relationship with God. Brakke brings evidence from the *Didascalia Apostolorum* (230 CE) and the *Apostolic Constitutions* (380 CE), third- and fourth-century works compiled in Syria, with potential influence on the rabbis.

41. For a more in-depth discussion of amoraic sources about the ba'al keri in JT Yoma, see Kiperwasser, "Immersion," 311–321. According to Boyarin, Jews in the Land of Israel felt that sexuality could be controlled to a much greater extent than did Babylonian Jews, who believed that men could not live without sex. This might explain why the final piece of the sugya on BT Yoma 88a has no parallel in the Tosefta or the Yerushalmi. See Boyarin, *Carnal Israel*, 33–35, 46–47, 141. Also see Satlow, *Tasting the Dish*, 319, and Koltun-Fromm, *Hermeneutics of Holiness*, 201, 234.

42. See also JT Berakhot 3:4, 6c.

43. This is also not mentioned where the Bavli discusses sexual relations in connection with the prohibitions listed in M. Yoma 8:1.

44. When Rabbi Yose is mentioned without the patronymic, he is Rabbi Yose bar/ben Ḥalafta. See Mordechai Margoliot, *Encyclopedia leḥakhmei hatalmud vehage'onim*, vol. 2 (Tel-Aviv: Yavneh Publishing House, 1981), 522.

45. David Biale, *Eros and the Jews: From Biblical Israel to Contemporary America* (New York: Basic Books, 1992), 57; Dawn M. Hadley, *Masculinity in Medieval Europe* (London: Longman, 1999), 2.

46. In Björn Krondorfer's Introduction to *Men's Bodies, Men's Gods: Male Identities in a (Post) Christian Culture* (New York: New York University Press, 1996), 7, he argues that in late antiquity, Christian men considered nocturnal emissions as signs of an imperfect bodily state and prayed to God for mercy, thinking that male virility was not in man's power but in God's alone.

47. We also need to consider statements in BT Nidah that are attributed to amoraim in the Land of Israel, including those of Rabbi Yohanan and Rabbi Yitzhak. As Rabbi Yohanan said, "Anyone who emits semen wastefully is liable to the death penalty" (BT Nidah 13a–b); Rabbi Yitzhak of the School of Rav Ami said, "It is as if he spilled blood, having wasted his seed" (BT Nidah 43a). See Satlow, *Tasting the Dish*, 246–264, for a more in-depth discussion of this material.

48. See Koltun-Fromm's larger discussion in *Hermeneutics of Holiness*, 193–194, on the rabbinic move to distance holiness from sexual renunciation, making Yom Kippur an important locus for this discussion.

Notes to Chapter 9

49. Satlow, "Try to Be a Man," 31–40. Alexander, *Gender and Timebound Commandments in Judaism*, 193, discusses the relationship between a father's Torah study and his reproductive capacities, as well as the tension reflected in T. Berakhot 2:12–16 between the biologically reproducing body and Torah study, a tension manifested in whether the ba'al keri needs to immerse or not before reciting Shema or studying Torah.

50. Michael L. Satlow's "Try to Be a Man" 89, no. 1, 29–31, refers to BT Nidah 31ab to support the idea that male self-restraint in sexual relations ensured male offspring. BT Nidah makes the point that if men restrained themselves on their stomachs so that their wives would emit seed first, their children would be male. See BT Nedarim 20ab and Satlow's discussion, where he argues that men who allow themselves to lose control during intercourse produce female children. He concludes that when males act like men, they are responsible for the birth of males, but when they allow nature to "take its course" and do not exercise their more mature manly attributes, they produce female offspring. Also see Koltun-Fromm, *Hermeneutics of Holiness*, 179–195.

51. Himmelfarb in *A Kingdom of Priests*, 164–170, argues that the decline of priestly ancestry among Jews after the Temple was destroyed generated a widespread and thorough embrace of a definition of the Jewish people based on ancestry. As the tractate draws to a close, biological progeny become a significant factor in determining the rabbis' future.

52. Michele Emanatian, "Metaphor and the Expression of Emotion: The Value of Cross-Cultural Perspectives," *Metaphor and Symbolic Activity* 10, no 3 (1995): 164. See her references to Mark Johnson, *The Body in the Mind: The Bodily Basis of Meaning, Imagination and Reason* (Chicago: Chicago University Press, 1987), and George Lakoff and Mark Johnson, *Metaphors We Live By* (Chicago: University of Chicago Press, 1980). See also Gail Labovitz, "Is Rav's Wife 'a Dish'?," 147–148.

53. In Ezekiel 40–47, the prophet sees a detailed vision of a new Temple.

54. Interestingly, the ba'al keri is not included in this list. It also happens that the ba'al keri is the only individual who does not have to bring a sin offering. See Leviticus 12:1–8 regarding woman after childbirth and Leviticus 15, esp. 15:16–18, regarding the man who has a seminal emission.

55. The reference here to nidah in Zeḥariah does not mean menstrual impurity. It is a way of referring to uncleanness from sin.

56. Possibly the idea of the community ridding itself of impurities is rooted in the more ancient underpinnings of Yom Kippur, alluded to in Leviticus. See Milgrom, *Leviticus 1–16: A New Translation with Introduction*

and Commentary, 1066–1070, where he argues that inui (self-denial) was not initially part of the ten-day New Year's festival that culminated on the 10th day of Tishrei with jubilation and merriment. Inui was associated with rites undertaken during times of personal emergency when the people needed to purge themselves of their sinful behavior in order to reverse the calamity. Priests could enact this rite whenever needed. But when the high priest could no longer declare such an emergency fast day, the penitential aspects of the rite were transferred to the 10th day of Tishrei, and the two rites were combined into one.

57. As Elizabeth Castelli argues, early Christians wanted to remove social markers between men and women to achieve one of the objectives attributed to Jesus in the Gospel of Thomas: "Behold I myself shall lead Mary so as to make Mary male, that she too may become a living spirit like you males, for every woman who makes herself male will enter the kingdom of heaven." Renouncing marriage and sexual relations enabled this to occur. Elizabeth A. Castelli, "I Will Make Mary Male: Pieties of the Body and Gender Transformation of the Christian Women in Late Antiquity," in *Body Guards: The Cultural Politics of Gender Ambiguity*, ed. Julia Epstein and Kristina Straub (Philadelphia: Routledge Publishing, 1991), 30.

AFTERWORD

1. Gaston Bachelard, *The Poetics of Space* (Boston: Beacon Press, 1994), 6.

2. Following Bachelard's line of thinking about the houses we construct in our imaginations, inhabited space transcends geometric space, inviting human complexity and idiosyncrasy to beset the household. See John R. Stilgoe, Foreword to Gaston Bachelard, *The Poetics of Space* (Boston: Beacon Press, 1994), vii.

3. In saying this, I do not discount that in many instances in rabbinic literature, the rabbis resurrect the Temple and its memory of practices, imagining, for example, that fasting takes the place of sacrificial offerings in BT Berakhot 17a.

4. For example, Mary Beard, in *Women and Power*, stresses the degree to which women have been silenced and asks us to think about how to "resuscitate women on the inside of power" (79). Unfortunately, we have no template for what a powerful woman looks like (54). And so that leads me now to pose the question: What if we turn to the mother? Is there a way to get to the core of what mothering is so that we can think with it to redefine power?

5. Beard, *Women and Power*, 83, argues that "if women are not perceived

to be fully within the structures of power, surely it is power we need to redefine, rather than women."

6. Beard, *Women and Power*, 89, writes regarding our present-day reality, "We have not got anywhere near subverting those foundational stories of power [referring here to Greco-Roman myths] that serve to keep women out of it."

7. Peskowitz, *Spinning Fantasies*, 171.

8. Julia Watts Belser, "Privilege and Disaster: Toward a Jewish Feminist Ethics of Climate Silence and Environmental Unknowing," *Journal of the Society of Christian Ethics* 34, no. 1 (2014): 87. Also see Sarra Lev, "Talmud That Works Your Heart, 177–178; Peskowitz, *Spinning Fantasies*, 171; Fonrobert, *Menstrual Purity*, 9; and Boyarin, "Reading Androcentrism against the Grain," 29–30.

9. Sara Ruddick, *Maternal Thinking: Toward a Politics of Peace* (Boston: Beacon Press, 1989), 65–102. For a more recent analysis of mother-child relationships, claiming mothers as metaphorical Talmudic sages, see Benjamin, *Obligated Self*, 40–53.

10. Damien W. Riggs and Elizabeth Peel, *Critical Kinship Studies* (London: Palgrave Macmillan, 2016), 6.

11. Kath Weston, *Families We Choose: Lesbians, Gays, Kinship* (New York: Columbia University Press, 1991), 148.

12. Wasserman, *Jews, Gentiles, and Other Animals*, 236–237; Moulie Vidas, *Tradition and the Formation of the Talmud*, 9–11.

13. Wasserman, *Jews, Gentiles, and Other Animals*, 21, 234.

BIBLIOGRAPHY

· · ·

PRIMARY SOURCES

For Talmud variants, see the Friedberg Jewish Manuscript Society (https://fjms.genizah.org) and the Sol and Evelyn Henkind Text Data Bank of Talmudic manuscripts collected by the Saul Lieberman Institute for Talmudic Research at the Jewish Theological Seminary in New York.

Albeck, Ḥanokh, ed. *Sefer Beit Habeḥirah* (Menaḥem ben Solomon Meiri). Berlin, 1922.

———. *Shishah Sidrei Mishnah*. 6 vols. Tel-Aviv: Dvir, 1957–1959.

Albeck, Ḥanokh, and Julius Theodor, eds. *Midrash Beraishit Rabbah*. Berlin, 1903–1929.

Azulai, Ḥayim Joseph David. *Sefer Torat haḥidah: Al hatorah*. Jerusalem: Oz vehadar, 1994.

Bavli (Babylonian Talmud). Vilna: Romm, 1880–1886. (Standard printed edition.)

Buber, Solomon. *Midrash Eikhah Rabbah*. Vilna: Romm, 1899.

———. *Midrash Tanḥuma*. Vilna: Romm, 1913.

———. *Pesikta Rabbati*. Jerusalem: Zikhron Aharon, 2011–2012.

Edels, Samuel Eliezer (Maharsha). *Hidushei Aggadot*. Vilna: Romm, 1880–1886 (in standard printed edition of the Bavli).

Josephus. *Jewish Antiquities*. Translated by H. St. J. Thackery. 9 vols. Cambridge, MA: Harvard University Press, 1957–1961.

———. *Jewish War*. Translated by Louis H. Feldman. 10 vols. Cambridge, MA: Harvard University Press, 1926-1965.

Kahana, Menaḥem. *Sifrei Bamidbar*. Jerusalem: Magnes, 2011.

Lieberman, Saul, ed. *Tosefta*. 5 vols. Jerusalem: Jewish Theological Seminary, 1955–1988.

Maimonides, Moses (Rambam). *Mishneh Torah*. Jersualem: Shivtei Frankel, 2007.

Mandelbaum, Bernard. *Pesikta derav Kahana*. New York: Jewish Theological Seminary, 1962.

Margulies (Margoliot), Mordekhai, ed. *Vayikra Rabbah*. Jerusalem: Ararat, 1953–1960.

Midrash Rabbah: Al ḥamishah ḥumshei Torah veḥamesh megillot. Jerusalem: Levin-Epstein, 1878.

Recanati, Menaḥem. Harekanati al hatorah (Devarim). In *Sifrei Halevushim,* edited by Mordekhai ben Abraham Jaffee. 7 vols. Jerusalem: Zikhron Aharon, 1999–2000.

Schechter, Solomon, ed. *Avot derabi Natan.* Vienna: Knöpflmacher, 1887.

Weiss, Isaac Hirsch, ed. *Sifra.* Vienna: Ya'akov Hakohen Shlosberg, 1862.

Yerushalmi (Jerusalem Talmud). Venice: Bomberg, 1523–1524. (Facsimile edition based on Leiden manuscript.)

Zuckermandel, M. S., ed. *Tosefta.* Jerusalem: Wahrmann Books, 1970.

SECONDARY SOURCES

Achrati, Ahmed. "Hand and Foot Symbolisms: From Rock Art to the Qur'an." *Arabia* 50, no. 4 (2003): 464–500.

Alexander, Elizabeth Shanks. *Gender and Timebound Commandments in Judaism.* Cambridge: Cambridge University Press, 2013.

———. "Ritual on the Threshold: Mezuzah and the Crafting of Domestic and Civic Space." *Jewish Social Studies* 20, no. 3 (2014): 100–130.

Amaru, Betsy. "The Killing of the Prophets: Unraveling a Midrash." *Hebrew Union College Annual* 54 (1983): 153–180.

Antler, Joyce. *You Never Call! You Never Write! A History of the Jewish Mother.* New York: Oxford University Press, 2007.

Arendell, Terry. "Conceiving and Investigating Motherhood." *Journal of Marriage and Family* 62 (2000): 1192–1207.

Arthur, Linda B. Introduction to *Religion, Dress and the Body*, edited by Linda B. Arthur, 1–8. Oxford: Berg, Oxford International, 1999.

Bachelard, Gaston. *The Poetics of Space.* Boston: Beacon Press, 1994.

Baker, Cynthia M. "The Queen, the Apostate, and the Women Between: (Dis)Placement of Women in Tosefta *Sukka.*" In *A Feminist Commentary on the Babylonian Talmud: Introduction and Studies*, edited by Tal Ilan, Tamara Or, Dorothea M. Salzer, Christine Steuer, and Irina Wandrey, 169–173. Tübingen: Mohr Siebeck. 2007.

———. *Rebuilding the House of Israel: Architectures of Gender in Jewish Antiquity.* Stanford: Stanford University Press, 2002.

Bal, Mieke. *Death and Dissymmetry: The Politics of Coherence in the Book of Judges.* Chicago: University of Chicago Press, 1988.

———. *Lethal Love: Feminist Literary Readings of Biblical Love Stories.* Bloomington: Indiana University Press, 1987.

Balberg, Mira. "Artifact." In *Late Ancient Knowing: Explorations in Intellectual History*, edited by Moulie Vidas and Catherine Michael Chin, 17–35. Berkeley: University of California Press, 2015.

———. *Blood for Thought: The Reinvention of Sacrifice in Early Rabbinic Literature*. Berkeley: University of California Press, 2017.

———. "The Emperor's Daughter's New Skin: Bodily Otherness and Self-Identity in the Dialogues of Rabbi Yehoshua ben Hanania and the Emperor's Daughter." *Jewish Studies Quarterly* 19 (2012): 181–206.

———. *Purity, Body, and Self in Early Rabbinic Literature*. Berkeley: University of California Press, 2014.

———. "Rabbinic Authority, Medical Rhetoric, and Body Hermeneutics in Mishnah Nega'im." *AJS Review* 35, no. 2 (2011): 337–339.

Balberg, Mira, and Simeon Chavel. "The Polymorphous Pesah: Ritual between Origins and Reenactment." *Journal of Ancient Judaism* 8, no. 3 (2017): 292–343.

Barry, Jennifer. *Bishops in Flight: Exile and Displacement in Late Antiquity*. Berkeley: University of California Press, 2019.

Batten, Alicia J., Carly Daniel-Hughes, and Kristi Upson-Saia. "Introduction: What Shall We Wear?" In *Dressing Judeans and Christians in Antiquity*, edited by Kristi Upson-Saia, Carly Daniel-Hughes, and Alicia J. Batten, 1–18. Surrey: Ashgate, 2014.

Baumgarten, Elisheva. *Practicing Piety in Medieval Ashkenaz: Men, Women, and Everyday Religious Observance*. Philadelphia: University of Pennsylvania Press, 2016.

Beard, Mary. "Priesthood in the Roman Republic." In *Pagan Priests: Religion and Power in the Ancient World*, edited by Mary Beard and John North, 17–48. London: Duckworth, 1990.

———. *Women and Power: A Manifesto*. New York: Liveright, 2017.

Becker, Adam H. "Beyond the Spatial and Temporal *Limes*: Questioning the 'Parting of the Ways' Outside the Roman Empire." In *The Ways That Never Parted: Jews and Christians in Late Antiquity and the Early Middle Ages*, edited by Adam H. Becker and Annette Yoshiko Reed, 373–392. Tübingen: Mohr Siebeck, 2003.

Beer, Moshe. "Al ma'asei kaparah shel ba'alei teshuvah besifrut hazal" [On penances of penitents in the literature of "hazal"]. *Zion* (1981): 159–181.

Belser, Julia Watts. "Crying Out for Rain: The Human, the Holy and the Earth in the Ritual Fasts of Rabbinic Literature." *Worldviews* 13 (2009): 234–236.

———. "Disability and the Social Politics of 'Natural' Disaster: Toward a Jewish Feminist Ethics of Disaster Tales." *Worldviews* 19, no. 1 (2015): 51–68.

———. "Opulence and Oblivion: Talmudic Feasting, Famine, and the Social Politics of Disaster." *AJS Review* 38, no. 1 (2014): 89–107.

———. *Power, Ethics, and Ecology in Jewish Late Antiquity: Rabbinic Responses to Drought and Disaster*. New York: Cambridge University Press, 2015.

———. "Privilege and Disaster: Toward a Jewish Feminist Ethics of Climate Silence and Environmental Unknowing." *Journal of the Society of Christian Ethics* 34, no. 1 (2014): 83–101.

———. *Rabbinic Tales of Destruction: Gender, Sex, and Disability in the Ruins of Jerusalem*. New York: Oxford University Press, 2018.

———. "Reading Talmudic Bodies: Disability, Narrative, and the Gaze in Rabbinic Judaism." In *Disability in Judaism, Christianity, and Islam: Sacred Texts, Historical Traditions, and Social Analysis*, edited by Darla Schumm and Michael Stolzfus, 12–18. New York: Palgrave Macmillan, 2011.

———. "Returning to the Flesh: A Jewish Reflection on Feminist Disability Theory." *Journal of Feminist Studies in Religion* 26, no. 2 (2010): 127–132.

Benjamin, Mara H. *The Obligated Self: Maternal Subjectivity and Jewish Thought*. Bloomington: Indiana University Press, 2018.

Benovitz, Moshe. "Time-Triggered Positive Mitzvot as Conversation Pieces." *Hebrew Union College Annual* 78 (2007): 45–90.

Ben-Yehuda, Nahum. "Jewish Dress and Religious Identity in the Land of Israel during the Roman Era: The Talmudic Dress Code." Master's thesis, Bar-Ilan University, 2012.

Berkowitz, Beth A. *Execution and Invention: Death Penalty Discourse in Early Rabbinic and Christian Cultures*. New York: Oxford University Press, 2006.

Biale, David. *Eros and the Jews: From Biblical Israel to Contemporary America*. New York: Basic Books, 1992.

Bokser, Baruch. "Approaching Sacred Space." *Harvard Theological Review* 78, no. 3 (1985): 279–299.

———. "Ma'al and Blessings over Food: Rabbinic Transformation of Cultic Terminology and Alternative Modes of Piety." *Journal of Biblical Literature* 100, no. 4 (1981): 563–572.

———. *The Origins of the Seder: The Passover Rite and Early Rabbinic Judaism*. Berkeley: University of California Press, 1984.

———. "Ritualizing the Seder." *Journal of the American Academy of Religion* 56, no. 3 (1988): 443–471.

Bonfante, Larissa. "Nudity as a Costume in Classical Art." *American Journal of Archaeology* 93, no. 4 (1989): 543–570.

Bordo, Susan. *Unbearable Weight: Feminism, Western Culture, and the Body.* Berkeley: University of California Press, 1993.

Bourdieu, Pierre. "Cultural Reproduction and Social Reproduction." In *Knowledge, Education, and Social Change*, edited by Robert Brown. London: Tavistock, 1973.

———. "The Kabyle House or the World Reversed." In *The Logic of Practice*, translated by Richard Nice, 271–283. Cambridge: Polity Press, 1990 [1970].

———. *Outline of the Theory of Practice.* Cambridge: Cambridge University Press, 1977.

Boyarin, Daniel. *Carnal Israel: Reading Sex in Talmudic Culture.* Berkeley: University of California Press, 1993.

———. *Dying for God: Martyrdom and the Making of Christianity and Judaism.* Stanford: Stanford University Press, 1999.

———. "Hellenism in Jewish Babylonia." In *The Cambridge Companion to the Talmud and Rabbinic Literature*, edited by Charlotte E. Fonrobert and Martin S. Jaffee, 336–364. Cambridge: Cambridge University Press, 2007.

———. "Internal Opposition in Talmudic Literature: The Case of the Married Monk." *Representations* 36 (1991): 87–113.

———. "Rabbinic Resistance to Male Domination: A Case Study in Talmudic Cultural Poetics." In *Interpreting Judaism in a Postmodern Age*, edited by Steven Kepnes, 118–141. New York: New York University Press, 1995.

———. "Reading Androcentrism against the Grain: Women, Sex, and Torah-Study." *Poetics Today* 12, no. 2 (1991): 29–53.

———. *Socrates and the Fat Rabbis.* Chicago: University of Chicago Press, 2009.

———. *Unheroic Conduct: The Rise of Homosexuality and the Invention of the Jewish Man.* Berkeley: University of California Press, 1997.

Brakke, David. "The Problematization of Nocturnal Emissions in the Early Christian Church." In *Man and Masculinities in Christianity and Judaism: A Critical Reader*, edited by Björn Krondorfer, 336–352. London: SCM Press, 2009.

Bronner, Simon J., ed. *Jews at Home: The Domestication of Identity.* Oxford: Littman Library of Jewish Civilization, 2009.

Bibliography

Brown, Peter. *The Body and Society: Men, Women, and Sexual Renunciation in Early Christianity.* New York: Columbia University Press, 1989.

———. *Society and the Holy in Late Antiquity.* Berkeley: University of California Press, 1982.

Broyde, Michael J. "A Special Supplement: Hair Covering and Jewish Law; Biblical and Objective (*Dat Moshe*) or Rabbinic and Subjective (*Dat Yehudit*)." *Tradition: A Journal of Orthodox Jewish Thought* 42, no. 3 (2009): 97–179.

Buc, Philippe. *The Dangers of Ritual: Between Early Medieval Texts and Social Scientific Theory.* Princeton: Princeton University Press, 2001.

Burroughs, Catherine B., and Jeffrey David Erenreich. *Reading the Social Body.* Iowa City: University of Iowa Press, 1993.

Carsten, Janet. *After Kinship.* Cambridge: Cambridge University Press, 2004.

Carsten, Janet, and Stephen Hugh-Jones. Introduction to *About the House: Lévi-Strauss and Beyond*, edited by Janet Carsten and Stephen Hugh-Jones. Cambridge: Cambridge University Press, 1995.

Castelli, Elizabeth A. "I Will Make Mary Male: Pieties of the Body and Gender Transformation of the Christian Women in Late Antiquity." In *Body Guards: The Cultural Politics of Gender Ambiguity*, edited by Julia Epstein and Kristina Straub, 29–49. Philadelphia: Routledge, 1991.

———. *Martyrdom and Memory: Early Christian Culture Making.* New York: Columbia University Press, 2004.

Chapman, Cynthia. *The House of the Mother: The Social Roles of Maternal Kin in Biblical Hebrew Narrative and Poetry.* New Haven: Yale University Press, 2019.

Chin, Catherine M., and Moulie Vidas. Introduction to *Late Ancient Knowing: Explorations in Intellectual History*, edited by Catherine M. Chin and Moulie Vidas, 1–13. Berkeley: University of California Press, 2015.

Clark, Elizabeth. "The Lady Vanishes: Dilemmas of a Feminist Historian after the 'Linguistic Turn.'" *Church History* 67 (1998): 1–31.

Clark, Kenneth. *The Nude: A Study in Ideal Form.* Princeton: Princeton University Press, 1953.

Cohen, Aryeh. *Rereading Talmud: Gender, Law and the Poetics of Sugyot.* Atlanta: Scholars Press, 1998.

Cohen, Gerson D. "Hannah and Her Seven Sons in Hebrew Literature." In *Studies in the Variety of Rabbinic Literature*, 420–429. Philadelphia: Jewish Publication Society, 1991.

Cohen, Getzel. "Travel between Palestine and Mesopotamia during the

Hellenistic and Roman Periods: A Preliminary Study." In *The Archaeology and Material Culture of the Babylonian Talmud*, edited by Markham J. Geller, 186–224. Leiden: Brill, 2015.

Cohen, Shaye J. D. "The Matrilineal Principle in Historical Perspective." *Judaism* 34, no. 1 (1985): 5–13.

———. "Menstruants and the Sacred in Judaism and Christianity." In *Women's History and Ancient History*, edited by Sarah B. Pomeroy, 273–299. Chapel Hill: University of North Carolina Press, 1991.

———. "Purity and Piety." In *Daughters of the King*, edited by Susan Grossman and Rivka Haut, 103–116. Philadelphia: Jewish Publication Society Press, 1992.

Cohen, Stuart A. *The Three Crowns: Structure of Communal Politics in Early Rabbinic Jewry*. Cambridge: Cambridge University Press, 1990.

Cohn, Naftali S. *The Memory of the Temple and the Making of the Rabbis*. Philadelphia: University of Pennsylvania Press, 2013.

———. "When Women Confer with Rabbis: On Male Authority and Female Agency in the Mishnah." *Journal of the Society of Textual Reasoning* 6, no. 2 (March 2011).

Collard, Christopher, Martin J. Cropp, and Kevin H. Lee. *Euripides: Selected Fragmentary Plays with Introductions, Translations and Commentaries*, vol. 1. Liverpool: Liverpool: Aris & Phillips, 1995.

Connelly, R. W. *Masculinities*. Berkeley: University of California Press, 1995.

Cooper, Kate. "Apostles, Ascetic Women, and Questions of Audience: New Reflections on the Rhetoric of Gender in the Apocryphal Acts." *Seminar Papers* 128, no. 31 (1992): 147.

———. *The Virgin and the Bride: Idealized Womanhood in Late Antiquity*. Cambridge, MA: Harvard University Press, 1996.

Crane, Diana. *Fashion and Its Social Agendas: Class, Gender, and Identity in Clothing*. Chicago: University of Chicago Press, 2000.

Dal Bo, Federico. *Massekhet Keritot: A Feminist Commentary on the Babylonian Talmud*. Tübingen: Mohr Siebeck, 2013.

Dalton, Krista. "Teaching for the Tithe: Donor Expectations and the Matrona's Tithe." *AJS Review* 44, no. 1 (2020): 49–73.

De Verteuil, Roger. "The Scapegoat Archetype." *Journal of Religion and Health* 5, no. 3 (1966): 209–225.

Delaney, Carol. "Cutting the Ties That Bind: The Sacrifice of Abraham and Patriarchal Kinship." In *Relative Values: Reconfiguring Kinship Studies*, edited by Sarah Franklin and Susan McKinnon, 445–467. Durham: Duke University Press, 2001.

DeVries, Hent. *Religion and Violence: Philosophical Perspectives from Kant to Derrida*. Baltimore: Johns Hopkins University Press, 2002, 169.

Diamond, Eliezer. *Holy Men and Hunger Artists: Fasting and Asceticism in Rabbinic Culture*. Oxford: Oxford University Press, 2004.

Dillon, Matthew. *Girls and Women in Classical Greek Religion*. New York: Routledge, 2002.

Douglas, Mary. *Natural Symbols: Explorations of Cosmology*. London: Routledge, 1996.

———. *Purity and Danger: An Analysis of Concepts of Pollution and Taboo*. London: Routledge, 2002. Originally published 1966.

———. "Social Preconditions of Enthusiasm and Heterodoxy." In *Forms of Symbolic Action: Proceedings of the 1969 Annual Meeting of the American Ethnological Society*, 69–87. Seattle: American Ethnographical Society, 1969.

Eliav, Yaron Z. "The Material World of Babylonia as Seen from Roman Palestine: Some Preliminary Observations." In *The Archaeology and Material Culture of the Babylonian Talmud*, edited by Markham J. Geller, 153–185. Leiden: Brill, 2015.

Elman, Yaakov. "Acculturation to Elite Persian Norms and Modes of Thought in the Babylonian Jewish Community of Late Antiquity." In *Neti'ot leDavid: Sefer hayovel leDavid Halivni*, edited by Yaakov Elman, Ephraim B. Halivni, and Zvi Steinfeld, 31–56. Jerusalem: Orhot, 2004.

———. "Babylonian Baraitot in the Tosefta and the 'Dialectology' of Middle Hebrew." *AJS Review* 16, no. 1–2 (1991): 1–29.

———. "'He in His Cloak and She in Her Cloak': Conflicting Images of Sexuality in Sassanian Mesopotamia." In *Discussing Cultural Influences: Text, Context, and Non-Text in Rabbinic Judaism*, edited by Rivka Ulmer, 129–164. Lanham, MD: University Press of America, 2007.

———. "Middle Persian Culture and Babylonian Sages: Accommodation and Resistance in the Shaping of Rabbinic Legal Tradition." *Cambridge Companion to Rabbinic Literature*, edited by Charlotte Elisheva Fonrobert and Martin S. Jaffee, 165–197. Cambridge: Cambridge University Press, 2007.

Emanatian, Michele. "Metaphor and the Expression of Emotion: The Value of Cross-Cultural Perspectives." *Metaphor and Symbolic Activity* 10, no. 3 (1995): 163–182.

Emrani, Haleh. "'Who Would Be Mine for the Day!' Irano-Judaic Marriage Customs in Late Antiquity." *Iranian Studies* 49, no. 2 (2016): 217–231.

Feintuch, Yonatan. "Bein kohanim laḥakhamim: Al aggadah aḥat beheksherah haraḥav bevavli Yoma" [Between priests and rabbis: An analysis of an Aggadah and its wider context in Bavli Yoma]. *Meḥkerei Yerushalayim besifrut ivrit* 23 (2010): 1–14.

———. "Uncovering Covert Links between Halakhah and Aggadah in the Babylonian Talmud: The Talmudic Discussion of Yom Kippur Afflictions in B. Yoma." *AJS Review* 40, no. 1 (2016): 17–32.

Fine, Steven. *This Holy Place: On the Sanctity of the Synagogue during the Greco-Roman Period*. Notre Dame: University of Notre Dame Press, 1997.

Finkelstein, Louis. *Torat Kohanim*. New York: Jewish Theological Seminary, 1956.

Fitzgerald, William. *Slavery and the Roman Literary Imagination*. New York: Cambridge University Press, 2000.

Fonrobert, Charlotte Elisheva. "Education as Filiation: BT *'Eruvin* 72b–73a." *Nashim: A Journal of Jewish Women's Studies and Gender Issues* 28 (2015): 9–29.

———. *Menstrual Purity: Rabbinic and Christian Reconstructions of Biblical Gender*. Stanford: Stanford University Press, 2009.

———. "When the Rabbi Weeps: On Reading Gender in Talmudic Aggadah." *Nashim: A Journal of Jewish Women's Studies and Gender Issues* 4 (2001): 56–83.

Foucault, Michel. *Discipline and Punish: The Birth of the Prison*. Harmondsworth: Penguin, 1979.

———. *The History of Sexuality: An Introduction*, vol. 1. New York: Random House, 1978.

Fraade, Steven D. "Ascetical Aspects of Ancient Judaism." In *Jewish Spirituality: From the Bible through the Middle Ages*, edited by Art Green, 253–288. New York: Crossroad Publishing, 1987.

———. "Facing the Holy Ark, in Words and in Images." *Near Eastern Archaeology* 82, no. 3 (2019): 156–163.

Fraenkel, Yonah. *Sipur ha'agadah: Aḥdut shel tokhen vetzurah* [The Aggadic narrative: Harmony of form and content]. Tel-Aviv: Hakibbutz Hameuḥad, 2001.

Franklin, Sarah, and Susan McKinnon. "Introduction: Relative Values: Reconfiguring Kinship Studies." In *Relative Values: Reconfiguring Kinship Studies*, edited by Sarah Franklin and Susan McKinnon. Durham: Duke University Press, 2001.

Franklin, Susan. "The Anthropology of Biology: A Lesson from the New Kinship Studies." In *The Cambridge Handbook of Kinship*, edited by Sandra Bamford, 107–132. Cambridge: Cambridge University Press.

Bibliography

Friedman, Shamma. "Habaraitot batalmud habavli veyaḥasan lemakbiloteihen shebatosefta" [The Baraitot in the Babylonian Talmud and their relationship to parallels in the Tosefta]. In *Atara leḥayim: Meḥkarim besifrut hatalmudit veharabbanit likhvod professor Ḥayyim Zalman Dimitrovski* [Atara leḥayim: Studies in the Talmud and medieval Rabbinic literature in honor of Professor Ḥayyim Zalmon Dimitrovsky], edited by Daniel Boyarin, Marc G. Hirshman, Menahem Schmelzer, Shamma Friedman, and Israel Ta-Shma. Jerusalem: Magnes Press, 2000.

———. "Perek ha'ishah rabah babavli: Betzeruf mavo klali al derekh ḥeker hasugya" [A critical study of Yevamot X with a methodological introduction]. In *Meḥkarim umekorot: Ma'asef lemada'ei hayahadut* [Texts and studies: Analecta Judaica I], edited by H. Z. Dimitrovsky, 275–441. New York: Jewish Theological Seminary of America, 1977.

———. *Talmudic Studies: Investigating the Sugya, Variant Readings, and Aggada*. New York: Jewish Theological Seminary, 2010.

Frymer-Kensky, Tikvah. *Studies in Bible and Feminist Criticism*. Philadelphia: Jewish Publication Society, 2005.

Gafni, Isaiah. "The Institution of Marriage in Rabbinic Times." In *The Jewish Family: Metaphor and Memory*, edited by David Kraemer, 13–30. Oxford: Oxford University Press, 1989.

Gager, John G. "Body-Symbols and Social Reality: Resurrection, Incarnation, and Asceticism in Early Christianity." *Religion* 12 (1982): 345–364.

Galor, Katharina. "Domestic Architecture." In *The Oxford Handbook of Jewish Daily Life in Roman Palestine*, edited by Catherine Hezser. Oxford: Oxford University Press, 2010.

Gardner, Gregg E. "Competitive Giving in the Third Century CE: Early Rabbinic Approaches to Greco-Roman Civic Benefaction." In *Religious Competition in the Third Century C.E.: Jews, Christians, and the Greco-Roman World*, edited by D. Rosenblum, L. C. Vuong, and N. P. DesRosiers, 81–92. Göttingen: Vandenhoeck & Ruprecht, 2014.

———. *The Origins of Organized Charity in Rabbinic Judaism*. New York: Cambridge University Press, 2015.

Gawlinski, Laura. "Theorizing Religious Dress." In *What Shall I Say of Clothes? Theoretical and Methodological Approaches to the Study of Dress in Antiquity*, edited by Megan Cifarelli and Laura Gawlinski, 161–178. Boston: Archaeological Institute of America, 2017.

Gillespie, Susan D. "Beyond Kinship: An Introduction." In *Beyond Kinship: Social and Material Reproduction in House Societies*, edited by Rosemary

A. Joyce and Susan D. Gillepsie, 1–21. Philadelphia: University of Pennsylvania Press, 2000.

Gilmore, David. *Manhood in the Making: Cultural Conceptions of Masculinity*. New Haven: Yale University Press, 1990.

Gordon, Benjamin D. "Sightseeing and Spectacle at the Jewish Temple." *AJS Review* 43, no. 2 (2019): 271–292.

Gray, Alyssa M. *A Talmud in Exile: The Influence of Yerushalmi Avodah Zarah: On the Formation of Bavli Avodah Zarah*. Providence: Brown University, 2005.

Green, Deborah A. *The Aroma of Righteousness*. University Park: Pennsylvania State University Press, 2011.

Green, William Scott. "What's in a Name? The Problematic of Rabbinic 'Biography.'" In *Approaches to Ancient Judaism: Theory and Practice*, edited by W. S. Green, 77–96. Missoula, MT: Scholar's Press for Brown University, 1978.

Grey, Matthew. "Jewish Priests and the Social History of Post-70 Palestine." PhD diss., University of North Carolina, 2011.

Gribetz, Sarit Kattan. "Consuming Texts: Women as Recipients and Transmitters of Ancient Texts." In *Rethinking 'Authority' in Late Antiquity: Authorship, Law, and Transmission in Jewish and Christian Tradition*, edited by A. J. Berkovitz and Mark Letteney, 178–206. New York: Routledge, 2018.

———. "The Mothers in the Manuscripts: Gender, Motherhood and Power in the Toledot Yeshu Narratives." In *Toledot Yeshu in Context: The Jewish "Life of Jesus" in Ancient, Medieval, and Modern History*, edited by Daniel Barbu and Yaacov Deutsch, 99–129. Tübingen: Mohr Siebeck, 2019.

———. *Time and Difference in Rabbinic Judaism*. Princeton: Princeton University Press, 2020.

Gross, Simcha M. "Irano-Talmudica and Beyond: Next Steps in the Contextualization of the Babylonian Talmud." *Jewish Quarterly Review* 106, no. 2 (2016): 248–255.

———. "Rethinking Babylonian Acculturation in the Sassanian Empire." *Journal of Ancient Judaism* 9 (2018): 280–310.

Grossman, Susan. "Women and the Jerusalem Temple." In *Daughters of the King*, edited by Susan Grossman and Rivkah Haut, 15–37. Philadelphia: Jewish Publication Society, 1992.

Gruchcow, Lisa. *Writing the Wayward Wife: Rabbinic Interpretations of Sotah*. Leiden: Brill, 2006.

Hadley, Dawn M. *Masculinity in Medieval Europe*. London: Longman, 1999.

Haendler, Cecilia. "Women and Priests in Tractate Hallah: Gender Readings in Rabbinic Literature." *Melilah Manchester Journal of Jewish Studies* 13 (2019): 86–102.

Halbertal, Moshe. *On Sacrifice*. Princeton: Princeton University Press, 2012.

Halbwachs, Maurice. *On Collective Memory*. Edited and translated by Lewis A. Coser. Chicago: University of Chicago Press, 1992.

Halivni, David Weiss. Introduction to *Mekorot umesorot: Bava batra*. Jerusalem: Magnes Press, 2007.

———. *Midrash, Mishnah, and Gemara: The Jewish Predilection for Justified Law*. Cambridge, MA: Harvard University Press, 1986.

Harvey, Susan Ashbrook. "Asceticism." In *Late Antiquity: Guide to the Postclassical World*, edited by G. W. Bowersock, Peter Brown, and Oleg Grabar. Cambridge, MA: Harvard University Press, 1999.

Hasan-Rokem, Galit. "Material Mobility vs. Concentric Cosmology in the Sukkah: The House of the Wandering Jew or a Ubiquitous Temple?" In *Things: Religion and the Question of Materiality*, edited by Dick Houtman and Birgit Meyer, 153–179. New York: Fordham University Press, 2012.

———. "Polymorphic Helena: Toledot Yeshu as a Palimpsest of Religious Narratives and Identities." In *Toledot Yeshu ("The Life Story of Jesus") Revisited: A Princeton Conference*, edited by Peter Schäfer, Michael Meerson, and Yaacov Deutsch, 247–282. Tübingen: Mohr Siebeck, 2011.

———. *Web of Life: Folklore and Midrash in Rabbinic Literature*. Translated by Batya Stein. Stanford: Stanford University Press, 2000.

Hatlie, Peter. "Images of Motherhood and Self in Byzantine Literature." *Dumbarton Oaks Papers* 63 (2009): 41–57.

Hauptman, Judith. "From the Kitchen to the Dining Room: Women and Ritual Activities in Tractate Pesachim." In *A Feminist Commentary on the Babylonian Talmud: Introduction and Studies*, edited by Tal Ilan, Tamara Or, Dorothea M. Salzer, Christine Steuer, and Irina Wandrey, 109–126. Tübingen: Mohr Siebeck, 2007.

———. "Hadavar masur lenashim: Nashim betiksei dat beitiyim" [The matter is turned over to women: Women and domestic religious ritual]. *Sidra* 24–25 (2010): 83–111.

———. "A New View of Women and Torah Study in the Talmudic Period." *Jewish Studies, an Internet Journal* 9 (2010): 249–292.

———. *Rereading the Rabbis: A Woman's Voice*. Boulder, CO: Westview Press, 1998.

———. "The Talmud's Women in Law and Narrative." *Nashim: A Journal of Jewish Women's Studies and Gender Issues* 28 (2015): 30–50.

Hayes, Christine Elizabeth. *Between the Babylonian and Palestinian Talmuds: Accounting for Halakhic Difference in Selected Sugyot from Tractate Avodah Zarah.* New York: Oxford University Press, 1997.

Hengel, Martin. *The Atonement: The Origins of the Doctrine in the New Testament.* Minneapolis: Fortress, 1981.

Herman, Geoffrey. "Priests and Amoraic Leadership in Sassanian Babylonia." In *Proceedings of the Twelfth World Congress of Jewish Studies,* 59–68. Jerusalem: World Union of Jewish Studies, 2000.

Hezser, Catherine. "The Halitzah Shoe: Between Female Subjugation and Symbolic Emasculation." In *Jews and Shoes,* edited by Edna Nahshon, 47–64. New York: Berg, 2008.

———. *The Social Structure of the Rabbinic Movement.* Tübingen: Mohr Siebeck, 1997.

Himmelfarb, Martha. *A Kingdom of Priests: Ancestry and Merit in Ancient Judaism.* Philadelphia: University of Pennsylvania Press, 2006.

Hume, Lynne. *The Religious Life of Dress: Global Fashion and Faith.* London: Bloomsbury, 2013.

Ilan, Tal. "Haem she'akhlah et benah" [The mother who ate her son]. In *Bein Yosephus lehazal* [Josephus and the rabbis], edited by Tal Ilan and Vered Noam, 2:713–730. Jerusalem: Yad Ben Zvi, 2017.

———. *Integrating Women into Second Temple History.* Peabody, MA: Hendrickson, 2001.

———. *Jewish Women in Greco-Roman Palestine.* Tübingen: Mohr Siebeck, 2006.

———. *Massekhet Hullin: A Feminist Commentary on the Babylonian Talmud.* Tübingen: Mohr Siebeck, 2017.

———. *Massekhet Ta'anit: A Feminist Commentary on the Babylonian Talmud.* Tübingen: Mohr Siebeck, 2008.

———. *Silencing the Queen: The Literary Histories of Shelamzion and Other Jewish Women.* Tübingen: Mohr Siebeck, 2006.

Ilana, Pardes. *Countertraditions in the Bible: A Feminist Approach.* Cambridge, MA: Harvard University Press, 1992.

Israeli, Anat, and Inbar Raveh. "'He Did Not Embarrass Her': Motherhood and Shame in Talmudic Literature." *Nashim: A Journal of Jewish Women's Studies and Gender Issues* 33, no. 1 (2018): 20–37.

Jastrow, Marcus. *A Dictionary of the Targumim, the Talmud Bavli and Yerushalmi, and the Midrashic Literature.* New York, 1926.

Jay, Nancy. *Throughout Your Generations Forever: Sacrifice, Religion, and Paternity*. Chicago: University of Chicago Press, 1992.

Johnson, Mark. *The Body in the Mind: The Bodily Basis of Meaning, Reason, and Imagination*. Chicago: Chicago University Press, 1987.

Jones, Serene. *Feminist Theory and Christian Theology: Cartographies of Grace*. Minneapolis: Fortress, 2000.

Josephus. *The Jewish War*. Translated by H. St. J. Thackeray and R. Marcus. London: William Heinemann, 1926.

Joslyn-Siemiatkoski, Daniel. "The Mother and Seven Sons in Late Antique and Medieval Ashkenazi Judaism: Narrative Transformations and Communal Identity." In *Dying for the Faith, Killing for the Faith: Old-Testament Faith-Warriors (1 and 2 Maccabees) in Historical Perspective*, edited by Gabriela Signori, 127–146. Leiden: Brill, 2012.

Kahana, Avi. "Asiyat haparokhet leveit hamikdash" [The making of the temple's parokhet]. *Ketoret Shiloh* (2009): 201–209.

Kalmin, Richard L. "The Adiabenian Royal Family in Rabbinic Literature of Late Antiquity." In *Tiferet leyisrael: Jubilee Volume in Honor of Israel Francus*, 61–77. New York: Jewish Theological Seminary of America, 2010.

———. "The Formation and Character of the Babylonian Talmud." In *The Cambridge History of Judaism IV: The Late Roman-Rabbinic Period*, edited by Steven T. Katz, 840–876. Cambridge: Cambridge University Press, 2006.

———. *Jewish Babylonia between Persia and Roman Palestine*. Oxford: Oxford University Press, 2006.

———. *Migrating Tales: The Talmud's Narratives in Their Historical Contexts*. Berkeley: University of California Press, 2014.

Kampen, Natalie. "Houses, Paintings, Family and Emotion." In *Family in the Greco-Roman World*, edited by Ray Laurence and Agnata Strömberg. London: Continuum International Publishing Group, 2012.

Kanarek, Jane. "All Are Obligated: Sacrifice, Sight and Study." In *Introduction to Seder Qodashim (FCBT V)*, edited by Tal Ilan, Monika Brockhaus, and Tanja Hidde, 213–223. Tübingen: Mohr Siebeck, 2012.

———. "Memorializing the Temple through the Maternal Practice of Arakhin." Accessed June 2020 at http://thegemara.com/memorializing-the-Temple-through-the-maternal-practice-of-arakhin/.

———. "Pilgrimage and Piety: Rabbinic Women and Vows of Valuation." *Nashim: A Journal of Jewish Women's Studies and Gender Issues* 28 (2015): 61–74.

———. "Rewriting Arakhin: Women and Tannaitic Vows of Valuation." *AJS Review* 40, no. 2 (2016): 261–277.

Karras, Ruth Mazo. *Unmarriages: Women, Men, and Sexual Unions in the Middle Ages*. Philadelphia: University of Pennsylvania Press, 2020.

Kessler, Gwynn. *Conceiving Israel: The Fetus in Rabbinic Narrative*. Philadelphia: University of Pennsylvania Press, 2009.

Kiel, Yishai. "Confessing Incest to a Rabbi: A Talmudic Story in Its Zoroastrian Context." *Harvard Theological Review* 107, no. 4 (2014): 401–424.

———. "Fasting and Self-Deprivation in the Babylonian Talmud in Light of Zoroastrian Ideology." *Jewish Studies, an Internet Journal* 12 (2013): 1–28.

———. "Study versus Sustenance: A Rabbinic Dilemma in Its Zoroastrian and Manichaean Context." *AJS Review* 38, no. 2 (2014): 275–302.

Kiperwasser, Reuven. "The Immersion of Ba'alei Qerain." *Jewish Studies Quarterly* 19 (2012): 311–338.

Klawans, Jonathan, *Purity, Sacrifice and the Temple: Symbolism and Supercessionism in the Study of Ancient Judaism*. Oxford: Oxford University Press, 2006.

Klinzing, Georg. *Die Umdeutung des Kultus in der Qumrangemeinde und im Neuen Testament* [The Reinterpretation of the culture of the community of Qumran in the New Testament]. Göttingen: Vanderhook and Ruprecht, 1971.

Knohl, Israel, and Shlomo Naeh. "Milu'im vekipurim." *Tarbits* 62 (1993): 17–44.

Koltun-Fromm, Naomi. *Hermeneutics of Holiness: Ancient Jewish and Christian Notions of Sexuality and Religious Community*. New York: Oxford University Press, 2010.

———. "Non-Jewish Sources for Late Ancient Jewish History." In *A Companion to Late Ancient Jews and Judaism, Third Century BCE–Seventh Century CE*, edited by Naomi Koltun-Fromm and Gwynn Kessler. Hoboken, NJ: Wiley, 2020.

Koren, Sharon Faye. *Forsaken: The Menstruant in Medieval Jewish Mysticism*. Waltham, MA: Brandeis University Press, 2011.

Kosman, Admiel. *Gender and the Dialogue in the Rabbinic Prism*. Berlin: Walter De Gruyter, 2012.

Kosman, Admiel, and Avraham Ofek. *Masekhet nashim hokhmah, ahavah, ne'emanut, teshukkah, yofi, min, kedushah: Keri'ah besipurim talmudiyim verabaniyim ushenei midreshei shir* [Tractate Nashim: Wisdom, love, faithfulness, passion, beauty, sex, holiness: Readings in talmudic and rabbinic stories and two midrashic poems]. Jerusalem: Keter, 2007.

Kosut, Mary, and Lisa Jean Moore. "Introduction: Not Just the Reflexive Reflex; Flesh and Bone in the Social Sciences." In *The Body Reader*, edited by Lisa Jean Moore and Mary Kosut, 1–26. New York: New York University Press, 2010.

———. "Vulnerable Bodies." In *The Body Reader*, edited by Lisa Jean Moore and Mary Kosut, 27–30. New York: New York University Press, 2010.

Krauss, Samuel. *Talmudische Archaologie*, vol. 1. Leipzig: G. Fock, 1910–1912.

Krondorfer, Björn. Introduction to *Men and Masculinities in Christianity and Judaism: A Critical Reader*, edited by Björn Krondorfer, xi–xxi. London: SCM Press, 2009.

———. *Men's Bodies, Men's Gods: Male Identities in a (Post) Christian Culture*. New York: New York University Press, 1996.

Labovitz, Gail. "A Man Spinning on His Thigh: Gender, Positive Time-Bound Commandments and Ritual Fringes: Mishnah Mo'ed Katan 3:4." *Nashim: A Journal of Jewish Women's Studies and Gender Issues* 28 (2015): 75–87.

———. *Marriage and Metaphor: Constructions of Gender in Rabbinic Literature*. Lanham, MD: Rowman & Littlefield, 2009.

———. *Massekhet Moed Katan: A Feminist Commentary on the Babylonian Talmud*. Tübingen: Mohr Siebeck, 2022.

———. "Is Rav's Wife 'a Dish'? Food and Eating Metaphors in Rabbinic Discourse of Sexuality and Gender Relations." In *Love—Ideal and Real—in the Jewish Tradition from the Hebrew Bible to Modern Times*, edited by Leonard J. Greenspoon, Ronald A. Simkins, and Jean A. Cahan, 147–170. Omaha: Creighton University Press, 2008.

Lakoff, George, and Mark Johnson. *Metaphors We Live By*. Chicago: University of Chicago Press, 1980.

Lapin, Hayim. "The Construction of Households in the Mishnah." In *The Mishnah in Contemporary Perspective*, edited by Alan J. Avery-Peck and Jacob Neusner, 55–80. Leiden: Brill, 2006.

Lavee, Moshe. *The Rabbinic Conversion of Judaism: The Unique Perspective of the Bavli on Conversion and the Construction of Jewish Identity*. Leiden: Brill, 2018.

Lefkowitz, Mary R. "The Motivations for St. Perpetua's Martyrdom." *Journal of the American Academy of Religion* 44, no. 3 (1976): 417–421.

Lehman, Marjorie. "Dressing and Undressing the High Priest: A Talmudic

View of Mothers." *Nashim: A Journal of Jewish Women's Studies and Gender Issues* 26 (2014): 52–74.

———. "Feet in the Rabbinic Imagination and the Prohibition against Wearing Shoes on Yom Kippur." *AJS Review* 43, no. 2 (2019): 319–338.

———. "The Gendered Rhetoric of Sukkah Observance." *Jewish Quarterly Review* 96 (2006): 309–335.

———. "Imagining the Priesthood in Tractate Yoma 2:1–2 and BT Yoma 23a." *Nashim: A Journal of Jewish Women's Studies and Gender Issues* 28 (2015): 88–105.

———. "Rabbinic Masculinities: Reading the Ba'al Keri in Tractate Yoma." *Jewish Studies Quarterly* 22 (2015): 109–136.

———. "Reading the Gendered Rhetoric of Yom Kippur." In *Introduction to Seder Qodashim*, edited by Tal Ilan, Monika Brockhaus, and Tanja Hidde, 33–56. Tübingen: Mohr Siebeck, 2012.

———. "Reimagining Home, Rethinking Sukkah: Rabbinic Discourse and Its Contemporary Implications." In *Jews at Home: The Domestication of Identity*, edited by Simon J. Bronner. Oxford: Littman Library of Jewish Civilization, 2009.

———. "Rereading Beruriah through the Lens of Isaac Bashevis Singer's Yentl." *Nashim: A Journal of Jewish Women's Studies and Gender Issues* 31 (2017): 123–145.

Lehman, Marjorie, Jane L. Kanarek, and Simon J. Bronner. Introduction to *Mothers in the Jewish Cultural Imagination*, edited by Marjorie Lehman, Jane L. Kanarek, and Simon J. Bronner, 1–20. Liverpool: Liverpool University Press, Littman Library of Jewish Civilization, 2017

Lerner, Paul Frederick, Benjamin Maria Baader, and Sharon Gillerman. *Jewish Masculinities: German Jews, Gender, and History*. Bloomington: Indiana University Press, 2012.

Lev, Sarra. "Talmud That Works Your Heart: New Approaches to Reading." In *Learning to Read Talmud: What It Looks Like and How It Happens*, edited by Jane L. Kanarek and Marjorie Lehman, 175–202. Boston: Academic Studies Press, 2016.

Levine, Baruch A. *The JPS Torah Commentary: Leviticus*. Philadelphia: Jewish Publication Society, 2003.

Levine, David. "Why No Women in the Beit Midrash?" In *Introduction to Seder Qodashim (FBCT V)*, edited by Tal Ilan, Monika Brockhaus, and Tanja Hidde. Tübingen: Mohr Siebeck, 2012.

Lévi-Strauss, Claude. *Structural Anthropology*. New York: Basic Books, 1963.

Bibliography   329

Libson, Ayelet Hoffman. *Law and Self-Knowledge in the Talmud*. Cambridge: Cambridge University Press, 2018.

Lichtenstein, Aharon. "On the Assassination of Prime Minister Yitzchak Rabin, z"l. Accessed June 2020 at https://www.etzion.org.il/en /assassination-prime-minister-yitzchak-rabin-zl.

Lieberman, Saul. *Tosefta kifeshuta* IV. New York: Jewish Theological Seminary, 1992.

Liebowitz, Etka. "A New Perspective on Two Jewish Queens in the Second Temple Period: Alexandra of Judaea and Helene of Adiabene." In *Sources and Interpretation in Ancient Judaism: Studies for Tal Ilan at Sixty*, edited by Meron M. Piotrkowski, Saskia Dönitz, Geoffrey Herman, and Tal Ilan, 41–65. Leiden: Brill, 2018.

Lubhéid, Eithne. *Pregnant on Arrival: Making the Illegal Immigrant*. Minneapolis: University of Minnesota Press, 2013.

Mandel, Paul. "'Lo hayu yamim tovim leyisrael kaḥamishah asar be'av ukheyom hakipurim': Al hamishnah ha'aḥaronah shel masekhet ta'anit vegilguleiha" ["There were no happier days for Israel than the Fifteenth of Av and the Day of Atonement": On the final Mishnah of Tractate Ta'anit and its transmission]. *Teudah* 11, no. 5 (1996): 148–178.

Marciak, Michal. "Izates and Helena of Adiabene: A Study on Literary Traditions and History." PhD diss., Leiden University, 2012.

Margalit, Natan. "Priestly Men and Invisible Women: Male Appropriation of the Feminine and the Exemption of Women from Positive, Time-Bound Commandments." *AJS Review* 28, no. 2 (2004): 297–316.

Margoliot, Mordechai. *Encyclopedia leḥakhmei hatalmud vehage'onim*, vol. 2. Tel-Aviv: Yavneh Publishing House, 1981.

Marx, Dalia. "Tractate 'Qinnim': Marginality or Horizons." In *Introduction to Seder Qodashim*, edited by Tal Ilan, Monika Brockhaus, and Tanja Hidde, 253–272. Tübingen: Mohr Siebeck, 2012.

———. *Tractates Tamid, Middot and Qinnim: A Feminist Commentary on the Babylonian Talmud*. Tübingen: Mohr Siebeck, 2013.

———. "Women and Priests: Encounters and Dangers as Reflected in 1 Samuel 2, no. 22." *Lectio Difficilior* 1 (2011): 1–22.

Matthews, Shelly. "Thinking of Thecla: Issues in Feminist Historiography." *Journal of Feminist Studies in Religion* 17:2 (2001): 46–54.

Meyer, Michael. *Response to Modernity: A History of the Reform Movement in Judaism*. Detroit: Wayne State University Press, 1995.

Milgrom, Jacob. *Leviticus 1–16: A New Translation with Introduction and Commentary*. New Haven: Yale University Press, 1998.

———. *Leviticus 23–27: A New Translation with Introduction and Commentary*. New York: Doubleday, 2001.

Mills, Sara. *Discourse*. London: Routledge, 2004.

Milnor, Kristina. *Gender, Domesticity, and the Age of Augustus: Inventing Private Life*. Oxford: Oxford University Press, 2005.

Moore, Lisa Jean, and Mary Kosut. *The Body Reader*. New York: New York University Press, 2010.

Naumov, Goce. "Embodied Houses: The Social and Symbolic Agency of Neolithic Architecture in the Republic of Macedonia." In *Tracking the Neolithic House in Europe: Sedentism, Architecture, and Practice*, edited by Daniela Hofmann and Jessica Smyth. New York: Springer, 2013.

Neis, Rachel Rafe. *The Sense of Sight in Rabbinic Culture: Jewish Ways of Seeing in Late Antiquity*. New York: Cambridge University Press, 2013.

Neusner, Jacob. *The Documentary Foundation of Rabbinic Culture: Mopping Up after the Debates with Gerald L. Bruns, S. J. D. Cohen, Arnold Maria Goldberg, Susan Handelman, Christine Hayes, James Kugel, Peter Schaefer, Eliezer Segal, E. P. Sanders, and Lawrence H. Schiffman*. Atlanta: Scholars Press, 1995.

———. *Judaism: Evidence of the Mishnah*. Chicago: University of Chicago Press, 1981.

———. *The Reader's Guide to the Talmud*. Leiden: Brill, 2001.

Noam, Vered. "Nes pakh hashemen: Haumnam makor leverur yaḥasam shel ḥazal laḥashmona'im" [The miracle of the cruse of oil: Questioning its use as a source for assessing the sages' attitude toward the Hasmoneans]. *Zion* (2002): 396–400.

Oppenheimer, Aaron. "Kedushat haḥayim veḥeruf hanefesh be'ikvot mered bar-kokhba" [Sanctity of life and martyrdom following the Bar Kochba Revolt]. In *Kedushat hahayim veḥeruf hanefesh: Kovetz ma'amarim shel Amir Yekutiel* [Sanctity of life and martyrdom: Studies in memory of Amir Yekutiel], edited by Isaiah M. Gafni and Aviezer Ravitzky. Jerusalem: Zalman Shazar Center for Jewish History, 1992.

Or, Tamara, *Massekhet Betsah: A Feminist Commentary on the Babylonian Talmud*. Tübingen: Mohr Siebeck, 2010.

Ortner, Sherri. "Gender Hegemonies." *Cultural Critique* 14 (1989–1990): 35–80.

———. "Is Female to Male as Nature Is to Culture?" *Feminist Studies* 1 (1972): 5–31.

Osiek, Carolyn, and David L. Balch. *Families in the New Testament World: Households and House Churches*. Louisville, KY: Westminster John Knox Press, 1997.

Panken, Aaron D. *The Rhetoric of Innovation: Self-Conscious Legal Change in Rabbinic Literature*. Lanham, MD: University Press of America, 2005.

Parker, Holt. "Loyal Slaves and Loyal Wives: The Crisis of the Outside-Within and Roman *Exemplum* Literature." In *Women and Slaves in Greco-Roman Culture*, edited by Sandra R. Joshel and Sheila Murnaghan, 152–173. London: Routledge, 1998.

Patai, Raphael. *The Hebrew Goddess*. New York: Ktav Publishing House, 1967.

Peletz, Michael G. "Neither Reasonable nor Responsible: Contrasting Representations of Masculinity in a Malay Society." *Cultural Anthropology* 9, no. 2 (1994): 137.

Penniman, John David. *Raised on Christian Milk: Food and the Formation of the Soul in Early Christianity*. New Haven: Yale University Press, 2017.

Perkins, Judith. *The Suffering Self: Pain and Narrative Representation in the Early Christian Era*. London: Routledge, 1995.

Peskowitz, Miriam B. *Spinning Fantasies: Rabbis, Gender, and History*. Berkeley: University of California Press, 1997.

Ramsey, Gillian. "The Queen and the City: Royal Female Intervention and Patronage in Hellenistic Civic Communities." *Gender and History* 23, no. 3 (2011): 510–527.

Rapp, Claudia. "Figures of Female Sanctity: Byzantine Edifying Manuscripts and Their Audience." *Dumbarton Oaks Papers* 50 (1996): 313–333, 335–344.

Regev, Eyal. *The Temple in Early Christianity: Experiencing the Sacred*. New Haven: Yale University Press, 2019.

Reynolds, Gabriel Said. "On the Quran and the Theme of Jews as Killers of the Prophets." *Al-Bayān Journal* 10, no. 2 (2012): 9–32.

Rich, Adrienne. *Of Woman Born: Motherhood as Experience and Institution*. New York: Norton, 1986.

———. *On Lies, Secrets, and Silence: Selected Prose 1966–1978*. New York: Norton, 1980.

Riggs, Damien W., and Elizabeth Peel. *Critical Kinship Studies*. London: Palgrave Macmillan, 2016.

Roach, Mary Ellen, and Joanne Bubolz Eicher. "The Language of Personal Adornment." In *The Fabrics of Culture: The Anthropology of Clothing and Adornment*, edited by Justine M. Cordwell and Ronald A. Schwarz. New York: Mouton, 1979.

Romney-Wegner, Judith. *Chattel or Person? The Status of Women in the Mishnah*. New York: Oxford University Press, 1988.

Rooke, Deborah W. "Breeches of the Covenant: Gender, Garments and the

Priesthood." In *Embroidered Garments: Priests and Gender in Biblical Israel*, edited by Deborah W. Rooke, 20–37. Sheffield: Sheffield Phoenix Press, 2009.

Rosaldo, Renato. "Notes Toward a Critique of Patriarchy from a Male Position." *Anthropological Quarterly* 66, no. 2 (1993): 81–86.

Rosen-Zvi, Ishay. *Demonic Desires: "Yetzer Hara" and the Problem of Evil in Late Antiquity*. Philadelphia: University of Pennsylvania Press, 2011.

———. "Haguf vehamikdash: Reshimat mumei hakohanim bemishnah vemekomo shel hamikdash beveit hamidrash hatana'i" [Temple and the body: The list of priestly blemishes in the Mishnah and the place of the Temple in the Tannaitic House of Study]. *Mada'ei hayahadut* 43 (2005–2006): 49–87.

———. "Haishah hanitzevet: Tefillat Ḥannah biderashot ḥazal" [The standing woman: Hannah's prayer in rabbinic exegesis]. In *Tarbut yehudit be'ein hasaarah: Sefer hayovel leYosef Ahituv* [Jewish culture in the eye of the storm: A jubilee book in honor of Yosef Ahituv], edited by Avi Sagi and Nahem Iman, 675–698. Ein Tzurim: Hakibbutz Hameuḥad, 2002.

———. *The Mishnaic Sotah Ritual: Temple, Gender and Midrash*. Leiden: Brill, 2012.

———. "Orality, Narrative, Rhetoric: New Directions in Mishnah Research." *AJS Review* 32, no. 2 (2008): 243–249.

———. "Yetzer hara, miniyut ve'isurei yiḥud: Perek beantropologiya talmudit" [Yetzer hara, sexuality and yihud: A chapter of Talmudic anthropology]. *Theory and Criticism* 14 (1999): 55–84.

Ruane, Nicole J. *Sacrifice and Gender in Biblical Law*. New York: Cambridge University Press, 2013.

Rubenstein, Jeffrey L. *The Culture of the Babylonian Talmud*. Baltimore: Johns Hopkins University Press, 2003.

———. *The History of Sukkot in the Second Temple and Rabbinic Periods*. Atlanta: Scholars Press, 1995.

———. *Stories of the Babylonian Talmud*. Baltimore: Johns Hopkins University Press, 2010.

———. *Talmudic Stories: Narrative Art, Composition, and Culture*. Baltimore: Johns Hopkins University Press, 1999.

Ruddick, Sara. *Maternal Thinking: Toward a Politics of Peace*. Boston: Beacon Press, 1989.

Safrai, Chana, and Avital Campbell Hochstein. *Nashim baḥutz—nashim bifnim: Mekomam shel nashim bamidrash* [Women out–women in: The

Bibliography

place of women in the Beit Midrash]. Tel-Aviv: Miskal-Yedio Aḥaronot and Hemed, 2008.

Safrai, Shmuel Ze'ev, and Chana Safrai. *Mishnat Eretz Yisrael: Massekhet Yoma*. Jerusalem: E. M. Liphshitz, 2010.

Salomon, Nanette. "Making a World of Difference: Gender, Asymmetry, and the Greek Nude." In *Naked Truths: Women, Sexuality, and Gender in Classical Art and Archaeology*, edited by Ann Olga Koloski-Ostrow and Claire L. Lyons, 197–219. London: Routledge, 1997.

Satlow, Michael L. "'And on Earth You Shall Sleep': 'Talmud Torah' and Rabbinic Asceticism." *Journal of Religion* 83 (2003): 204–225.

———. "Jewish Constructions of Nakedness in Late Antiquity." *Journal of Biblical Literature* 116, no. 3 (1997): 429–454.

———. *Jewish Marriage in Antiquity*. Princeton: Princeton University Press, 2001.

———. *Tasting the Dish: Rabbinic Rhetorics of Sexuality*. Atlanta: Scholars Press, 1995.

———. "'Try to Be a Man': The Rabbinic Construction of Masculinity." *Harvard Theological Review* 89, no. 1 (1996): 19–40.

Sawicki, Jana. *Disciplining Foucault: Feminism, Power, and the Body: Thinking Gender*. New York: Routledge, 1991.

Schäfer, Peter. "Rabbis and Priests, or: How to Do Away with the Glorious Past of the Sons of Aaron." In *Antiquity in Antiquity: Jewish and Christian Pasts in the Greco-Roman World*, edited by Gregg Gardner and Kevin Osterloh, 155–172. Tübingen: Mohr Siebeck, 2008.

Schiffman, Lawrence. "The Conversion of the Royal House of Adiabene in Josephus and Rabbinic Sources." In *Josephus, Judaism, and Christianity*, edited by Louis H. Feldman and Gohei Hata, 293–312. Leiden: Brill, 1987.

Schmelzer, Menahem H. "How Was the High Priest Kept Awake on the Night of Yom Ha-Kippurim?" In *Studies in Jewish Bibliography and Medieval Hebrew Poetry: Collected Essays*. New York: Jewish Theological Seminary of America, 2006.

Schorsch, Ismar. "From Wolfenbüttel to Wissenschaft: The Divergent Paths of Isaak Markus Jost and Leopold Zunz." In *The Leo Baeck Institute Year Book* 22, no. 1 (1977): 109–128.

Schüssler Fiorenza, Elisabeth. "Cultic Language in Qumran and the New Testament." *CBQ* 38 (1976): 159–177.

Schwartz, Daniel R. "God, Gentiles, and Jewish Law: On Acts 15 and Josephus' Adiabene Narrative." In *Geschichte—Tradition—Reflexion: Festschrift für Martin Hengel zum 70*, edited by H. Cancik,

H. Lichtenberger, and Peter Schäfer, 263–282. Tübingen: Mohr Siebeck, 1996.

———. "Two Pauline Allusions to the Redemptive Mechanism of the Crucifixion." *Journal of Biblical Literature* 102, no. 2 (1983): 259–268.

Schwartz, Seth. *Josephus and Judean Politics*. Leiden: Brill, 1990.

———. *Were the Jews a Mediterranean Society? Reciprocity and Solidarity in Ancient Judaism*. Princeton: Princeton University Press, 2010.

Scott, Joan Wallach. *Gender and the Politics of History*, 28–50. New York: Columbia University Press, 1988.

Shai, Secunda. *The Talmud's Red Fence: Menstrual Impurity and Difference in Babylonian Judaism and Its Sasanian Context*. Oxford: Oxford University Press, 2020.

Shemesh, Aharon. "Letoledot mashma'am shel hamusagim 'mitzvat ase umitzvat lo taaseh'" [Toward a history of the terms "positive and negative commandment"]. *Tarbitz* 72, no. 1 (1993): 133–149.

Shlezinger-Katsman, Dafna. "Clothing." In *The Oxford Handbook of Jewish Daily Life in Roman Palestine*, edited by Catherine Hezser, 193–211. Oxford: Oxford University Press, 2010.

Siegal, Michal Bar-Asher. *Early Christian Monastic Literature and the Babylonian Talmud*. New York: Cambridge University Press, 2013.

Simon-Shoshan, Moshe. "Talmud as Novel: Dialogic Discourse and the Feminine Voice in the Babylonian Talmud." *Poetics Today* 40, no. 1 (2019): 105–112.

Siverstev, Alexei M. *Households, Sects, and the Origins of Rabbinic Judaism*. Leiden: Brill, 2005.

Smith, Jonathan Z. *Imagining Religion: From Babylon to Jonestown*. Chicago: University of Chicago Press, 2004.

———. "The Temple and the Magician." In *Map Is Not Territory: Studies in the History of Religions*, 289–310. Leiden: Brill, 1978.

———. "Trading Places." In *Relating Religion: Essays in the Study of Religion*, 215–229, Chicago: University of Chicago Press, 2004.

Snitow, Ann. "Feminism and Motherhood: An American Reading." *Feminist Review* 40 (1992): 32–51.

Spencer, F. Scott. *Salty Wives, Spirited Mothers, and Savvy Widows: Capable Women of Purpose and Persistence in Luke's Gospel*. Grand Rapids, MI: Eerdmans, 2012.

Stein, Dina. "Collapsing Structures: Discourse and the Destruction of the Temple in the Babylonian Talmud." *Jewish Quarterly Review* 98, no. 1 (2008): 1–28.

———. "A Maidservant and Her Master's Voice: Discourse, Identity, and Eros in Rabbinic Texts." *Journal of the History of Sexuality* 10, no. 3, 4 (2001): 379–397.

Steinmetz, Devorah. "Agada Unbound: Inter-Agadic Characterization of Sages in the Bavli and Implications for Reading Agada." In *Creation and Composition: The Contribution of the Bavli Redactors (Stammaim) to the Aggada*, edited by Peter Schäfer and Jeffrey L. Rubenstein, 293–337. Tübingen: Mohr Siebeck, 2005.

Stern, Sacha. *Time and Process in Ancient Judaism*. Portland, OR: Littman Library of Jewish Civilization, 2004.

Stiebert, Johanna. *First-Degree Incest and the Hebrew Bible: Sex in the Family*. London: Bloomsbury T&T Clark, 2016.

Stilgoe, John R. Foreword to *The Poetics of Space*, edited by Gaston Bachelard. Boston: Beacon Press, 1994.

Stökl Ben Ezra, Daniel. "Fasting with Jews, Thinking with Scapegoats: Some Remarks on Yom Kippur in Early Judaism and Christianity, in Particular 4Q541, Barnabas 7, Matthew 27 and Acts 27." In *The Day of Atonement: Its Interpretations in Early Jewish and Christian Traditions*, edited by Thomas Hieke and Tobias Nicklas, 168–187. Leiden: Brill, 2012.

———. *The Impact of Yom Kippur on Early Christianity: The Day of Atonement from Second Temple Judaism to the End of the Fifth Century*. Tübingen: Mohr Siebeck, 2003.

Swadding, Judith. *The Ancient Olympic Games*. London: British Museum, 1999.

Swartz, Michael R. "The Choreography of Blood in Mishnah Yoma." In *Jewish Blood: Reality and Metaphor in History, Religion, and Culture*, edited by Mitchell B. Hart, 70–82. London: Routledge, 2009.

———. "Liturgy, Poetry, and the Persistence of Sacrifice." In *Was 70 CE a Watershed in Jewish History? On Jews and Judaism before and after the Destruction of the Second Temple*, edited by Daniel R. Schwartz, Zeev Weiss, and Ruth A. Clements, 393–412. Leiden: Brill, 2012.

———. "Ritual Is with the People: Sacrifice and Society in Palestinian Yoma Traditions." In *The Actuality of Sacrifice: Past and Present*, edited by Alberdina Houtman, Marcel Poothius, Joshua Schwartz, and Joseph Turner, 206–227. Leiden: Brill.

———. "Yoma from Babylonia to Egypt: Ritual Function, Textual Transmission, and Sacrifice," *AJS Review* 43, no. 2 (2019): 339–353.

Ta-Shma, Israel Moses. "Karet." In *Encyclopaedia Judaica*, 2nd ed., edited by Michael Berenbaum and Fred Skolnik. New York: Macmillan Reference, 2007.

Tropper, Amram. *Keḥomer beyad hayotzer* [Like clay in the hands of the potter]. Jerusalem: Zalman Shazar Center, 2011.

Tzuberi, Christiane. "'And the Woman Is a High–Priest': From the Temple to the Kitchen, from the Laws of Ritual Im/Purity to the Laws of Kashrut (Toharot)." In *Introduction to Seder Qodashim (FCBT V)*, edited by Tal Ilan, Monika Brockhaus, and Tanja Hidde, 167–175. Tübingen: Mohr Siebeck, 2012.

Urbach, Ephraim E. *The Sages: Their Concepts and Beliefs*. Translated by Israel Abrahams. Jerusalem: Magnes Press, 1975.

Valler, Shulamit. *Massekhet Sukkah: A Feminist Commentary on the Babylonian Talmud*. Tübingen: Mohr Siebeck, 2009.

Vidas, Moulie. *Tradition and the Formation of the Talmud*. Princeton: Princeton University Press, 2014.

Walker, Lynne, and Vron Ware. "Political Pincushions: Decorating the Abolitionist Interior 1787–1865." In *Domestic Space: Reading the Nineteenth-Century Interior*, edited by Inga Bryden and Janet Floyd, 58–83. Manchester: Manchester University Press, 1999.

Wardle, Timothy. "Who Is Sacrificing? Assessing the Early Christian Reticence to Transfer the Idea of the Priesthood to the Community." In *Ritual and Metaphor: Sacrifice in the Bible*, edited by Christian A. Eberhar, 99–114. Atlanta: Society of Biblical Literature, 2011.

Wasserman, Mira Beth. *Jews, Gentiles, and Other Animals*. Philadelphia: University of Pennsylvania Press, 2017.

Watts, Edward Jay. *The Final Pagan Generation: Transformation of the Classical Heritage*. Berkeley: University of California Press, 2015.

Weisberg, Dvora. "Clothes (un)Make the Man: *bMenaḥot* 109b." In *Introduction to Seder Qodashim: A Feminist Commentary on the Babylonian Talmud*, edited by Tal Ilan, Monika Brockhaus, and Tanja Hidde. Tübingen: Mohr Siebeck, 2012.

———. *Massekhet Menaḥot: A Feminist Commentary on the Babylonian Talmud*. Tübingen: Mohr Siebeck, 2020.

Weiss, Avraham. *Hithavut hatalmud bishlemuto* [The Talmud Bavli as a literary unit]. New York: hamosad lezikhron Aleksander, 1943.

Weiss, David Halivni. *Midrash, Mishnah, and Gemara: The Jewish Predilection for Justified Law*. Cambridge, MA: Harvard University Press, 1986.

Weiss, Susan. "Under Cover: Demystification of Women's Head Covering in Jewish Law." *Nashim: A Journal of Jewish Women's Studies and Gender Issues* 17 (2009): 89–115.

Weston, Kath. *Families We Choose: Lesbians, Gays, Kinship*. New York: Columbia University Press, 1991.

Wimpfheimer, Barry Scott. *Narrating the Law: A Poetics of Talmudic Legal Stories*. Philadelphia: University of Pennsylvania Press, 2011.

Wolf, Sarah. "'Haven't I Told You Not to Take Yourself Outside of the Law?' Rabbi Yirmiyah and the Characterization of a Scholastic." *AJS Review* 44, no. 2 (2020): 384–410.

INDEX

. . .

Aaron, 4, 5, 22, 89, 216, 219, 250n44, 256n2, 257n9, 277n60
Abaye, 44, 63–64, 95, 97, 119, 129, 151–52, 158, 227n26, 258n15, 286n18
Abba Shaul, 119
Abraham, 83
abstinence, of sexuality/sexual relations, 104, 106, 111, 122
accountability, of the high priest, 179
Adiabene, 65, 70, 237n22, 241–42n47
adultery, 67, 68, 91, 137, 138
Ahashverosh, 114
Amalek, 41–42
Ammonites, 41
animals, sin transference onto, 46, 87
Antler, Joyce, 57, 88
Ark of the Covenant, 109–10
aroma, sexual arousal and, 112–13
asceticism, 105–6, 132, 179, 273n24
ash, removal of, 37–40
at-homeness, following Yom Kippur, 282–83n93
atonement: bodily affliction as, 141; fasting and, 128; prayer and, 168; process of, 159; rite of, 13; sacrifices for, 206–7n68; for sin, 42
avodah, 3, 22–25, 216n24
Avtalyon, 5, 100, 161
Avtinas, house of, 58
Avtinas chamber, 28

ba'al keri: classification of, 175; defined, 16; exclusion of,

166; impurities of, 305–6n18; purification ritual of, 167, 168, 169–71, 174, 304–5n14, 304n13; self-definition of, 309n40; sexual satisfaction of, 173; sin offerings and, 310n54
Babylonian rabbis, authority of, 6
Bachelard, Gaston, 27, 181, 311n2
backup wife, 22, 23
Baker, Cynthia, 21, 22, 197n9, 214n13, 214n15, 215n17, 249–50n40, 295n7
Bal, Mieke, 105, 114, 124, 271n14, 283n1, 302n50
Batsheva, 42, 113, 277n56
Baumgarten, Elisheva, 141, 292n56
Bavli Yoma, overview of, 2, 9–10, 11, 12–18
bayit: defined, 198n11; future, 178–79; mezuzah requirements and, 30; overview of, 21; rabbinic notions of, 27; rethinking of, 184–85; significance of, 197n9
Beer, Moshe, 141, 293n62
Ben Azzai, 68, 69, 242–3n54
benefactors, need for, 61
Ben Ilas/Ilam, 74
blessing, of the priests, 206n68
bloodlines: disruption of, 4, 17, 43, 55; generativity within, 70; of the high priest, 5, 23, 82, 85, 117, 176; leadership within, 54; protection of, 135–36
bodily affliction, as atonement, 141
bodily discharges, 115–16, 166, 278n65, 303n6. *See also* seminal emission
body, naked, 96, 265n53

Boyarin, Daniel, 11, 104, 117–18, 229n36
braids, hair, 80–81, 112
brides, 108–9, 151, 291n54
brother-brother relationship, 268n69

casting lots, 40–41, 44
celibacy, 17, 104, 106
chastity, 106
children: father-son relationship, 47–52, 200n30, 267–68n64; gender determination of, 310n50; as mamzerim, 91, 115, 116; mother-begotten, 72; naming of, 59, 60; nurturing of, 299n27; parental connections with, 88; self-denial of, 152, 299n27; separation from, 53; significance of, 177, 186; teaching of, 67, 68; of temporary wives, 119. *See also* mother-son relationship
Chrysostum, John, 120, 281n84
clothing/priestly garments/tunic, 88–93, 94–95, 259n16, 259n18
Cohn, Naftali, 14, 53, 233n55
collective memory, 16
commandment: of ash removal, 37–38; discipline regarding, 146; of mezuzah, 31; negative, 148, 297–98n20; positive, 148, 297–98n20; of Torah teaching, 64. *See also specific commandments*
communication, within spinning rituals, 90–92
competition, of masculinity, 38–39, 227n24
confession, liturgical formula for, 14
Cooper, Kate, 72, 197n6
court, non-priests within, 39
cultural memory, religion as, 16
cultural reproduction, 4

David, 40, 42, 43, 114, 277n56
death, as praiseworthy act, 83
desert, experiences within, 137
Dinah, 139, 140, 291n51
disease, remedies for, 158
divorce, conditions for, 91
Doeg the Edomite (son of Yosef), 59, 60–62, 87
droughts, effects of, 179
Dubiel, removal of, 13

eglah arufah, 42, 45–47
Eliezer ben Yaakov, 68–70, 90, 91–92, 118
Elijah, 119–20
Elkhanah, 242n48
emergencies, rites within, 206n66, 311n56
Esther, 113, 114

fasting: atonement and, 128; within the Bible, 292n56; practice of, 210n86, 217–18n28; pregnancy and, 152–57, 300n37; self-induced suffering as, 292–93n59; significance of, 289–90n43, 292n55; as suffering, 140–42
father-son relationship, 47–52, 200n30, 267–68n64
Fonrobert, Charlotte, 11–12, 78, 214n15, 223n4, 229n36, 290n46, 295n1
food: children and, 152, 299n27; metaphor of, 130–31; sexual innuendos regarding, 130–32, 134, 143; significance of, 134
foot washing, 114–15, 277–78n61
forgiveness, 142, 173–76
Friedman, Shamma, 9

Gabriel, removal of, 13
Gamru, house of, 58
God: as Hope of Israel, 125–26,

165; sexuality and, 108, 111, 123; spiritual cleansing by, 177

gold, 62–63, 89

golden tablet, 62, 66–67, 68

Gray, Alyssa, 11

Gross, Simcha, 132

hair braids, significance of, 80–81, 112

Halbwach, Maurice, 16

Halivni, David Weiss, 9

hand size, significance of, 76–77, 251–52n54

hand washing, 114–15

Ḥanina ben Teradyon, 151

Hannah, 60, 89, 242n48

Ḥarsom, Eleazar ben: father rejection by, 99–102; as rabbi, 263n46; removal of, 93–94, 98, 264n51; social standing of, 99; Torah study by, 269n71; tunic of, 93–94, 95–96, 101

Hayes, Christine, 11

heifer, sacrifice of, 46

Helene: as nazarite, 241–42n47; overview of, 62–70, 87; significance of, 56, 57, 241n46

high priest: accountability of, 179; asexual nature of, 105; clothing of, 89–90, 95; disqualifications of, 22–23, 75, 80, 199–200n26, 216–17n24, 248n28; full-body immersions of, 114; hand size of, 76–77, 251–52n54; legal status of, 24–25; marriage of, 23–25, 34, 216n24; negative description of, 219–20n38; purity rituals of, 29–30, 106–7, 114–15, 207–8n73; rabbis *versus*, 5; sequestration of, 22, 27, 28, 75, 107, 216n21, 273n27; sexuality of, 75; significance of, 5; substitute, 23, 217n26, 218n29; succession

of, 73–74; weeping by, 47; wives of, 23–24, 122, 182; Yom Kippur preparations by, 22, 27, 75, 107, 273n27. *See also* priests

Hillel, 100, 101

holiness, 34, 35, 215n19

Holy of Holies, 77, 107, 109, 111, 179

house leprosy, 32–34, 221–22n50

houses/households/housekeeping: as codependent environment, 145; collapsing, 58–60; desert, 137; elements within, 181; fractured, 56; as home spaces, 19; impurity within, 19–20; insecurity within, 183; karet punishment within, 147; legal matters regarding, 210n86; relationships within, 181–82, 196n2; scarcity within, 145; significance of, 85–86; structure of, 127–28; within the Temple, 38, 208n74; by women, 38, 224n10, 295n8; women's bodies and, 20

Hugras, Levite, 58

human beings, donation of, 60–61

Ilan, Tal, 1, 120, 195n1

immersion: items needed for, 114; prayer and, 168; privacy within, 174; repentance *versus*, 165; requirements for, 115, 167–68; ritual of, 168, 169–71; significance of, 174–75. *See also* purification

impurity, 164, 168, 172. *See also* seminal emission

incense, 77, 113, 276n53

incest: consequences of, 122; example of, 96, 279n75; laws regarding, 135–36, 289n38, 289n41

Inclination, sexuality and, 121

Index

inherited leadership, 117
insecurity, male, 2–3
intellectual competition, between
    rabbis, 227n24
inui nefesh. *See* self-denial
Israelites: complaints of, 132–34;
    households of, 137; manna for,
    128, 130; Noahide laws and, 135;
    Pharaoh and, 140
Issur, 244n12

Jacob, 88, 139
Jerusalem, 50–51, 52
Jesus, 49
Jews, sexuality and, 105–6
Joseph, 88, 96, 100, 114
Josephus, 65, 108, 210n84, 240n40,
    242n50, 242n51, 253n68
judgment, 130, 137–38, 160

Kamtzar, Ben, 58–59, 60
karet, 141, 146–50, 163, 283n2,
    294n65, 296n12, 297n17
keruvim (cherubs), 108, 110, 120,
    123
Ketina, Rav, 107, 108
Kimhit: behavior of, 81–83; charac-
    teristics of, 84; house of, 71–74;
    influence of, 246n19; kinship ties
    of, 76–81; modesty of, 80, 156,
    249–50n40; as mother exemplar,
    74–76; overview of, 85–86, 87, 182
kings, authority of, 42
kinship, 4, 5, 252n55
Klawans, Jonathan, 142, 144,
    199n21, 201n39, 207n69, 209n83,
    210n83
knife, purification ritual of, 50,
    51–52

Laban, 139
leprosy, house, 32–34
Leviticus, 12–14

Libson, Ayelet, 157, 285n8, 293n59,
    300n37, 301n44

Ma'ariv, 168, 307n27
mamzerim, children as, 91, 115, 116
manna, 127–36, 137–38
Mar bar Rav Ashi, 157
marriage: of the high priest, 23–25,
    34, 216n24; on the Sabbath,
    216n24; for sexuality, 118–19;
    temporary, 280n76; Torah study
    within, 122
martyrdom, 71, 83–84, 253–54n68,
    255–56n79
Marx, Dalia, 14–15, 38, 199n16,
    209n78, 223n6, 224n9, 227n24,
    258n13, 258n14, 268n66
masculinity: construction of, 3; of
    the priests, 38–39; of the rabbis,
    3, 36–37, 52–54, 103–4, 226n24
master-disciple relationship, 4, 54,
    57, 69, 117, 157, 234n4
master-servant relationship, 101
materiality, within the Temple,
    67–68, 183, 239n38
meat, sacrificial, eating of, 208n77
men: insecurity of, 2–3; marginal-
    ization of, 3–8; sexual weaknesses
    of, 113; signs from God to, 184
Menasseh, 50–51, 52, 231–32n52,
    232n53
menstruation, 23, 106, 165–66, 178,
    279n76
metaphor, significance of, 130
mezuzah: overview of, 26–32; re-
    quirements for, 218n32, 220n40,
    220n42; reward and, 31–32;
    significance of, 218n34
mezuzot, requirements for, 221n48
Milgrom, Jacob, 60, 206n66, 236n16
mishkal, 60
modesty, significance of, 81–83
Moses, 135, 137, 303n6

mother-child relationship, 185
mother(s): destabilization of, 57; of
 Doeg the Edomite (son of Yosef),
 60–62; Helene, 62–70; martyrdom
 of, 71, 83–84, 254–55n74,
 255–56n79; problematizing of,
 93–99; rabbis' viewpoint of, 57;
 significance of, 56–57, 185, 186;
 transmission power of, 101; value
 of, 151–52; as vessel, 88
mother-son relationship: biblical
 antecedents for, 88–93; dysfunction within, 98; martyrdom
 within, 71; overview of, 55–56;
 power of, 56–57; sexual overtones
 within, 96, 97, 98; significance of,
 83, 101, 102, 182
Munbaz, 62–70
murder, by/of priests, 44–45, 47–48

nakedness, within the Temple, 96
negative commandments, 148,
 297–98n20
Nehardean virgins, 119, 120
Ne'ilah, 164, 168
Neusner, Jacob, 10
nivreshet, 62, 63–64
Noahide laws, 135
non-priests, within the court, 39

parent-child relationship, self-
 denial within, 152
Parhedrin chamber, 27–29, 30,
 218–19n36
parokhet, 89, 107–8, 258n13,
 259n19
Passover, 14, 206n67, 298n20
penis, significance of, 115–16.
 See also seminal emission
Peskowitz, Miriam, 90, 241n46,
 242n53, 243n57, 258n13, 258n14
Pharaoh, Israelites and, 140
pikuaḥ nefesh, 152–57

positive commandments, 148,
 297–98n20
Potiphar, wife of, 100, 113
power: of bloodlines, 85; of
 celibacy, 106; of clothing, 88,
 90; of food, 130; of incense, 113;
 of Joseph, 282n91; of kings, 42;
 of manna, 137–38; of martyrs,
 83–84; of mothers/mother-son
 relationship, 56–57, 71, 83, 101,
 185, 255n74; of odors, 221n47,
 276–77n55; prestige and, 160–61;
 of priests, 33, 55, 176; of rabbis,
 2, 6, 15, 39, 53, 117, 126–27, 155,
 158, 184; relations of, 200n33;
 of sexuality, 114, 130
prayer, 164, 166, 168
pregnancy, 152–57, 300n37,
 307–8n31
priest-fathers, sons and, 47–52
priest-priest relationships, 36
priests: blessings of, 206n68;
 casting lots by, 44; confession
 by, 14; disempowerment of, 161;
 falsifications of, 116–17; family
 relationships of, 7; garments
 of, 89–90, 95–96, 258–59n15;
 housekeeping by, 38; house
 purity role of, 32–33; as husbands, 182; identification of,
 197n10; judgment of, 115–16;
 kings *versus*, 42; masculinity of,
 38–39; murder by, 44–45; murder
 of, 47–48; purification of, 169,
 215n19; rabbis *versus*, 3, 6–7,
 17–18, 200n33; sexuality of, 105,
 106–12; sins of, context within,
 40–47; weeping by, 229n36;
 women *versus*, 112–17.
 See also high priest
procreation, sexuality for, 111–12,
 121, 271n14, 281n81
profane houses, 32–34

Index   343

punishment, of karet, 141, 146–50, 163, 283n2, 294n65, 296n12, 297n17

purification/purity: of ba'al keri, 167, 168, 169–71, 174, 304–5n14, 304n13; following pregnancy, 307–8n31; following seminal emissions, 106–7, 169, 216n23, 303n6; following sexual relations, 306–7n25, 307n26; following urination, 115–16, 278n65, 303n6; importance of, 53; laws regarding, 164; ritual of, 50, 51–52, 75, 106–7, 114–15, 215n19, 277n60, 308n35; rituals for, 168; sexual, 165–67; from sin, 178; timing regarding, 172

rabbis: ancestry of, 5; asceticism and, 132; authority of, 3–4, 145, 158, 159–60, 201n37; court control of, 39; cultural memory of, 16; emotional wounding of, 227n24; as father-like figures, 36–37; focus shift within, 2; household of, 20; influence of, 184; judgment by, 130, 160; masculinity of, 3, 36–37, 52–54, 103–4, 226n24; mothers and, 57, 69–70; power of, 126–27; priests *versus*, 3, 6–7, 17–18, 200n33; rise of, 197n10; sexuality of, 104–5, 117–23; Temple rites and, 4; vulnerability of, 157–62; weeping by, 47, 229n36

Rabbi Tzadok, 45–47, 53
Rabbi Yose, 137
Rabbi Yossa, 169
Rachel, 244n12
Rava, story of, 282–83n93
Rav Ami, 131–32
Rav Assi, 131–32
Rav Dimi, 173–74, 175

RavHuna bar Yehudah, 94
Ravina, story of, 59, 60–62
Rav Shmuel bar Yehudah, 94, 226n20, 247–48n25, 256–57n3, 262n40
Rehav'am, 43
Rehumi, Rav, 282–83n93
Reish Lakish, 110–11
relationships: brother-brother, 268n69; father-son, 47–52, 200n30, 267–68n64; master-disciple, 4, 57; master-servant, 101; parent-child, 152; priest-fathers, 47–52; priest-priest, 36; teacher-disciple, 101. *See also* mother-son relationship

religion, as cultural memory, 16
ritual, controlled environment of, 26. *See also specific rituals*
Rosen-Zvi, Ishay, 14, 104, 117–18, 196n3, 211n93, 225n15, 237–38n24, 242n48, 242n51, 271n10, 281n85
Rubenstein, Jeffrey, 11, 204n59, 204n60, 206n67, 286n19
Ruddick, Sarah, 185, 312n9

Sabbath, 171–72, 216n24
sacrifices: for atonement, 206–7n68; eating of, 208n77; of a heifer, 46; human, 48–49; removal of ash from, 37–40; sin, transference through, 46, 87
saliva, impurity within, 75, 80
Samuel, 41, 60, 89
Sassanian Babylonia, 57, 104
Satlow, Michael, 104, 265n55, 276n52, 280n81, 282n88, 283n93, 310n50
Saul, 40, 41–42
scapegoat, 46, 49, 50
self-denial: bodily, 136; children and, 152; commandment of,

126, 148; example of, 287n29; experience of, 131; interpretation of, 136; leniencies within, 150–53; manna and, 129; non-gendered view of, 146–50; overview of, 127–28; process of, 311n56; rabbi objections regarding, 141; requirements of, 183; sexual relations and, 138–40; women and, 149; within Yom Kippur, 103, 104, 206n66

seminal emission: causes of, 175, 273n27; as good omens, 173–76; impurity of, 23, 74, 106–7, 120–21, 165–66, 169, 248n28; purification following, 216n23, 303n6; significance of, 166, 184; types of, 305–6n18

sequestration, of the high priest, 22, 27, 28, 75, 107, 216n21, 273n27

sexual immorality, consequence/benefit of, 121

sexuality/sexual relations: abstinence of, 104, 106, 111; in the Bavli, 104–5; competition within, 289n38; food *versus*, 130–31, 134, 143; function of, 103; glorification through, 184; of the high priest, 75; illicit *versus* licit, 138–40; inui nefesh and, 138–40; of Jews, 105–6; marriage and, 118–19; miracles regarding, 114; necessity of, 135; overview of, 177; for procreation, 121; purification following, 306–7n25, 307n26; social revolution of, 124; within the Temple, 106–12, 123–24; as "way of the world," 291n53

sexual purity, law regarding, 165–67

Shavout, 206n67

Shekhem, 139, 140, 291n51

Shema, recitation of, 63–65, 70

Shema'yah, 5, 100, 161

Shim'on, 75, 248n29

Shim'on ben Yehotzadak, 43

Siegal, Michal Bar-Asher, 132, 272n22, 288n32

sin: animal transfer of, 46; atonement for, 42, 48; ba'al keri and, 310n54; bloodline disruption regarding, 43; of David, 40, 42, 114, 277n56; of priests, 40–47; purification from, 178; transference of, 87

slavery, social death and, 301n44

Smith, Jonathan, 26, 201–2n40

sotah rite, 67, 70, 242n48, 242n51

spinning wool, 90–91, 259–60n19

Stemberger, Gunther, 125

Stökl ben Ezra, Daniel, 14, 230n40, 244n10, 271n11, 281n83, 285n10

suffering, 130, 140–42, 292–93n59

synagogues, mezuzah within, 32

Syrian Christian culture, sexual abstinence within, 104, 122

tablet, golden, 62, 66–67, 68

teacher-disciple relationship, 101

Temple: bayit within, 136–37; benefactors within, 61; chambers within, 26; destruction of, 110, 112; destructuring within, 144; donations to, 62; exceptionalism of, 31; expense within, 56; gold within, 62–63; holiness within, 35, 215n19; housekeeping work within, 38, 208n74; house structures within, 182; human donations to, 60–61; immersion requirements for, 165; materiality within, 67–68, 183, 239n38; nakedness within, 96; objects within, 181; priestly service within, 14–15; rabbinic household and, 20; sanctity of, 33; sexuality within, 106–12,

Index   345

123–24; social standings within, 99; undignified spaces within, 31; weaknesses within, 70; women's roles within, 93, 261n32
terumat hadeshen, 37–40
timing, within purification rituals, 172
Torah: passing on of, 158–59; study of, 69, 122, 242–43n54
Toraitic law, 135
transference, of sin, 87
tunic, 88, 94–95, 259n16, 259n18

Uriah, 42
urine, impurity of, 115–16, 278n65, 303n6

veil, making of, 259–60n19
Vidas, Moulie, 10–11, 203–4n55, 203n54
virility, seminal emissions and, 173–74, 309n46

washing, 114–16, 151. *See also* immersion; purification
Wasserman, Mira, 9, 10, 11, 15, 186
water, significance of, 178–79
Watts Belser, Julia, 11, 12, 140–41, 184, 200n26, 211n90, 236n13, 237n19, 255n75, 285n9, 287n27, 290n45, 292n58
weaving, 87, 88–93, 90
weeping, 47, 135, 229n36
wet drapery, artistic style of, 96
whispering, significance of, 155
wife: backup, 22, 23, 216n24; of the high priest, 23–24, 122, 128; as "his house," 1, 20, 21–26, 34, 38, 56, 144, 177, 214n15, 280n80, 295n7; marital commitment of, 122–23; temporary, 118–19
Wimpfheimer, Barry, 11, 260n27
Wissenschaft des Judentums, 8

women: as benefactors, 61; bodies of, house metaphor and, 20; bodily agency of, 127, 146; earnings of, 90, 259–60n19, 264n49; enforcement significance of, 68–69; housekeeping work of, 38, 224n10, 295n8; marginalization of, 3–8; men's desire for, 130–31, 143; mezuzah requirements and, 30, 218n32; positive/negative commandments for, 297–98n20; priests *versus*, 112–17; rabbinic household making by, 2–3; self-denial regarding, 149; sexuality and, 112–17; spinning rituals of, 90–92, 259–60n19; as symbols of decline, 285n9; Temple roles of, 93, 261n32; viewpoints regarding, 213n8; weeping by, 229n36

Yehudah ben Beteirah, 22–23, 25, 28–29, 158, 216n24, 218–19n36, 218n34, 220n39, 220n40, 220n42, 305n17, 307–8n31
Yehudah Hanassi, 154
Yirmiyah bar Abba, 141
Yishmael (son of Kimhit), 78–80, 243–44n5, 244n11, 251–52n54
Yishmael, as "mother-born," 72
Yishmael ben Piabi/Pabi, 92, 93, 94, 95, 261n30, 262n41, 263n44, 263n46
Yitzhak, Nahman bar, 109, 173, 175
Yom Kippur: asceticism within, 179; at-homeness and, 282–83n93; avodah within, 247–48n25; bodily self-denial within, 20; distinctions of, 12–14; focus of, 2; high priest preparations before, 22, 75, 107, 273n27; historical significance of, 145; house and, 1; leniencies within, 150–53; prayer

within, 164; prohibitions within, 125, 138; scapegoat ritual within, 46; self-denial practice within, 103, 104, 206n66; sequestration prior to, 22, 27, 28, 75, 107, 216n21, 273n27; sexuality and, 120, 216n23; spiritual cleansing within, 177

Yosef, disappearance of, 60

Zoroastrian culture, sexuality within, 17, 96, 104, 135, 266n55